Anti-Semitism in British Society, 1876–1939

Anti-Semitism in British Society

1876–1939

Colin Holmes

Holmes & Meier Publishers, Inc
New York

First published in the United States of America 1979 by
HOLMES & MEIER PUBLISHERS, INC.
30 Irving Place, New York, N.Y. 10003

Library of Congress Cataloging in Publication Data

Holmes, Colin, 1938–
Anti-Semitism and British society, 1876–1939.

Bibliography: p.
Includes index.
1. Antisemitism—Great Britain. 2. Jews in
Great Britain—Public opinion. 3. Public opinion—
Great Britain. 4. Great Britain—Politics and
government. I. Title.
DS146.G7H64 1979 301.45′19′24041 78–21023

ISBN 0–8419–0459–6

PRINTED IN GREAT BRITAIN

Contents

Preface

This book developed out of my interest in Jewish immigration into Britain, with which I began to occupy myself in the late 1960s. I was soon pushed beyond this study by the appearance of books by John Garrard and Bernard Gainer and, as a result, I turned towards the more general question of anti-semitism in Britain. It was John Davey, then at Edward Arnold, who suggested that a work which ended in 1906 – which at that point was my outer chronological limit – would be of less interest than one which pushed ahead as far as 1939. I accepted his challenge and the present book is a child of such circumstances.

In writing it I have incurred a number of debts which I should like to place on record. I shall always be grateful to C. C. Aronsfeld, of the Institute of Jewish Affairs, who was the first editor to commission an article from me and who, since the early days, has been generous in his help, enthusiasm and encouragement. Professor Chimen Abramsky was also helpful at an early stage of my work, particularly in relation to bibliographical detail. More recently I have benefited from my exchange of ideas with Michael Biddiss, Alan Lee and Richard Thurlow and from the general sharpening of my thoughts in seminars at different universities. My postgraduate students have also provided me with fresh insights into the problems I discuss. In particular, I have benefited from the contact I have had with Kenneth Lunn, whose thesis on the Marconi scandal is an important contribution to our understanding of rich-Jew anti-semitism present in Britain before 1914, and from my reading of Joe Bennett's detailed study of East End responses to Jewish immigration. I am also indebted to Barbara Hill for her interest, encouragement, help and criticism, all of which have succeeded in enriching a companionship which now spans a decade. Outside the academy I am grateful for the help given to me in relation to a number of obscure matters by Jan and Helena Heller and Barry Kosmin of the Board of Deputies, who helped me in a deceptively casual manner.

So much for 'superstructural' emphases. At this point it is salutary to remind ourselves that academic work is a consumer of cash and without financial resources little can be achieved – a further proof that Clapham was right in emphasizing that economic history is the most fundamental branch of history. With regard to financial help, I gratefully acknowledge the assistance of the Knoop Fund at Sheffield. Little could Douglas Knoop have realized as he speculated on the Liverpool commodity exchange the kind of works his gains would help to bring forth. In later stages of my study I was helped by a grant from the Social Science Research Council.

I should also mention that like all other historians I am in the debt of archivists, librarians and libraries. My thanks here must go to Gordon Phillips of *The Times* for the courtesy and consideration he has shown to me on my visits to New Printing House Square and the patience with which he has answered my enquiries. Robin Price of the Wellcome Institute has also been diligent on my behalf. I am also indebted, in various ways, to the staff of the British Library, the Bodleian, the Public Record Office, the Royal Anthropological Institute, the University Library at Sheffield and the Wiener Library, as well as the staff of the public libraries in three great northern cities at Liverpool, Manchester and Sheffield. Among individuals holding archival material I am indebted to Timothy Tindal-Robertson of the Britons for access to his file on *The Protocols*.

Although I alone am responsible for the details and emphases in the book, the information which was drawn from the various sources listed above was put together for me in readable form by Beryl Moore and Pat Chessum, who typed with quiet competence and a pleasing efficiency. The meticulous task of compiling the index was expertly undertaken by Vic Gilbert.

Throughout these processes of production I count myself fortunate in having as my publisher Edward Arnold, who at a time of commercial panic resisted the challenge to inject the principles of the supermarket into publishing. John Davey, who commissioned the book, and Fay Sharman and Susan Loden, who saw it delivered, maintained a continuous interest in it.

Finally, on a personal note, I wish to emphasize that the book would never have appeared without the help of my parents. I regret my father did not live to see it finished. The book also owes a great deal to the organizational efficiency of Joyce Holmes who provided an oasis of quiet in which I could work and who also found time to read and comment on the manuscript, despite all the demands made upon her by our daughter, Rachel. Since I believe there are lessons to be learnt from this book and, hopefully, the future will most fully belong to Rachel it is to her that I have decided to dedicate it, reminding her that, 'Wisdom is the principal thing; therefore get wisdom: and with all thy getting get understanding,' (Proverbs IV. 7).

Sheffield
July 1978

Part I

1 Background

There are historical themes and subjects which often inspire fierce and widely differing views and anti-semitism is one of them. 'If you want to keep out of trouble', it has been written, 'there are about five subjects you should never mention in a speech or in print. Either in praise or dispraise or even natural curiosity. One of them is anything to do with Jewish culture or Jewish people.'[1] An exaggeration, without doubt, and one which might be countered by quoting a Jewish source that we could do with more studies of anti-semitism and, in particular, accounts written by Gentiles.[2]

Of course, difficulties and sensitivities concerning particular topics are relative. It is much easier to write of certain themes in some societies than others and it is also the case that difficulties can be greater in some epochs than others. Anyone who writes now on anti-semitism can hardly be unaware that he is working in an age which has witnessed an orgy of persecution and death, and, more generally, in a climate which has encountered the emergence of guilt feelings in certain sections of Western society concerning the treatment of other races. Such developments have undoubtedly affected attitudes and opinions and, in some respects, inhibited analytical progress. Indeed, a review of Robert Skidelsky's long awaited biography of Oswald Mosley, after noting that the author had referred to Mosley's anti-semitism as 'the greatest blemish on his whole career', went on to comment: 'That ought to satisfy the critics but I fear it will not, for Mr Skidelsky [attempts] to explain it, and there are quarters which will not forgive even an explanation of a phenomenon they rightly detest.'[3] Tensions can clearly begin to mount once description gives way to analysis.[4]

My theme in the following pages is anti-semitism in Britain between 1876 and 1939 and, before moving any further, we ought to engage in some definitions, bearing in mind that anti-semitism is notoriously difficult to define. The term is not employed here to mean an opposition towards all semitic peoples but is used in its more conventionally accepted sense of a hostility towards Jews. It can happen that Jews become caught up in conflict situations in which the fact that they are Jews is not an issue. But these are not our concern, since anti-semitism is defined broadly as a hostility towards Jews as such. In its most extreme expression between

1876 and 1939 it assumed the form of an ideological racist anti-semitism, when a genetic based hostility was manifested towards all Jews, who were regarded as a totally unassimilable element in society and as exercising a dangerous influence on their non-Jewish environment. In addition one can detect another strand of opposition in the tendency to refer to Jews in categorical rather than *ad hoc* terms, in other words to lump them together and to ascribe qualities to them but to do so without the injection of genetic elements. Finally, it is possible to find a more restricted opposition, towards individual Jews and groups of Jews – poor immigrants, rich financiers, international Jews, revolutionary Jews, for example – when the Jewish origins of such individuals or groups were emphasized as affecting the nature of the conflict which had developed between them and the Gentile world. Hence, because they were Jews, immigrants could pose special problems to British society. Hence, within a general opposition to finance capital, there could be specific hostility to Jewish finance. Such responses implied a wider antipathy and, as will become apparent, boundaries between sections of Jews could not always be neatly drawn and maintained. Although all the forms of anti-semitism referred to here found expression in the form of social discrimination against Jews as Jews, my emphasis in the following pages is mainly upon anti-semitic attitudes and my intention is to illustrate, analyse and categorize the essential qualities of such thought and the patterns of emphasis and expression it assumed.[5]

It is possible for anti-semitic ideas to exist among individuals and in societies where Jews are not present.[6] But all sections of the British Isles have witnessed some Jewish settlement. A custodian of Irish Jews was appointed in the thirteenth century and authentic references to Jews in Ireland appeared two centuries earlier. In Scotland settlement occurred much later than this. There were applications for trade and residence in Edinburgh in 1691 but the first community, also in Edinburgh, was not established until 1816. In Wales too, no organized existence was recorded in the middle ages although individual Jews certainly lived there. It was not until 1768, in fact, that the first community was settled in Swansea.[7]

In England, by contrast, an organized Jewish life existed in medieval times. It is possible that the occasional immigrant entered the country before the Norman Conquest but it is generally accepted that 'the first Jews of medieval England were Norman imports': members of the Rouen community came in the wake of the Conqueror and settled in London, which is the only place in England where Jews are definitely known to have established themselves before the middle of the twelfth century.[8] This medieval Jewish community maintained an existence until Edward I's expulsion order of 1290. This does not mean that there were no Jews in England from the late thirteenth century until the official acceptance of their readmission in 1664. It has been emphasized that 'the exclusion of the Jews from any land, however rigidly it may be prescribed by law, is unlikely to be absolute' and this was certainly the case in England.[9] Indeed, from medieval times onwards individual Jews were called in to help in some special capacity, often in their role as medical men or financiers, and a scattering of nominally converted Jews, the Marrano community, maintained an existence in the sixteenth and early seventeenth century. Furthermore, there was official connivance at the settlement of Jews in the Cromwellian years. But it was not until 1664 that the residence of the Jews in England was legally authorized for the first time since the great expulsion.

From around this time – the religious status of Jews was not legally secured until 1673 – it is possible to write about a continuous Jewish community in England, contributing to and sharing in social activity while maintaining its own forms of social organization. And, as we have just noticed, communities were formed later in other areas of Britain. The majority of the community during the early years of the resettlement were Sephardi Jews, those of Spanish, Levantine, Mediterranean descent, although there were Ashkenazi Jews, of Franco, German, Polish background, some of whom entered England after the 1648 and 1651 attacks upon Jewry in Poland by Bogdan Chmielnitzki, the Polish king of the Cossacks.[10] In the course of the eighteenth century the number of Ashkenazi Jews increased still further until by the middle of the century there were two distinct groups of Jews in Britain. These were so different in terms of status, condition and appearance that by the end of the century a German traveller could comment: 'Dress, language, manners, cleanliness, politeness, everything distinguishes them [the Ashkenazim] much to the advantage of the former [the Sephardim] who have little to distinguish them from Christians.'[11]

Over the course of the next century as a result of migration, a component inseparable from Jewish history, the number of Ashkenazi Jews was to increase even more. Some came from central Europe but, from the middle 1860s and certainly from 1870, the outstanding factor in the history of the Jewish community in Britain was the influx of Ashkenazi Jews from Russian Poland.[12] This was part of a general westward migration from Russia, Austria-Hungary and Romania which went mainly towards America, 'the goldene medina', and to a lesser extent to western Europe and South Africa. It gathered momentum in 1881–2 during the pogroms which followed the assassination of Alexander II, reached a new high point in 1891–2 when administrative measures by the Tsarist autocracy resulted in the uprooting of large numbers of Russian Jews, and attained an unequalled peak in 1903–4, in the wake of the pogroms instigated by the Russian authorities. There was in fact an upward curve of movement by Jews out of the Russian Empire and it has been estimated, although figures cannot be entirely accurate, that one million Jews left eastern Europe for the west between 1881 and 1905. The majority of these – almost three quarters, in fact, – came from Russia itself and over 80 per cent of them went to America, with an imprecise number, although probably more than 100,000, coming to Britain.[13]

But immigration from eastern Europe was not the only numerical accretion to Anglo-Jewry in the late nineteenth century. There was also a settlement of some German Jews, a number of whom like Ernest Cassel, Felix Semon and Edgar Speyer were later to play an important role in

British society, particularly during the reign of Edward VII. The consequence of all these developments was that an Ashkenazi stamp was firmly imprinted upon Anglo-Jewry, which reached the apex of its power within 'the Cousinhood'.[14]

Although this end-of-century migration has captured much attention, Jewish immigration into Britain did not end in 1914. The events of the Russian Revolution encouraged a further refugee immigration between 1917 and 1920 and this was supplemented shortly afterwards by the influx of Jews fleeing from the tightening screw of Hitlerite persecution after 1933. This most recent immigration was on a smaller scale and concentrated into a much shorter time span than that of the late nineteenth century and whereas the earlier movement from the Russian Empire had been composed largely of working-class Jews or those who had few visible means of support on arrival, the influx of the 1930s into this 'strange country' was mainly middle class and professional in character.[15]

The community which developed from the Restoration resettlement succeeded over the course of time in establishing an effective institutional life to preserve and defend its interests. By the end of the seventeenth century both the Sephardi and Ashkenazi Jews were organized to look after their own and in the years which followed significant additions were made to the community's institutions. The Board of Deputies, the legal representative of the Jewish community, was established in 1760; the Jews' Free School was officially founded in 1817; the *Jewish Chronicle*, the voice of the older Jewish families, appeared in 1841; and the Jewish Board of Guardians was established in 1859 to relieve the poverty and improve the condition of the Jewish poor. In all this, as well as in the early establishment of synagogues for both Sephardi and Ashkenazi groups, we can discern an intention to protect Jewish interests and guarantee a future existence for the community.

In tentative fashion we can also plot the growth in numbers of the community, although there can be no doubt that any attempt to make an assessment of the size of the Jewish population built up over the years is fraught with difficulty. Until capitalism found it useful and necessary to engage in the measurement of resources in the nineteenth century no accurate figures were available and even after official surveys had been introduced it still remained difficult to assess the size of the Anglo-Jewish community. 'Comprehensive detailed surveys of Anglo-Jewry have been rare', one commentator has remarked, 'and there is no absolutely authoritative statistical evidence, because the census does not classify the inhabitants by religion.'[16] From what does exist it would seem that the medieval community in England was the least important numerically – as well as culturally – in Europe, that soon after the resettlement it numbered 3,000–4,000 and that by the 1753 Jew Bill its size had grown to 8,000.[17] By 1850 we are dealing with a community in Great Britain of approximately 35,000 and between 1850 and 1939 this grew tenfold.[18] It is apparent from this that the years which are of prime concern to us here were remarkable for a significant population jump, albeit from a very small base. At no time, however, did Jews constitute a large percentage of the total population. They were 0·1 per cent of the population of Britain in 1850 and in 1880, 1900, 1910 and 1939 they constituted only 0·17 per cent, 0·38 per cent, 0·53 per cent and 0·8 per cent, respectively.[19]

Although this point is worth making, it does not have a significance regarding anti-semitism which some might try to suggest. The size of the Jewish community is not necessarily a crucial variable in creating anti-semitism. In England at the time of the 1753 Jew Bill, Jews were only one tenth of 1 per cent of the total population, yet this did not prevent the emergence in certain quarters of fears about Jewish power.[20] In Germany Jews formed only 1·25 per cent of the population of the German Empire in 1870 and this figure diminished as time went on, yet anti-semitism existed there and increased as the relative size of the Jewish population declined.[21] Jews were often perceived as a linked international minority; consequently it could be believed that national details did not tell the whole story.

Although the Jewish community was never large in absolute or relative terms it was spatially concentrated. From its beginnings at the time of the Conquest throughout medieval times the Jewish settlement remained basically urban and lived close to the sources of much of the host community's wealth. There was no strict ghetto but Jews tended to live close to a market and, where possible, a royal castle.[22] From its beginnings, therefore, the Jewish community possessed an urban character, it was very strongly represented in London and, even within urban centres, was inclined to congregate in certain areas. These characteristics were to remain important features of Jewish life. Indeed, this concentration was such that by the middle of the eighteenth century, when proposals to naturalize Jews were being discussed, 'outside the metropolis practically nothing was known of Jews: many eighteenth-century Englishmen had never seen one' and some of those who had were probably acquainted only with the poor Ashkenazi hawker who peddled his wares from time to time in their district.[23] This concentration in London continued into the following century: it has been estimated that in 1850, when Anglo-Jewry numbered about 35,000, approximately 18,000–20,000 Jews lived in the capital. It is true that some degree of geographical dispersion had taken place by this date as the wealthier members of the community had drawn themselves apart in terms of residence and as provincial communities had been founded with the active support of leaders of the London community.[24] Nevertheless, the figures for the number of Jews living in London in 1850 show its continuing attraction in a period when dispersion was taking place and its importance was further increased once the immigration from the Russian Empire was under way.

Once here the immigrants settled mainly in the East End of London and within that part of the city they were concentrated in Stepney. The 1903 Royal Commission on Alien Immigration noted that at the time of the 1901 census there were 53,537 Russians and Poles (mainly Jews) in London out of a total Russian-Jewish population of 95,245 and of these 43,000 were in Stepney, where there was a total alien population of 54,310. This meant that aliens constituted 18·19 per cent of the population in

Stepney – unofficial figures placed it as high as 21·15 per cent – and Russian Jews made up 14·4 per cent of the inhabitants, although it has to be recognized that certain parts of the borough, such as Whitechapel, had a higher proportion of foreigners than other constituent areas like Mile End.[25] Strangeways in Manchester and the Leylands area of Leeds took on similar characteristics. It was in such centres that, at least in the short term, the great majority of the immigrants lived and worked in a 'self-contained milieu which encompassed a whole range of social and cultural life.'[26] This pull of London has continued into recent times[27] and assumes a relevance therefore not only to the debate surrounding Jewish immigration but also to the later campaign by Mosley in the East End of London.[28] What is being suggested here is that Jews were 'visible' in a spatial, geographical sense. Such a concentration could not only aid in the creation of social problems by placing additional pressure on scarce resources in particular areas; it could also be used by those hostile to the Jewish community to add to a more generalized picture of Jewish power and influence.

Jews were 'visible' in another sense: it has been remarked that, in spite of the efforts of scholars to show the participation of Jews in various trades and professions in the middle ages, finance and its offshoots, such as commodity dealing and the sale of pawns, were the major sources of employment.[29] Those who were admitted to England at the time of resettlement were also primarily interested in finance. Their descendants and the assortment of newcomers who swelled the ranks of the community also carried on this tradition in the following century and as late as 1850 activities other than in finance were peripheral.[30] After 1850 a greater occupational variation became apparent, some of which was related to the immigration from the Russian Empire. But even so, employment bunching was still present. The newcomers settled in a narrow range of occupations outside finance, such as tailoring, where there was an 'extensive concentration of Jews,'[31] boot and shoe making and also in the furniture trades, where Jewish workers came to be employed mainly by Jewish capitalists, many of whom had themselves been 'greeners' only a short time before.

Coexistent with this trend was the increase in the number of professional men within Anglo-Jewry, which became more pronounced in the late nineteenth century.[32] But here again we are dealing with a concentrated rather than a diffused development, with Jews finding employment mainly in the medical, legal and educational professions.[33] During these same years Jews also became more generally involved in business; even so, Jewish businessmen were not spread across the whole business spectrum but were concentrated in the manufacture and supply of consumer goods.[34] Furniture making, which increased in importance in the East End, the jewellery trades, the boot and shoe trades, retail tailoring and the fur trade were the areas which attracted Jewish attention and it was here where, even if they did not have a monopoly, they had an influence out of all proportion to their numbers in the general population. The overall effect of such changes over the course of a century was that by 1950 there was 'a large enough contingent of traders and businessmen, particularly in the smaller settlements in the provinces, to lend the community a specifically commercial air in the sight of the nation.'[35] However, although these broad patterns are apparent, it is difficult to be precise on many matters since 'statistics about Jewish economic life are a very scarce commodity in Britain' and discussion is restricted by the fact that 'Anglo-Jewish sociologists . . . have preferred to concentrate on such comparatively barren and inward looking subjects as Jewish identity and the extent (or lack) of Jewish cohesiveness'[36] rather than upon the community's socio-economic structure.

After discussing these characteristics we can proceed to a consideration of the attitudes which developed towards the Jewish community, or sections of it, in order to discover the nature of the hostility which Jews had to face and the disabilities they encountered. No attempt is made to engage in a detailed analysis and attention is concentrated mainly on the years immediately preceding those which come in for detailed analysis and discussion.

It is nevertheless important to comment on hostility expressed earlier than this and, with reference to medieval society, there were two conspicuous developments. It was in England that the charge of ritual murder was raised at Norwich in 1144 when the body of a young skinner's apprentice was discovered. It was rumoured that he was killed by Jews 'who had enticed him away from his family and crucified him after synagogue service on the second day of Passover, in mockery of the passion of Jesus'. This was, in fact, 'the first recorded instance in the medieval world of the infamous ritual murder accusation, which subsequently caused the Jews throughout Europe untold misery.'[37] A later accusation came at Lincoln in 1255 in the case of 'Little' St Hugh of Lincoln, a legend which was recounted by the Prioress in Chaucer's *Canterbury Tales*, and which became firmly embedded in English folklore. These accusations do not stand alone as evidence in England of medieval opposition to Jews as Jews. In 1290, as we have already mentioned, Jews were expelled from the country and although such an act was difficult to enforce in an absolute sense, it provided an example which was to be emulated elsewhere.

As we have noticed, it was not until the seventeenth century that Jews were officially readmitted to England and, although at first the law ignored them, they soon found themselves touched by its provisions. The country was still Christian and legal restrictions were placed upon those who did not share this faith and, indeed, for some time even upon those Christians who were not communicants of the Church of England. The major instances of opposition to Jews in the eighteenth and nineteenth centuries developed out of this kind of situation and, in the sense that Jews were denied social rights because they could not subscribe to an oath supporting the Church of England rather than being singled out as Jews for discrimination, the principle behind the hostility cannot be regarded as specifically anti-semitic in intention, although in practice it might assume that form. It should also be realized that whatever reasoning lay behind the restriction it succeeded in creating and sustaining an image of Jews as a problem.

The other major limitation which Jews could encounter centred upon the restrictions affecting those who were foreign-born. It was generally possible for foreigners to obtain naturalization through Parliament but this was not open to Jews since such petitioning was available only to those professing the Christian religion. And the impression that Jews were outside the nation and ought to remain there was clearly brought home at the time of the 1753 Jew Bill, which would have enabled the naturalization of Jews applying for this privilege by specific Act of Parliament and consequently would have drawn them closer into the body of the nation. The bill, which was calculated to appeal to the interests of rich Jews, 'naturalized no one: all it did was to modify the statutory requirements for naturalization so that Parliament in future cases could, if it wished, naturalize professing Jews, a thing impossible under existing law.'[38] But the project proved abortive. The measure, which was passed in the spring of 1753, was repealed in the autumn before it had helped to naturalize anybody, after a fierce debate which at times assumed an anti-semitic character, and it was not until 1825 that the sacramental test for naturalization was abolished.[39]

This was part of a process by which over time the various disabilities affecting religious groups outside the Church of England, including Jews, were gradually removed. In the early nineteenth century, for instance, the 1828 Test and Corporation Acts, which had closed the great offices of state and membership of town corporations to all who were unable to take the Church of England communion, were repealed. Very little changed as a consequence of such legal developments. They merely rationalized a *de facto* practice, since many Protestant dissenters had in fact enjoyed office for years by means of an annual Indemnity Act. However, as a result of the 1828 measure, no more Indemnity Acts would be required and the Catholic Emancipation Act of the following year left Jews as the only section of British society denied civic rights on religious grounds. But it should be emphasized that such official restrictions did not totally hinder the community since, although Jews lived under legal disabilities, they nevertheless 'enjoyed many of the realities of security and respect if without their legal foundations.'[40]

The removal of those restrictions which continued to affect Jews was not achieved until the mid-Victorian years. An unsuccessful attempt to change the situation was made in 1830 but it took twenty-eight years before a measure was passed which enabled Jews to become eligible for the House of Commons. Another eight years were to pass before a Jewish peer could take his seat in the House of Lords, and it was not until 1885 that the first Jewish peer was admitted to the Upper House. Of wider significance was the fact that in 1871 the whole range of oaths and declarations which restricted Jews was repealed and, once the Promissory Oaths Act of 1871 became law, Jews 'were placed at last on precisely the same footing as regards political rights as their Christian fellow subjects with one or two insignificant exceptions.'[41]

This history of Jewish emancipation has been told often enough so that only the bare significant details have been referred to here. What it displayed on the one hand was an example of liberal toleration, the belief that it was socially undesirable to discriminate against individuals and groups on the basis of their religion. On the other, it reflected the hope that through the processes of emancipation the Jew would forsake his separateness and move closer to British society. But such views did not possess a total social dominance and there were two major strands of opposition which were raised against Jews throughout the years of the emancipation debate. In the course of the prolonged discussion they were charged with foreignness and divided loyalties and also with possessing a low moral character as evidenced by their concentration upon financial gain. Both sets of charges provide a significant link with later expressions of anti-semitic hostility.[42]

Thus, by the time this study opens Jews had been freed from their former disabilities, as they had been in every other major European country except Russia, where emancipation had to wait for the Revolution. But the community which rejoiced in such progressive developments had also experienced hostility directed against its members. We are unable to say how widespread such opposition was. Indeed, it is difficult to estimate the extent of anti-semitism even in contemporary society, where a greater variety of techniques can be employed in the investigation.[43] What can be said with certainty, however, is that opposition had been manifested towards Jews from medieval times onwards. In particular, it is not without significance for later expressions of hostility that for much of the nineteenth century Jews in Britain were treated as a difficult case, a social group whose emancipation was achieved only after a prolonged debate, which in itself was likely to induce an impression that Jews must be a special minority, an awkward element in society. By 1876, therefore, it was not only religious images of Jews which gave rise to antagonism. The social structure of the Jewish community – in particular the concentration of Jews in business, especially as middlemen – and the sojourning image which attached to a minority scattered over the earth whose history had been one of migration, exposed it, or sections of it, to charges of an undue concentration upon material gain and a shaky allegiance to British society.[44] It is clear, in fact, that the conflicts after 1876 were influenced by these prior images of Jews which were present in British society. With that awareness as the starting point of our discussion, we will first indicate how there were in addition specific situational pressures at work helping to generate anti-semitism, before attempting to present a total picture of the conflicts which occurred between 1876 and 1914.[45]

2 A nation within a nation?

Shortly after James Picciotto had written about the secure position of English Jewry in 1875, the first instances of an anti-semitism which was to recur at frequent intervals down to the First World War began to manifest itself in British society.[1] In surveying these attitudes an initial emphasis is placed upon those expressions of hostility which revealed an underlying concern with 'Britain for the British', which stressed that the scarce resources of British society should reside in those who might be labelled 'British', and that there was a British culture and way of life which was worth preserving. The elusive nature of such concepts did not deter those who took up the battle on their behalf.

The fall of Gladstone's first ministry in 1874 opened the way for Disraeli to form his second government in that year and to dominate British politics down to 1880, until he too slipped from what he called the 'greasy pole'. For the first time Britain had a prime minister who was born a Jew, although in some Gentile minds this had been overcome by baptism into the Church of England. In others, the origins of the 'potent wizard',[2] coupled with his passion for ostentation created unease, but it was not until the Bulgarian Horrors that a significant anti-semitic opposition manifested itself.

The 1875 version of the Eastern Crisis had its immediate origins in the attempt by the Bulgarian Christians to free themselves from Turkish rule. The response of the Turks was to massacre the Christians. Once more the question of British policy towards the Balkans was raised and Disraeli pursued the traditional one of supporting the Turks, who were regarded by the Foreign Office as a useful counterweight against Russian pretensions and aspirations in that part of the world. However, Gladstone, who was leading the parliamentary opposition, came out strongly in support of the Bulgarian Christians and in 1876 added a new dimension to nineteenth-century political controversy through his elevated attack upon the Turks in his pamphlet *The Bulgarian Horrors and the Question of the East*. The country was deeply divided over the war and considerable moral and political passion was aroused, as Gladstone's pamphlet clearly revealed. Indeed, 'few political issues have raised such venemous feelings', Robert Blake has written in his life of Disraeli. 'Munich and Suez are the nearest equivalents in recent times.' But neither of these displayed the degree of vehemence which characterized the earlier controversy.[3]

It was against this background that hostility towards Disraeli began to appear. Goldwin Smith, who had been Regius Professor of Modern History at Oxford between 1858 and 1866 and who became the first Professor of English and Constitutional History at Cornell University, was soon into the fray.[4] This was hardly surprising. Smith's first newspaper assignment was with the *Morning Chronicle* in 1850 and it was in this paper that he wrote a series of anonymous articles attacking Disraeli who, it was suggested, after asking for office in Sir Robert Peel's administration (1841–6), had proceeded after a refusal of the request to engage in a bitter opposition to the government. It was an opposition which Smith, an ardent Peelite, found himself unable to forgive. Disraeli soon discovered the authorship of the articles and henceforth a bitter feud persisted between the two of them.[5] The hostility was exacerbated thirteen years later when Smith advocated the cession by Britain of Gibraltar and the Ionian Islands. Disraeli told the House, in a remark which was generally regarded as being aimed at Smith, that colonial policy was the affair of statesmen rather than professors and rhetoricians and the British Empire must not be left to 'prigs and pedants'.[6] A few years later, in 1870, Disraeli extended his assault on Smith in his novel *Lothair*, in which an Oxford professor, universally taken to be Smith, was classified as a 'social parasite'.[7] In its turn this prompted Smith to write to *The Times*, that great clearing house of public opinion, where he referred to Disraeli's remarks as 'the stingless insults of a coward'.[8]

At this stage the conflict had not been characterized by any reference to Disraeli's Jewish origins and reflected little more than an adolescent exercise in personal abuse between grown men. But after the publication of *Lothair*, Smith's attacks became increasingly severe and "with an illogical defiance of liberal principle [he] seized every opportunity of assailing Disraeli's race.'[9] Disraeli came to be described as 'this Semite',[10] his vindictiveness became 'truly Oriental'[11] and it was argued that England was being led astray by his 'Hebrew flashiness'.[12] It was during the Eastern Crisis that this personal anti-semitism, this hostility towards an individual Jew, was extended into an attack upon sections of the Jewish community.

It has been claimed that Disraeli's origins, although not determining his Eastern policy, influenced his contempt for Bulgarian nationalism and helped to blind him to an appreciation of the appeal which the traditions of Orthodoxy and the Eastern Roman Empire could exercise over certain influential public figures.[13] But Smith's position was an extreme one. The whole issue of the Bulgarian Horrors, as the crisis was popularly called, was discussed by him within a framework of predominantly Jewish influences and interests. 'Had England been drawn into this conflict', he wrote, 'it would have been in some measure a Jewish war, waged with British blood to uphold the objects of Jewish sympathy or to avenge Jewish wrongs.'[14] It has to be said that there were Jewish financial interests in Turkey which Disraeli might have been under pressure to defend.[15] But Smith's analysis was too simple and narrow sighted, ignoring as it did not only the argument that a defence of Turkish interests would act as a counter to Russian ambitions in the

Balkans but also the national benefit which a stable Turkish influence would provide in preserving the Near East route to Britain's imperial interests in Asia.[16] Smith's concentration was elsewhere. Reference to the undesirable influence of Jewish interests had by now become a pronounced feature of his work and in his opening statement on the Eastern controversy in the *Contemporary* he also proceeded to engage in a criticism of Jewish emancipation, to attack Jewish racial exclusiveness as evidenced in the teachings and practice of Judaism, and to state that strict or 'genuine' Jews could not be patriots.[17]

It was hardly to be expected that such assertions would go unchallenged and they were in fact taken up by Hermann Adler, the Chief Rabbi, who attempted to refute Smith's assertion through an analysis of 'the teachings of Judaism and a history of the Jews', in the course of which he emphasized that no section of British society was more ready to make national sacrifices than 'that which [professed] the ancient, primaeval faith of Judaism'.[18] The encounter was sterile. In his reply Smith merely reaffirmed his position, stressing the difference between Englishmen and Jews and reiterating that 'genuine Jews' could not be patriotic.[19] Judaism, it was claimed, was characterized by a racial exclusiveness and in the mind of a strict Jew race was always triumphant over country.[20]

Smith was not a lone voice at this time raising these issues and injecting an anti-Jewish aspect into the discussion of British foreign policy. Other contemporary comments displayed a willingness to attack Disraeli on account of his origins. Hence the *Church Times* could refer to 'the Jew Premier',[21] John Bright, the veteran radical, could arraign Disraeli 'for his native blood' and even Lord Derby, the prime minister's close friend, admitted that Disraeli's mental processes were those of a 'foreigner'.[22] Elsewhere, reference was made to 'an oriental dictator', pursuing a 'Hebrew' policy,[23] but 'the nadir of bad taste'[24] was reached by E. A. Freeman, the Oxford historian, who was quite prepared to attack 'the Jew' for his 'drunken insolence' and to write about the Queen, when she visited Disraeli at Hughenden, as 'going ostentatiously to eat with Disraeli in his ghetto'.[25]

So much for the anti-semitism which surrounded the discussion in Britain of the Bulgarian crisis. It arose at a time when war seemed to threaten and, in such circumstances, the individual and collective hostility directed against Jews indicated how tenuous the threads of toleration could be and how the wisdom of Jewish emancipation could be questioned. And this was not the only war situation before 1914 when Jewish interests were subjected to such scrutiny. A similar debate was heard at the time of the Boer War.

The South African War, which lasted between 1899 and 1902, was the first major war in which Britain was involved after the cessation of the hostilities in the Crimea in 1856 and it was fought against a background of discontent and opposition within British society. Ostensibly it was started to protect the interests of the Uitlanders who, in Arendt's words, had tumbled onto the wharves of Africa and hurried up country to exploit the mineral wealth of the Transvaal.[26] The Boers, the descendants of the early Dutch settlers, retreated before this influx, recoiled before the prospect of a gold mining industry developing in the Transvaal and, it was argued, proceeded to make life difficult for the newcomers, to the extent of denying them social rights. In contrast to this assessment of the situation it was pointed out in some quarters that the Uitlander capitalists had systematically and deliberately inflamed relations with the Boers, while it was additionally emphasized that Uitlander voices which cried for war in these circumstances were not always those of British subjects but in many cases belonged to Jewish capitalists with an indeterminate concept of nationality.[27]

It was through these latter emphases that an anti-semitism developed which assumed a conspiratorial tone, with the claim that Jewish capitalists in South Africa received support from Jewish financial groups in Britain itself. The war, some said, was being fought for their benefit. This was clearly apparent in the widely influential writings of J. A. Hobson and was in fact prominently referred to in Radical and Socialist circles,[28] where it was not unusual to find it being asserted that 'the capitalists who bought up or hired the Press both in South Africa and in England to clamour for war [were] largely Jews and foreigners.'[29] In reality the issue of anti-semitism within the context of the South African War is a complex matter and, since it assumed mainly conspiratorial tones (although charges of Jews shirking their military responsibilities were also made), a discussion of it is reserved until later.[30] But it might be noted here that it was yet another instance when war or the threat of war called into question Jewish national loyalties.

Both the Eastern Crisis of 1875 and the Boer War triggered off hostility against Jews which stressed their tenuous attachment to British society. But these were not the only situations in which a sharp distinction was drawn between what was regarded as the essential incompatibility of certain Jewish and British interests. Similar strands of thought can also be discerned in the debate which developed after 1881 over Jewish immigration.[31] As we have already noticed, there was a significant westward movement by Ashkenazi Jews from the Russian Empire during the late nineteenth century down to the First World War. Although the majority of Jews went to America, an elusive number, probably around 100,000, settled in Britain. Those immigrants who came to Britain, whether for permanent settlement or in search of a temporary refuge on their way to America, tended to congregate in certain areas such as Leeds, Manchester and the East End of London.[32] In considering expressions of hostility which emerged in response to this immigration, we might make a start by referring to those which reflected opinion in the East End, the area which had to bear the brunt of Jewish immigration.[33]

There were, in fact, three main strands of opposition. The influx from eastern Europe occurred at a time of conjunctural crisis in the East End when a series of hard winters and the trade depression of the mid-1880s 'highlighted and reinforced the more long-term tendencies towards industrial decline'.[34] The sudden increase in the number of Jewish immigrants exacerbated certain social problems in the area and, at first, attention was directed towards the effect of immigration upon the labour market. At that time, when social problems were discussed, reference was frequently made to the residuum, the excess supply of labour in the East End. It was this surplus, it was argued, which weakened the bargaining power of labour while simultaneously helping to sustain grossly exploitative sectors of the economy. In other words, there was already considerable discussion about the sweated industries and immigration added a further dimension to the debate. Sentiments expressed in the East End displayed considerable repetition and it would be tedious to present a large number of them but some indication of what was agitating opinion in east London can be gleaned from the East End press.

In the early days of immigration there was an almost unanimous opinion that immigrant elasticity lay at the heart of the sweating problem or, at least, was a major contributory factor to it. The *Eastern Argus*, a paper closely associated with the brewing interests and the Conservative Party, was in no doubt on this score:

> A number of men and women ... land on our wave-beaten shores in a destitute condition, and offer to do work at any price. ... [This] undermines all our commercial arrangements and drives English labour out of the labour market. All the 'sweating system' in the East of London is carried on by cheap foreign labour.[35]

Other contemporary opinion, while opposed to the sweating system and unsympathetic to Jewish immigration, was nevertheless prepared to accept that Jewish immigrants were only one contributory factor.[36] In this sense, therefore, the *Argus* took an extreme line, although on other aspects of the immigration debate it adopted a more cautious approach. For instance, it did not clearly spell out that the foreign labour beating on the shores of Britain was made up of Jews. In this respect its reaction was anti-alien rather than anti-semitic, although it needs to be understood that the hostility was in fact directed towards Jewish immigrants.[37] But where the *Argus* trod delicately, others were prepared to spell out that the immigrants were Jews. The *East London Advertiser*, a Conservative organ, provides a clear illustration of this. In 1888 in a discussion of the sweating problem, its readers were informed:

> Competition is ... at the bottom of all this evil – foreign competition for the most part. The swarms of foreign Jews who have invaded the East End labour market are chiefly responsible for the sweating system and the grave evils which are flowing from it. ... If this foreign immigration can be checked half the battle against the sweating system will be over.[38]

Here was an explicit reference to Jewish economic competition and it was echoed elsewhere. The *Eastern Post and City Chronicle*, another important East End newspaper source, while not adopting a consistent attitude on the effects of immigrant competition, could nevertheless claim that the issue was

> how to prevent the Jew driving the Gentile out of the land. ... It seems to be coming almost to a state as existed in Egypt just prior to the exodus.[39]

The whole question of the reactions of the East End as reported through the local press, the shifts in emphasis, the links these had with changes in ownership control and the emergence of specific local problems, is a topic in itself and no attempt can be made here to indicate even the tip of such developments. But it can be safely claimed that with varying degrees of explicitness and consistency there was, certainly in the early days of immigration, a tendency to identify the undercutting Jewish immigrant as a significant element contributing to the economic problems of east London and, on this basis, to oppose his presence in the East End. This should not create any surprise; indeed, a belief that immigration resulted in labour displacement and wage reductions was a widely held assumption which remained undisputed until late 1887.

Such a charge was of course closely related to another, which stressed that the Jewish immigrants were heavily pauperized. It was because they were in this condition, it was argued, that they were prepared to work at any level of wages, or at least, a level at which Englishmen, with more developed ideas about their 'standard of comfort', would starve. Such competition was persistent, it was emphasized, because of the existence in Britain of charities, such as the Jewish Board of Guardians, which encouraged a flow of pauperized immigrants who knew full well that they would receive succour and support from their kinsmen.[40] Where free entry was defended in the face of such beliefs, it rested upon different factors, which referred to the logic of free trade, the sacred right of asylum and a belief that immigration levels were declining.

It is important to recognize that this East End opposition to Jewish immigration came to centre around different issues at different times. Down to the late 1880s the emphasis was upon undercutting, but the second major wave of hostility which developed in the years preceding the 1905 Aliens Act displayed a much greater concern with the impact made by Jewish immigrants on the housing market. The issue was spelt out quite clearly in the *East London Advertiser* in 1898 when it was claimed that displacement was becoming a threat in the very centre of the Empire and there was a danger that 'the greatest industrial area in the capital city of Europe will be entirely populated by Yiddish speaking aliens.'[41] It was indeed difficult to separate the immigrants from the housing problem. A tight housing market, powerless 'greeners', straight from the Russian ghettos, and unscrupulous Jewish landlords, who were prepared to buy up property and turn out established tenants in favour of their own kinsmen whom they then proceeded to exploit, were frequently stressed as key factors in the problem. The case was succintly put in 1903, although the major components were present in the 1890s.

> The evils of housing in London are always intensified in districts where alien landlords rule.... The alien on his arrival knows no sanitary laws ... and falls an easy prey to the rack-rent landlord, who in these districts is frequently an alien Jew. It is the Jew alien landlord who sets the pace in the East End; he imposes excessive demands and goes one or more worse than the British landlord. He is merciless and unscrupulous, has elastic ideas of what constitutes a habitable dwelling, and while ostensibly more respectful of the

> laws and authorities than the British householder, nevertheless manages to get round both. . . . The Jewish landlord would not succeed in his methods were not his chief victims the alien tenants, for he is able with these people to raise the rents above the market rate. Aliens will insist on crowding together in certain quarters. They are more helpless than the British tenant, who migrates more easily and is more persistent in resisting oppressive demands.[42]

It was not suggested that the influx of Jewish immigrants and the activities of Jewish landlords were by themselves responsible for all the housing problems which blighted the East End. Such developments had to be considered in conjunction with pressures resulting from the extension of the City, the construction of commercial buildings on sites which had formerly been given over to residential property, as well as the demolition of large areas for railway extensions, all of which added to pressures on accommodation in the East End.[43] But a recognition that the Jewish presence was a contributory factor to the situation is reflected in the priority given by sections of the Jewish establishment to the policy of dispersal and in the effects made through the Four Per Cent Industrial Dwellings Company Ltd and the East End Dwellings Company Ltd to reduce the congregation of Jews and secure the immigrants against unscrupulous landlords.[44]

If anyone were in doubt about the tension which could be stirred by the housing issue, they had only to take account of the situation which developed in Bethnal Green. The housing shortage there was acute even if the situation was worse in other parts of the East End and it was given an added edge by the rapid growth of Jewish residents in new model dwellings and tenements.[45] This was evidenced in 1898 when the London County Council completed the Boundary Street scheme of model dwellings and the displaced inhabitants who were unable to pay the LCC rents for the replacement accommodation were extruded into the outlying areas to compound an already chronic housing shortage. The other side of the coin – and it was this which led to tension – was that approximately half the tenants in the Boundary Street model dwellings were Jewish and, perhaps unavoidably, a causal connection between displacement of long established families and the presence of Jews in the new model dwellings grew up. Attention was directed particularly to an area known as 'Jew's Island' in the very heart of Bethnal Green and it was here in June 1903 that the periodic harassment to which Jews were subjected erupted into open violence, with stone throwing, looting and serious injury.[46] This was a vivid reminder, in a powerful language, that native East Enders, as well as Jewish observers and East End editorial opinion, linked Jews to the housing problem. It was such a belief which sharpened ethnic relations in the East End between 1900 and 1904, at a time when Jewish immigration was increasing in the wake of further Russian persecution. It is not without interest that relations seem to have improved as the supply of unoccupied houses increased, in other words as the pressure on housing diminished in intensity.[47]

It is often difficult to categorize reactions such as these, arising out of competition in the housing and employment markets. They were seldom specifically anti-semitic but, as will be frequently emphasized, anti-semitism can shelter behind a different facade. However, such hesitancy in categorization vanishes once we turn to other matters raised in the immigration debate. Another major expression of hostility towards Jewish immigrants laid emphasis upon certain special cultural attributes, such as their hygienic habits and social separateness. Particular concern was expressed over this last issue.[48] The *East London Advertiser*, for instance, commented at the close of the century:

> People of any other nation, after being in England for a short time, assimilate themselves with the native race and by and by lose nearly all their foreign trace. But the Jews never do. A Jew is always a Jew. No doubt this is due to their [sic] desire for the formation of a new Hebrew nation, a fact which inclines them to look upon themselves as pilgrims in a strange land.[49]

It was, in fact, a persistent theme that Jews kept themselves apart. '"When in Rome do as the Romans do"' was observed as a guide to social behaviour by 'every race except the alien Jews', it was claimed. It was pointed out that Jews ignored local 'customs', 'religious observances', 'days of rest', and contravened established morality.[50] Even the *East London Observer*, which with its independent outlook usually sprang to the defence of the immigrants, referred in the early days of the immigration to the 'Ishmaelite complex' which it believed it could detect among the immigrants in the East End, although by the end of the century it was claiming, by contrast, a belief in the assimilative qualities of the Jews. Striking a well known and frequently rehearsed Liberal chord, it claimed that 'individual freedom', 'opportunities for education' and 'general prosperity' had reduced the attraction of remaining socially exclusive.[51]

Charges about social separateness were present not only in the East End press: they were echoed by various East End representatives who gave evidence before the 1903 Royal Commission on Alien Immigration. In the course of this investigation the Commission listened to Whitechapel and the Mile End being referred to as 'Jerusalem' or 'a second Palestine'[52] and they heard James William Johnson of the British Brothers' League complain about the immigrants who lived 'according to their traditions, usages and customs' in a way which was wholly deleterious to the Englishman.[53] And if that particular aspect of immigrant life soon ceased to occupy the *Observer*, it nevertheless continued to be concerned about the hygienic or sanitary habits of the newcomers. Jewish districts were singled out for their dirt and squalor in contrast to which 'the districts of the most benighted Chinese and Hindoos, to say nothing of the poor Irish and English, were simply paradise.'[54] Once again, similar, although more exaggerated comment, appeared elsewhere, as in the claim that

> Foreign Jews . . . either do not know how to use the latrine, water and other sanitary accommodation provided, or prefer their own semi-barbarous habits and use the floor of their rooms and passages to deposit their filth. Even in places where caretakers see that yards and closets are cleared away every morning dirt and destruction follow the same day.[55]

Throughout the East End campaign there were claims that there was nothing in this hostility which could be regarded as anti-semitic.[56] The issue is complicated but there is in fact sufficient evidence to indicate that, certainly in connection with the kind of cultural opposition to Jewish immigrants we have just been considering, such protestations and qualifications were not universally valid.[57] In the course of such responses there was a tendency to contemplate a mythical golden age, before the Jews came, when the problems which faced the East End did not exist. Attention fondly turned towards a time when 'good old names' appeared over shop doors, when the streets of east London belonged to Englishmen, and women with clean white aprons, with their children about them, sat on their doorsteps during the summer evenings busily engaged in their needlework, though doubtless with half an eye left over for possible scandal – in short, a time 'when people were fairly happy and contented'; a time when, although there was 'a small extent' of overcrowding, occasional periods of 'bad trade' and situations when the East End did not display 'its best side', tradesmen were nevertheless 'prosperous on the whole', and houses were 'filled by English people leading [for the most part] decent and cleanly English lives'.[58]

This past, it was believed, had vanished under the cumulative weight and competition of a Jewish yoke. Hence the cry was for help, for protection, for legislation to keep out the immigrants or for the Hirsch scheme to settle the immigrants in Argentina and thereby guarantee 'an avenue of escape for them – and for us'[59] or, in some cases, for almost anything that would take them out of the East End. 'I say let these Jews have an island to themselves and let them live on one another,' Walter Trott, a stallholder, told the 1903 Royal Commission. '[They] live like rats in a hole – I cannot find words bad enough for them myself.'[60] How many of the East Enders shared similar attitudes is impossible to say. It has been rightly noticed that the majority of the East Enders who gave evidence before the 1903 Royal Commission were hostile to Jews in varying ways and the hostility seemed greater in 1903 than in the 1880s[61] but we have no accurate means of assessing proportions of hostility, tolerance and acceptance.[62]

These particular expressions of opposition to Jewish immigration were only one facet of the hostility which developed towards Jewish immigrants. As we shall discuss later, there was some concern about the physical endowment of the immigrants, which involved claims that they had a propensity to transmit diseases to the receiving society, in addition to which there were fears of Jewish dominance and hints of Jewish conspiratorial activity, although these were mainly directed against rich Jews.[63] There were, furthermore, instances of organized opposition as indicated by the British Brothers' League as well as evidence of discrimination.[64] In short, the immigration led to a variety of responses and reactions. We have focused upon certain specific responses in the East End because these have been relatively neglected. It is important, nevertheless, to realize that similar types of argument were to be heard outside east London. The majority of these opinions have been discussed elsewhere and there is little point here in engaging in a massively detailed reiteration of them. Rather than this, a selection of attitudes will be taken from individuals on different points of the political spectrum, in an attempt to illustrate that even outside the East End hostility arose out of what was considered to be a conflict of interests. These individuals did not suddenly find their livelihoods were threatened because of Jewish immigration, they did not have to concern themselves directly with the East End housing situation, they did not live cheek by jowl with the immigrants, but they did believe, at various times, that the Jewish newcomers threatened their conception of an ideal society. Hostile strains of this kind can be illustrated from what might broadly be termed the left and the right.

We have already discussed East End fears about Jewish undercutting and this theme had a wider currency. Nothing along these lines worried the solid phalanx of Liberal opinion, of course, which tended to endow the immigrant with a shower of Smilesean virtues so that he became a veritable symbol of self help, hard work, self denial, and deferred gratification.[65] At its highest and most exaggerated point this way of thinking was illustrated by Charles Rolleston. He could stereotype the Gentile as a worthless degenerate, whose social fate it was to be replaced by a Jewish alien who

> enters the lists of the national struggle . . . endowed with a more than average capacity for work, together with an intense instinct for gain. Neither a loafer nor an idler, he appreciates the value of time and money; he is sober, self denying and intelligent, working with the supreme object of placing himself on a wealthier and better position. . . . He is not a hopeless degenerate, but very progressive. . . . When this man gets on in life so as to afford better food and healthier surroundings . . . [he becomes] in the second and third generation . . . a self respecting businessman, thoroughly English in sentiment.[66]

But to others the situation could be construed differently. It was precisely because it was believed that the Jewish immigrants were endowed with such qualities, as a result of their historical experience, that they were attacked. To the young Beatrice Potter, involved in the East End as an investigator attached to Charles Booth's survey team, there was indeed ample evidence to support a great deal of what Rolleston was to write a few years later. In her analysis of the East End tailoring trade she emphasized 'the love of profit as distinct from other forms of money earning' that prevailed among the Jewish immigrants, who were regarded as 'a race of producers with an indefinitely low standard of life' and 'apparently without the capacity for combination'.[67] But, at this juncture, as the Liberal clapped his hands and worshipped the immigrant as the personification of capitalism, Miss Potter proceeded to take a conflicting view. While Jewish workers were extremely law abiding, she commented that they were nevertheless prepared to engage in competition, 'unrestricted by personal dignity of a definite standard of life and unchecked by the social feeling of class loyalty and trade integrity'. All told, the immigrant Jew, 'though possessed of many first class virtues' was nevertheless, in her opinion, 'deficient in that highest and latest development of human sentiment – social morality'. Such an individual personified

> the economic man, seeking employment or profit with an absolute mobility of body and mind, without pride, without preference, without interests outside the struggle for existence and welfare of the individual and family. We see these assumptions verified in the Jewish inhabitants of Whitechapel; and in the Jewish East End trades we may watch the prophetic deduction of the Hebrew economist [Ricardo] actually fulfilled in a perpetually recurring bare subsistence wage for the great majority of manual workers.[68]

What is evident in Beatrice Potter's work is a hostile stereotype of Jews in east London, a categorical rather than an *ad hoc* treatment which discounts variety within that community. After all, if every Jew were a capitalist, how are we to account for Jewish Socialists and the existence of Jewish trade unions?[69] Such criticisms have in fact been made of Beatrice Potter's comments.[70] But it is important to recognize that while it is now currently unfashionable to refer to racial or ethnic group characteristics of any kind, this has not always been the case and when Beatrice Potter engaged in generalizations about the social behaviour of Jewish immigrants and referred to a Jewishness which grew out of a cumulative cultural experience she was not alone in doing so. In this particular instance she was, in fact, reflecting a belief in Lamarckianism which was a powerful current working through much social science in the late nineteenth century.[71]

Among those who held similar attitudes was J. A. Hobson who, although involved in the intellectual movement which eventually took him into the Labour Party, was still at this time a Liberal. Hobson was prepared to use Beatrice Potter's work in the *Nineteenth Century* quite extensively in his own *Problems of Poverty* which appeared in 1891. In this he was keen to emphasize that there was much to be said for the immigrants as individuals. They did not introduce 'a lower morality' in the areas where they settled, nor were they 'quarrelsome and law breaking'. But, like Beatrice Potter he presented an image of the Jewish immigrant as Ricardo's 'economic man':

> From the point of view of the old Political Economy, they are the very people to be encouraged, for they turn out the largest quantity of wealth at the lowest cost of production. If it is the chief end for a nation to accumulate the largest possible stock of material wealth, it is evident that these are the very people we require to enable us to achieve our object.[72]

Such qualities, however, did not appeal to Hobson, who at this stage of his life was busily engaged in rejecting laissez faire capitalism and all its implications. It was because the Jewish immigrant displayed these qualities that he was 'such a terrible competitor'. In his own words:

> He is the nearest approach to the ideal 'economic' man, the 'fittest' person to survive in trade competition. Admirable in domestic morality and an orderly sitizen, he is almost devoid of social morality. No compunction or consideration for his fellow worker will keep him from underselling and

> over-reaching them; he acquires a thorough mastery of all the dishonourable tricks of trade which are difficult to restrain by law; the superior calculating intellect, which is a national heritage, is used unsparingly to enable him to take advantage of every weakness, folly and vice of the society in which he lives.[73]

Hobson, like Beatrice Potter, was therefore prepared to discuss Jews in categorical terms. The attitudes of both are complex and this is hardly the place to engage in a detailed analysis: it is sufficient to show that they both engaged in this kind of writing, and to recognize that while they could isolate characteristics in the immigrants which Liberals also found, their developing opposition to laissez faire capitalism led them to take a jaundiced view of such qualities. And, to repeat, it is also necessary to recognize that in engaging in such categorical thinking they were neither unique nor deviant. So, while a body of East End opinion could complain about undercutting because of its effect upon the local labour situation, others far removed from the daily life of the East End could exercise their minds over the undercutting issue, not because they or those close to them were directly affected – indeed they might benefit as consumers – but because such activity offended and clashed with their conception of social morality, with their particular view of the world.

Turning from individual viewpoints to the organizational expression of attitudes towards Jews, we might at this point refer to responses by sections of the British labour movement. In 1892, 1894 and again in 1895, the Trades Union Congress passed motions urging the government to prohibit the landing of all pauper aliens who had no visible means of support. The extent of this opposition is impossible to determine although it was certainly not unanimous. It was strong among boot and shoe workers, cabinet makers and costermongers but other union leaders regarded the problems faced by labour as the result of difficulties inherent within capitalism rather than as the specific consequence of immigration.[74] It should be noted, too, that the resolutions referred to alien rather than Jewish immigration: there was no objection to Jews as such, although, as in other instances, it is difficult to disentagle anti-alien from anti-Jewish sentiment and on some occasions an antipathy directed specifically towards Jews did emerge. In these cases the hostility was very similar to that present in the work of Hobson and Beatrice Potter, stressing that immigrant Jews had a special thirst for mastership, that is to become capitalists and exploiters of labour. The Jewish immigrant was perceived as a supreme individualist, 'a man undeterred either by social consequences or personal sentiment from making whatever sacrifice was necessary in order to become an entrepreneur, "a sweating master"'.[75] But it was believed that this heresy could be removed through positive action directed towards the immigrant. Consequently, we can detect attempts by trade unions to unionize the immigrant, to remould his economic personality within the light of his British experience. But this was not an easy task: there were suspicions on both sides and its was not until after the First World War that Jewish unions began to merge into the British trade union movement.[76]

How did other sections of British labour respond to the presence of immigrant Jews in Britain? A fair amount of attention has been devoted to the general question of Socialist attitudes towards Jews and it is no exaggeration to say that every stone has been upturned to demonstrate that anti-semitism was prevalent within the ranks of the left.[77] But if we refer to details emerging in the course of the debate over immigration, it can be said that the major groups in existence during these years – bodies such as the Socialist League, the Social Democratic Federation (SDF), the Independent Labour Party (ILP), the circle around Robert Blatchford and the *Clarion* newspaper, as well as the Fabians – expressed very little overt hostility towards the Jewish newcomers, although exceptions to the rule can be found.

The immigrant Jews employed in the sweated workshops of the East End were regarded by the Socialist League as victims, together with British workers, of the capitalist system. Consequently, there was no point in attacking 'the blarsted furriners';[78] instead of this 'grimly grotesque' ploy, it was suggested that attacks should be directed towards the system itself. It was indeed strange, the League could reflect, digging into the ribs of the restrictionists, that many of those who attacked the poor immigrants had a different, more favourable perception of rich Jews.[79] Down to 1892 when the League ceased to exist – it had been founded in 1884 by William Morris as a breakaway group from the SDF – it did not hesitate to point out what it regarded as inconsistencies within the arguments of those who attacked Jews, while drawing attention to the fundamental structural problems facing society which were disguised by concentrating hostility upon Jewish immigrants.[80]

A similar line was taken by H. M. Hyndman's SDF group, which had begun life as the Democratic Federation but assumed its larger title in 1884. The SDF opposed restrictions upon entry from the time it began coverage of the issue in 1893. The TUC resolution of that year urging immigration control was dismissed as unsocialistic. The danger was that once controls were applied Socialist refugees could be kept out of Britain, in addition to which it was believed that there were alternative ways of solving problems which could arise from immigration. Like the Socialist League, the Marxist-orientated SDF was concerned to point out that the problems associated with immigration stemmed essentially from deficiencies inherent within the capitalist system. Any other emphasis was dust thrown in the eyes of the workers, mere 'tokenism' however attractively presented, with the object of blinding them to the real causes of their problems.[81]

In some respects the ILP followed a similar course. It was argued that attempts to interest workers in a campaign over immigration diverted attention from the real problems they faced. Thus while J. Bruce Glasier could speculate whether anti-alienism was always necessarily inhumane, and J. Havelock Wilson, the seamen's leader, could argue in favour of legislation against cheap alien labour, such anti-alien attitudes were not representative. The drift within the Party was against restriction and, even where an opposing sentiment existed, it did not always give rise to any overt opposition towards Jews as such.[82]

In *Clarion*, through which after 1891 Blatchford propagated his own brand of socialist enthusiasm, it was argued initially that immigration should not be restricted, that the problems which were associated with it should be dealt with by legislation against the sweating system. But individual writers were allowed to express their own opinions on the immigrants, which at times led to a high degree of viciousness, as when Quinbus Flestrin in his account of 'An East End Sunday' referred to a Jewish street trader in Houndsditch as 'The Nose' and commented that 'wherever you looked you saw a nose, such large noses, too.'[83] Also in line with this policy of allowing individual expression, Howard Hall was given a platform in 1895 from which he argued in favour of immigration restriction on the grounds that the aliens intensified competition for employment and by their cheaper labour held back the advance of Socialism.[84]

After this initial interest in the early 1890s *Clarion* did not take much interest in the issue until 1903–5 at the time when controversy was rife about the prospect of legislation. At this point in time, and certainly after 1904, the paper was in favour of restriction, although extremism was frowned upon. Even so, this did not mean that all discussion was restrained, as was shown in an article called 'Exchange is sometimes a robbery'. Although it was noted that the immigrants were 'downtrodden' and 'debased' as a result of their experience under the Russian despotism, the writer continued: 'I fear we can only look upon these poor creatures as so much poison injected into the national veins.'[85] It was admitted to be a cruel comment but, so it was claimed, since the immigrants were characterized by unscrupulous commercial methods and unclean habits and their presence was often a menace and an injury to the English working classes, this was something which had to be stated. Not everyone agreed and *Clarion* itself soon carried an attempt by the writer to limit the extent of his damaging remarks.[86] But this came too late to avoid a sharp retort from *Justice*, which complained about 'a most strikingly unsocialist and anti-semitic attack upon the Jewish workers'.[87] In fact, of course, the remark was not clearly anti-semitic; it was, rather, a vicious attack upon immigrants who happened to be Jews. The fact that they were Jewish was not stressed explicitly as a cause for concern but, as reaction to the remark indicates, it was difficult to steer a course between anti-alienism and anti-semitism.

Unlike the *Clarion* circle and the other groups, the Fabians referred only sparingly to alien immigration and, on wider matters, as a corporate body they 'expressed no opinion on the Jewish question'.[88] This is not entirely unexpected. 'Fabians disagreed among themselves as much as they did with non-Fabian socialists', it has been written, 'and it is generally difficult to refer to a Fabian doctrine.'[89] The most we can say in relation to alien immigration is that the Society did express a corporate response at its annual meeting on 12 May 1905, when those present accepted the executive committee's resolutions opposing legislation to exclude aliens. But the Society was not tempted into a specific discussion about the entry of Jews and the desirability or otherwise of a Jewish presence in Britain.[90]

If these inevitably selective attitudes constitute the general trend of Socialist opinion expressed in the course of the immigration debate, there were nevertheless instances when a specific opposition to Jewish immigrants was clearly spelt out. As we noticed earlier, Beatrice Potter referred in hostile terms to the inherited trasitions among the newcomers which could lead to a concentration upon self seeking activity and an absence of any wider social morality.[91] In the same tradition, Keir Hardie, who for many personified the ILP, Blatchford, Harry Quelch, the editor of *Justice* and Ben Tillett of the dockers' union, all engaged in this type of criticism.[92] In each instance it was suggested that the immigrant Jews had a special propensity for 'getting on' in capitalist society and absorbing its values; in view of this it comes as no surprise to discover that Socialists were less restrained in discussing rich Jews than they were in their references to Jewish immigrants. Indeed, it was quite possible for a discussion about immigration to become a vehicle for attacks of a vaguely conspiratorial character to be mounted on rich Jews in British society.[93]

In the light of such sentiments it has become fashionable in certain quarters to take the left to task for its anti-semitism.[94] And, in some respects, it is a valuable exercise to remind ourselves that anti-semitism has not been the sole prerogative of the right, of what have often been called reactionary forces. It is important, nevertheless, to keep a sense of proportion. The pendulum should not be allowed to swing too far in its new direction. Consequently, after acknowledging that anti-semitic stereotypes were present on the left, we might now remind ourselves that anti-semitic hostility could also be found on the right. An archetypal figure in this respect was Arnold White.[95] White described himself as an author who was interested in social problems and throughout his working life he moved from one bandwagon to another, involving himself in matters of the day and feverishly trying to project himself as an authority on a variety of social problems. After all, he had to earn a living and in the late nineteenth and early twentieth centuries he, and many in similar position, were willing contributors to the condition-of-England debate. It was in the course of this that he became involved in writing about Jews, including within the scope of his work references to rich Jews as well as their poorer immigrant brethren.

When White first concerned himself with the issue of Jewish immigration while collecting material for his book, *The Problems of a Great City*, he did not single out the immigrants on the grounds that they were Jewish. It was an influx of 'pauper foreigners' to which he referred and his apprehension at the arrival of the immigrants was related to what he perceived as their effects upon the labour market, their insanitary habits and, he believed, their susceptibility to Socialism, which offended his sense of moral principle.[96] Faced with this type of situation he had no doubt about his response. He was in favour in 1888 of refusing entry to pauper foreigners[97] and was prepared to apply this rule to all who fell into this category, even those who were fleeing from persecution.[98] Action of this kind, he realized, would meet opposition from sentimental liberals, the Jewish community and free traders, but he regarded himself as having different priorities from these groups: 'As the choice lies between renewed suffering abroad and renewed suffering at home', he wrote, 'I choose the former from considerations of justice and humanity to our own kith and kin.'[99] At this point White's response to the immigration issue, although clearly nationalist, nevertheless managed to avoid the overt expression of anti-semitism. His ostensible concern was with pauper foreigners.

This was soon to change. As early as February 1888 he had declared that he could not refrain from introducing the work 'Jew' into the immigration debate.[100] But it was the effect of his experiences in Russia which led him more openly into a consideration of the Jewish composition of the immigration and into the area of anti-semitism.[101] He went on the first of his five journeys in 1890, straight into the heart of an anti-semitic country, where there was no close season for the Jews – or indeed, for most of the other ethnic minorities who lived within the Tsar's Empire.[102] White travelled to Russia as the emissary of Baron Maurice de Hirsch, the noted Jewish philanthropist, who was anxious for Jews to settle in colonies in Argentina as an alternative to continued persecution in the Russian Empire and who believed that White, with his interest in emigration, colonization and Jewish matters, would be well suited to talk to the Russians about the Hirsch scheme. In the course of these discussions White was not entirely convinced by what the Russian bureaucracy told him about the Jews. He was prepared to say, in fact, that the image of the Jew which prevailed in St Petersburg corresponded more closely to the 'inner consciousness' of the administrators than in did to reality.[103] But even so, he was sympathetic to the problems facing the Russian authorities. 'The Russian nature', he believed, 'was self indulgent, impulsive, kind hearted, generous and passionate' and had to contend with the 'masterful' Jewish intellect and Jewish 'assiduity', as well as 'the deadly resolve to get on', and the 'self denial' and 'ambition' which characterized Russian Jewry.[104]

All told, the Russian experience created a deep impression and by the 1890s White was convinced that the threat of Jewish power which he had encountered in Russia was extending itself and becoming a feature of British social life. He came to believe that his early writing on Jewish immigration had been 'superficial', 'unconvincing' and 'even irrelevant',[105] and began to refer to a Jewish question which was racial and international in character.[101] More precisely, his writing came to incorporate two particular emphases. One of these concerned the aloofness of the Jews. In his view it had to be recognized that the crux of the immigration question was

> not that of numbers, nor of habits, nor of occupations of the immigrants but the fact that, good or bad or indifferent the orthodox immigrants belong to a race and cling to a community that prefers to remain aloof from the mainstream of our national life, by shunning intermarriage with Anglo-Saxons.[107]

In addition, in pursuit of the wider Jewish question, he began to concern himself with the development of a Jewish materialist imperium within the British Empire, whose allegiance to Britain was undermined by its connections, 'both by blood and religion' with Jewish communities elsewhere.[108]

How could these problems be solved? White offered several courses of action at different times. He continued to argue for control over the entry of Jews into Britain and, in an attempt to divert the stream of immigration, suggested that as an alternative to the Hirsch scheme which had been pronounced impracticable, and in place of Zionism, that Jews should be settled in Turkish Armenia, 'rich in soil, benign in climate, half populated and inhabited in part by a semitic race which [would] get no harm from contact with the Jews'.[109] Any surplus population which developed in Turkish Armenia could move into the Holy Land.[110] For those who did not accept this form of exclusion from Gentile society, White suggested a policy of assimilation, the breaking of the cultural bonds which united Jews to each other.[111] In understanding White's advocacy of this it needs to be realized that at times his general comments suggested his acceptance of a belief in the inheritability of acquired characteristics[112] and some of his specific remarks about ethnic groups assumed a similar neo-Lamarckian tone.[113] Against such a background it was possible to speculate that the intermarriage of Jew and Gentile could lead to the injection of some worthwhile commercial qualities into British society.[114]

White wrote a good deal about Jews – too much one is tempted to say – and the comments which have been made on the model Aliens Act which he drew up for consideration, describing it as 'remarkable for imprecision, confusion of mind and absolute impracticability', have a relevance to a good deal of what he wrote.[115] In fact, it says something about the quality of advice which was on offer on such matters that White could be turned to as some kind of authority.[116] But, if persistence prevails and we cut through the mass of repetition, prejudice, ego-projection, sycophancy and half digested detail, it is apparent that White's attitudes towards Jews were not an isolated feature of his work. He was a staunch nationalist, with a belief in England's 'national purpose' and a believer in what he regarded as a Christian-based society. On these counts he was suspicious of Jews. And to someone who distrusted modernity – the growth of industry, a commercial society in which money could be made rather than earned – and the physical manifestation of such developments in the urban Babylon, who preferred instead to vaunt the claims of agriculture and the restorative powers of contact with the soil, the Jews were suspect on a wider front. Had they not been emancipated by the very processes he detested? Were they not occupationally concentrated in finance and commerce, where they could corner the market and create wealth out of rumour? And were they not urban dwellers *par excellence*?[117] Like those of Beatrice Potter and Hobson, his references to Jews have to be considered within the context of his wider philosophy of life.

Hostility expressed elsewhere on the 'right' also assumed a 'Britain first' dimension. The Tory Party did not involve itself with anti-semitism and it was quick to reprimand those MPs whose activity seemed to draw them towards sources which did.[118] There were, nevertheless, a number of members, particularly those with interests in the East End, who flirted, Janus-like, with these dark powers. Prominent in this respect was the member for Stepney, Major William Eden Evans-Gordon, who sat on the 1903 Royal Commission and played a leading role in the immigration debate. His concern arose from what he perceived as the recreation of Wilna and Lodz in the East End of London and the social consequences inherent in that development.[119] 'East of Aldgate', he wrote, 'one walks into a foreign town' and, reversing the image for effect, claimed that when visiting the towns of western Russia within the Jewish pale of settlement he was surprised to find himself in the 'familiar surroundings of the East End'.[120] Within east London he believed he could detect the development of a separate community, 'a solid and permanently distinct block – a race apart, as it were, in an enduring island of extraneous thought and custom' – and it was from this that Evans-Gordon's apprehensions developed. He argued that this 'sentiment of difference' between Hebrew and Gentile and its social consequences in terms of housing, employment and social behaviour, led a proportion of each community to disregard the other's welfare and it was in the light of this belief, and no doubt with an awareness of political self interest as MP for Stepney, that he took his stand.[121]

Evans-Gordon's work, *The Alien Immigrant*, was one of the many publications written to influence public opinion in the debate over immigration and similar arguments were offered by those with related political views when they gave evidence before the 1903 Royal Commission. A. T. Williams, a member of the LCC and someone who was to become involved with the British Brothers' League – in which Evans-Gordon was also to assume a prominent position – was anxious to tell the Commission, when referring to foreign Jews, that 'their habits are so different to ours.'[122] He went on to expand this, providing the Commission with impressions which were to enjoy a wide currency during the immigration debate:

> The aliens will not conform to our ideas, and, above all, they have no sort of neighbourly feeling. English Jews will associate far more, and Germans will, but these Russian Poles do not appear to be able to budge an inch. A foreign Jew will take a house, and he moves in on a Sunday morning, which rather, of course, upsets all the British people there. Then his habits are different. You will see the houses with sand put down in the passages instead of oilcloth or carpet. These are little things but they all serve to make a difference. He will use his yard for something. He will store rags there, perhaps – mountains of smelling rags, until the neighbours all round get into a most terrible state over it, or perhaps he will start a little factory in the yard, and carry on a hammering noise all night, and then he will throw out a lot of waste stuff, offal, or anything like that – it is all pitched out, and in the evening the women and girls sit out on the pavement and make a joyful noise, I have no doubt, and on the Sunday the place is very different to what the English are accustomed to. Most extraordinary sights are seen. In one place last summer there was a kind of leads to a house with other

> houses backing on to it, and two alien families put out their beds on the leads and two married couples slept out on the leads, much to the amusement of all the surrounding neighbourhood. These are little things, but they serve to show that their habits are not such as will enable them to associate.[123]

This suggestion of immigrant Jewish separateness and a perception of conflicting norms of social behaviour between the immigrants and other East Enders was also retailed to the commission by J. L. Silver, who took time off from his desk as editor of the Conservative-orientated *Eastern Post and City Chronicle*, to express his attitudes before a different type of audience.[124] Much more obscurely, Joseph Banister, whose implacable hostility towards Jews extended over thirty years, turned his journalist's training into account and argued that one of the objects of Jewish immigration, and the reason it was supported by rich Jews, was to damage the 'race pride' of the British, their love of their country, and subject it to cosmopolitan pressures.[125] A similar concern was apparent in the statements by William Stanley Shaw, an early leading light in the British Brothers' League, who, although claiming at one point that he was not anti-semitic, could nevertheless raise and lament the spectre of London becoming 'an important Jewish city on the Thames' by 1913 unless drastic steps were taken to reduce this frightening possibility.[126]

On the right as well as the left it is clear that minds were exercised about a Jewish presence in British society as a result of the processes of immigration and even after the 1905 Aliens Act the issue remained alive. For instance, David Hope Kyd, the prospective Tory MP for Whitechapel, reminded the electorate in 1906 that Stuart Samuel, the sitting member, whom he unsuccessfully opposed, was pro-alien and it was 'no good sending to Parliament a man who stands up . . . for the *foreign* Jews.'[127] Rather, consideration should be given to the return of someone who could speak for the English in Whitechapel.

We might examine finally in this initial discussion of expressions of hostility towards Jews before 1914 various writings which appeared in the *Eye Witness* and the *New Witness*. The former, which boasted a string of well-known contributors, began life on 22 June, 1911, becoming the *New Witness* on 7 November, 1912. It had Hilaire Belloc as its first editor, although this role was assumed from June 1912 by Cecil Chesterton.[128] The general orientation of both journals was Liberal but they adopted an anti-Liberal Party stance and proceeded mainly to attack the parliamentary system, expose corruption and oppose those measures which seemed to limit the freedom of the individual.[129] A fair proportion of the comment was hostile towards Jews in a conspiratorial sense, particularly at the time of the Marconi scandal, and will be considered later, as will the National League for Clean Government with which the *New Witness* was associated; but it is possible to discern other expressions of anti-semitism which might properly be discussed here.[130]

It was not long after it commenced publication that the *Witness* turned its attention to what it called 'the Jewish question'. But what did this entail? On this it had no doubt:

> In the first place it is unique: there is no other case in history of the presence of a race not specially segregated by accident or by law, maintaining through long vicissitudes of various policies, its identity and its vigour in the midst of alien elements.[131]

But it was not merely that the Jews kept themselves apart – and here we can detect the charge which was raised at the time of the Eastern Crisis, in the East End during the years of high immigration and in the course of Arnold White's discussion of the Jews – it was also believed that this created tension and conflict.

> The mere acceptance of the Jewish race, the mere recognition of its presence does not rid either the Jewish people or the great majority of foreign peoples among whom they find themselves of an acute problem attached to that very presence.[132]

In an attempt to reinforce his argument the writer was keen to emphasize that

> The passion against the Jew has blazed out at the summit as at the nadir of our material civilization. The antagonism has borne its fruit in the most refined and the most sceptical as in the stoutest and simplest of European societies. And it is precisely today and precisely in a generation, when a particular and very noble republican philosophy of the state spread throughout Europe, was supposed to have laid the spectre for ever, that that spectre is beginning to reappear in unexpected places, with menacing power, and is promising a terrible future.[133]

The essential nature of the conflict between Jew and Gentile could in fact be summed up in the following terms. The enmity was 'fatally coincident with the presence of an alien race amidst a race differentiated into passionately conscious nationalities; of an uprooted race present amidst a race rooted in locality and soil; of a race bereft alas! of its shrines in the midst of a Europe whose religion [was] alive with shrines'.[134] These were the grounds of conflict and talk about a deliberate Jewish conspiracy aiming at power and domination, which was to appear in the coverage of the Marconi affair, was not emphasized – indeed, it was firmly dismissed.[135]

So much for the problem. In more positive vein it was suggested that there was a responsibility upon thinking men to offer some solution or otherwise European society was going to undergo a repetition and perpetuation of the 'oppression, injustice and enduring hatred' which had been evident in the past. In order to avoid what the *Witness* called this 'lamentable conclusion', it was suggested that there were three possible policies:

> The first – and that still most generally held in Western Europe – is to regard the matter as solved; vaguely to suppose the absorption of the alien race as feasible, and its presence for the moment as something at once absurdly separate and yet *not* separate from the life of the community as innocuous. The second policy is that of exclusion. The third policy is to grant the Jew recognition and privilege.[136]

These were the only courses open to any human organism which discovered it carried a foreign body. But which course should be adopted?

It was claimed that there were historical arguments against absorption. Experience suggested that it had never properly occurred in the past. 'The historic successes', the 'historic opportunities' and the 'historic failures' of the Jew had all failed to make him merge his race. But there was, furthermore, another powerful argument against absorption: wherever the course had been tried it had worked against the society which had fostered it. The experience of Poland, the Dreyfus affair in France and Britain's immigration policy all showed the dangers of pursuing it. In each case 'irritation' had developed between Jewish and non-Jewish elements.[137] In other words, emancipation should be rejected.

But was exclusion the answer? This was 'the most obvious and the shortest way of dealing with an alien body'.[138] However, in the case of Jews it had proved impossible to exclude them on a permanent basis. There had been many attempts to implement such a policy but none had proved absolutely effective and there was no machinery which could secure it. 'Though not of us they are with us – and with us for good.'[139] What, then remained? The solution, it was suggested, was privilege. In other words, special recognition was required. Customs had to be developed and regulations framed to meet the exceptional case. Jewish names should be registered, and there should be 'special and definitely Jewish representation in the councils of government'. In short:

> To tell the truth, to admit that the Jew is the Jew and with his immense pride of race and his indefatigable tenacity will remain what he is, to recognize it, to stamp it as a special exception upon the body of our laws is the way out.[140]

It was only through such a policy, the *Witness* believed, that social relations between Gentile and Jew would be transformed from a 'cryptic and abominably dangerous' basis to one which was 'healthy and regular'.[141] It had to be realized that Jews would never become Englishmen.

If such an analysis sounds familiar, it is because it was repeated at a later date and, in this respect, forms a bridge between pre-war and post-war anti-semitism. Both the contents and the structure of the arguments which appeared in the *Witness* formed the basis of Hilaire Belloc's *The Jews*, published in 1922.[142]

In conclusion, we have been concerned in this chapter with expressions of anti-semitism in which a conflict was posited over certain standards, values, beliefs, and recognized guides to social action. In pursuing these we have considered the 1875 Eastern Crisis, the South African War, the Jewish immigration from 'the land of bondage',[143] as well as comment in the pages of the *Witness*. In all this, with the exception of the generalized hostility of Belloc, we have been involved with charges made against sections of the Jewish community by other sectional interests, which sometimes arrogated to themselves the right to speak on behalf of the nation. However, in the case of the *Witness* hostility was expressed towards more than a section of Jewry and referred to Jews in general.

In approaching such conflicts there has been a general tendency to couch analysis within the framework of a scapegoat theory and to treat

Jews as innocent recipients of hostility, whose activities and interests were essentially irrelevant to an understanding of such situations. And no one could deny that the interests of those forces which opposed Jews were crucial in helping to generate the conflict. The Eastern Crisis in 1875, for example, provided such groups with an opportunity to question the emancipation process, to suggest that a Jew premier could not be expected to pursue a British policy, as well as a chance to engage in personal abuse. There were clearly forces which were waiting for such a political opening. But the particular circumstances during which they raised their voices did have certain ingredients which must not be overlooked. It is important, for instance, to underline that Jewish business interests were significantly represented in Turkey, where conditions were particularly favourable for certain types of enterprise and that Jews also had considerable financial interests there – to the extent that A. J. Mundella took it for granted that 'the Jews and Turkish bondholders' were intimately associated groups.[144] This, coupled with the fact that Disraeli was 'a Jew of Jews'[145] despite his baptismal certificate, need to be considered when a discussion takes place as to why the Jewish factor was brought into the debate. However, no specifically Jewish policy was pursued by the Foreign Office and indeed Jews were themselves divided in their attitudes towards the war;[146] the cry of Jewish influence as well as the cheap, vituperative jibes at the expense of Disraeli's origins which were triggered off by the Near East conflict distorted a complex situation. But such charges, if they are to be understood, have to be considered with a knowledge of Jewish economic interests in the Turkish Empire as well as in the light of Disraeli's perceptions of the Gentile world and its images of him.

In considering reactions at the time of the Boer War, it is similarly important to mention that there was a pronounced Jewish involvement in South African society in the late nineteenth century. Indeed, such activity has been eulogized in certain quarters.[147] Even so, this did not mean that the South African War was a Jewish war, fought by 'Britons true' for Jewish interests. *Clarion* was wide of the mark when it reproduced the jibe 'Britannia Rulth the wavth ma tears', which had originally appeared in the *Daily News*.[148] But such accusations, it can reasonably be argued, have to be considered against a short term Jewish influence, exercised through financial links upon the nature of developments in southern Africa.[149]

One of the hostile charges laid by contemporaries, particularly by the political left, in the immigration debate was that because of their cultural-historical experience the immigrant Jews had a special racial attachment to values associated with laissez faire capitalism. If studied from a present day standpoint and in the light of prevailing attitudes regarding what we mean by racial characteristics, such statements are suspect. But they need to be considered in a context in which racial categorization was common.[150] It has to be recognized that while such categorization was apparent among those who opposed immigration, it was also present in the writings and speeches of those Liberals who supported the immigrants.

Both pro- and anti-Jewish forces had a similar perception of the qualities of the immigrants: they differed, however, in their assessment of the social utility of such qualities.[151] And, in order to understand why such categorizations could occur, it is also necessary to take into account observable social behaviour, in the sense that insecurity and the need to overcome legal and financial problems before families could be brought over from Russia led many newcomers to engage in 'an unlimited application to work'.[152] In other words, an image was projected of Ricardo's 'economic man'. However, even with such a commitment there was no automatic, universal passport to success in the immigrant trades and, furthermore, some of those who did raise their status soon tumbled back into the ranks of the proletariat – in considerably less than the space of three generations.[153]

It is also necessary to retain a sense of perspective in discussing specific allegations which arose during the immigration controversy. Cries were heard that Britons should have jobs, Britons should have houses, British ways and customs should predominate and if anyone had the temerity to ask 'why?' there was a ready reply. Britain was for the British. It can hardly be doubted that all these sentiments have to be taken into account in explaining much of the hostility which Jewish newcomers had to face. They arrived in east London at a time of economic difficulty and uncertainty and these circumstances provided the major preconditions for the emergence of such views, although popular conceptions of Jews, derived from a variety of sources, would also almost certainly influence the ways in which the immigrants were perceived. But this does not mean that everything in the various claims made about their activity can be discounted. Allegations of sweating, undercutting, and of competition in the housing market were the main economic charges which were heard and which deserve attention here.

It should be noted first of all that there was a Jewish involvement in sweating, even if it is wide of the mark to suggest that the Jews deliberately perpetuated the system.[154] The sweated trades were a reflection of inadequate social control over sectors of the economy where market forces had free rein and they were not an exclusively Jewish preserve. But within that context it should be recognized that, for a variety of reasons, Jewish immigrants tended to work with their own kith and kin and linguistic as well as other cultural barriers, in addition to Gentile hostility, limited the occupational mobility of Jewish labour. Hence Jewish sweaters could draw upon a regular supply of weak, unorganized newcomers with which to sustain a system of exploitation.[155] As far as we can tell this did not seriously affect skilled British workers but the impact of cheap Jewish labour, and the extent to which it 'split' other sections of the labour force in the East End, is less clear.[156] What is more certain is that some local tradesmen were hit by Jewish competition.[157]

Forced out of Russia, shunted across land and sea to Britain, directed into and virtually confined within a new ghetto, in many respects the Jewish immigrants had little say in what was happening to them. But those who were themselves suffering from the pressure on housing in the

East End, another main irritant which came to be built into the immigration debate, did not care to unravel the layers of historical experience which brought the newcomers to east London. They believed that the Jews exacerbated the housing problem and sixty years on from the crisis Gartner could write: 'Jewish immigrants intensified the East End's deep rooted problem of house accommodation by preventing the population from declining as its houses were pulled down.'[158] With varying degrees of lucidity and coherence, in organized or inchoate ways, this was what many inhabitants of Bethnal Green and Stepney and the other voices who joined them for a variety of motives, were trying to say.

However, it was not chiefly in relation to the employment and housing issues that clearly pronounced anti-semitic hostility manifested itself. Anti-semitism, it has been argued, emerged mainly in the course of the wider cultural clash with Jewish immigrants. In this connection attention has been directed towards the charge of Jewish separateness which was made against the immigrants and evidence would suggest that this was not a figment of fevered imaginations. It was indeed a feature of the immigrant quarter which was critically referred to at the time in the *Jewish Chronicle:*

> If poor Jews will persist in appropriating whole streets to themselves in the same district, if they will conscientiously persevere in the seemingly harmless practice of congregating in a body at prominent points in a great public thoroughfare like the Whitechapel or Commercial Road, drawing to their peculiarities of dress, of language and of manner, the attention which they might otherwise escape, can there be any wonder that the vulgar prejudices of which they are the objects should be kept alive and strengthened? What can the untutored, unthinking denizen of the East End believe in the face of such facts but that the Jew is an alien in every sense of the word – alien in ideas, in sympathy and in interests from the rest of the population, utterly indifferent to whom he may injure so long as he benefits himself, an Ishmael whose hand is against everyone, and against whom the hand of everyone may rightly be.[159]

Similar impressions of separateness and a distinct social cohesiveness have also remained with those who were nourished by the immigrant community, whether in east London or in Soho, Whitechapel's spillover in the West End.[160] And, in a comment on the consequences of such tendencies, it has been written:

> It was to be expected that conflict between local habitants and immigrants would arise as a result of their mutually exclusive styles and cultures.[161]

Related to this dispute was the claim that Jews contravened established hygienic standards, and it is important here to draw a distinction between the charges that were made. Religion imposed certain standards of personal hygiene upon Jews which should make us suspicious about accusations of personal uncleanliness.[162] As for the wider charge concerning social hygiene, it has to be remembered that standards in Whitechapel were not, in any case, 'sensitively high'.[163] Furthermore, the East End was for the most part an underprivileged area, an overlooked territory with an inadequate social infrastructure which did little to inculcate high standards of social hygiene. But given all that, it has been concluded that on arrival the newcomers added to this a 'seeming ignorance and indifference to sanitary arrangements'.[164]

Thus, hostility towards Jewish immigrants developed not merely as a consequence of sentiment within the receiving society but also depended upon the existence of an identifiable core of grievances. But these circumstances were soon transcended. Once under way the conflict could not be contained within strict limits. It could be exploited for personal political gain by David Hope Kyd, among others.[165] It could lead to someone like the Reverend G. S. Reaney writing as if the whole mass of East End problems could be laid at the door of the immigrants.[166] It could result in the emergence of economic fantasies derived from the impact of immigration upon particular trades such as tailoring and the boot and shoe trade, both of which were undergoing unsettling processes of economic transformation.[167] It could encourage individuals such as Joseph Banister and William Stanley Shaw to raise respectively fears of Jewish cultural and territorial dominance.[168] In short, once under way the debate fed upon itself.

This brings us, finally, to the *Witness*. The charge of Jewish separateness which appeared there was frequently made by others, sometimes by way of praise but more often as a form of criticism. In this latter respect, as we have noticed, it was prominently present in the work of Goldwin Smith and Arnold White as well as various contributors to the immigration debate and it was repeated elsewhere.[169] It was a charge to which Jewish communities were susceptible for two reasons. A degree of Jewish separateness based upon religious conviction has characterized some sections of the Jewish community throughout the life of the Diaspora – and within the hostility displayed in the *Witness* there was a tinge of religious opposition.[170] In addition to this sacred element, there was a secular tendency towards separateness from receiving societies which characterized Jews as well as certain other 'sojourning' groups and which had been reinforced in the case of many Jewish communities – and other minorities – by persecution, which was itself related in part to a pre-existing separateness. The whole problem was, in short, a tangled web of interactionist sentiment.[171]

At the same time, separateness has not been universally pursued by Jews and has been stronger at certain times than others – hence the inaccuracy of the stereotype which was projected in the *Witness*. In particular, some successful and wealthy Jews – or their children – have not always found it necessary to stay within the community and it is perfectly clear that before 1914 in Britain there were Jews who were prepared to 'marry out'. And the British aristocracy, which has always been prepared to marry socially inferior persons provided adequate compensation were forthcoming, was certainly not totally averse to such unions. Hence it is not difficult to unearth alliances between 'Jewish hieresses and scions of the British aristocracy'.[172] In 1878, for example, the earl of Rosebery married a Rothschild – although his mother strongly disapproved and so did influential elements in the Jewish community – and evidence of intermarriage has led to the comment that the charge of Jews being unassimilable 'passes understanding'.[173] In some instances intermarriage went the other way with wealthy Jews marrying into well established families in order to secure individual respectability, as when Ernest Cassel married into a Roman Catholic background and, secretly, adopted its faith.[174] But, at the same time, there were many rich and powerful Jewish families who never contemplated or indulged in any of this, preferring instead to maintain their historic links with their ethnic background. There were, furthermore, Jews like Lord Swaythling, who was deeply opposed to any such desertion from the community and believed so strongly in his views that he was prepared to insist upon it in his will, as a condition for his beneficiaries.[176] Reactions to the prospect of assimilation were clearly mixed but even if we add to the activities of the rich and powerful, whose lives are easier to plot and discuss, those more anonymous Jews who exercised their personal prerogative and rejected their origins, there was no wholesale abandonment by Jews of their faith and culture and everything which that involved for social behaviour. In short an awareness of the grossness of any charge of universal Jewish separateness should not allow us to lose sight of the core which gave the image its birth and sustained its life.

Two important concluding emphases might now be made. On the one hand it has been suggested that an understanding of the hostility we have analysed needs to take account of the interests and activities of both sides in the conflict equation. But it has also been argued that while anti-semitism reflected irreducible social irritations, in the course of the conflict these became simplified and distorted.[177] Anti-semitism arises through a process of subtle complexity.

3 The health and morals of the nation

There was a strand of thought in the late nineteenth and early twentieth centuries which emphasized the hazards to the health, physical efficiency and morals of the nation which a Jewish presence encouraged. This brand of anti-semitism was directed almost exclusively towards the Jewish newcomers to British society.

A number of medical men and scientists expressed fears about the dangers to health which could result from alien immigration, but this did not necessarily lead them to comment specifically upon Jews in this respect. For instance, Karl Pearson, who had been Goldsmid Professor of Applied Mathematics and Mechanics at London since 1884, discussed the influx of aliens in the revised version of *National Life from the Standpoint of Science* in which he urged the exclusion of the undesirable alien, the habitual criminal, the mentally defective, the congenital pauper and the insane, without any concentration or emphasis upon Jews.[1] It was only later, in the 1920s in fact, that Pearson wrote a full scale analysis of Jewish immigration.[2] Before 1914, while he was concerned about the quality of the national stock, it was alien rather than Jewish influences which principally caught his interest and, although the two were often synonymous, Pearson's overt stress remained upon aliens.

Pearson was a commanding figure in the academic sciences but the concerns which exercised him were widely discussed outside academic circles. Among the contributions made by medical men none was more forthright than Robert Reid Rentoul.[3] This Liverpool doctor was a prolific writer in the cause of 'eugenic principles' and it was to be expected that a consideration of immigration would attract him since these matters were regarded as especially relevant to the alien immigrant.[4] His particular contribution to this debate was displayed in his pamphlet, *The Undesirable Alien from the Medical Standpoint*, which was published in Liverpool in 1905. 'Salus Populi Suprema Lex', his readers were told and they were invited to consider Herbert Spencer's assertion that 'to be a good animal is the first requisite to success in life and to be a nation of good animals is the first condition to national prosperity.' These remarks, which prefaced Rentoul's analysis, provided the framework within which he approached matters of social importance. The same emphasis was apparent in his other work, where he could proclaim, 'heredity is the great cause', and prophesy that the attempt to build an imperial race from degenerates was doomed to failure.[5] But in none of this, it should be made clear, was there a bias towards anti-semitism. Rentoul's concern was with Britain for the British, with the interests of what he called 'our native poor and hungry', as well as the imperial strength of the country.[6] But this did not encourage him to single out Jews from other aliens and to engage in a specific hostility towards them.

Elsewhere, however, it is possible to find discussion which was specifically concerned with Jewish immigration, as in the hearings of the 1903 Royal Commission on Alien Immigration. In giving his evidence before this body Dr F. A. C. Tyrrell contended that trachoma, a disease of the eyes, was 'very largely a disease of race . . . the Jewish people are peculiarly prone to trachoma.' From this standpoint he was anxious about their addition to British society.[7] But, as is often the case, medical opinion was not unanimous, as was shown when Dr S. F. Murphy was later called and questioned specifically on this matter by Major Evans-Gordon. It was put to the witness that trachoma was prevalent among Jewish immigrants and it was asked whether an inspection of the immigrants on arrival would be an advantage. Murphy replied:

> No, I do not think so. I think I know the condition of the eye that was referred to and I find it generally in overcrowded districts, whether occupied by aliens or Christians. It is very common among the poor Irish – trachoma.[8]

Discussion about the incidence of consumption among Jewish immigrants was also inconclusive.[9] What is more certain is that whether or not according to medical opinion of the day Jewish immigrants were susceptible to certain diseases, the 1905 Aliens Act required the authorities to prevent the immigration into Britain of any alien found to be suffering from loathsome diseases.

Apart from scientists and doctors, the potential health hazards of immigration also attracted the interest of journalists and polemicists. Prominent in this respect was Robert Sherard, author, journalist, translator and biographer, whose interest in poverty and sweating was shown in *The White Slaves of England* (1897) and *The Cry of the Poor* (1901). This concern with social problems also encouraged Sherard to pay some attention to Jewish immigration and it was in this connection that he visited America in 1900, travelling steerage class to discover how aliens were treated by the New York Immigration Board. The results of this survey appeared in the *Daily Express* and subsequently in book form under the title, *At the Closed Door*, and this was followed by a series of articles which appeared in the *Standard* newspaper in 1905.[10] The latter, which sparked off a heated correspondence in the *Jewish Chronicle*, have been described as 'vicious' and although 'the word "Jew" [was] conspicuous by its absence occasionally . . . Sherard's xenophobia [switched] to overt anti-semitism.'[11] No one would argue against the articles being vicious. It was a feature which jumped straight from the pages of Sherard's report, as when readers of the *Standard* were informed that while 'splendid specimens' of Russians, Lithuanians, Hungarians and Slovanians could be seen in Hamburg, 'clean, sturdy, open-faced, sweet creatures' ready to put 'their strong arms' and 'clean hearts' at the disposal of America and Canada, one could also see

> the very opposites of these – filthy, ricketty jetsam of humanity, bearing on their evil faces the stigmata of every physical and moral degeneration, men and women who have no intention of working otherwise than in trafficking.[12]

These individuals, he reminded his readers, were destined for England and the dangers of admitting such immigrants should not be underestimated. In a clear attempt to send a *frisson* of horror through his audience he informed them that 'a variety of skin diseases, of curious and abnormal character' were present among the intending newcomers and occasionally the cases were 'such as to baffle the diagnosis of the doctors'.[13] Several comments might be made on this. First of all, Sherard did not spell out that his references were to Jews – although, in fact they were and his readers would have recognized them as such. Furthermore, his attempt to draw a distinction between the physical quality of those immigrants entering America might well have been valid as a result of the existence of more stringent American immigration procedures at this time.[14] But given that, in drawing such a distinction, his quoted remarks indicate that he did lapse into anti-semitism and there were other occasions when traces of anti-semitism did openly break through in his references to Jewish physical characteristics, as when he wrote:

> Long ages of hunger and suffering have brutalized a race which of all races is the most intelligent. The faces that, under matted and verminous locks, peer out into the streets are scarcely human. They are the faces of imbeciles, of idiots, ape-faces, dog faces – all that is hideous and most profoundly pitiful. These people are clad in rags and live in kennels, where they ply their trades. In the doorways and the mire of the thoroughfare little children are moving about. Their half naked bodies are black with filth and red with sores.[15]

In such writing, where the emphasis was upon undesirable Jewish physical attributes among ghetto Jews, there was more than a suggestion that it was necessary to take account of social influences upon physical endowment. In other words, there was a Lamarckian influence.[16]

Articles which stressed the physical arguments against admitting ghetto Jews also appeared under John Foster Fraser's name in the *Yorkshire Post* in 1903.[17] Like Sherard two years later, Fraser emphasized the difference between the physical state of the immigrants departing from Hamburg for America and Britain. 'The scabby headed, the soreeyed, the vermin infested' were those destined for the latter.[18] In short, Britain received from the Continent 'inferior physical material', the 'pictures of crushed humanity'.[19] Both Sherard and Foster Fraser were engaged in an attempt to secure some restrictionist legislation on immigration and Fraser pointed out that at the time he was writing there was no provision 'to turn back cases of smallpox, scarlet fever, measles, diptheria or indeed anything but plague, yellow fever and cholera'. The result was that 'the unwashed verminous alien' could land in Britain and add 'the refuse of the earth' to the existing population.[20]

Although Fraser was opposed to the entry of Jews – as with Sherard 'alien' was a euphemism for 'Jew' – partly because of their physical excresences, he did not emphasize that the diseases were directly related to an unalterable, universal Jewish endowment. It is true that there were remarks in his writing which give the impression of a generalized physical quality among Jews – hence his reference to 'the odour of Vilna' being brought to Whitechapel.[21] But, as in Sherard's case, there was usually a suggestion that the physical problems he found among the intending Jewish immigrants were evidently related to their social experience in the Russian Empire and the historical impact of this upon their physical constitution.[22] By 1908, indeed, when Fraser was writing a series of articles for the *Sunday Chronicle* on aspects of industrial life in the large towns of England, Ireland and Scotland, he showed in his article on 'The Jews in Yorkshire' that such fears were in the past and although he was not entirely reconciled to their presence in Britain, he was no longer concerned about their association with disease. By now he could categorically state: 'The Jews are a healthy people. Excepting consumption they have a peculiar immunity from disease.'[23] He had been influenced in this direction – he openly acknowledged it – by the work of Dr William Hall who made a thorough study of the health and habits of Jews in Leeds, in the course of which he did a good deal to dispel some of the wilder accusations levelled against Jews and their association with particular diseases, even if such work was probably more impressive to educated, professional opinion than it was at a popular level.[24]

What was probably the most vicious hostility towards Jews on account of their danger to the health of the nation came not from Sherard or Foster Fraser, whose work was not very easy to categorize in this respect, but from Joseph Banister. Banister was born on 6 December 1862 in St Pancras, the son of a cow-keeper and died on 12 April 1953 in the same borough. He was described on his death certificate as 'a retired journalist', living at Mill Lane in Hampstead. His first traceable contribution to anti-semitic literature came in 1901 and his last in 1934 and throughout these years he engaged in a savage and unremitting hostility towards Jews, although it is likely that his work had only a limited circulation and appeal. Nevertheless, even if he did not exercise any degree of influence his work is worth analysing and discussing as an illustration of what might be regarded as a particularly savage brand of anti-semitic hostility.

The work with which he opened his discussion of anti-semitism, *England under the Jews*, went through three editions between 1901 and 1907, although it is probable that the print was very small on each occasion and in fact the second edition seems to have disappeared altogether. He added to his ideas between 1901 and 1907 and the fullest expression of his hostility is contained in the third edition. As the title of his work suggests, Banister was anxious – indeed, obsessed, – about the power and influence, amounting to domination, which he believed Jews exercised in British society and it was an obsession expressed at times in conspiratorial terms.[25] But apart from this fear of Jewish domination and his wish to communicate this message to his fellow Britons, Banister was pathologically concerned about what he called the 'alien immigration plague', the presence of 'Asiatic invaders', and the 'semitic sewage' which was spilling into Britain.[26]

In keeping with this he launched into a vicious attack upon Jewish physical characteristics and propensities, in the course of which he proceeded to develop a complaint about Jewish odour, in language which was remarkable for its total lack of restraint. 'They may have bathed in Jordan a couple of thousand years ago', he wrote, 'but very few of them appear to have bathed in anything else.' Consequently, he believed, 'a Yiddish rookery in east London' was 'as hard on the olfactory nerves as a Chinese warren in San Francisco'.[27] The difference between Britons and the 'real aliens', which was the point he was trying to make, was apparent not just in this sense, he argued, but also in terms of physical characteristics. In this respect Jews were made visible 'not only by their repulsive Asiatic physiognomy, their yellow oily skins, their flat feet, fat legs and loathsome skin and scalp diseases' but also by the smell which they emitted. In view of this, he mused, it was easy to understand why 'the Chosen One' had a nose 'of such extraordinary size and thickness', since without it, 'how could he have survived the many centuries he was doomed to associate only with the members of his own tribe?'[28]

But his stress was not solely upon the repulsive physical appearance of Jews and unpleasant olfactory associations. He was also obsessed with what he perceived as the Jewish propensity to carry and spread disease and thereby infect and weaken other elements in the population. It was a message which, in common with other aspects of his thought, was vividly presented, as when he invited his readers to share his suggestion that 'the unpopularity of the bath among the members of the Wandering Tribe' accounted for the 'extraordinary extent' to which they were susceptible to 'blood and skin diseases'. Jewish blood 'like that of other Oriental breeds' was regarded by him as 'loaded with scrofula'.[29] Other anti-semites could attack Jews for their aloofness, their separateness, but, as his comments would suggest, Banister did not share this concern. Indeed, he warned against the mingling of blood:

> If the gentle reader desires to know what kind of blood it is that flows in the Chosen People's veins, he cannot do better than take a gentle stroll through Hatton Garden, Maida Vale, Petticoat Lane, or any other London 'nosery'. I do not hesitate to say that in the course of an hour's peregrinations he will see more cases of lupus, trachoma, favus, eczema, and scurvy than he would come across in a week's wanderings in any quarter of the Metropolis.[30]

Diseases of the skin seemed in fact to hold out a peculiar, obsessive, fascinated horror for him and he could claim that

> One particular deplorable result of the popularity of scrofula among our imports is the extraordinary extent to which the native element is becoming infected. Many a young Englishman accustomed to travel on the railways in London is as bald as a billiard ball from letting his head rest against a cushion that had been touched by the favus afflicted scalp of a Jew.[31]

Banister's *England under the Jews* appeared when the issue of Jewish immigration was under active consideration and thirty years on from this in *Hints to London Editors* Banister rose to a defence of Hitler.[32] Throughout the intervening years he was not inactive; he was in fact busily engaged in conducting his vendetta against the Jewish enemy and at no time did he attempt to disguise his hatred. Indeed, he claimed that wherever there were semites anti-semitism would exist and only 'neurotic nancies' who loved every race but their own would be unaffected by its influence.[33] Such forthrightness was far removed from the hesitancy and trimming which was apparent in so many others who interested themselves in various aspects of the Jewish question.[34]

His work had other salient qualities. Contrary to what is generally assumed, some American evidence would suggest that stereotypes can often express ambivalent emotions and, by way of illustration, it has been argued that they 'may blend affection and contempt as the southern image of the Negro has often done' or might 'mingle pity and censure, as eastern views of the Indian did in the last century'. Furthermore, and directly relevant to the discussion here, it has been remarked that 'in the case of the Jew especially diverse and conflicting attitudes have always existed side by side in American minds', so that 'attractive' elements could mingle with 'unlovely' ones.[35] In Banister's case, however, unlike that of some of his contemporaries, the hostility was unrelieved and his work was conspicuous for the absence of any kind of balance. He did at one point refer to the 'more pleasing points of the Jewish character', but used this as an opportunity to attack the 'beautiful home life' of Jews, 'the superior purity of their women', 'their wonderful industry', and 'their general sobriety'.[36]

Apart from its unremitting and unqualified opposition to Jews, Banister's work was further characterized by the comprehensive nature of the Jewish stereotype which he presented in his work. It was a construction which contained both ego and id elements and is interesting on account of this. Again it has been suggested in American studies that hostility towards Jews is usually directed towards their status, power and influence in society: in short, in Freudian terminology, it is a form of ego-hostility. By contrast, it has been suggested that aversion towards Negroes has its basis elsewhere and is generally characterized by its concentration upon the perceived laziness and sexuality of the Negro as well as its association of him with dirt and filth. In brief, it is presented as arising from the id.[37] In Banister's work, however, both elements were directed against Jews. Whereas his attacks upon Jewish political and journalistic influence, which constituted a good part of *England under the Jews*, reflected the ego-dimension of his anti-semitism, his frequent references to the dirt, disease and stench which prevailed among Jews added an id-type hostility to his work.

Banister's anti-semitic crusade was conducted in a language remarkable then and now for its persistent viciousness and violence. Respectable writers felt strongly obliged to display some caution in what they wrote and were schooled in the art of self restraint and it was in such terms that debates on issues of public importance were conducted. But for someone like Banister, operating on the edges of society, publishing much of his own work, such inhibiting restrictions had little appeal and restraining influences fell away. This was particularly apparent in his use and choice of imagery.

Some discussion has already taken place about the nature and significance of the use of illustrative images by anti-semitic agitators and it has been suggested that 'likening the enemy to a vicious animal is more than a metaphor of abuse because the agitator's use of this metaphor is so persistent, so overwhelming, that in effect it usurps the place of its object in the perception of the audience.'[38] It has also been argued that in indulging in such constructions 'the agitator confines himself in his imagery to animals of the "unrespectable" kind, rodents, reptiles, insects and germs' and this is fully supported from an analysis of Banister's writings.[39] Here we find references to Jews as 'parasites', 'Yiddish money-pigs', as spreaders of 'lupus and leprosy microbes', as 'oof-pigs', 'oof birds', 'Yiddish bloodsuckers', as well as 'Jewish oof-hogs'.[40] In addition to all this, throughout *England under the Jews* there was a persistent stress upon Jews as disease carriers, germ agents who were responsible for a great variety of loathsome skin and scalp diseases. Microbes and germs are not, of course, visible to the naked eye, to our everyday perceptions; they wreak their destruction in insidious, silent fashion and are all the more dangerous for that.[41]

Banister's campaign against Jews was very much a personal affair. *England under the Jews* was privately produced and most of his later works had similar origins although two of these, *Jews and the White Slave Traffic* and *Our Judaeo-Irish Labour Party*, were published by the Britons with whom he was associated.[42] However, the fact remains that Banister was essentially a lone wolf, a kind of 'underground' figure in the sense referred to by Norman Cohn, who lived in a subterranean world where pathological fantasies disguised as ideas were produced.[43] No one who contributed to the debate over Jewish immigration equalled the extent of his obsession with disease and no one wrote out his hostility in the same violent form. Had he been writing in Tsarist Russia or Hitlerite Germany he might well have secured patrons and it is not inconceivable that his work would have been taken up in influential quarters. In British society, however, he remained a curiosity, consigned to a feverish impotence, lashing out at 'swarms of gambling house keepers, hotel porters, barbers, "bullies", runaway conscripts, bath attendants, street musicians, criminals, bakers, socialists [and] cheap clerks' from Germany, 'cooks waiters and street-walkers' from France, 'organists, ice-cream poisoners, chestnut vendors, anarchists [and] beggars' from Italy, whose influence, added to that of the Jews, was bound to have 'a demoralizing and deteriorating effect' upon their English hosts.[44]

The potential threat to the nation through physical disease and degeneration was not the only avenue through which immigration was perceived as destroying national life. From time to time reference was made to alien criminality and the danger which it posed to society. This charge, that the nation's social health and well being were under siege, was part of the campaign waged against alien immigration by Sir Howard Vincent who, after a military career, had been appointed the first director of the CID at Scotland Yard; it was also present in the work of Vincent's successor, Sir Robert Anderson.[45] In each case, we should note, the concern was most frequently directed towards *alien* rather than *alien Jewish* criminality.

As a matter of fact, it would seem that in the early years of the present century alien Jewish criminality was not a pronounced social problem. Aliens committed more crimes proportionately than the British but alien Jews – if these are taken as synonymous with Russian and Poles – under-contributed to the amount of crime committed by foreigners at this time and a pro-Jewish source has suggested that alien Jewish crime became of even more diminishing significance in the years which followed up to 1914.[46] Nevertheless, alien criminality – which to some was synonymous with *Jewish* criminality and was referred to as if it were an ethnic quality – continued to be discussed and worried over, if necessary in defiance of statistics, in the early part of the present century. Particular concern was expressed in this connection about the adequacy of the 1905 Aliens Act in protecting Britain against undermining criminal influences and six years after the Act was passed such concern reached a peak with the dramatic incident involving shooting, burning and sudden death in Sidney Street.[47]

Forces hostile to alien Jews had little capital on which to draw for a concerted campaign based on alien Jewish criminality but reference to Sidney Street is a necessary reminder that crime and political activity could be related. In the course of the immigration debate suggestions were made linking alien Jews with particular political philosophies which opponents could classify as dangerous, un-English or undesirable. The 1880s and 1890s were, of course, the heyday of anarchism, the time of Joseph Conrad's *Secret Agent*, and it was sometimes assumed that London was the secret international headquarters of the movement where anarchist crimes were planned. And London itself was not immune from anarchist attack. The House of Commons, the Tower, Greenwich Observatory, London Bridge and Nelson's Column were all subjected to bomb outrages.[48] Discussion of such dramatic activity took place in blurred terms. Anarchists and Socialists were indiscriminately linked in many minds and, although Russian-Jewish immigrants were not prominent in either group, since foreigners were involved alien Jews were 'ineluctably embraced in the resulting odium'.[49] Nevertheless, most of the hostility directed towards anarchists and Socialists did indeed stress *alien* rather than *Jewish* origins and on this occasion was not a mask for a disguised attack upon Jews. In so far as any alien group was selected for attention it tended to be the Italians but several commentators did seize upon the situation to stress an alien Jewish involvement.

W. H. Wilkins, for instance, informed his readers about secret Jewish revolutionary societies, whose existence, he claimed, could not be doubted. In addition he claimed that there were pamphlets in circulation in the

East End, written in Yiddish, which were described as 'breathing the vilest political sentiments'.[50] Wilkins was not alone in making emphases of this sort. It comes as no surprise to find him joined by Arnold White who took every opportunity to link anarchists and alien Jews and proceeded to play upon Lord Salisbury's exaggerated, indeed obsessive, fear of anarchism, by telling him that 'an undue proportion of the dangerous anarchists in this country are foreign Jews.'[51] It was a charge which was to be repeated a few years later in the *Standard*, whose political orientation has already been demonstrated in the discussion of Robert Sherard's reports from Europe, and which could claim in 1901 that the East End anarchist was 'almost invariably a Jewish immigrant'.[52] What can be detected here is an exaggerated identification of Jews with political upheaval, with 'the visionary violence of Continental Socialism'[53] and we can witness it being used by those who were prepared to advance other arguments against alien Jews and who were not slow to incorporate this additional item in their armoury. However, it was difficult to sustain an argument that Jews had any prerogative over anarchism or any special association with it and the difficulty was clearly recognized by Major Evans Gordon when he commented in a letter to *The Times* that a concentration on such matters obscured the more important social and economic problems which east European (that is Jewish) immigrants created.[54]

In discussing alien Jewish criminality and the forms of political activity which came to be linked with it, it has been argued that the image of alien Jews and their activity which opponents offered for public consideration bore little relation to reality. But there was one additional, related area of concern which had a firmer factual base. After sustaining an argument similar to that advanced here, and de-emphasizing the Jewish connection with crime, anarchism and socialism, Lloyd Gartner proceeded to remark:

> It is otherwise with the most scandalous social problem cast up by the tides of immigration, decorously termed 'the social evil', meaning prostitution. Its full chronicle has not yet engaged historical attention, but the evidence demonstrates the variety and extent of the Jewish connection with commercialized vice. The principal 'contribution' made by Jews was the supply of girls to the entrepôts of the system in Buenos Aires, Bombay, Constantinople, and elsewhere, fresh from the East European Pale and London.[55]

Throughout the course of the debate over alien immigration suggestions were made that aliens were involved in this particular form of sexual exploitation. This was a feature of Wilkins's work in 1892;[56] a concern about 'alien vice' was present in Evans Gordon's attempt to influence the direction of the immigration debate;[57] evidence about alien prostitutes was given by police witnesses and others before the 1903 Royal Commission enquiry into alien immigration; and similar claims were made in the recollections of those who had engaged in philanthropic work to combat white slavery and prostitution.[58]

However, there were also specific attacks on Jews for their involvement in prostitution rackets. In one instance it was emphasized in 1887 by

Arnold White during a deputation to the Home Office on the subject of pauper immigration. In an attempt to make his point, White quoted the Chief Rabbi, Hermann Adler, who had remarked that the overstocked labour market and the continuance of Russian persecution which caused thousands of girls to arrive in Britain without any means of subsistence were the forces which lay behind 'the extension of the social evil', even into the Jewish community.[59] Later, at the height of concern about alien immigration, Joseph Banister waded into the attack. Readers were told that 'the aliens' especially the Jews', proneness for the viler forms of vice' was 'even greater than their criminality'.[60] And, whereas White used the comments of the Chief Rabbi as a lever in his discussions with the Home Office, Banister supported his assertion with evidence from 'the pro-alien organ, *Reynolds's Newspaper*', after which he proceeded to refer to the Jewish involvement in the white slave trade on the basis of comment in the *Jewish Chronicle*.[61] This Jewish involvement in commercialized vice was not special to England, Banister argued, and the widespread presence of 'the daughters of Israel' among the ranks of prostitutes gave the lie to elevated claims about the superior purity of Jewish women.[62]

As Gartner's comment would suggest, a temptation to write off these charges as gambits in a political battle without any substance to them should be resisted. In 1886 the *Jewish Chronicle* noticed that the Jewish Ladies' Association for Preventative and Rescue Work had just issued its first report and this was indicative of the concern within the community about a Jewish involvement in vice.[63] A similar anxiety could be detected two years later when the same paper felt obliged to refer to Jewish prostitution in the East End as 'a blot upon our community at large'.[64] It was a problem which, in spite of such disapproval, showed no signs of disappearing. In 1898 seven leading western rabbis addressed an open letter to their east European colleagues, begging them to cooperate in combating what was described as 'this dreadful disgrace'. They urged them to warn parents and children of the dangers of emigrating to a far away land of which they knew nothing and to guard against bridegrooms who, once out of Russia, found monetary gain and a capacity for exploitation superseding their affection.[65] But the problem continued, as was evident in 1909, when a private Jewish International Conference for the Suppression of the Traffic in Women and Girls was held in London, soon after the Board of Deputies had begun to take a closer interest in such matters because of the implications for the Jewish community of Jews being connected with commercialized vice.[66]

Jewish involvement occurred in a number of different ways. It was not unknown for silken tongued, smooth talking operators to persuade Jewish women to leave their homes in Russia on the basis of promises of a better life in the new world and then proceed by various means to 'place' them in brothels or under the control of *souteneurs* in Britain or some far flung corner of the world. In other instances unaccompanied women immigrants who arrived in London without much financial support and ignorant of the language could find themselves befriended and offered a 'home', only to discover that they had been taken up by racketeers and placed in a brothel. Alternatively, immigrant women who 'suffered a fate worse than death' while living in the ghetto were sometimes set on the road to prostitution through such an experience.[67] In some instances, however, impersonal rather than personal forces wreaked their influence, in the sense that the influx of Jewish female workers into the East End added to the oversupply of labour and drove some of those unable to find suitable employment into the ranks of prostitution.[68] This overstocking of the labour market, it was argued in certain quarters, also encouraged the spread of prostitution among other sections of the population.[69]

Sexual hostility towards newcomers is not uncommon in receiving societies and an examination of British attitudes towards aliens in the late nineteenth century and early twentieth century provides one illustration of this. It is, in fact, particularly common when immigrant groups are male-dominated.[70] But we have noticed that it can also be directed towards women immigrants. Now that we have become more confident about understanding human behaviour, responses of this kind might be regarded as little more than the projection of sexual frustrations onto those who are 'different'.[71] And it is quite possible that those individuals who wrote about prostitution among Jews and a Jewish connection with commercialized vice in the late nineteenth and early twentieth centuries thereby vicariously satisfied some individual sexual need. At the same time, they might also have gratified a prurient interest in others. In addition to this it can be said with confidence that campaigners like White and Banister were eager for any weapon with which they could beat the Jewish minority – or sections of it.

But, even if details about the absolute and relative number of Jewish prostitutes and 'bullies' defy extraction, and if, as needs to be emphasized, Jews did not exercise a monopoly in commercialized sex, and did not involve themselves in it through any special ethnic proclivity, this does not allow us to obscure or ignore the fact that there was a Jewish participation in vice and that it was on a scale to worry an admittedly sensitive Jewish establishment, whose records bear witness to a continuing problem and a persistently matching concern.[72] This involvement was not very noticeable in the East End although one or two streets in the Jewish quarter became known as red light areas; the principal 'contribution' which Jews made to that world where sex could be bought and sold like any other commodity was in the distribution of prostitutes on an international scale on the basis of an extensive contacts system.[73] What started for some as a journey to London in search of a fuller and freer life, far away from legal restrictions and pogroms, ended with them catering to clients in remote places in South America, Asia and the Near East whence they had been brought by Jewish middlemen dealing in human merchandise.[74]

In conclusion, then, there was a widely expressed concern about the state of the nation in the late nineteenth and early twentieth centuries. Pearson discussed issues in relation to a 'usefulness to our body social'[75] and Rentoul claimed that, 'to be a good animal is the first requisite to success in life and to be a nation of good animals is the first condition to national prosperity' and planned his arguments and policies accordingly.[76] Similarly, Sidney Webb could turn his attention to the prospect of 'degeneration of type', 'race deterioration if not race suicide' and contemplate the prospect of the country falling to the Irish, the Jews or even the Chinese as a result of the regulation of families by 'the self controlled and foreseeing members' of each class of British society.[77]

From the 1880s there was indeed a general preoccupation among politicians and commentators with the health of the nation; talk of racial degeneration – actual or prospective – as well as national decline was in the air and the cry was for 'efficiency', which it was hoped would rival that of Germany and Japan and restore the country to its former greatness. 'At the present time', the *Spectator* claimed, 'and perhaps it is the most notable social fact of this age, there is a universal outcry for efficiency in all the departments of society, in all the aspects of life. We hear the outcry on all hands and from the most unexpected of persons. . . . Give us Efficiency or we die.'[78] It is against this kind of backcloth that the ideas we have been discussing should be considered.[79]

About the fact – or perceived fact – of the nation's decline, there was little dispute among all these writers. But they could approach this matter in quite different ways, even when they were concerned with the specific impact of immigration upon the nation. Pearson and Rentoul limited their comments to aliens or, in referring to Jewish immigrants, did so without placing them under any special odium. But the circumstances allowed others to go further. In the writings of Banister, Foster Fraser, Sherard and Wilkins – the political journalists – there was a willingness, a rashness, a compulsion to settle upon Jewish immigrants to a greater or lesser degree and to emphasize a specifically Jewish contribution to the country's social problems and to the decay and decline of England.

Much of this writing was transparently polemical, geared to shifting issues of the moment and fixed on surface rather than structural issues. As such it was unlikely to make a major contribution towards an alleviation of Britain's problems but this should not lead us to assume that it was all wind. Accounts by Sherard and Foster Fraser about the physical condition of Jewish immigrants en route to Britain need to be considered against the possibility that the social conditions within the pale of settlement might still have been reflected in different ways in the physical condition of numbers of intending immigrants.[80] And the existence of American immigration control procedures meant that it *was* easier to gain entry into Britain, as Sherard and Foster Fraser suggested. Furthermore, allegations about a Jewish involvement in prostitution, it has already been argued, were more real than some might believe.

But we should also unearth the exaggeration and distortion which was reflected in the debate. Although the overcrowded conditions in the pale would almost certainly affect the physical well being of some Jews obliged to live there, this impact does not seem to have been as dramatic or general as that described by Sherard, whose description of intending Jewish immigrants portrayed them generally as physical Frankensteins. Exaggeration was also present in the discussion of diseases carried by the immigrants. Inevitably some disease could be found among them as in every migrating group. At the time, in the early twentieth century, doctors were divided on the kind of diseases which were present among the Jewish newcomers and also on their susceptibility to them, but the Royal Commission in 1903 chose to accept that the incidence of disease and the threat which was posed to the receiving society on this account were not significant.[81] This helps to highlight the lurid fantasies which were spun around this theme.[82] As for other charges, a false perspective was also revealed in the association of Jews with anarchism, Socialism and political crime. And the link which, for instance, Banister endeavoured to establish between Jews and organized prostitution, while reflecting the situation in a part of the white slave trade, exaggerated and distorted that particular issue.[83]

The whole debate falls into a recognizable pattern which was to be repeated elsewhere. We can detect opposition expressed for the most part towards a section of Jews rather than to the whole community – although boundaries could be ambiguously drawn. We can refer to a set of issues over which some dispute and difference was possible – in this case health, political activity and prostitution. We can detect wild exaggerated charges emerging from such differences. We can observe hostility operating on different levels, with instances of restraint and nice calculation and examples of startling crudity. And, whatever its form, we can find such hostility being pronounced against a declared love of England and the English or, at other times, Britain and the British.

4 Dark legends

In the midst of so much debate about Jews as a result of the immigration controversy, we should not lose sight of the fact that other tensions could generate hostility towards Jews. It is in this connection that we turn to Sir Richard Burton.

Burton was one of the most impressive figures of Victorian England. He was, in the words of a contemporary writer,

> a bold and original thinker, a profound student of men and things ... a rare genius, if a wayward one, and one of the most remarkable personalities of our day and generation.[1]

Even at a distance from this kind of Victorian hagiography Burton's memory can still attract considerable interest and effusive praise. Hence he has been described by a recent biographer as

> a Renaissance Victorian ... a soldier, poet, translator, ethnologist, amateur physician, botanist, zoologist and geologist as well. A celebrated swordsman and superb raconteur.[2]

Both sources, it need hardly be stressed, are closely involved in the Burton legend but there is a general testimony to the intellectual calibre and stature of Burton, and a universal recognition that he succeeded in imposing himself upon a range of interests, particularly those of an exotic, unusual or 'different' character. Leaving aside this mass of polymathic involvement, we shall concentrate on Burton's attitudes towards Jews, and especially his posthumous work, *The Jew, the Gypsy and El Islam*, which appeared in 1898. Before its publication, the *Jewish Chronicle* could write of him on the occasion of his death in 1890 as 'a great student of oriental matters', whose 'references in his many learned works to the Jews were usually, if not invariably, marked by the tolerance and respect of a scholar.'[3] By 1906, however, in a reference to Thomas Wright's recent biography of Burton, it was clear that this image had changed. He was now described as 'a British anti-semite', indeed as 'one of the few modern British anti-semites', as well as a learned author of indecent literature.[4] It was apparent from the *Chronicle's* remarks that Burton's posthumous work had been a major force in bringing about this revision of opinion.

The book had an involved history. For part of his life Burton was employed in government service and the material for the essay on the Jews was collected while he was consul at Damascus between 1867 and 1871.[5] From existing evidence it seems likely that he began work on it after he was removed from the consulship and before he was appointed to the less prestigious post as consul at Trieste in 1873.[6] According to W. H. Wilkins, who wrote the preface, Burton was in fact ready to publish in 1874 and indeed wished to go ahead in 1875 but 'an influential friend who was highly placed in the official world' advised against this on account of the hostility which the work expressed towards the Jews.[7] Burton was eager for advancement within the government service – he was particularly anxious to be appointed to the consular post at Tangier, Morocco – and, swayed by the suggestion that publication of the book might damage his career prospects, it would seem that he was prepared to withhold its publication. This, at least, is the account of events provided by Wilkins.

Burton's own comments throw less light on the genesis and manoeuvering which lay behind the progress of the book, although we do know, on the basis of a letter of 12 May 1887 to a publisher, Gratton Geary, that the manuscript was then ready and Burton was aware that it could well offend public sensibilities. 'You must tell me that you want it, or rather that you are not afraid of it', he was led to comment.[8] If, as Wilkins suggests, Burton did withhold the manuscript in expectation of future promotion, the plan misfired. In 1886 Lord Rosebery, the foreign secretary, had to make an appointment to the consulship in Tangiers but Burton was not favoured with the post. Consequently, he took up the manuscript once more. But it would seem that he was persuaded by his wife, Isabel, to delay its publication for a short while, until March 1891 in fact, by which time he would no longer be in government service. Burton agreed, but he died five months before his date of retirement. It was then the intention of his widow to publish the manuscript but she had not accomplished this by September 1896 when she rejoined her 'earthly master'[9] and so the harvest of death guaranteed that it fell to Lady Burton's biographer and friend, W. H. Wilkins, to prepare the manuscript for publication.

A version of the book appeared in 1898 under the Hutchinson imprint and it has 'always been an embarrassment to Burton biographers, who usually skirt the issue of his anti-semitism'.[10] The reasons for his biographers' sensitivity can be readily appreciated. Chapter 4 of the book consisted of a recital of what he considered to be the cruel and vindictive teaching of Judaism, followed by a catalogue of Jewish crimes, in the course of which Burton made it plain that he believed there had been a Jewish involvement in ritual murder:[11]

> The Jews murdered Padre Tomaso and Ibrahim Amárah at Damascus. In the same year they made away with a Greek boy at Rhodes, a Greek boy disappeared from Corfu and an attempt was made to murder a Mohammedan.[12]

The work encountered a generally hostile reception. For instance, the reviewer in the *Athenaeum* commented that the influential friend who advised Burton in 1875 not to publish the essay showed better judgement than the literary executors. It was concluded that the indictment against the Jews was 'too serious to be advanced by any responsible writer without ample proof', yet there was no attempt to prove the accusation. Furthermore, the 'savage style of writing' harmed Burton's reputation. There was hardly any influence of scholarship: the work was more like that of 'a party pamphleteer'. It amounted to little more than 'a violent attack, in clumsy English, unsupported by evidence', and it was suggested that Lady Burton would have been wise to consign it to the flames.[13] Similar harsh words were present in the *Critic*. In its opinion *The Jew* was 'decidely anti-semitic' and once again it was suggested that the book ought not to have appeared. Burton, it was said, 'was certainly unfortunate in his choice of literary executors'.[14] Elsewhere, the *Bookman* found the essay 'for the most part fiercely, fanatically anti-semitic' and, on the basis of its accusations against the Jews in the absence of supporting evidence, detected 'the taint of *Judenhetze* . . . over the whole treatise'.[15] By contrast, however, the *Spectator* adopted a more generous approach. Burton's claim that the application of the teachings of the Talmud lay at the heart of the hostility which was expressed towards Jews was dismissed as a 'defective fancy' but the chapters on the Jews were considered to be 'worth recovery despite their prejudice'.[16]

This is how matters appeared on the surface but beneath this there were other powerful currents at work. In his preface Wilkins indicated that in its published form the work was not fully complete. In fact, he was quite specific about a section which had been omitted:

> In the exercise of the discretion given to me, I have thought it better to hold over for the present the Appendix on the alleged rite of Human Sacrifice among the Sephardim and the murder of Padre Tomaso.[17]

Wilkins had no doubt that what remained was anti-semitic but he did not feel justified 'in going contrary to the wishes of an author' and suppressing 'an interesting ethnological study merely to avoid the possibility of hurting the susceptibilities of the Hebrew community'.[18] Wilkins was fully conscious of the fact that English Jews would shrink with 'abhorrence and repudiation before ritual murder' but, in his view, this did not mean that such a charge was without foundation when directed against 'their less fortunate Eastern bretheren'.[19]

Clearly some battle had been going on behind the scenes and this is confirmed in a recent account of Burton's life:

> Even Wilkins could not bring himself to publish the most offensive portion of 'The Jew' – a section on the alleged ritual murder among the Sephardic Jews of Damascus, and the murder of one Padre Tomaso in 1840. The manuscript of this portion was 'sold' in 1908 to Manners Sutton, who tried to publish it. But a suit brought by D. L. Alexander, who held that the manuscript had been only loaned to Wilkins, prevented publication.[20]

What are we to make of this? We can in fact reveal more clearly what was happening by using new manuscript material and placing events within their appropriate historical context.

An examination of the minute book of the Board of Deputies of British

Jews for 14 March 1897 indicates the beginnings of what was to be a long campaign to control the publication of Burton's manuscript. It was noted at this meeting that the publication of Burton's essay *Human Sacrifice amongst the Sephardim or Eastern Jews* had been announced and at this stage of the discussion it was unanimously resolved that the press who were present at the Board meeting should be requested either to abstain from reporting the discussion of the question (except such passages as the Board might sanction) or else to withdraw while the subject was under consideration. In reply to this the representative of the *Jewish Chronicle* indicated that he would have to follow his instructions to report everything. Consequent upon this the press were requested to withdraw – which they did. Following the Board's private discussion of the matter it was unanimously resolved that the solicitor of the Board should obtain a copy of the book. If it were found to contain matter which, in the opinion of the law and parliamentary committee of the Board, consitituted a defamatory libel on the Jewish community or any section of it, or was calculated to bring it into contempt and hatred, it was agreed that a criminal prosecution should be started against the proprietors, editors, publishers, printers, and any other persons responsible for the publication of the book. Alternatively, an action should be initiated against any such one or more persons as the committee determined. The solicitor of the Board was instructed accordingly and empowered to take all appropriate aid and advice. A copy of the resolutions was forwarded to interested parties. At the same time, it was resolved that no action should be taken on W. H. Wilkins's invitation to meet the solicitor and secretary to the Board.[21]

Following this, and after meetings of representatives of interested parties, it was announced on 8 April 1897 by the solicitor and secretary that the book was about to be published in an abridged form.[22] The law and parliamentary committee of the Board was still apprehensive about the situation, so it was decided to buy four copies and at the same time prepare a case for submission to Sir Edward Clarke QC and Mr H. S. Q. Henriques for their opinion. In addition, in an attempt to prevent the reproduction of the book in European countries, it was decided to send letters to Jewish leaders in France, Germany, Austria, Italy, Switzerland, Russia and the United States, informing of what was happening and urging them to be on the *qui vive* for an announcement of the book and then to take such steps as they might be advised in the matter. It was also resolved that a similar course should be adopted with regard to the important centres in the east and that a guarantee fund should be started with a view to providing for the expenses which would be incurred in the exercise. It was decided to approach Rothschilds' on this.[23] For almost a month nothing happened. Publication was still awaited on 13 May 1897[24] and in the summer it seemed likely that the book would not appear[25] but shortly afterwards it was reported that it had been referred to as one of Hutchinson's autumn publications.[26]

On 17 April 1898 it was reported to the Board that a copy of a work called *The Jew, the Gypsy and El Islam* had appeared: it was the book on *Human Sacrifice* in 'a very altered state' with at least 150 pages omitted.[27] It was resolved that the book should be referred to the parliamentary committee with power to take such steps as it thought appropriate. At the same time, the hope was expressed that members of the Jewish community would use their discretion and refrain from rushing into print.[28] At its next meeting the law and parliamentary committee heard the view expressed that although some passages in the book contained defamatory statements which reflected on the Jews as a body, any legal proceedings would be unsuccessful.[29] The Board received and accepted this report at its meeting a few days later but added that it was the duty of the Board to act if at any time the appendix referred to in the preface to the existing book were published and was found to contain matter which constituted a defamatory libel on the Jewish community or was calculated to bring into contempt and hatred the Jewish community or any section or members of the community.[30]

For a time this was where the matter rested. But in 1908 a member of the National Vigilance Society brought it to the notice of the Board that the publication of the omitted section was being contemplated. When approached on this matter the publishers maintained that their client was the owner of the copyright and they intended to publish.[31] Unfortunately, the reports of the law and parliamentary committee to which the matter was once more passed, are incomplete for this period but in February 1909 it was reported at the Board itself that arrangements had been made for the purchase of the Burton manuscript. The consideration was £10 to the trustees of Lady Burton's estate and one shilling to Mr Wilkins's representatives. The assignee was the president of the Board.[32] Shortly afterwards in view of a request from the solicitors to the Burton family it was resolved that the president should be authorized to undertake not to publish the Burton manuscript once it had been assigned to him, as it was in March 1909.[33]

But the matter did not quite end there. In 1911 it was reported that a hearing had taken place in the King's Bench Division over Burton's manuscript, the controversial appendix on *Human Sacrifice amongst the Sephardim or Eastern Jews*, and, in effect, it was a continuation of the struggle between Jewish interests and those intent upon publishing the manuscript. Although Fawn Brodie refers to the 1911 case she does not place it in its appropriate context, nor does she seem to realize that D. L. Alexander, who brought the 1911 action was president of the Board of Deputies and had in fact played a prominent role on behalf of the Board ever since the publication of Burton's essay was threatened in 1897.[34]

In the 1911 action Alexander asked for an order which would require the defendant, Henry Frederick Walpole Manners Sutton, to deliver up the manuscript on human sacrifice and all extant copies of it. Alexander also asked for an injunction which would restrain Sutton from printing or dealing with the manuscript 'or doing any acts in derogation of the plaintiff's right to publish the MS. and obtain copyright therein'.[35] The defendant, Sutton, claimed that the manuscript was his property since he had purchased it from Sotheran and Co. of 140 Strand, London. The plaintiff's case was opened by Montague Sherman who went through the history of the manuscript. After describing the events leading up to the publication of *The Jew, the Gypsy and El Islam* Sherman indicated that following this the offensive appendix was taken by W. H. Wilkins to Sotheran and Co. for sale and in 1908 Sutton purchased the manuscript from this source. But in March 1909, as already indicated,[36] the manuscript was assigned to Alexander, as president of the Board of Deputies, by the surviving executors of Isabel Burton, the executors of Elizabeth Fitzgerald who had died in 1902 and who had been an executor of Isabel Burton, and the executors of Wilkins, who had died in 1905.[37] It was argued in court that the plaintiff had a valid title to the manuscript as Wilkins had no power to part with it. Yet the firm with which Sutton was once a partner, Cope, Fenwick and Co., proposed now to publish the manuscript. It was this which the action was designed to prevent. For his part the defendant's counsel argued that his client was an innocent purchaser, and that no affirmative proof had been produced to show that Wilkins had no right to sell the manuscript. It was made clear that for his part, Sutton was quite willing to sell it. However, Mr Justice Lawrence held that a good title to the manuscript had been proved in the plaintiff. Consequently, he ordered it to be delivered up and granted an injunction restraining the defendant from printing or otherwise dealing with it.[38]

So much for the book and the swirling currents of opinion and action it produced. The feature of Burton's work which generated the hostility and aroused the apprehensions of the Jewish community was the suggestion of a Jewish involvement in violence and, in particular, ritual murder. In putting forward this libel Burton was not breaking new ground. In medieval times in Britain, as we have already noticed, the charge had been directed against the Jews in Norwich and Lincoln, both of which centres were to establish their own martyrs on this account.[39] But it was even older in origin than this and blood libel claims can be traced back into the ancient world.[40] Nevertheless, it might be regarded as unusual or eccentric for such an accusation be considered in the nineteenth century. But, in fact, it underwent a revival at this time. In 1882 the charge, which normally involved a claim that a Christian child had been killed at Eastertime, with a view to the Jews obtaining Christian blood for their Seder celebrations, was heard at Tisza-Eszlar in Hungary and following this a series of allegations occurred, culminating in the major show trial in Russia of Mendel Beiliss which dragged on from 1911 to 1913.[41]

Indeed, even before it had to face the problem of Burton's work on human sacrifice among the Jews, the Board of Deputies had been concerned about a report in the *Globe* newspaper from its Cairo correspondent, which referred to the revival of the ritual murder charge in Alexandria. In the opinion of the Board, the tone of this communication implied that, although the accusation had been generally discredited, there was evidence which could be adduced to support the allegation and, furthermore, the writer had tried to strengthen his argument by introducing what was regarded as a garbled version of the Damascus affair of 1840.[42] The Board noted that the report in the *Globe* had led to the Chief Rabbi, Dr

Hermann Adler, calling upon the paper to drop the allegations but no retraction had been forthcoming. In view of this, the Board took up the matter and the vice-president – at this time it was D. L. Alexander – persuaded the editor to publish the following paragraph:

> It is with quite as much surprise as regret that we hear of Jewish feeling in England being hurt by the letter which we published from our Cairo correspondent on the 18th of April, regarding the old allegation against the Jews of killing Christian boys at the Passover. Most assuredly neither our correspondent nor we had the smallest intention to cast a stigma on the Jews and if the letter is fairly open to the charge of doing so, we are sorry for it.

Such a statement was acceptable to the Board.[43] When we consider Burton's book, therefore, we should regard it as one element in an ancient tradition which had given considerable trouble to the Jewish community and which, in fact, continued to create apprehension into recent times.[44]

Apart from his excursion into one particular sensitive area of anti-Jewish sentiment, there is other evidence on Burton's attitudes towards Jews. Just before taking up residence in Damascus where he was to accumulate material for *The Jew*, Burton had been in South America and in *The Highlands of Brazil*, which was published in 1869, had written about the Mineiro, and noted that among these people Jewry served 'as a synonym for all devilry' but he felt it necessary in a footnote to distance himself from such opinion.[45] It was in his later work that a different sentiment was indicated.

Burton's specifically hostile references to Jews are in fact located in two works – *The Jew, the Gypsy and El Islam* and an earlier publication, *Lord Beaconsfield. A Sketch*, which was probably published in 1882. According to a recent opinion Burton was interested in and envious of Disraeli's career and, in an indirect reference to the Beaconsfield pamphlet, the same writer has commented:

> Eventually he wrote a half-admiring, half-hostile pamphlet that revealed a sense of kinship. Both men appeared half alien to other English men, Burton because he had been reared in France, Disraeli for being a Jew, a handicap his baptism into the Church of England as a boy only moderated. Both were able writers, witty, arrogant, and intellectual, and both paid penalties for their superiority.[46]

This is an interpretation which is favourable to Burton but one which hardly corresponds with the details of the pamphlet. Burton was basically intent upon showing that Disraeli was a Jew and that this dominated his political career. According to Burton the fact that Disraeli had been baptized was of no significance: 'Even the waters of baptism', he commented, could 'not wash away blood'.[47] Indeed, the fact that his 'semitic brain' had dominated his politics needed to be revealed, and could be, since 'the hour of reserve' had 'past away'.[48] It was of no deep regret to Burton that subscriptions to Beaconsfield's national memorial came in only slowly. After all, he commented, Disraeli was only a 'little great man' as opposed to someone like Cavour, the architect of Italian unification, who was clearly 'a great, great man'.[49] A reading of Burton's slim pamphlet soon makes it clear that in common with a number of anti-semites Burton found it difficult to accommodate himself to Disraeli's attitudes and activities.[50]

But the pamphlet contained more than an attack upon Disraeli. It encompassed Burton's views about the role of Jews in society and a first reading of the text might encourage support for Brodie's view that it was written in half admiring tones or, to express it differently, that it constituted an example of what has recently been called 'bright racialism' in which we are treated to an account of the glories of another group.[51] After all, references were made to the 'energy', 'foresight' and 'tenacity' which had resulted in the Jew emerging as 'the dominant figure of the day, the ethnological phenomenon of the world', where he was rapidly becoming 'the master', while to underline the new power of the Jews Burton affirmed that none of the European thrones could be compared for stability with 'the office stool of the house of Rothschild'.[52] Praise indeed. But behind the *apparent* admiration lay a deep sense of fear. Burton was engaged in building up an image of the Jews which would bring home the threat they posed to non-Jewish interests.[53]

How was this thrust home? In a powerful section of the pamphlet Burton aimed to reveal to the public the extent of Jewish power and the nature of its influence – matters which, he believed, were not widely appreciated. He began by saying that there was scarcely a titled house in England that was not 'leavened with Jewish blood', although since the process was disguised through religious 'conversion' the general public hardly suspected what had happened. And what its unsuspecting members did not realize was that although the Jew could profess himself 'a Deist, possibly an Agnostic', in reality, 'at heart', he was, according to Burton, 'a Talmudist', mostly able to convert his missionaries through his superior intelligence. This increase in Jewish power was not merely personal and inchoate in character. Burton claimed that it had an organizational base in what he called the Société Universelle Israélite, whose heart was in Paris but whose limbs were everywhere.

At this point students of anti-semitism will only be too aware that we are moving into the imagery and language of *The Protocols of the Elders of Zion*, a good twenty years before that particular publication was launched upon its influential and dangerous journey throughout the world. It was precisely because the Jew was 'going too fast' that hostility against him could be expected and, if people did not realize how fast the Jew was moving in European society, then Burton's pamphlet was designed to tell them. At the same time it was intended to reinforce other widespread arguments which were directed against Jews. The threat of a *Judenhetze*, it was argued, would not disappear until 'high authorities' in the Jewish world forbade 'the abuse of usury, especially amongst the poor', and something was done about Jewish monopolies in the spirit trade as well as the Jewish ownership of 'gambling and immoral establishments'. According to Burton 'these infamies' would have to be abated before the Jews could 'vaunt' that they were a 'holy people' and exchange the 'antipathies' of the world for its 'sympathies'.[54]

The 'pheonomenal position' which the Jews enjoyed, and which Burton acknowledged, was considered as arising out of 'a peculiar racial vitality'. In the past, he argued, Jewish social life had always been characterized

> by its 'one idea-ness', by its absolute concentration of thought; by its comprehensive far-reaching views and by its strong bond of common belief. . . . Hence when this stupendous organization devoted all its energies to the principle of self interest, it easily distanced the rest of mankind and created for itself the monopoly of wealth, which is the monopoly of power.[55]

Such qualities continued into the present and, in line with this, Burton argued that Disraeli was successful precisely because he shared in and enjoyed this Jewish experience, since he was 'a Hebrew of the Hebrews' and it was by this light alone that it was possible to peer into 'his dark places'. Consequently, his policy was dictated by his 'semitic brain'; his 'Hebrew blood made him love those who loved his people and hate with a fiery racial hate, all who did not.' Faced with this Burton consoled himself with the hope that Beaconsfield would be 'the last of race' to vitiate 'the sound condition and constitution of his party' and weaken the standing of the country.[56]

Clearly then, although *The Jew, the Gypsy and El Islam* was important, the earlier pamphlet on Beaconsfield should not be ignored by anyone seeking an understanding of Burton's attitudes towards Jews in general and Disraeli in particular. Interest in the earlier publication goes beyond this, however. Themes which occurred in the Beaconsfield pamphlet were repeated in the later essay. Although it was the aura of ritual murder in *The Jew, the Gypsy and El Islam* which captured public curiosity and concern, the work was wider in scope. An emphasis on the capacity of Jewish communities to survive united in the face of dispersion appeared in both publications,[57] as did a stress on the increasing power of the Jews,[58] and the view expressed in the Beaconsfield pamphlet, that Burton was able to reveal secrets about the Jews which other observers could not, was also repeated.[59]

So far the emphasis has been upon Burton's ideas, their character and element of continuity. But the significance and ramifications of *The Jew, the Gypsy and El Islam* go beyond Burton. The book was edited for publication by W. H. Wilkins and through this a link is established with a wider area of anti-Jewish hostility. Wilkins was born in 1860, the son of a Somerset farmer. After a private education and a short lived excursion into banking he went up to Cambridge, where he graduated in 1887. After leaving university he settled down to a literary career in London as well as acting for a time as private secretary to the earl of Dunraven. In 1892 he began to edit a periodical, the *Albermarle* and also published novels under the pseudonym of de Winton but his best known work was done in the field of biography. He died on 22 December, 1905.[60]

Wilkins is in no sense a front rank Victorian figure but he is of more significance than would be realized from a recent vague reference to him as 'a Mr Wilkins'.[61] In addition to his editing, his novels and biographies, Wilkins also became caught up in the debate over Jewish immigration. Why he did so is obscure, although it might be significant that the earl of Dunraven was involved in the agitation and helped to run the Association for Preventing the Immigration of Destitute Aliens.[62] Whatever the reason, Wilkins was one of the many who participated in the immigration debate. In this connection he published an article on destitute foreigners in the *National Review*, he wrote on the immigration problem in the United States in the *Nineteenth Century*, and also contributed to Arnold White's anti-alien publication, *The Destitute Alien in Great Britain*, where he dealt in some detail with the social problems resulting from the presence of Italian immigrants in Britain. This last interest was also reflected in *The Alien Invasion*, which appeared with a dedication to Dunraven. In the following year, 1893, he returned once more to the theme of Jewish immigration in his paper 'The Bitter Cry of the Voiceless Toilers with special reference to the seamstresses of East London', read at a London conference of the Women's Emancipation Union on 16 March 1893.[63]

For someone with Wilkins's attitudes, the opportunity which arose from his association with Lady Isabel Burton to marshal evidence of a different but certainly more damaging kind against the Jewish community, was probably not unwelcome. But the significance of Wilkins's role has been lost on those who have concentrated upon the general features of Burton's life, and the extent of Wilkins's contribution to anti-Jewish sentiment has also been missed by those who have focused their attention solely upon his role within the immigration debate. In fact, Wilkins provides a personal bridge between the immigration debate and the much wider issue of anti-semitism in British society.[64]

Eight years after Wilkins's death the reverberations of *The Jew* were still being felt. Those who were aware of the suppressed appendix and, more importantly, had knowledge of its whereabouts, were not slow to arouse an interest in it when a suitable opportunity presented itself. It has been remarked that *The Jew* was published at a time when agitation about the Dreyfus case was sweeping through Europe[65] and it is hardly surprising that with the onset of the Beiliss affair in Russia in 1911 an interest should revive in certain circles in this particular aspect of Burton's work. The charge against Beiliss, the superintendent of a brickworks in Kiev, was that he had committed ritual murder and it was an accusation of this nature which the Tsarist authorities attempted to prove over the course of two weary years between 1911 and 1913.[66]

There was no widespread British reaction to events in Russia, just as there had been little interest in the earlier instances of blood accusation trials which had taken place in eastern Europe in the 1880s and 1890s.[67] However the incident did stir some correspondence in *The Times* where Frederick Pollock commented that the notion of Jews engaging in sacrificial killing was an all but exploded myth and other letters were critical of the medieval sources which were supposed to justify the accusation.[68] The tone of the letters was strikingly similar to that which Charles Wright had adopted in the wake of the Tisza-Eszlar ritual murder case in 1882, when he commented that the charge 'ought long since to have been thrown in the lumber room of exploded opinions'.[69] There is no doubt, in fact, that the majority of the correspondents were hostile to the charges brought against Beiliss and this sentiment was also fully reflected in a composite intellectual protest of 1912 compiled by a number of prominent personalities.[70]

But there was another side to the coin as evidenced when F. A. Floyer informed readers of *The Times* that 'those interested in the truth of the matter' should refer to Burton's book where, he claimed, evidence was adduced 'in proof of the practice of ritual murder'.[71] This was an isolated defence of Burton's work in 1912, but in the following year, under the influence of the Beiliss affair, an article on Burton's suppressed book by F. Hugh O'Donnell, which appeared in the *New Witness*, made it clear that in some circles the issue was still alive.[72] O'Donnell's writings – which did not satisfy all readers of the *Witness* – indicate how contemporary anti-semitic circles could interpret the events surrounding *The Jew*.[73] In brief, the suppression of Burton's complete manuscript through the action of the Board of Deputies, 'that Imperium Judaeorum in Imperio Britannico', that 'Semitic Inquisition', which could 'ruin British officials and stifle British letters',[74] was presented as an example of 'shekel-power'.

O'Donnell's argument ran as follows. Burton had tried during his time as consul in Damascus to delve deep into the ritual murder accusation and it was the publication of his findings which the Jewish community would not tolerate, just as it was not prepared to endure his exposé of the Jewish usurers who had battened upon the population of Syria. London Jews, he argued, were always prepared to back the eastern Shylocks and the London community, which could be increased by any 'stuttering alien' who paid 60 shillings 'to become a Citizen of England, an Heir of Magna Charta, a Samuello-von-Isaac-von-Meyer de Stuart de Plantagenet de William the Conqueror', was portrayed as the centre of the 'world wide web' where the Judaean spider sucked his prey. In short, the intervention of the London Jewish community in Burton's activity in Syria, its earlier action in the Damascus affair to secure the lives of Jewish subjects charged in 1840 with the alleged ritual murder of Padre Tomaso, and its successful campaign to prevent the publication in full of *The Jew, the Gypsy and El Islam*, were presented by O'Donnell as evidence of the existence of an organized Jew power which could assume the form, where necessary, of the 'Judean International'.[75]

Since any mention of Burton's anti-semitism has been a severe embarrassment to 'the Burton industry' which has tended to produce highly romantic and coloured pictures of the great man, there are very few published leads available which help us to understand why Burton engaged in his attacks upon Jews.[76] Some explanation, however, is necessary and in trying to understand this aspect of his work it is a reasonable speculation – it would be unwise to place it higher than this – that his stay in Damascus marked a turning point in his perception of Jews.

It has been suggested that prior to his appointment in Syria he was questioned by the Foreign Office about his alleged anti-semitism as well as other matters which might be raised as objections to his being offered the consulship in Damascus.[77] But it is not clear that Burton's attitudes towards Jews did in fact give grounds for concern, although the Foreign Office was certainly anxious about his well known opposition to missionary activity and his well attested sympathy with Mohammedans; both sets of attitudes could create tension in a city of seething, clamant faiths like Damascus and it was these aspects of Burton's character and outlook which exercised officials in London.[78] As for Jews, we know that in his work on Brazil published in 1869 he had commented favourably, even if in qualified terms, about them.[79]

In retrospect, the Foreign Office was right to concern itself about Burton's suitability for the Damascus post. The city was a hot bed of warring factions, needs and beliefs, an erratic compound of different races, where prodigious tact and lightness of touch were vital in any consul. It was here that Burton came unstuck. In the course of his stay he managed to alienate local Christian opinion as well as run foul of the Wali, the Turkish governor-general of Syria, towards whom both Burton and his wife developed 'a pronounced antipathy' and whose rule he was to describe as nothing less than an autocracy.[80] But in addition to these sources of friction, and as well as incurring the suspicion of Sir Henry Elliot, the British ambassador in Constantinople, and G. Jackson Eldridge, the consul-general in Beirut, Burton alienated certain Jewish moneylenders who were based in Syria and were under British government protection. He was personally appalled by the high rates of interest which three of these men charged to Syrian villagers, many of whom found themselves totally in hock to them. There was an obligation upon the consul to enforce payment of these debts as well as guarantee the interests of the moneylenders and hitherto this practice had been pursued. But Burton's sense of moral outrage could not be contained and it became known that in him these particular Jews had an enemy rather than a protective friend. He made it clear, in fact, that he would assist only in the recovery of those debts which were such that if they were between British subjects were recoverable through the consular courts.[81]

Faced with lending in what was normally a high-risk situation and without the sympathy of the British government's representative, some of the moneylenders were anxious to reduce Burton's authority. The chance to attempt this came in August 1870 when, through prompt action, he managed to control a potential conflict situation between Jews and Christians. It was brought to Burton's attention that the threat of massacres in Damascus had been stirred up by certain Jewish moneylenders who wished to take advantage of the situation to buy up property and that two Jewish boy servants had acted as agents. Burton reproved the boys and temporarily took away the British protection of their masters. The situation was thereby calmed but consequent upon this Jewish moneylending interests wrote to London protesting about what they regarded as Burton's anti-semitism and Sir Moses Montefiore and Sir Francis Goldsmid presented the letters to the Foreign Office, thereby doubtless adding weight to the conern which was being registered there about Burton's suitability for the work which the Damascus post entailed.[82]

Such doubts were further inflamed by a private incident at Nazareth on 5 May 1871 involving a Copt, Greek Christians and a party which included the Burtons.[83] Shortly afterwards Burton was cleared in court of all blame and responsibility for the incident but this decision came too late to save him. By 25 May the Foreign Office was advising Elliot in Constantinople that Burton would be transferred elsewhere. It took only his dabbling in the affairs of the Shazlis, an esoteric Muslim sect which had been secretly converted to Christianity in 1870 and for whom he proposed a separate settlement outside Damascus under British protection, for the Foreign Office to decide on his recall.[84]

The incident-packed stay in Damascus has been discussed in some detail to provide an indication of the complex issues which Burton encountered and to underline that in part these involved Jewish interests with which he came into conflict. There is no direct evidence, it would seem, clearly linking Burton's later hostility towards Jews with these particular events but it has been suggested that his Damascus experiences and, more particularly, the trauma of his recall, led him during his ensuing period of unemployment to spend time in the British Museum writing his diatribe against the Jews.[85] In this connection it has been remarked that 'like many men who have difficulty with particular Jews and jump easily to an indictment of the whole people, his rage became generalized.'[86] And those who are brave enough to believe that the dead, excessively intricate recesses of Burton's mind can be revealed on Clio's couch, might speculate further and add to this social explanation of his hostility the idea that an element of identification with Jews would heighten his perception of their activities in Damascus.[87]

Although the links between Burton's experiences of Jews in Damascus and his later anti-semitism are elusive, there are pieces of evidence which would suggest that these years were significant in the evolution of his thought. We have been informed that he had been collecting material during his consulship on the alleged ritual murder of Padre Tomaso and this was a charge which not only appeared in *The Jew* but, it was claimed, was also defended by Burton in conversation.[88] Research and discussion 'on the spot' in Damascus seem to have convinced him of the authenticity of the charge that a ritual murder had been committed in 1840. Apart from this, there were some similarities between his own recall and the Tomaso affair, in the sense that on both occasions representatives of the Jewish community in London intervened. In his case he was also concerned about the involvement of the Alliance Israélite Universelle which, during his consulship in Damascus, took up the cause of the Jews in Syria and from that time onwards held a privileged place within his canon of suspicion and hostility.[89] Was it his personal experience of such activity which led towards his belief in the existence of an international Jewish network engaged in the defence and furtherance of Jewish interests?

On a concluding note, the hostility which Burton did display was expressed in part along religious lines and, according to his own lights, was concerned with the consequences which flowed from the cruel teachings of Judaism. Such teaching, he argued, had led to the perpetration of violence against non-Jews and to a participation in ritual murder. This was at the core of his hostility as it was expressed in *The Jew*. In an age when Darwinism in a multitude of forms became increasingly fashionable, it is clear that the implications of the Jewish religion, as they were understood by individual commentators, still held an interest and indeed anti-semitism could be defined by some as involving an attack upon Judaism.[90]

But a reading of *The Jew* and his earlier, slim pamphlet on Disraeli, reveal that additional stresses were present in Burton's work. He was also hostile towards what he perceived as a Jewish influence in forms of economic enterprise which, socially and morally, he regarded as undesirable. It was in this connection that his work indicated traces of a concern about Jews 'going too fast', as contemporaries would have it, which allowed some observers to slide into the belief that Jewish power was such that it could manipulate society in its own interests. Indeed, it is possible to discern these suggestions in Burton's work, for instance in his discussion of the Alliance Israélite Universelle, where his reference to its limbs spreading far and wide over the earth revealed the use of an imagery which was to become increasingly common in later years.[91] In short, he perceived the Jew not as part of a trembling, insecure minority group, but of one showing 'intense vitality' and 'purpose', endowed with 'energy' and 'foresight' as well as a 'marvellous tenacity' – qualities which had made the Jew 'the dominant figure of the day', the 'ethnological phenomenon' of a world where he was rapidly becoming the master and where, by implication, he could be an overpowering, and terrifying enemy.[92] In believing this, Burton was not alone.

5 Our new masters?

'The deadliest kind of anti-semitism', it has been claimed, has turned upon the belief that all Jews everywhere formed a conspiratorial body set on ruining and then dominating the rest of the world. Such a belief was simply 'a modernized, secularized version of the popular medieval view of Jews as a league of sorcerers employed by Satan for the spiritual and physical ruination of Christendom'.[1] This conviction, that social developments were 'ordained by a secret organization of Jews', it has been further argued, 'helped to prepare the way for the near extermination of European Jews'.[2] These developments are associated with a strain of anti-semitism which developed after the appearance in Russia in 1903 of *The Protocols of the Elders of Zion*, the influence of which, although reaching its high point in Nazi occupied Europe, has continued on a world wide basis until the present day. This particular manifestation of anti-semitism is considered later since it was not until just after the First World War that *The Protocols* appeared in an English translation.[3] However, long before then fears about Jewish power and influence in society, and a perceived ability by Jews to manipulate circumstances to their own advantage had made their presence felt in Britain.

The definitions of anti-semitism current elsewhere at the beginning of the century show that a powerful driving force behind the hostility was related to a perceived increase in social and political power among Jews in the years following their emancipation. For instance, in its discussion of anti-semitism in 1907 the *Grosse Meyer* could refer to anti-semitism being a reaction against 'the growing economic and political influence of the Jewish population, freed from its former restrictions'.[4] And in Britain, occasionally during the immigration controversy, but principally at the time of the South African War, in the debates over the Marconi affair and the Indian silver scandal, as well as in the emergence of anti-German sentiment in the years preceding the First World War, concern was expressed in certain quarters about a perceived increase in Jewish power and social influence. Jewish forces were in some instances described as having sufficient power to 'fix' situations in their own interest, in others they were considered as attempting to take over and ruin British society, and on occasions such dominance was treated as an assured fact. We might now turn to consider claims of this kind which were levelled against Jews and the circumstances in which they arose, before attempting to provide a fuller context for the emergence and persistence of such attitudes.

Among the strands of opposition towards Jews which developed in the course of the debate over immigration, this fear of Jewish domination was openly heard in the East End. Whereas the defenders of Jewish immigration could isolate and praise particular qualities of the immigrants, such as their hard work and their proverbial thrift and diligence, it was precisely on those grounds and the consequences which resulted from the employment of such qualities that others, who saw their livelihoods or values being threatened, were prepared to oppose the immigrants and the immigration. Some of this hostility reflected a fear of Jewish dominance, as was clearly demonstrated in a letter which appeared in the East End, written by an anti-immigrant source, although one purporting to be Jewish, which was brought to the attention of the 1903 Royal Commission on Alien Immigration. The letter presented a defence of Jewish immigration ('we maintain we have a perfect right to enter and settle in England'), coupled with an assertion of Jewish superiority ('you will pardon me if I say that we consider ourselves far superior to the English people') and, significantly, a threat of Jewish domination ('we dominate your House of Commons; we dominate your daily and weekly press; we shall shortly dominate your local boards and your councils; enough to spoil you if need be, as our ancestors spoilt the Egyptians').[5]

Similar fears were expressed by others who became involved in East End life. We have already noticed that William Stanley Shaw, whose activity in the British Brothers' League is considered later, could claim that by 1913, unless changes were made, London would become an important Jewish city on the Thames.[6] This fear, coupled with opposition to the prospect of future Jewish control over British society, was also evident in the editorial comment that the Jewish newcomers were set upon seizing control of the British Parliament with the intention of putting 'the Britishers out of existence altogether'.[7] Related fears and sentiments were echoed elsewhere, as when the *East London Leader* claimed:

> With the sceptre of finance the Jew also dominates the politics of the world. . . . It is the Jewish mind that is guiding the religious and moral movements in society in our day, and in secret the Jew is forging the chains with which he is preparing to load those miserable Gentiles who are looking on in their folly.[8]

However, the East End did not have a monopoly over opinions such as these. In *The Modern Jew*, published in London in 1899, Arnold White commented that the purpose of his work was, 'to make the people of England think'. But what had they to consider? On this occasion White stressed:

> If they refuse to think betimes, they will wake up one morning only to discover that they have parted with the realities of national life, and are dominated by cosmopolitan and materialist influences fatal to the existence of the English nation.[9]

The threat of Jewish domination was suggested obliquely in this – 'cosmopolitan and materialist influences' was a well-known long hand for 'Jewish influences' – and, soon afterwards, the avenues through which an explicit Jewish power was exercised were also revealed when he wrote about Jewish interests in the worlds of high finance and the European press.[10]

These agencies of finance and the press were regarded as providing the base for what White perceived as the increase in Jewish social power. He was particularly concerned about Jewish financial influence which he believed was a major feature of business life in the capitals of central and western Europe; it was apparent, he claimed, in London, Paris, Berlin, Frankfort and Vienna.[11] In fact, Jewish financial power was such that in his view – and he shared it with others – the house of Rothschild could have brought the Russian government to heel in 1894 by declaring that it would not assist the Tsar's ministers in raising funds on the international money market until the condition of Jews in Russia was transformed.[12] Jews, he believed, had a particular facility for making money in the commercial conditions of the late nineteenth century. Money no longer had to be earned; it could be made. And in this situation the Jew was particularly well equipped to survive. 'There is', White commented, '[an] element which seems to be almost universal in the Semitic race – viz. the inborn proclivity to perceive with lightning glance the right moment to "corner" the market.'[13] Such financial expertise and power, White stressed, was evident in England:

> In the art of hypnotizing large communities of shareholders into the belief that something is to be made out of nothing, there is no equal to the immigran [sic] Hebrew when he begins to prosper. His success has been imperial. It has introduced a new and dangerous element in modern society. . . . Since the fall of Barings the Jewish financial houses live in lonely supremacy. In Johannesburg there is but one non-Jewish firm of the first rank.[14]

Jewish press influence, which was linked to the growing importance of 'cosmopolitan finance', was the other agency through which, he believed, Jewish interests could manipulate society.[15] How else, he asked, was it possible to explain the opposition to the celebration of Trafalgar Day except by the fact that

> Some of the newspapers which opposed Nelson's commemoration were owned and inspired by people who have not a drop of English blood in their veins, and whose claim to articulate English thought and feeling is neither more nor less than that of the other domiciled aliens who are known for what they are. This manipulation of the Press by a handful of philosophic Semites who have no more predilection for England than for France, and who regard political questions from a pecuniary and cosmopolitan, and not from a British, standpoint, is an evil which exists, is growing and must be abated.[16]

We have, then, in White's work a prospect of Jewish financial and press power. It was believed that a combination of such influences was dangerous, since 'scattered over the face of the earth the Jews [maintained] a secret and indissoluble bond of common interest.'[17] In White's view, it was an influence which could lead to Jewish domination and run counter to British interests. 'Subterranean and invisible influence' could be brought to bear on policy.[18] After all, the Jews had 'a complex and mysterious power denied to any other living race'[19] and the financial backing which could underwrite this power was particularly threatening and central to an understanding of anti-semitism. 'The beginnings of modern anti-semitism', he wrote, '[were] due to the new appreciation of the growing financial power of the Jewish race.'[20] Thus, although White's opposition to Jews could be expressed along lines of Britain for the British, it is obvious that he quaked at the fear of Jewish power leading to Jewish domination. In fact, of course, the two themes were interlinked as was apparent when, after his reference to Jews as 'a new and growing power', which he viewed with concern, he could stress that such power was even more dangerous because 'like the Gulf Stream they remain apart from the mass of the ocean around them.'[21]

White played a major part in the debate over Jewish immigration and in his day was one of the leading commentators on 'the Jewish question' in Britain. Throughout the time he wrote on such matters he had a nodding acquaintance with influential sections of British society and was able to place his work in the leading journals and newspapers of the time. By contrast, as we have noticed, Joseph Banister had no such connections and the majority of his work before 1914 was privately printed.[22] We have also remarked that Banister's hostility towards Jews was characterized by his obsession with the existence of disease among Jews and the prospect of its transmission to the rest of society. But anti-semitic thought patterns often assume a mixed character, and Banister's work was additionally marked by the stress it placed upon the threat of Jewish power and dominance. In this respect, the title of his major work, *England Under the Jews*, is certainly not without significance.

Banister's remarks, characterized by their usual crudities, included references to 'our cowardly Jew-dominated rulers', as well as 'our Yiddish conquerors and their reptile Press' and he claimed that one of the difficulties, in discussing the 'alien immigration plague' was that the press was controlled by Jews, 'our Asiatic invaders', and those sections of it which were not controlled by them were still unreliable since they were afraid of losing advertising revenue if they were hostile towards Jews. This belief in Jewish press control was a constant emphasis in his literary career.[23]

Both White and Banister devoted a good deal of their lives to 'the Jewish question' but a concern about Jewish financial and press power was evident among others who displayed a less tenacious hostility towards the Jews than they. Indeed, widespread references concerning Jewish financial and press power occurred at the time of the Boer War. It was suggested in certain quarters that the war had come about mainly to satisfy certain financial interests who wished to preserve and extend their influence in southern Africa and it was around this issue that charges were pressed against sections of the Jewish community.

A useful way into examining this aspect of the South African situation is provided by the writings of J. A. Hobson, remembered chiefly for his unorthodox contribution to economic studies although his work, prolifically produced, was much wider in scope than this. Hobson was sent to South Africa in 1899 by C. P. Scott of the *Manchester Guardian* when it seemed that a war might be imminent. His assessment of the situation out there appeared in the *Manchester Guardian* and eventually provided material for *The War in South Africa*, *The Psychology of Jingoism*, as well as *Imperialism, A Study*, which appeared in 1902. *The War in South Africa* contained a chapter on 'For whom are we fighting?' and in discussing this Hobson said that it was difficult to deal with the question 'without seeming to appeal to the ignominious passion of Judenhetze'. Nevertheless, he persisted and claimed that resources in southern Africa had passed under the control of 'a small group of international financiers, chiefly German in origin and Jewish in race' and, in his opinion, the war was being fought for their benefit. He believed there was a community of Jewish interests at work which grew out of their exploitation of the goldfields, their control of the dynamite monopoly, their influence on the stock exchange, their grip on the loan and mortgage business, their domination of the liquor trades and their ownership of the Johannesburg press, as well as other activities. This influence, he believed, was also reflected in the social life of Johannesburg which he described as 'the New Jerusalem'[24] and, partly on the basis of these perceptions, he was encouraged to launch into a hostile categorical reference to Jews. In writing about their role in South African life he asserted:

> The Jews are par excellence the international financiers.... They fastened on the Rand ... as they are prepared to fasten upon any other part of the globe.... Primarily they are financial speculators, taking their gains not out of the genuine fruits of industry, even the industry of others, but out of the construction, promotion and financial manipulation of companies.[25]

In short, Hobson was keen to convey an impression of 'Jew power'[26] at work in southern Africa, a 'Jew-Imperialist design',[27] in the course of which Jews came to be labelled as parasites.

What is interesting in the present context is the way in which Hobson perceived this power. It was not dependent solely upon Jews in Johannesburg; their influence and success were related to their external connections. Jews in South Africa, he argued, could count upon Jewish press influence in London as an aid in their designs[28] and, as his analysis developed, it stressed that a strong network of interests was busily engaged in financial manipulation and pursuing sectional benefits at the expense of what he regarded as British interests. In other words, Hobson suggested that an organized international Jewish power was at work. His prior discussion of Jewish immigrants and rich Jews in British society had been characterized by a categorical rather than an *ad hoc* treatment of Jews and his assessment of the South African situation had the effect of extending his analysis so that it no longer merely discounted sectional or individual Jewish differences but proceeded to assume the existence of a strong degree of international Jewish unity. In essence, it has been graphically described as an analysis which saw the Jews as 'manipulators of the press both in their own preserve and in Britain through their connections with their bretheren', who through their activity 'drugged the public [and] appealed to blood lust by perverting the true springs of patriotism'. The consequence was that British policy danced to their 'diabolical tune'.[29] Or, in more restrained terms, it has been suggested that:

> His South African experiences convinced Hobson that the war was the outcome of a deliberate conspiracy planned and executed by a small group of self seeking capitalists who had systematically exacerbated divisions between the Afrikaner and British groups.[30]

Hobson's analysis has received a good deal of attention, which is wholly appropriate since it was widely circulated by those opposed to the war.[31] Furthermore, it was not an idiosyncratic view but was a major expression of a well worked contemporary theme. In Liberal circles, for instance in the South African Conciliation Committee, the idea of a "capitalist conspiracy' was being put forward in September 1900 in the course of which it was suggested that the Unionists were the tools of financiers, mainly Jewish, who would pour out British blood to secure high profits. In what have been called the 'slick Paper' pamphlets issued by the Conciliation Committee Jews were usually referred to in restrained long hand form as 'cosmopolitan capitalists', whereas in leaflets printed by other agencies for mass distribution there was an open reference to 'Jewish financiers'.[32] But in each case it was clear that Jews were the focus of attention.

This claim that the South African War was being fought for Jewish interests was not confined to Liberal opinion but was also present in Labour circles. This was made clear when the TUC meeting in September 1900 debated the issue and there were numerous references to taxpayers' money being used to secure control of the South African gold fields for 'a number of cosmopolitan Jews, most of whom had no patriotism and no country'.[33] Similar sentiments were echoed by others, such as when John Burns referred to a British army which 'had become in Africa the janissary of the Jews'[34] and on the occasion when the *Labour Leader*, the mouthpiece of the Independent Labour Party, adopted a position on the South African War directly on the basis of Hobson's analysis[35] and gave prominence to the analysis contained in *The War in South Africa*.[36] Elsewhere, Robert Blatchford's *Clarion* shared a similar position and quoted with approval the claim made by H. W. Massingham in the *Ethical World*:

> Modern imperialism is really 'run' by half a dozen financial houses, many of them Jewish, to whom politics is a counter in the game of buying and selling 'securities' and the people are convenient pawns.[37]

Although a concession is made here to other influences as well as Jewish, in the case of *Clarion* it has to be balanced against a later cryptic remark about 'the suffering Uitlanders of Jewhannesburg'.[38]

Similar analyses were forthcoming on the Marxist-influenced left.

Unlike *Clarion*, the Social Democratic Federation did not engage in hostility towards the Jewish immigrants entering Britain and it was less concerned than the Independent Labour Party and trade union opinion about the economic effects of the immigration, in particular the threat which might be posed to the standard of living built up over the years by British labour. Yet, at the same time, it did draw critical attention to the behaviour of Jewish finance and the Jewish press. Jews were regarded as have a special relationship to capitalism. 'The Jew financier' was referred to as 'a living type of the international capitalist',[39] as 'the personification of international capitalism',[40] and Jewish capitalists were considered dangerous not only because they possessed economic power but also because they were interested in using it for political purposes. According to *Justice* capitalist Jews exercised an 'enormous' and 'injurious' influence in the French, German and Austrian press[41] and the situation was not much better in Britain. In all cases the danger was that Jews acted not in national interests but in accord with their fellow Jew capitalists throughout the world.[42] This influence, it was argued, was already at work in English politics,[43] as developments in southern Africa made abundantly clear.[44] It was in this kind of situation that Hyndman could raise the prospect of 'an Anglo-Hebraic Empire in Africa' and urge:

> It is high time that those who do not think that Beit, Barnato, Oppenheim, Rothschild and Co. ought to control the destinies of Englishmen at home, and of their Empire abroad, should come together and speak their mind.[45]

In the month in which war broke out Hyndman wrote about 'The Jews' War in the Transvaal' in which he argued that 'the Jew influence' in England was being used to favour the outbreak of a war in southern Africa. 'Beit and Eckstein, Barnato and Oppenheim, Steinkopf and Levi', he argued, were 'the true born Britons' who were dragging the country into a war which would have to be paid for in the money and blood of others and it was claimed that Salisbury, the prime minister, was being drawn into a war by 'a Jew clique' whom he could not master.[46] The article was not universally approved of within the SDF. A. Lewis, J. B. Askew and Theodore Rothstein were individual members who protested about its tone and emphasis and they were joined by E. Belfort Bax who found it strange that the South African War should be attributed by some members not to capitalists in general, or to 'the financial capitalist' in particular, but to 'financial Jew *as Jew*'. 'There is', he commented, 'no getting over the fact of this *as Jew*, seeing that otherwise the introduction of race would be quite irrelevant.'[47] Nevertheless, editorial policy stood firm and at the beginning of November 1899 Harry Quelch, the editor, who had little personal sympathy for rich Jews, published an article defending the attack which had been made upon Jewish interests. In it he maintained there was every justification for calling the South African War 'a Jew capitalist war' but agreed that the fostering of an anti-semitic movement would injure Socialism. As a consequence the issue was allowed to fizzle out in the next issue.[48]

It is clear from this that a number of sources, of differing political complexions, regarded the South African business as a Jews' war. Rich

Jewish financial and press interests in Britain and South Africa were identified as the driving forces behind government policy, deliberately directing it for their own ends at the expense of British interests. In some instances, as the war continued, opinions changed and the role played by Jewish influences came to be written down. This was significantly apparent in Hobson's analysis.[49] On a cautionary note it should also be said that on some occasions the precise nature of the evidence is difficult to evaluate because of a reluctance to engage in a clear attack upon Jewish interests. However, reticence was often difficult to maintain and sufficient comment is available for us to say that there was a strong strand of contemporary Liberal and Labour opinion which regarded the Boer War as a war fostered by Jews for Jewish gain.[50] It is also apparent that there were striking similarities in the images which were presented of Jewish economic power, spilling over into politics and influencing government policy and, furthermore, such analysis was not confined to Britain. It appeared on the Continent where Albion could be depicted under Jewish control – a claim which understandably found favour years afterwards in National Socialist circles.[51]

Moving forward a few years we can detect additional uneasiness about 'Jew power' in the Marconi and Indian silver financial scandals which were unearthed in the years immediately preceding the first World War. A history of 'the Marconi scandal' – the term was coined by Cecil Chesterton who was to play a prominent part in exposing it – has already been written and consequently it would be superfluous to engage in a detailed account of the affair but a brief reference to the chronology of events is nevertheless called for.[52] Its origins lay in the armaments race with Germany and the Admiralty's wish to be in instant touch with British vessels throughout the world. A chain of wireless stations throughout the Empire would achieve this and it was with the aim of creating such a network that the government began to undertake negotiations with industrial firms. These began in March 1910 with the Marconi Company and in particular with the managing director, Godfrey Isaacs, who was a brother of the attorney general, Sir Rufus Isaacs. By November 1911 it was public knowledge that the government and the Marconi Company were engaged in discussions and in March 1912 Herbert Samuel, the postmaster-general, provisionally accepted the Marconi tender. Before the contract was publicly announced or ratified, Godfrey Isaacs went to the United States and took up a parcel of new shares on preferential terms in the American Marconi Company whose share capital it had been agreed to enlarge, and in April 1912 he generously offered a number of such shares to Harry Isaacs, his brother, who offloaded some to Rufus Isaacs, who in turn successfully offered some of his holding to the chancellor of the Exchequer, Lloyd George. It was this arrangement which provided the basis for the scandal. The American company was not directly involved in the contract and had not entered into talks with the government but it would have been a beneficiary if the British government did in fact officially sign an agreement with the English Marconi Company, as it did in July 1912.

Questions began to be asked and in the autumn of that year a parliamentary select committee was appointed to investigate the share dealings of ministers. The enquiry continued into the summer of 1913 and in the course of the investigations, in April 1913 in fact, the original contract given to the Marconi Company was cancelled. The report of the parliamentary committee split along party lines, with the Liberals declaring that no impropriety had occurred, whereas the Conservatives, although they agreed that the ministers had not been corrupt, accused them of grave impropriety and lack of respect for the House. Once this report was out of the way the question of providing the wireless network could be taken up again and in July 1913 the postmaster-general signed another agreement with the English Marconi Company. It was perhaps ironical that by August 1914 and the outbreak of war the wireless network remained unfinished and incomplete. Such in outline was the history of the Marconi affair. This is not the place to engage in a complete survey of the reactions which emerged during the scandal. Instead, the discussion is limited to those with an anti-semitic flavour and, in particular, those which displayed a concern about an increasing Jewish power in society.[53]

In this connection the role of the *Eye Witness*, later to become the *New Witness* is crucial but we will first consider the reaction of Leo Maxse's *National Review*. This journal, which was bought by Maxse's father in 1893, had a Conservative tone but was out of tune with the Conservative Party at this time, so that over the Marconi scandal, for instance, Maxse was critical of the Unionist press for not encouraging the *real* Conservative Party into more direct political action. This had a parallel in the *Witness*, where most of the staff were Liberals but had given up hope of the Liberal Party for much the same reasons as Maxse had come to despair of the Conservatives. Both journals had lost faith in the party system and the party press. Maxse opposed the former because he believed that the collusion which was attendant upon party politics prevented Conservative ideology being put into practice and he disliked the party press because, in his opinion, it was under the control of Jews, monopoly capitalists and wire pullers and was actively engaged in supporting the party system. Apart from these issues many of his leaders expressed in the form of 'Episodes of the Month' were hostile to Germany. He was obsessed with the idea that Germanic influences were at work in every part of British life and in all this there was a persistent suggestion that German Jews were busily engaged in working for the submission of Britain to Germany. Jewish power was apparent to Maxse both in finance and journalism and particularly in the 'pro-German' papers which he alluded to as 'the Potsdam Press',

> which knowingly or unknowingly, is wirepulled in the interests of Germany and against the interests of this country largely through the instrumentality of cosmopolitan Jews who repay the excessive hospitality they enjoy here by, to use a well-known phrase, 'working for the King of Prussia'.[54]

An alleged Jewish manipulation and domination of this kind was constantly emphasized in references to the 'heavy Hebrew control of several "British" newspapers',[55] the 'Hebrew press'[56] and 'Hebrew journalists at the beck and call of German diplomats'.[57] On other occasions attention was turned towards Jewish financial power as when reference was made to 'cosmopolitan financiers domiciled in London in order to do 'good work' for the Fatherland'.[58] Rich Jews of this stamp were perceived as far more dangerous than their poorer kinsmen who had captured attention during the immigration debate. Hence the *Review* could state:

> Much has been said, much has been written, about the pauper alien, and in many cases he is a curse and a pest, but he is nothing like so dangerous to national well-being or to our national security as plutocratic aliens who divide their energies between maintaining a fiscal system which sweats the Englishman for the benefit of the foreigner and intriguing on behalf of the beloved Fatherland, though curiously enough several of them have not even the excuse that they are of German origin.[59]

Such references indicate that the *Review*, in effect Maxse, found it necessary in its analysis of contemporary society to refer to the workings of a malign Jewish influence. Sometimes the comments were directly made; on other occasions they lurked behind a familiar 'cosmopolitan financier' façade. In commenting upon this Maxse himself denied that his analysis was in any sense anti-semitic. To his mind it was only when hostility was expressed towards all Jews that anti-semitism was involved, and, as he reminded his readers, there were Jews for whom he had 'the greatest respect'.[60] But on the basis of the working definition I have adopted,[61] Maxse would be regarded as anti-semitic and even in terms of Maxse's own definition, there are statements made during the Marconi scandal which reveal his anti-semitism.

It was in respect of the *Le Matin* libel action that Maxse showed himself capable of ascribing qualities to Jews. On one occasion when accusations had been made against ministers in the *Eye Witness* it was decided eventually to take no action in the courts. However, as the issue continued to simmer a clear attack upon the probity of ministers appeared in the French newspaper, *Le Matin*, and on this occasion it was decided to initiate proceedings. But the circumstances gave rise to some questions. The action was not defended and Lloyd George and Rufus Isaacs were therefore able to make a statement of their own position without challenge and to win the case. It was presumably hoped that this would restore the ministers' probity. Another interesting feature of the case was that the ministers briefed the two leading counsel in the Conservative Party, Edward Carson and F. E. Smith, thereby silencing two possible opponents across the House. It was this action which Maxse referred to as an instance of 'Semitic sliminess'.[62] The cross currents were curious and Maxse's objections reflected his belief in a Jewish plot. More generally, he also thought that there was a deliberate attempt in the press to 'hush up' the whole Marconi affair and the scandal helped to confirm his well-known suspicion of Jewish press control.[63]

Although Maxse took a keen interest in such developments, the journal primarily associated with the anti-semitic aspect of the Marconi scandal was not his *National Review* but the *Eye Witness*, which began its life in June 1911 and became the *New Witness* on 7 November 1912.[64] The combination of corruption in high places with a Jewish involvement meant that the affair was tailor made for coverage in the *Witness* and on 8 August 1912 it was stated that collusion to benefit financially from a government contract had taken place.[65] The standard accounts of the scandal reveal that at this juncture Herbert Samuel and Rufus Isaacs contemplated suing the *Witness* for libel over its accusation of improper behaviour, although Samuel believed there were arguments against doing so since the circulation of the paper was small and its income minimal. Furthermore, restraint was counselled on the grounds that an action by the first two Jews who had entered a British cabinet could result in unwelcome publicity for the whole community. In addition, Samuel, who had been characterized in February 1911 as the 'excessively correct' Lewis in H. G. Wells's *New Machiavelli*, was to comment, 'one does not wish to soil one's hands with the thing.'[66] Isaacs was also inclined to let the issue rest but left the matter in Prime Minister Asquith's hands and Asquith advised against any action.[67] Although a united front was taken by the politicians there remained a threat that Godfrey Isaacs, the managing director of Marconi, would sue on the grounds that reference had been made to a conspiracy. But he was prevailed upon by his brother not to do so.[68]

The article on 8 August 1912 marked the onset of the campaign against prominent Jews involved in the Marconi affair. Implications which were to assume an increasing importance started to be made when the *Witness* asked:

> What progress is the Marconi scandal making? We ask the questions merely from curiosity and under no illusions as to the inevitable end of the affair. Everybody knows the record of Isaacs and his father, and his uncle, and in general of the whole family. Isaacs' brother is Chairman of the Marconi Company, it has therefore been secretly arranged between Isaacs and Samuel that the British people shall give the Marconi Company a very large sum of money through the agency of the said Samuel, and for the benefit of the said Isaacs.[69]

Very soon, as the campaign grew, conspiratorial Jewish activity and a Jewish abuse of social power came to lie at the centre of the *Witness*'s presentation of the case and in direct terms it was claimed that

> Samuel, in the presence of several competitors, privately favoured with his patronage the Company run by Isaacs' brother and secretly negotiated with it a contract so very advantageous to the chosen – shall we say people?[70]

Two specific developments were seized upon to embroider this theory of Jewish conspiracy. First of all, it was noticed that Gerald Montagu, a banker and close relation of Herbert Samuel, had allowed his name to be used in the purchase of some Marconi shares made on behalf of a client of the Amsterdam firm of Wertheim and Gompertz. But the *Witness* was not prepared to believe the defence that Montagu was a mere middleman.[71] It wanted the public to be told whose interests lay behind that entry on the share register. The *Witness* also wanted to know whether Wertheim and Gompertz were connected with the 'group of Amsterdam

Jews [who] were especially prominent in boosting Marconi during the boom' which occurred in the early months of 1912.[72] From this point, in December 1912, this Amsterdam connection began to assume an importance in the *Witness*'s coverage as was revealed in the following week when it attributed the check in the falling price of Marconi shares to 'systematic buying' and claimed that those who bought 'were the same Amsterdam Jews who created the original boom and whom we now know to be in close touch with the Samuel family through the mysterious Wertheim and Gompertz'.[73]

It has been remarked that this is 'an outstanding example of how rumours and snippets of information could be fitted together to create a scandal'.[74] Only the previous week statements in the *Witness* about the role of the Amsterdam Jews had been couched in more moderate terms. At that stage Dutch advices had been regarded as prominent in boosting Marconi shares during the boom. Now they were held to be directly responsible for creating the boom. Also, in that earlier edition, the relationship between the Amsterdam Jews and the Samuels was in some doubt. At that point it was asked: 'Were Messrs Wertheim and Gompertz in any way connected with that group [that is, the Amsterdam Jews]? And what was the relationship between that group and the Samuel group in London?'[75] A week later the *Witness* was presenting the answers to these questions to the parliamentary select committee, set up on 11 October 1912 to enquire into the Marconi contract. Amsterdam Jews, it was said, were linked to the Samuel family through Wertheim and Gompertz. The answers were assertions, made in the absence of evidence, the purpose of which was to suggest Jewish clannishness and secret dealings for the benefit of Jews within the context of the cosmopolitan world of Jewish finance.[76]

The other important incident which encouraged the *Witness* to write about Jewish conspiracy was the ministers' action against *Le Matin* which, like the *National Review*, it regarded with great suspicion. *Le Matin* was described, in the absence of evidence, as 'the Jew financial organ of Jew financial organs', its editor, Stephen Lausanne, was referred to as 'the Jews of Jews' and the whole business, it was believed, smacked of a prearranged plan which would enable the ministers to save their reputations. In brief, a Jewish financial journal sued by peccant Jewish financial operators was hardly the context out of which enlightenment would emerge. Or, as the *Witness* cynically expressed it, 'decidedly, the penitent David could not have offered a more convenient "leg up" to Jonathan.'[77]

A great deal of the writing in the *Witness* on the Marconi affair came from Cecil Chesterton but some of the most vicious comment which emphasized and opposed Jewish dominance came from F. Hugh O'Donnell, whose writing displayed these characteristics from the moment he came into the orbit of the *Witness* in 1912.[78] In a letter he referred to his impression that 'the Press, the Parliament, the theatre, the music hall, the bar, the teashop, the tobacconist, all kinds of trades' reflected 'the appalling ascendancy' of the Jews, who were purposefully engaged, he believed, in individual and collective activity towards the achievement of such dominance.[79] Hilaire Belloc, at that stage the editor of the *Witness*, made a cautious response but an editor's qualification was a godsend to O'Donnell, since it gave him yet another opportunity to pick up his pen and engage in further correspondence, thereby keeping himself before the readers of the *Witness* and impressing himself upon those who were running the journal. The theme of his reply was that 'the vast and increasing domination of this gifted Asiatic tribe in almost every department of English life' made 'the struggle for life proportionately harder for the inferiorly equipped Englishman of the twentieth century'. Indeed, the fact was 'the Jew wins and must win in what are called modern conditions.'[80]

It was not long after launching himself in such a manner in the correspondence columns that O'Donnell began to write a regular feature called 'Twenty Years After' for the *New Witness*.[81] There were clearly forces within the *Witness* circle who wanted such views expressed and he now had a platform from which he could transmit his obsessive concern about England being transformed into 'a transplanted and magnified Ghetto-ridden and Ghetto-eaten West Poland' under Jewish dominance.[82] As he described it, such dominance as existed before the First World War was both wide ranging and significant:

> After my long absence from Parliament naturally I sought again the glimpses of the moon, and as I had still many acquaintances within the assembled wisdom, I found a hearer's place without difficulty. The walls and furniture and the attitudes of the honourable ones had not altered much; but in everything else what a revolution, not sublime! The Jew Kings were come, but the Parliament of England was gone. I was pointed out a Jew King of opium and a Jew King of railways, and a Jew King of petrol, and a Jew King of silver, a Jew King of soap, and a Jew King of salt and soda and nickel; while lesser Princes and Powers of the Oriental Immigration showed their swarthy profiles in equal distribution of patronage among the subjugated natives. I heard that they ran India, exploited China, corresponded with Hechts and Erlangers and Camondos and Schiffs and Guggenheims etc. etc. in three or four continents, advised the monarchy on law and justice, hold what is commonly called the Ministry of Posts, Telegraphs and Ways of Communication. Why, why did not Mr Speaker wear the robe of the Grand Rabbinate? The tribe had recently induced those Christians to spend £230,000 000 and tens of thousands of Christian lives in order to secure its African mines and investments. Canaan-on-Thames was, indeed, a Promised Land.[83]

Since, in O'Donnell's vision of the world Jews were able to 'fix' so much and commanded so much, since the Jew was, he claimed in a later article, the king of the age, it is hardly surprising that Jews were able to arrange the Marconi contract according to their own and their friends' advantage.[84]

It has already been noticed that the original contract lapsed on 30 April 1913 in the wake of public agitation but eventually negotiations were started up again which led to a new agreement being signed in the following July. O'Donnell warned that another boom would take place if such a contract were signed and expressed his opinion with characteristic sharpness. 'Does not the British taxpayer emphatically prefer to pay for his own British Government wireless system', he asked, 'instead of paying Scharkstein and Schtinkstein to work our electrical agency in connection with the Judaean Financial-Intelligence Departments round the globe?'[85] The British Empire was likened to a gambling hell where the pickings went to the Jews and the Marconi scandal was merely one illustration of the innate capacity of the Jews to organize society for their own material advantage:

> Beyond all possibility of a doubt Rufus Isaacs – of a notorious Jew financial family, insolvent member of the Stock Exchange, skilful commercial lawyer, knowing every turn of company law practice – was the planning brain and the crafty will in the whole transaction. . . . The mean treachery of the Isaacs person is, of course, manifest. But that is of less moment. Isaacs had it in his blood and tribe. . . . Israel, like the leopard, changes his habitat but not his spots.[86]

We have already noticed Hilaire Belloc's cautious handling of O'Donnell, although both he and G. K. Chesterton had been hostile in public to Jewish interests since the time of the Boer War, and it was only under Cecil Chesterton's editorship of the *Witness* that O'Donnell, the former leader of the Irish Nationalists, was given full rein. But it is appropriate at this point to notice that Belloc's work also carried a fear of Jewish dominance. In *Emmanuel Burden* published in 1904 and in a number of following works, *Mr Clutterbuck's Election* (1909), *A Change in the Cabinet* (1909) and *Pongo and the Bull* (1910), we encounter the person of Mr Barnett, with his hooked nose, thick lips, gross body and greasy curls, all of which were well accentuated by G. K. Chesterton in the illustrations he provided for *Emmanuel Burden*. In the course of the novels plain Mr Barnett – that, of course, was not his real name – rose from financial ruin to commercial success and transformed himself socially from Mr Barnett to Lord Lambeth and finally into the duke of Battersea and it was the accumulation of power by real life figures, of whom Barnett was the fictional representation, that deeply concerned Belloc. This was expressed in fiction in *Mr Clutterbuck's Election* through William Bailey, who was cast in the role of a bluff, hearty Englishman. The narrator of this particular novel is unreliable and the consequence is that throughout the book the truth is usually the reverse of what he appears to say, and Bailey's reflections, which on the surface might appear as a caricature of anti-semitic reasoning, are intended to reflect a well founded, if exaggerated opinion. Bailey's reflections – 'he had gone mad upon the Hebrew race' – stretch over several pages of the novel and must necessarily be given in abbreviated form. Even so, the essence is soon apparent.

> He saw Jews everywhere: he not only saw them everywhere but he saw them all in conspiracy. He would not perhaps have told you that the conspiracy was conscious, but its effects he would have discovered all the same.
>
> According to him Lombroso was a Jew. . . . Half the moneyed backers of Roosevelt were Jews. . . . All actors and actresses *en bloc*, and all the foreign correspondents he could lay hands on were Jews. . . .
>
> It got worse every passing year; there were Jews at Oxford and at Cambridge, and at Trinity College, Dublin; the Jews overran India. . . .

> The disease advanced with his advancing age; soon all the great family of Arnold were Jews; half the English aristocracy had Jewish blood; for a little he would have accused the Pope of Rome or the Royal Family itself; and I need hardly say that every widespread influence, from Freemasonry to the International finance of Europe was Israelite in his eyes; while our colonial policy and especially the gigantic and successful struggle in South Africa, he twisted into a sort of petty huckstering, dependent upon Petticoat Lane.[87]

And what Belloc invited his readers to share at this time, he expressed in more personal terms to Nancy Astor. A letter of 10 December 1913 was written from London, or 'Marconi-on-Thames' as he preferred to call it and, rather earlier in that year, he wrote about a dinner party he attended at which 'Schuster' (Sir Felix Schuster) and Montagu (possibly Edwin Montagu) were present. In the course of this he commented:

> It will be a long time before they raid the Indian Treasury again – but that kind of man is our master today and they will rob[?] us or flay[?] us in some other direction. No one has the courage to defend his country against them.[88]

Here was a clear reference to the Jewish domination of Britain and mention of the Indian treasury serves as a reminder that the Marconi affair was not the only financial scandal to be discussed with anti-semitic overtones in the early years of the reign of George V.

Those anxious about such matters had a field day in 1912 when, parallel with the Marconi scandal, emerged the Indian silver scandal – the 'little Marconi case' as it has been called.[89] This time an attack was launched against Herbert Samuel's elder brother, Sir Stuart Samuel, Liberal MP for Whitechapel and a partner in the firm of Samuel Montagu, bankers and bullion dealers, which had been purchasing large quantities of silver on behalf of the secretary of state for India, whose under secretary was Edwin Montagu, Samuel's first cousin. The senior partner in Samuel Montagu was Lord Swaythling, Edwin Montagu's father. But, it might be asked, what lay behind such comment and why was the arrangement regarded with suspicion?

The history of the business was that in January 1912 Ernest Franklin, one of the partners in Samuel Montagu, had proposed to Sir Felix Schuster, who was chairman both of the finance committee of the Council for India in London and of Montagu's principal bankers, the National Provincial, that by obtaining its silver requirements secretly through Montagu the Indian government would not have to contend with speculators raising the price against it in the market. The proposals were accepted and between March and September 1912 £5 million pounds of silver was secretly bought by Montagu for the India Office. This was not the customary arrangement. The usual practice was for the secretary of state for India to inform the Bank of England of the India Office's silver requirements and the Bank then instructed brokers to buy the required amount. In 1906 an agreement had in fact been reached between the Bank and the secretary of state by which it was agreed that for the next seven years purchases should be made by the Bank on special terms.

When it became known what had happened it was interpreted in some quarters as a Jewish plot involving Stuart Samuel, Edwin Montagu, Felix Schuster, and the assistant under secretary of the India Office, Lionel Abrahams, through whom the business was transacted. Edwin Montagu was soon cleared of any impropriety but Stuart Samuel's role was considered to be particularly delicate and in November 1912 a select committee was established to discuss his position.[90] The conclusion reached by the enquiry was that he was disabled from sitting and voting in the House, although no suggestion of improper motive attached to him. He was subsequently disqualified as a member but less than three weeks after the report, in April 1913, was re-elected MP for Whitechapel with a reduced majority.

It was this situation which led to the charge that the workings of a Jewish plot had been revealed. This was evident in December 1912 when Major Glyn, a Conservative, referred in north Bedfordshire to Jewish control of the Liberal Party:

> What a party, which has two members of the family in the Government, another brother who is a Member of Parliament and another who is a member of the House of Peers and all of them are making money out of Indian finance. The Under-Secretary of State for India is a Mr Samuel; the Postmaster-General is a Mr Samuel, then there is Lord Swaythling, a pretty name for one who was a Samuel – the Infant Samuel – and also a Sir Something Samuel, all of whom were created by the Radical Party. All the silver for India is financed by the House of Samuel.[91]

And discussion continued. In contrast to Glyn, the young J. M. Keynes adopted a more balanced view. His account of events might be summarized as follows. The silver market was a narrow one, with a ring of speculators waiting to force up prices once the government appeared as a buyer and it could be regarded as desirable in such circumstances for the authorities to buy secretly in order to prevent the market moving against them. If it wished to do this 'there was only one firm in a position to buy large quantities of silver with the secrecy which was necessary if the speculators were to be defeated', and that was Samuel Montagu. But, since the under secretary of state had family links with Montagu and since Indian finance was a complicated business which few understood, the charge of venality was likely to be made. Good intentions could lead to obloquy and scandal.

This puts the best interpretation on events and fails to explain why it was thought necessary to by-pass all consultation with the Bank of England and why the India Office dealt directly with Montagus in defiance of existing custom and agreement. It is hardly surprising, therefore, that in such shadowy circumstances 'the question of Indian currency became almost interesting' to use Keynes's words, and even less surprising that in certain quarters suggestions of Jewish intrigue were heard. These murmurings continued not only in the *New Witness* but also in the extreme Conservative journal, *Our Flag*, where Rupert Gwynne, the Conservative MP for Eastbourne, wrote an account of the scandal in which, by adding a geneological table emphasizing the interlocking relationships of the Montagus and the Samuels, he left no doubt that in his opinion a crucial element in the affair was a Jewish willingness to abuse power and to flout accepted British custom and tradition for Jewish ends.[92]

So far we have been considering the charges that Jews were engaged in the manipulation of British society in their own interests or attempting to dominate it for their own ends and at this stage we ought to explain the currents and forces which lay behind such indictments. In some instances there is no need for any particularly sophisticated explanation. Sir Richard Burton's belief that there was an international Jewish power at work in society, was probably related to the involvement of the Alliance Israélite Universelle and prominent London Jews in the campaign to dismiss him from the consulate in Syria. His research conclusions led him to believe that international Jewish pressures had successfully 'hushed up' the murder of Padre Tomaso in Damascus in 1840 and he regarded similar forces as responsible for the ruin of his own career.[93] But in other cases, Joseph Banister's for instance, one feels that motivation must remain elusive, that behind the words lie other forces, now obscured from us, which would constitute an integral part of any explanation. But if we leave such difficulties, it is apparent that the major manifestations of concern about Jewish power occurred in relation to three sets of circumstances, the South African War, the Marconi and Indian silver scandals and the fear of German-Jewish designs, as expressed in the *National Review*. We will now consider the interaction of forces which led to a concentration upon such issues.

The suggestion that the South African War resulted mainly from the machinations of Jewish finance was heard quite widely in Socialist and Radical Liberal circles and has to be considered as emerging at a time when the influence of finance capital was being increasingly scrutinized.[94] And the attention paid to the power of Jewish finance over the South African War needs to be set against this wider interest, which had encouraged earlier claims that Egypt was being milked by financiers under the protective cover of the British administration.[95]

If, at the time of the Boer War, an emphasis was placed upon the way in which international Jewish power could allegedly move politics in its own interest, in the course of the Marconi scandal and the Indian silver affair the stress was upon jobbery, corruption, and on the 'fixing' of situations by Jews in their own benefit. Such developments were of particular concern to the *Witness* circle since they were anxious to expose all instances of government corruption and consequently gave a close scrutiny to the award of all government commercial decisions in their efforts to discover those which displayed any trace of party political patronage.[96] But, if Jews were involved, a heightened interest was created, since prominent members of the *Witness* group found it difficult to accommodate Jewish separatism within their ideal version of society. It was believed that there was 'no other case in history of the presence of a race not specially segregated by accident or law maintaining through long vicissitudes of various policies its identity and its vigour in the midst of alien elements'.[97] In general, the *Witness* group perceived Jews remaining aloof and separate but extracting what they could from society for themselves, and the

Marconi and Indian silver episodes together with the issue of Lord Swaythling's will confirmed this for them.[98]

There was an additional, wider sense in which Jews were of particular interest to the *Witness* circle. We have been told that 'the Jews needed but few years to be completely at home in the life of the nineteenth century. It was a century 'made for them' and they assimilated themselves completely to it.'[99] Such an adaptation had no appeal for the powerful Chester-belloc group at the *Witness*. In the view of Belloc and Chesterton, nineteenth-century capitalism was essentially usury, hence anti-Christian and the prominence of Jews in high finance merely underlined that capitalism was alien to Christian culture. In short, the *Witness* group, like the Socialists, although for different reasons, had a particular interest in finance and Jewish involvement in it.[100]

Leo Maxse's *National Review* was the other major source which emphasized the threat of Jewish power but, whereas the *Witness* concentrated upon the jobbery at the centre of politics, Maxse's fear was of the German dominance of England. The orientation of the *National Review* from its early days was towards a clearly asserted patriotism and this was continued after Maxse acquired his interest in 1893. His concern was with the country's greatness which, he believed, was under threat from Germany.[101] This was a fear generated by the Prussian defeat of France in 1871 and the growing industrial and commercial strength of the German Empire which led to an obsession about everything 'made in Germany'.[102] In the light of this there were numerous articles in the *National Review* which emphasized the growing military strength of Germany and raised the fear of a German invasion. Maxse's own stress, repeated *ad nauseam* in his 'Episodes of the Month', was upon the danger to national interests which was being worked by German Jews, the Cocoa Press, disgruntled ex-foreign office types, sentimentalists, cranks and hack journalists – the 'Potsdam Party' he labelled them – who through their various actions were busily engaged in creating the necessary conditions for the ultimate victory of Germany over Britain. In this respect, therefore, Maxse's hostility towards German Jews needs to be considered as part of his hatred of Germany and anything which appeared to work in the German interest.

But why should he have stressed German Jews in such writings? Why not simply refer to Germans? It was Maxse's sense of patriotism which prevented him from coming to terms with the international dispersion of Jews, and he seemed to believe that one consequence of the Diaspora was that Jews found it difficult to develop and sustain patriotic attachments. As a result, he argued, some Jews could intrigue for Germany because they assumed that Germany would come to dominate Europe, in which case they would receive benefits for having worked on its behalf.[103] And Maxse made it plain that when he referred to the machinations of German Jews he was referring as much to the nature of a particular attachment as to a place of origin. German Jews were, simply, those Jews who supported Germany.[104] While he could claim in magnanimous moments that there were loyal Jews, loyal to Britain that is, Maxse clearly believed that the loyalty of Jews, because of their history, was difficult to guarantee and, as tension mounted to August 1914, this question was never far away from his heated mind.[105]

But none of this takes the analysis far enough. It is perfectly true that we need to understand the general ideology of those groups which were hostile towards Jews if we are to make sense of their anti-semitism but if we wish to understand these responses, there are additional factors in the conflict equation to be brought out. The South African War, the Marconi scandal and the Indian silver affair were all concerned with the behaviour of Jewish financiers and high ranking politicians and in each case there was a base, a core, from which speculation about Jewish power and intrigue could draw strength. The claim that the South African War was 'a Jewish war' was in fact widely made at the time.[106] Such claims about the war and the nature of Jewish influence have to be considered in the light of a number of contemporary developments and there were particular aspects of the South African business which lent speciousness to the claim that the war was indeed being fought for Jewish ends. The role of Jews in the exploitation of the diamond fields, in the development of Kaffir trading on the London stock market and the importance of Jews in prominent South African concerns – Alfred Beit, Barney Barnato, H. Eckstein, the managing director of Wernher Beit and Company, and the Rothschild connection with Rhodes come to mind here – provided fertile ground for the emergence of such views.[107] It should be stressed, however, that such details do not clinch the claim that these individual Jews were working in a Jewish interest. In reality, the situation in South Africa was highly complex and although Jews were important in the short term in the development of mining interests, they were soon superseded by others, even though they retained an importance as middlemen between South African concerns and the London financial markets.[108] A recognition of this changing role of Jews in South Africa was in fact present in Hobson's work on imperialism published in 1902 but by then ideas about a war for Jewish interests had taken hold and indeed Hobson, whose ideas had been widely embraced by others, had himself significantly contributed to their influence.

As for the Marconi scandal and the Indian silver affair, in both cases Jewish politicians laid themselves open to the charges of jobbery and corruption through their close connections with the world of finance. Whatever complexities were present in these situations – and, as we have already indicated, there were plenty – there was an irreducible core of Jewish involvement. Nothing could wash away the fact that Godfrey Isaacs, Rufus Isaacs and Harry Isaacs, were at the centre of the Marconi scandals even if others were with them, just as Edwin Montagu, Stuart Samuel, the firm of Samuel Montagu and Sir Felix Schuster were equally vital to the Indian silver deal. All were Jewish. Worse, in the former case they were all related and in the latter nearly so. In this respect both situations provided almost ideal conditions for the emergence of ideas about Jewish jobbery and manipulation.

The other major conflict we considered arose from the claim that there were in Britain forces described as German-Jewish which were engaged in fostering German interests at the expense of Britain. Here again the activities of certain German Jews provided a focus of attention for Leo Maxse and the *National Review*. The meteoric financial rise of Sir Ernest Cassel, the successful financial dealings of Sir Edgar Speyer – stars in the small galaxy of power and privilege which dominated British society – caught his attention. But it was not simply the fact that a number of German Jews had achieved prominence in British society: many of these individuals were involved in attempting to maintain peace in the years before 1914 and were particularly prominent in the cause of Anglo-German friendship. But, to Maxse all this was treachery. Germany was the great beast. Friendship with her was repugnant to him and any efforts in that direction were likely to be interpreted as offering sustenance to the German foe.[109]

The main thrust of Jewish power was regarded as coming from the strength of Jews in what contemporaries liked to call 'la haute finance', as if to Frenchify the activity attributed a deeper element of mystery and power to it. And, in order to understand hostility to Jews on such grounds, we have not only to take account of the broader philosophy of those who objected to Jewish power and the presence of Jews as actors in the major issues but also to comprehend that there was more generally a prominent involvement of Jews in high finance, which was related to their historical experience as Jews. One consequence of Jewish history had been the emergence of a Jewish social structure which exposed Jews, or rather sections of Jews, to the charge that there was such a force as international Jewish finance power. The scandals of 1911–12 and the earlier claim that Jewish gold could send the country to war in South Africa, need to be considered more generally within the context of a powerful Jewish representation in finance, particularly in merchant banking, which thrived on personal, international connections.[110] In 1888, the *Banker's Magazine* noted such a development in a piece on the career of Sir Samuel Montagu, when it commented:

> The Jews have shown a marked excellence in what can be called the commerce of imperceptibles. They have no particular superiority in the ordinary branches of trade; an Englishman is quite their equal in dealing with ordinary merchandise, in machine making and manufacturing. But the Jews excel on every Bourse in Europe; they have a pre-eminence out of all proportion to their numbers or even their wealth.[111]

This historical experience of Jews, their dispersion and early concentration upon finance fitted them for such activity even if they did not monopolize it.[112] It was work which not only involved playing the role of middleman, thereby incurring an odium and hostility traditionally encountered by such groups, but doing so on an international scale. Such a function was in fact an essential ingredient of the increasingly complex world economic situation, but it does not require much imagination – though some seemingly lack it – to realize that a concentration in international liquidity occupations, whatever useful functions were provided, could be a base from which fears of a Jewish design with national or international implications might emerge. Or, as Hannah Arendt expressed it, 'actual international connections . . . naturally stimulated the general popular delusions concerning Jewish political power all over the world.'[113]

In so far as such power was personally symbolized, a good deal was made of the Rothschild influence.[114] The Rothschilds burst upon the European scene through their acquisition of wealth at the time of the Napoleonic Wars and their banking resources were soon evident on a wide scale as a result of a conscious policy decision not to serve any national government exclusively.[115] As a consequence of that decision branches were established in the major centres of western Europe.[116] But an extension of financial interests in this fashion created suspicions and consistent opposition and fear were displayed in some quarters to the Rothschilds. They came to represent wealth which could influence individuals and governments. They were said to dominate the prince of Wales[117] and to pose a danger to others. In 1893, for instance, *Justice* complained about a visit which Gladstone made to Lord Rothschild. It was described as 'an extraordinary visit' and whatever protestations were made to the contrary, there was clearly a fear that corruption might be brought in its train:

> Nobody has or honestly could, impute any impropriety to Mr Gladstone. But it is not nice at this juncture, when the foreign secretary is closely connected by marriage with the same intriguing financial house, to see Mr Gladstone hobnobbing with Lord Rothschild. We know what has come of this Rothschild influence in Vienna and Paris.[118]

A similar kind of fear – but directed at Lord Rosebery – was expressed a few years later by J. A. Hobson who was sure that politicians, like ordinary mortals, could resist anything except temptation and was convinced that a close association with financiers – particularly if they were Jewish – was undesirable.[119]

But it was not merely an influence over individuals which gave grounds for concern. Around the time of the South African War the Rothschilds figured throughout in the charges which were made about the British government being manipulated in order to protect or extend the interests of Jewish finance.[120] Indeed, it was claimed by some that the Rothschilds had such an influence over policy that they could make peace or war at their own pleasure.[121] And the whole of European politics could be discussed basically in terms of the dominance of this financial network. On the left this was viciously and trenchantly expressed in *Labor Leader* and the passage is worth quoting:

> The Rothschild leeches have for years hung on with distended suckers to the body politic of Europe. This family of infamous usurers, the foundation of whose fortunes was laid deep in the mire of cheating and scoundrelism, has spread itself out over Europe like a network. It is a gigantic conspiracy manifold and comprehensive. There is a Rothschild – a devoted member of the family – in every capital of Europe. Vienna, St Petersburg, Paris, London, Berlin, are each and all garrisoned and held for family purposes by members of this gang. This blood-sucking crew has been the cause of untold mischief and misery in Europe during the present century, and has piled up its prodi-

gious wealth chiefly through fomenting wars between States which ought never to have quarrelled. Wherever there is trouble in Europe, wherever rumours of war circulate and men's minds are distraught with fear of change and calamity, you may be sure that a hook-nosed Rothschild is at his games somewhere near the region of disturbance.[122]

It was not only on the left that such sentiments appeared as H. B. Marriott Watson's analysis a little later in the *National Review* clearly shows:

There are Rothschilds in London, in Paris, in Venice, in the various European centres of finance, and it is well-known that these branches of a big international firm work together. This constitutes what may be at any time a menace to Europe. If the people of Europe are content that a committee of Jews should determine international policy to any extent there is nothing more to be said on the subject.[123]

In short, there was a fear of Rothschild power particularly among socialist groups, but also elsewhere, which focused upon the influence which modern finance could wield. In the case of the Rothschilds here was a house which was internationally based, which excluded Gentiles from positions within the firm[124] and which was said to exercise a sway over national and international politics. Not all social commentators worried about the Rothschild influence, of course.[125] But for Socialist groups, suspicious about what they perceived as the growing power of capitalism and the activities of the 'golden international', and for nationalist groups, wary of international connections and any propensity to form a nation within a nation, there was a steady persistent echo of opposition.

Such hostility towards Jews in finance distorted complex situations and this might be underlined yet again. For example, contrary, to what was claimed in some quarters at the time, the Indian silver scandal might be considered as an attempt by Jews to prove their patriotism rather than an attempt to engage in a Jewish plot for Jewish interests. In this construction of events Jewish financiers – on this occasion Samuel Montagu and Company – could be portrayed as attempting to aid the state, while gaining business and prestige for themselves, by their suggestion that they might buy silver discreetly from clients as unknown brokers and dealers for the government. And if such a scheme were easier to suggest than carry out, this does not have to be accounted for in terms of a Jewish plot but considered in relation to the narrowness of the silver market. It is also clear that, contrary to what was asserted in certain quarters, Jewish bankers were sometimes unable or unwilling to further the interests of Jews – hence the continued involvement of Jewish banking houses in raising loans on the international money markets to support the Tsar's government in Russia. In other words, they were prepared to pursue policies which were considered to be in the business interests of the firms concerned and which were regarded as acceptable and desirable in wider financial and official circles, rather than those more narrowly based upon considerations for fellow Jews living under the shadow of the autocrat's sword.[126]

Jewish press power was the other agency which was regarded as furthering the advance of sectional Jewish interests. International finance depends upon rapidly acquired and sure information as to what is happening in various parts of the world and Jewish bankers and merchants had long recognized this. Consequently, the Rothschilds and the great Jewish banking house in Berlin, Bleichröders, had very quickly established their own private means of communication; in fact they often obtained news of events before government sources. And, as capitalism chased itself over the face of the globe as Marx predicted it would, the interconnectedness of the world and the need to know what was happening outside national boundaries encouraged financiers and businessmen to take an active interest in the press. It was to satisfy this need for information that news agencies came into being. Reuter initially established in Aix-la-Chapelle, moved to London in 1851. In 1849 Bernhard Wolff established a similar agency in Berlin and the Agence Havas was formed in Paris. These were the three great news agencies of Europe. Reuter and Wolff were both founded by Jews and it has been suggested that the founder of the Havas Agency might also have been of Jewish origin.[127] Soon, the step from supplying news to publishing it was bridged and the Jewish influence on the press before the First World War has evoked the admiration of sources sympathetic to Jewish endeavour.[128]

But while philo-semitic sources could stand back and admire Jewish initiative, others took a less sanguine view of events. Indeed, a diametrically opposed reaction was present in some quarters. In Britain, at a time when the press was becoming increasingly commercialized, it was suggested that Jewish financiers were prominent in the syndicates which were rapidly becoming more important than the old-style proprietor. J. A. Hobson warned of such a development in 1892 and a number of other anxious voices sounded about Jewish press influence. 'A Quarterly Reviewer' wrote about an 'Israelitish "ring"' behind the printing press in 1896 and at the turn of the century Arnold White envisaged the prospect of the British press falling to Jews just as he believed the European press had crumbled before them. Following this in 1901 Joseph Banister, giving the impression that Jewish control prevented the publication of his work, devoted half of *England under the Jews* to the variety of ways in which the press had succumbed, in an age of materialism, to Jewish influence.[129] A little later, Leo Maxse and F. Hugh O'Donnell could both write about a Hebrew press reflecting Jewish interests and, as war broke out, John Foster Fraser, himself a journalist, could refer to Jewish press control in Britain, America, France, Germany, Austria and elsewhere.[130] Similar comments appeared in the Socialist press, particularly in *Justice*, where fears were expressed about a Jewish press power in Britain acting 'in accord with their fellow capitalist Jews all over the world'.[131] Representatives of 'triumphant Jewry' regarded as wielding press power included Harry Oppenheim, 'Levi calling himself Lawson' and Harry Marks who had interests in the *Financial News* and the *Evening News and Post*. In addition, *Justice* was concerned to draw attention to an interest in the *Pall Mall Gazette*, bought by a Jewish capitalist called Löwenfeld and the involvement of a certain Steinkopf in the affairs of the *St James' Gazette*.[132] These were the 'poisoners of the wells of public information', running their organs in the interests of 'bishness' and finance who were urged to keep their operations within decent limits.[133]

The actual involvement of Jews in the British press cannot be delineated with any certainty since the history of the press is surprisingly and significantly underresearched.[134] Furthermore, difficulties are sometimes created by the vagueness of the charges which were raised about Jewish press control.[135] What we can do, however, is to indicate that in Britain as elsewhere there were prominent Jews with press interests which served to magnetize opposition. Mrs Rachel Beer née Sassoon owned and edited the *Sunday Times* between 1893 and 1904 and had an interest in the *Observer*. We also know that Harry Oppenheim was a prominent shareholder and a member of the financial syndicate which ran the Liberal *Daily News* before it was sold to the Cadbury interest in 1901. And, as the needs of the City for financial information continued to grow with the development of the London securities market, Harry Marks founded the *Financial News* in 1884 and edited it himself, although it did eventually pass out of his control. More significant to hostile critics interested in the role of Jews in Britain was the fact that the Levy-Lawson family ran the *Daily Telegraph*, that Sir Alfred Mond provided the finance for the *Westminster Gazette* and after 1910 controlled the *English Review* and that Reuter's news agency was the principal supplier of information on world events to the British press.[136]

We need to know far more about such matters before we can write with any certainty about 'influence' and whether individual Jews with Fleet Street connections acted in a Jewish interest; we should bear in mind particularly that the Fleet Street scene, both in terms of personnel and financial support, was subject to almost constant change. But Jewish financiers were prepared to involve themselves in Fleet Street and prominent Jews were represented there.[137] It was around the activities of Mond, Levy-Lawson and Reuter that, in so far as names were mentioned, the opposition was mainly although not exclusively concentrated. In short, in Britain, as elsewhere, although possibly to a lesser extent, a logical progression of their economic interests by certain Jews, displayed by their willingness to risk money in a new and developing market situation, provided a base from which the charge that news was being manipulated in the sectional interests of Jews and if necessary at the expense of the rest of society, could be made. In some instances one suspects that such charges were also derived in part from projecting a knowledge of European press influences into the British situation. It was, as we have noticed, an opposition conducted by disgruntled journalists like Banister, Socialists worried about any additional support to the power of the 'golden international', radical liberals like Hobson, who focused attention upon Jewish press magnates as part of their campaign against finance capital, as well as nationalist influences, like the *Witness* group and Maxse, who were concerned about the implications of power being wielded by a group which they regarded as having only a lightly held national allegiance and extensive international connections. Although much of this writing was pessimistic, Maxse believed that one day the press would once more come to reflect true British interests.[138]

So far we have been explaining a conflict between Jewish and non-Jewish forces in terms of an interactionist analysis. There were those in Britain who, for their own reasons, feared the prospect of 'Jew power' and a combination of this, together with the activities of individual Jews and the social structure of the Jewish community, led to the emergence of exaggerated and unsubstantiated fears of a general Jewish dominance of British society. At this point it might be further suggested that such fears were probably highlighted as a result of the emancipation process. The consequence of this was that Jews were free to pursue careers to the limits of their ability and whereas before, as every reader of Macaulay knows, certain Jews had been able to exercise at times a *de facto* influence in situations where legal restrictions had prevailed, such barriers were finally removed in Victoria's reign. Adjustments needed to be made by Jews and others to this new situation and it was not always easy to achieve this as Rufus Isaacs's career vividly testified. For anyone to move from a 'hammering' on the Stock Exchange in 1884 to the position of attorney general in 1910 and lord chief justice by 1913 was, by all accounts, a remarkable achievement and likely to excite jealousy, envy or admiration. And if, at this time, it were achieved by a Jew it was unlikely to go unnoticed.[139] More generally, the perception that emancipation gave Jews a changed status was almost certainly strengthened by the increasing importance of prominent Jews especially during the reign of Edward VII. The Sassoons, Ernest Cassel, Baron Maurice de Hirsch, Edward Levy-Lawson (later Lord Burnham), Felix Semon and others all became part of the King's inner circle, well known elements in his 'loud, sophisticated and byzantine' entourage, and with the entry of such Jews into the highest ranks of English society Jewish emancipation received the highest form of recognition and publicity.[140]

But while this could be regarded by some as a positive, desirable, social development, it could be interpreted by others in a quite different light. 'It is indubitable', Cecil Roth concluded in his discussion of such court Jews, 'that the association of the Jews in this manner with unornamental aristocracy around the throne and their identification with superabundant wealth, played a considerable part in the development of Anglo Saxon anti-semitism.'[141] And there is evidence to support this. A contributor to the Socialist press complained that the prince of Wales was 'practically in the hands of the Jews.'[142] Joseph Banister speculated whether or not the King were Jewish,[143] Arnold White lamented the congregation of Jewish financiers around the throne,[144] and old court favourites directed their envy and turned up their noses at the Jews – as well as the racing people and loose women – whom it was claimed the King preferred.[145] In short, the opening up of society was a double edged weapon. It conferred benefits upon individual Jews and it was also possible for society in the widest sense to benefit from allowing Jewish talent to flourish; but it could also generate hostility among those who perceived a threat from such developments and thus provide anti-semitism with a sharp cutting edge. To those who believed that the national loyalty of Jews could not be ultimately guaranteed and who entertained doubts about the social compatibility of Jews with the nation, emancipation was a frightening process – and more so if individual Jews were visibly accumulating power and influence.

But it was not simply the emancipation process which added a sense of urgency to the debates about 'Jew power'. In discussing earlier the 'health of the nation' it was argued that the physical condition of Jewish immigrants arriving in Britain became an issue as doubts were arising about the previously assumed prowess and efficiency of the 'imperial race'.[146] But 'the condition of England' debate, as we have already noticed in discussing Jewish immigration, had an economic dimension which was central to it and this also formed a background to the issue of 'Jew power'. By the 1880s the years of mid-Victorian equipoise seemed quite another world. The time when Britain still enjoyed a worldwide leadership in industrial production, when it was in Chambers's phrase, 'the workshop of the world', gave way to years when this supremacy was under threat from the productive forces of other countries, notably Germany and America. It was against this background that the debate over Jewish immigration took place at a national level and it was against this backcloth that Jewish power became an issue. Britain was portrayed as under threat, under siege and undergoing a change for the worse. The country, Maxse once suggested, was in danger of sinking to the status of the Isle of Man.[147] It was also claimed that old ways and standards from the golden age of the past were dying.[148] There was, we have been told, in the years preceding the first World War, before the lights went out all over Europe, 'an atmosphere of uneasiness, of disorientation, of tension' prevailing in British society.[149] And it should not be forgotten that it was in this ambience of national insecurity that 'Jew power' attracted the attention of certain groups and individuals, as a development which it was considered reflected Britain's decline and contributed to the arching burden of the country's problems.

6 Movements and measures against Jews

So far we have been concerned with hostile ideas and attitudes towards Jews. But hostility went beyond this in the sense that there were a number of situations involving action or attempts at organizing action against Jews. It is true that at no point between 1876 and 1914 did any government introduce discriminatory legislation specifically against Jews but unofficial, individual discrimination certainly existed.[1] In addition – and of interest here – Jews also found themselves targets of organized group hostility.

It is just after the turn of the century when interest began to revive in the process of Jewish immigration into Britain that the British Brothers' League was established, an organization which conducted an agitation against Jewish immigration between 1901 and 1905. Throughout its campaign there was a reluctance on the part of some members and associates to say that Jews were being attacked *as Jews* but such remarks should be treated with caution.

The League was formed on 25 February 1901[2] and was then founded 'officially' with great publicity on 9 May 1901 at Stepney Meeting House. The increase in immigration after 1900 and the social pressures this helped to exacerbate in the East End, particularly in the housing market, where complex problems could be explained in terms of the activities of Jewish immigrants,[3] provided the background to its emergence. This was the atmosphere in which the League was born and from its early days its membership was drawn from the East End and sections of the Conservative Party so that at its inaugural meeting it could claim the support of East End Conservative MPs such as Spencer Charrington (Mile End), Murray Guthrie (Bow), Thomas Dewar (Tower Hamlets) and Major William Eden Evans-Gordon (Stepney), who 'had no small share in the formation of the League'.[4] Although he was not present, the well known Liberal spokesman and MP for Poplar, Sydney Buxton, let it be known that he sympathized with the organization and its aims.[5] In addition to the MPs, prominence was given to William Stanley Shaw, a City clerk, who promoted the League and was its first president. The League was in fact Shaw's brainchild but he lacked the imagination, skill and finances to run a pressure group and this provided an opportunity for the involvement of the East End MPs and other interested parliamentary colleagues.

The original aims and orientation of the League were given in a handbill which was circulated in the East End. According to this manifesto thousands of alien paupers were pouring into London, 'driving English people out of their native parishes and literally taking the bread out of English mouths'[6] and such remarks were a prelude to an assertion that if America had found it necessary to introduce immigration restrictions – as it had in 1882, 1885, 1891 and 1893 – a smaller country such as Britain had an even greater need. It was claimed that legislation of this kind was necessary since

> The East of London is rapidly becoming the dustbin of Europe, into which all sorts of human refuse is shot. This is not a question of politics, still less of religion. It is of no consequence whether a foreign pauper believes in the Bible, the Talmud or the Koran.[7]

As will soon become apparent such sentiments proved especially difficult to maintain.

The organization was active between 1901 and 1905, at a time when immigration from eastern Europe was building up and the possibility of legislation to restrict the flow of newcomers into Britain was under discussion. During these years the importance of the League ebbed and flowed. A significant addition to its strength was announced on 25 May 1901 with the publication of a letter from Sir Howard Vincent, Conservative MP for Sheffield Central, who had played and was to continue to play a leading part in the anti-alien agitation and who now professed himself to be in full agreement with the aim of the League, 'to bring about legislation to stop the immigration into the country of alien paupers'.[8]

In the summer of 1901, although on the surface it seemed to have slipped into obscurity, the BBL continued to make progress and by June it had evolved a tight, hierarchical, administrative structure, with sections, wards, an executive committee and chairman. At the same time a revised manifesto was issued[9] and, in the following August, a second manifesto appeared in which the League's intention to work with Members of Parliament was indicated. In other words a link was acknowledged with the Parliamentary Alien Immigration Committee, which included all East End MPs, with the exception of Stuart M. Samuel, Liberal MP for Whitechapel. This was a group which had been formed in August 1901 with a view to urging upon the government the need for immediate legislation on the immigration question.[10] By the autumn of that year developments in the immigration debate were such that the *East London Observer* admitted that what it called the anti-alien movement was growing and the League's meetings were larger and more enthusiastic.[11] By now the *Jewish Chronicle* referred to the League as 'a combination of Primrose Leaguers and radical working men' and the significance of this *rapprochement* was symbolized by Sir Howard Vincent's name being accorded the place of honour in the second manifesto.[12]

By 1902 when the alien problem was being regarded in some quarters as 'the most pressing problem of east London life',[13] a large meeting was planned by the League for 14 January, overall arrangements for which devolved upon Harry F. Smith, 'the well known Conservative agent to the Conservative and Unionist Party in Bow and Bromley'.[14] The proceedings attracted considerable attention but lost the League the support of the *East London Observer*, which complained of exaggeration, misrepresentation and anti-semitism.[15] The meeting at the People's Palace began to strains of 'Soldiers of the Queen', 'God bless the Prince of Wales', 'There's no place like home' and 'Britons never shall be slaves' and speeches were heard from Major Evans-Gordon, Sir Howard Vincent, S. F. Ridley, H. S. Samuel, H. Robertson, Henry Norman, the Liberal MP for Wolverhampton South East, David Hope Kyd, prospective Unionist candidate for Whitechapel, A. T. Williams and Arnold White. Sydney Buxton, the Liberal MP for Poplar, wrote to express his sympathy with the aims of the League while regretting his inability to attend the meeting.[16] Resolutions were carried to the effect that East End social problems would never be solved until legislation was passed against the entry of destitute and undesirable aliens and in the course of all this strong ethnocentric voices were raised. Warming to his theme, A. T. Williams declared:

> I don't care for statistics. God has given me a pair of eyes in my head – and as I walk through Mile End or Cable Street, as I walk about your streets, I see names have changed; I see good old names of tradesmen have gone, and in their places are foreign names – the names of those who have ousted Englishmen into the cold (Loud cries of 'Shame' and 'Wipe them out').

The audience was also told by Henry Norman: 'This is England. It is not the backyard of Europe; this is not the dustbin of Austria and Russia.' It was suggested that a notice should be placed at the mouth of the Thames, saying, 'no rubbish to be shot here.'[17]

By 1902 the League had developed into an organization claiming 12,000 members, although only 1,500 or 1,600 paid their political dues which were regarded as optional.[18] But the League was of more significance than this might suggest. It makes no sense to discuss the movement in isolation, as other accounts have done. It was really one rung of an interlocking ladder. Another stave was the Londoners' League which had also been founded in 1901. In June of that year Murray Guthrie called a meeting of east London Conservative Associations to discuss the housing question and at a reconvened meeting the Londoners' League was formed with the aim of pressurizing the government to restrict immigration. It was hoped that this would save Tory seats in working class areas.[19] This body worked with the British Brothers' League. Its members campaigned for the BBL during its recruiting campaign in the autumn and winter of 1901 and it was the Londoners' League which ultimately controlled the management aspects of the BBL meeting in 1902 at the People's Palace. On a higher stave was the Parliamentary Alien Immigration Committee which, we have noticed, was founded in August 1901, and it was from this group that parliamentary support for the East End campaign was drawn and it was from within its ranks that effective control over the BBL was exercised.

The interconnection of these pressure groups was well recognized by some contemporaries as was shown when a *Jewish Chronicle* journalist reported that the League's organization which he found in the East End and, more particularly, the central executive committee, represented only the tail of the BBL. The dog was Sir Howard Vincent and the anti-alien Tory MPs.[20] This focus of power was also apparent to the government and was emphasized when William Stanley Shaw requested the Board of Trade to receive a BBL deputation on immigration in January 1902. The minister, refusing the request, replied: 'I beg to inform you that I have been in communication with Major Evans Gordon, from whom you will doubtless hear in due course.'[21]

The League openly acknowledged its indebtedness to the parliamentary support it received.[22] It was, nevertheless, sometimes embarrassed by it as a result of particular decisions taken within sections of the Tory Party or the Party as a whole, as over the decision to import cheap Chinese workers to work in the Rand mines after the South African War. This move was opposed by the British labour movement as detrimental to the position of white workers in South Africa and in clear conflict with the government's professed concern for the interests of labour, which was loudly expressed during the debate over alien immigration. This evidence of government inconsistency was quickly seized upon by the Tories' opponents. But, for its part, the League was obviously embarrassed by the situation; it was reduced to stating that such matters were outside its province and that it could not express an opinion on any subject other than that for which it was founded.[23]

Apart from its parliamentary support and with the notable exception of J. L. Silver, the ambitious editor of the *Eastern Post and City Chronicle* and A. T. Williams, who was on the LCC, the leadership of the BBL was distinctly unimpressive.[24] Without parliamentary support the BBL, would obviously find it difficult to maintain a momentum and with the early death of Silver in November 1902 and A. T. Williams's increasing interest in securing parliamentary election, the League was even more exposed and it was around this time that parliamentary support began to ebb away.

Towards the end of 1902 the anti-alien Tory MPs were apparently warned about their involvement with the BBL. The Conservative Party was increasingly unhappy about the association between certain MPs and the League and it might have been this official attitude which gradually led Tory restrictionists to concentrate more attention on the Immigration Reform Association (IRA).[25] Founded in February 1903 under the presidency of the earl of Donoughmore, this was opposed to the immigration of all those 'of bad character', immigrants who were 'defective in mind and body', those 'likely to become a charge or dependent on charity' and those 'suffering any loathsome or contagious disease'. At the same time, it was not in favour of altering the 'cherished right of asylum' for political offenders, or excluding those who could make a contribution to the country.[26] With Donoughmore as president, connections with the Tory Party, and funds which enabled it to publish such well-produced pamphlets as *Destitute Aliens*, *Criminality among Aliens*, and *Aliens and Overcrowding*, the IRA played a prominent role in the years between the publication of the Royal Commission on Alien Immigration report in 1903 and the introduction of legislation on the aliens issue in 1904.

The influence of this 'respectable' group within the anti-alien ranks has not yet been appreciated and, in the fullest account we have, its activity has been confused with that of the BBL. It has been suggested, for example, that as part of its anti-alien campaign the League organized a major demonstration in November 1903 to pressurize the government into legislation.[27] However, this misreads the situation and misses its significance. At a council meeting of the BBL in September 1903, the secretary indicated that he had been in correspondence with the secretary of the IRA 'which had engaged the People's Palace for a great public meeting to be held on the 10th of November'.[28] It was later reported that arrangements for the meeting were under the direction of Geoffrey Burchett, secretary of the IRA and Harry F. Smith, the Conservative Party agent, who had been involved in arranging the major 1902 protest meeting.[29] It was agreed in the BBL council that an application should be made for twelve platform tickets for the November demonstration and a procession should be provided.[30] The November 1903 meeting, contrary to what has been claimed, was therefore organized by the IRA and symbolized the relative decline of the BBL and the growing importance of 'respectable' anti-alien forces. In view of this there is no reason to be surprised that the November protest was 'on the whole a more restrained and sober performance than that of [almost] two years ago' (at the People's Palace).[31]

By 1903 hostility towards Jewish immigration was running high in parts of the East End. Indeed, the worst outbreak of violence against Jews, if press reports are to be believed, occurred in Bethnal Green in June 1903 over the housing issue, when Jews were attacked on the grounds that they were believed to have displaced some of the local population.[32] Against this background, the BBL continued its activity and a meeting did take place at Stepney Temperance Hall in March[33] but by the end of the year the *East London Observer* could scent the decline of the League and cynically refer to it as conducting public house meetings and passing resolutions which were guaranteed to shake the pillars of government to their foundations.[34] Shortly afterwards the sole indoor meeting for 1904 took place[35] and in 1905, almost as a last kick, the League was to be found campaigning in the Mile End by-election for the Liberal Unionist, H. Lawson, himself a Jew, but a hard liner on the immigration issue, against B. Strauss, the Liberal candidate.[36] By this time, however, a significant change had occurred in the membership of the League. The parliamentary link had gone; these members had transferred their allegiance to the IRA. It is no great surprise, therefore, that the 1905 Aliens Act which eventually emerged from the immigration battle did nothing to keep out the able bodied immigrants who competed with East End labour. Although the act closely represented the demands of the IRA it was, in terms of the BBL's programme, mere tokenism.[37]

This account of the BBL is similar in most respects to those which have appeared elsewhere, although none has previously stressed the interconnected nature of the BBL, the Londoners' League, the Parliamentary Alien Immigration Committee and the IRA. Furthermore, one analysis has seriously confused the activity of the first and last of these groups and also underestimated the extent of BBL sympathies – which stretched into the secretaryship of the Royal Commission on Alien Immigration.[38]

In the course of its history an attempt was made to prevent the campaign by the BBL assuming an anti-semitic flavour but this was not completely successful. A consideration of such matters casts further doubt upon existing interpretations of BBL history. It has been suggested in one account that the attempt by individual members to steer the BBL away from anti-semitism, by stressing that the immigration issue was 'not a question of politics, still less of religion', and that it was of no consequence 'whether a foreign pauper [believed] in the Bible, the Talmud or the Koran',[39] was difficult to maintain and that William Stanley Shaw, the promoter and first president of the BBL resigned from the organization in 1902 partly as a result of its increasingly anti-semitic character.[40] The fullest piece of evidence we have on Shaw's position and that on which the argument regarding the reasons for his resignation has been based, is his letter in the *East London Advertiser* in July 1902. The letter runs as follows:

> Sir, My attention has been called to a leaflet headed 'British Brothers' League' and signed by Messrs A. T. Williams LCC and F. E. Eddis, in the course of which it says, 'If you or any of your friends have suffered by the Alien Jews coming here, now is the time to say so.'
>
> As the organiser of the British Brothers' League I should like to say that the first condition that I made on starting the movement was that the word 'Jew' should never be mentioned and that as far as possible the agitation should be kept clear of racial or religious animosity.
>
> If the above leaflet was issued by the British Brothers' League, then the League has departed from its original policy. I am informed, however, that this leaflet was issued without the authority of the Executive Committee. Presumably Mr A. T. Williams LCC consulted Major Gordon MP before the leaflet was drawn up. In which case these gentlemen would appear to have executed a change of front since issuing their leaflet in February last.
>
> That leaflet, which was printed in both English and Yiddish, contained the following:
>
> 'Do not be deceived by people who are trying to make you believe that "alien", means "Jew". It does not! "Alien" means "foreigner", Religion has nothing to do with it.'
>
> Your obedient servant,
> William Stanley Shaw,
> Founder and Ex-President of the
> British Brothers' League.[41]

If we read the letter carefully it becomes apparent that although he disapproved of what he regarded as a stress upon overt anti-semitism, at no point did Shaw state that he left the League because it was becoming anti-semitic – indeed, he does not claim that he was no longer a member of the BBL. From other sources we know that Shaw was in dispute with the BBL by the time the letter appeared and had in fact resigned from the presidency in the April before the letter appeared in July; we also know that this was not the first occasion on which he had resigned as President.[42] Even so, nothing which has come to light regarding his 1902 resignation would suggest that it occurred because anti-semitism had permeated the movement. The official reason for Shaw's resignation presented in the first report and balance sheet of the League explained that he had found the work demanding more time than he could afford and had tendered his resignation rather than remain a figurehead.[43]

But behind this official explanation we also have to remember that Shaw was a notably egocentric character, obsessed about his position within the BBL, who even after the resignation of his office signed his letters as 'Ex-President of the British Brothers' League' – an action which did not go uncriticized.[44] From the beginning Shaw wanted to regard the BBL as his movement and yet he was gradually eased out of influence by more powerful and able associates. This was a development he referred to in an interview he gave to the *Jewish Chronicle* where he said that he resigned as president, 'because the game was not worth the candle'. He objected particularly to the activity of Conservative MPs who refused to support him and the League unless he were a tool in their hands.[45] It is also clear from reports of BBL meetings that by the spring of 1902 he was being overshadowed in the ranks of the non-parliamentarians by J. L. Silver and A. T. Williams.[46] In addition to these factors it is likely that tension existed within the central executive over the misappropriation of funds.[47] If we are seeking the background to Shaw's resignation it is to these developments rather than to his concern about an incipient anti-semitism within the BBL that we should direct our attention. The little we know about Shaw would suggest that he was not likely to worry too much about the development of a hostility towards Jews as Jews. He was later to emphasize the possible danger of London becoming 'an important Jewish city on the Thames' as Jews took over British national life[48] and as late as 1930 the Board of Deputies contemplated whether to take action against him for an alleged anti-semitic libel but decided against it.[49]

What else can we say about anti-semitism within the BBL? In particular how is it possible to discuss its own claim that it was anti-alien rather than anti-semitic? The organization was never tightly controlled despite its apparent hierarchy, and there was always a fluctuating membership and, since the League's dues were optional, disputes were possible as to who was a member. The result was that in some cases it was difficult to know whether what its opponents classified as evidence of the anti-semitic nature of the BBL reflected official or unofficial opinion or, indeed, much more than individual judgements. It is, then, a complex situation, but it would seem to have the following discernible characteristics.

The leadership, or at least sections of it, believed that any open suggestion of anti-semitism would harm the progress of the movement – hence the affirmation that the origins of the immigrants were unimportant.[50] At the same time, there was an awareness that extremists were present in the movement and because of this it was found necessary to warn members against what was judiciously called any 'warmth of language'.[51] They were advised particularly: 'Let us do all in our power to prove that ours is not an anti-semitic movement.'[52] Any lapse from a studious avoidance of the immigrants' origins was quickly seized upon by its opponents and the League could hardly fail to be aware of this.[53] The result was a constant emphasis by various spokesmen that the organization was not interested in Jews as such and counter claims by those hostile to it that, contrary to these assertions, such sentiments were at the core of the BBL's campaign. By contrast, no such equivocation was present or worried over in the literature distributed to encourage the formation of a British Sisters' League. Several thousand pamphlets appeared in the abortive attempt to form such an organization in which the emphasis was specifically directed towards an attack on Judaism.[54]

In the event it was difficult to control all those who sympathized with the League and this resulted in expressions of hostility and action which provided its opponents with ammunition for their case that the League, despite its claims, did involve itself in anti-semitism. All this must have exercised the patience of those within the League who wanted to mobilize a moderate campaign without stressing the immigrants' ethnic origins. In this respect the giant meeting held at the People's Palace in January 1902 proved particularly damaging. Arnold White, who was always eager to involve himself in any issue involving Jews, could not be contained. His major theme was that the government was in the pocket of the Jews and was immobilized over the immigration issue through Jewish financial influence. And almost in the same breath he went on to claim that the immigrants came to England because they 'wanted our money'. A section of the audience obviously identified with this and responded with cries of 'wipe them out' but the *East London Observer* seized upon what it regarded as a clear example of anti-semitic excess to castigate the League and its activity.[55] Furthermore, it was not only individuals like White who created difficulties for moderates. The crowds who left the People's Palace meeting indulged in attacks upon Jews and Jewish property.[56] And this was not an isolated instance. Earlier, at a meeting of the League in Stepney a 'working man' had

> rushed up to the platform and invited the meeting to vote on the question whether 'no more Jews should be brought into the country.'

The 'motion' passed on a show of hands.[57] Later, in the same vein, in the spring of 1902, when the St Georges branch of the League had organized a march through Bethnal Green to St Georges, the marchers, who numbered several thousand, chanted 'Go back to Jerusalem' as they went on their way past passive crowds of Jews and other aliens.[58] If East End Jews were apprehensive about the activities of the British Union of Fascists how much fear did these earlier cries generate among those close to the stains of the Russian pogroms?

Such activity was not repeated in the IRA, which from its formation in February 1903 was directly and tightly controlled by middle- and upper-class restrictionists. Its manifesto laid no stress upon the ethnic origins of the immigrants being an issue and its well produced publications such as *Destitute Aliens*, *Criminality among Aliens* and *Aliens and Overcrowding* were also discreet on this.[59] It comes as no surprise, therefore, to learn that the IRA rejected overtures from the BBL to affiliate or amalgamate even though liaison continued between the two.[60] There was an extremist element within the BBL which did not fit easily into the IRA. It should be remembered, nevertheless, that both organizations were in business to counteract what was regarded by them as Jewish immigration, whatever stresses and forms their arguments assumed.

In continuing this discussion of anti-semitism in action we might now leave the East End and turn to the Creagh affair. British public attention was first drawn to this outburst of anti-semitism, affecting the Jewish community in Limerick, with the publication of Julian Grande's letter in *The Times* on 1 April 1904. In this the condition of the Jews in Limerick was described as 'appalling'.[61] In this part of Ireland in 1871 there were only six Jews in Cork, two in Limerick and one in Waterford but by 1904 as a result of immigration there were thirty-five families in Limerick. The increase in the number of Jews was relatively insignificant in relation to the overall size of the population but 'Milesian' commented in another letter in *The Times* on 5 April that the invasion of 'low class Polish and Russian Jews' had created suspicion and jealousy among local artisans and traders.[62] And during these years we can certainly detect evidence of local hostility towards Jews. This was revealed in 1884 when an attack was made upon a Jewish home in Limerick, an incident which was sparked off by a Jew killing a chicken on Good Friday, in 1888 when members of the Cork trades council attacked local Jews as 'crucifying gipsies' and called for their expulsion on account of the activities of two Germans mistaken for Jews, and further, in incidents occurring in 1892 and 1896.[63] Finally, a few years later in 1904, it was claimed in Limerick that three quarters of all civil bill cases in Ireland's quarter sessions were brought by Jews against unsophisticated debtors, although these figures were hotly rejected by E. B. Levin, the local Jewish minister.[64] Irrespective of the facts, there was sufficient belief in Jewish malpractice for this economic base to provide the springboard for an outbreak of anti-semitism.

Limerick had a tradition of religious pride or bigotry, depending upon one's view, and consequently, it is hardly surprising that Jewish middlemen newcomers could not only encounter hostility on account of their economic activity in a backward community but that Father Creagh, a monk of the Redemptorist order, could inject a dimension of religious hostility into the conflict, and thereby convert an economic opposition into an anti-semitic crusade with menacing overtones. In his sermons which began on 12 January 1904 he told his flock that the Jews killed St Stephen, the first Christian martyr, as well as St James the Apostle and since then they had not hesitated to shed Christian blood. The blood accusation was also impressed on the minds of his listeners, although it was not suggested that such incidents still occurred. A crueller martyrdom, they were then told, based upon economic exploitation, was its modern equivalent.[65] This was only one dimension of Creagh's hostility towards Jews. He also stressed the threat of Jewish power. He preached that there were no greater enemies of the Catholic Church than the Jews and claimed that in France the Jews were in league with Freemasonry and had succeeded in attacking nuns and religious orders. Creagh prophesied that a similar policy would be pursued in Ireland if Jews seized power.[66] Whereas most exponents of what Richard Hofstadter called 'the paranoid style' tend to express fears of an attack by rival groups upon a national culture, Creagh stressed the vulnerability of his church and the probable dire fate of Catholicism in contention with Jewish influences: this provided him with an opportunity for attacking Jewish interests, playing upon the alien origins of Jews, stressing their different religion and exploiting the activities of some Jews who acted as middlemen.[67]

The effect of such speeches was the enactment of physical violence against Jews, as well as the institution of a boycott of Jewish businesses and businessmen. 'No Jew or Jewesses can walk along the streets of Limerick without being insulted or assulted', it was reported, and in addition to the business boycott there was a refusal to honour existing commerical obligations. Discontent was not restricted to Limerick; with encouragement it spread to the country areas where the peasantry was advised not to have any dealings with the Jews.[68] If Creagh was able to add an anti-semitic dimension to a conflict of economic interests, the situation was allowed to develop further since the police offered only passive protection to the Jews, who also found it difficult to obtain legal redress. At the same time Creagh had the support of some of the local press.[69]

A call was made by Limerick Jews for help and, in this situation, a heavy responsibility fell upon the Board of Deputies in London. The action of the Board consisted of petitioning the chief secretary for Ireland, writing to the lord lieutenant and engaging in discussions through the duke of Norfolk with the cardinal archbishop of Armagh.[70] The Archbishop promised to bring the matter to the attention of the bishop of Limerick but, in the event, it proved impossible to obtain an assurance from this latter source that pressure would be used to end the boycott. It was soon clear, in fact, that the Board could do little to influence the church. However, in order to ensure that Jews in Limerick did not go entirely unaided in these difficult circumstances the Board opened a fund for the sufferers and this agency, administered by Joseph Prag, was to help the worst affected.[71]

But the campaign had not been stopped and indeed it continued into 1905. In addition to persisting with the boycott the local Catholics set up stores which, ironically, were run upon the weekly payment principle to which so much opposition was voiced when it was practised by Jews. As a result of this local hostility and the attack upon its livelihood the Jewish community began to diminish. Although police protection was afforded against physical injury, the 'real evil', the boycott, which had originated as a political weapon against the imperialist British in the 1880s, remained in force.[72] It lasted in fact for two years by which time eighty members of the Limerick community had left, leaving fewer than forty still in the town. The matter ended only with the withdrawal of Creagh by his Order. He was eventually to leave Ireland and died in New Zealand in 1947. With his removal from the scene it has been written that 'a sad but uncharacteristic and atypical episode' came to an end but 'the congregation did not recover, either numerically or economically, from the evil impact.'[73]

The events in Limerick were felt chiefly at a local level but their history cannot be written purely in local terms. Creagh's hostility towards Jews was occasioned partly by his belief that Jewish influences helped to account for the expulsion of the Redemptorist Order from France. And the events in Ireland were not lost on the BBL. In April 1904 the movement passed a unanimous resolution of sympathy with Creagh for 'his noble work' against the Jews in Limerick.[74] In other words, outside influences were fed into the Limerick situation and there was also sympathy outside Limerick for Creagh's campaign.

A few years later, in 1911, it was the turn of south Wales to demonstrate its hostility towards Jews in an outbreak of local riots, which followed upon evidence of earlier trouble in the area. In the autumn of 1903, for instance, at Pontypridd a young girl claimed that she had been taken down to the synagogue by Jews, tied in sheets, pricked with needles and severely injured. Rumour grew that she had been abducted for ritual purposes for the first day of the Jewish New Year and, swayed by the girl's story, a crowd gathered and threatened and insulted all Jews who passed by after evening service at the synagogue. However, the police promptly intervened and the incident quickly died, particularly when the girl admitted that she had invented the whole story.[75] The disturbances of 1911, however, were more serious and took place against an extension of Jewish settlement in Wales and at a time of bitter industrial disputes.

The growth of settlements outside London was one of the features of Anglo-Jewry after 1850 and in line with this development a number of communities grew up in south Wales. With the increased immigration from Russia after 1881 it was natural that some of the newcomers should go to existing Jewish communities in the area. But, in addition, Jewish settlement was extended from areas like Swansea, Cardiff, Merthyr Tydfil, Aberdare, Pontypridd, Newport and Tredegar into centres such as Abertillery, Bargoed, Ebbw Vale, Rhymney and as far north as Brynmawr in Breconshire. At the beginning of the century all these small communities were experiencing considerable industrial unrest and social tension.[76]

The Cambrian Combine coal strike began in September 1910 and continued into August 1911 and following this the area was affected by the outbreak of the national railway strike in August 1911. It was against this troubled background that the disturbances occurred on Saturday, 19 August 1911, just over a month after riots had destroyed all of Cardiff's thirty or so Chinese laundries, at a time when the Chinese were being employed as strikebreakers during the seamen's strike.[77]

> Eye witness accounts give a graphic picture. Shortly before Saturday midnight 'a band of about 200 young fellows' began a tour of Tredegar, attacking Jewish shops and singing 'several favourite Welsh hymn tunes'. The shops were wrecked and the contents looted. The police, even when reinforcements had arrived from Ebbw Vale, were hopelessly outnumbered. On Sunday afternoon the local magistrates met and decided to apply for military help. Men of the Worcester Regiment arrived from Cardiff on Monday afternoon just in time to deal with fresh disturbances in the town. Already, however, there were rumours that the rioters intended to march over the mountains to attack Jews in other centres. On Monday and Tuesday nights Jewish shops were attacked and looted at Ebbw Vale and Rhymney. On Tuesday the disturbances spread down the valleys to Victoria, Cwm, Waunllwyd, Abertysswg and to Brynmawr. By mid-week, troops having been deployed in the main areas of disturbance, the Western Valleys were quiet. But on Wednesday evening a mob attacked Jewish premises at Bargoed in Glamorgan. The disturbances at Bargoed intensified on Thursday, when troops arrived; at Bargoed and Gilfach large gangs of rioters engaged in running fights with the infantry and the police on Friday night and Saturday morning. Meanwhile, two shops, the property of Jews, were destroyed by fire at Senghenydd. That weekend, however, the disturbances died away almost as mysteriously as they had erupted. They left behind a trail of destruction and disruption, the financial cost alone of which was estimated at over £16,000.[78]

Although this violence clearly involved Jews it needs to be asked whether ethnic considerations were present in the attacks. Why did the disturbances take place? How were they related to the socio-economic unrest through which the area was passing and, of crucial importance here, to what extent were they anti-semitic?

These are not easy questions to answer. A contemporary Socialist analysis stressed that the disturbances were economic rather than racial and any reference to anti-semitism was designed to direct attention from fundamental social problems resulting from capitalism and this view was reflected generally in the national press.[79] But what does more recent opinion make of the situation? According to one view the disturbances should be considered against the background of industrial unrest in south Wales. The railway stoppage, it was said, resulted in price rises and, in some cases, an increase in house rents by Jewish traders. But it has also been suggested that economic pressures alone did not create the conflict.[80] So where does this leave us?

An alternative explanation to that which would regard the attacks as random, capricious disturbances to social life would suggest that the industrial stoppages reduced earnings and encouraged the use of credit and thereby the indebtedness of some families to Jewish credit traders and shopkeepers, who could not only finance day-to-day purchases but also assist with the payment of rents. Jews did not have a monopoly of these trades – just as Jewish establishments were not the only ones against which violence was directed – but it is acknowledged they were involved in such activity. There was therefore an economic basis to the hostility. But other influences were present in the conflict situation. Jews had special characteristics which made them visible. At the close of the nineteenth century the east European Jews who settled in the valleys 'spoke little or no English and [were] essentially inward looking'[81] while in occupational terms they were concentrated as middlemen.[82] As such they could be regarded as alien oppressors and thereby incur a double odium. And if further help were required in directing attention to Jews it could come through a religious agency in the form of the Welsh Baptists. Religious differences created tension, particularly in the smaller communities where hostility tended to be concentrated. And this religious dimension to the hostility is underlined by the fact that the attacks on Jewish shops at Tredegar were carried out to the sound of Welsh hymn tunes.[83]

In short it was the economic role of certain Jewish middlemen coupled with the alien 'visibility' of the Jews at a time of socio-economic unrest which resulted in attention being directed towards the Jewish community. It was within this kind of context that respectable citizens – there is no evidence that the incidents were the responsibility of young hooligans – proceeded at Tredegar to attack only Jewish shops and at Ebbw Vale to indulge in a long denunciation of Jews, thereby indicating within the general unrest a specific hostility to Jews as Jews.[84] Unlike the case of Limerick, however, the action of the authorities prevented the emergence of a prolonged, deteriorating situation.[85]

So far we have been concerned with organized opposition to Jewish interests, in the East End, in Limerick and south Wales and such developments provide the clearest indication of anti-semitism in action. In each case the target was the Jewish newcomers. We have noted the activities of a number of pressure groups attempting to influence the government to legislate on the immigration issue and eventually, in 1905, an Aliens Act did appear on the statute book. However, it was an Act which offended ardent restrictionists, since it was less restrictive than the 1903 recommendations of the Royal Commision on Alien Immigration, and a watered down version of the 1904 Aliens Bill. In proclaiming the perennial right of asylum, in applying controls only to 'undesirable aliens' who came on 'immigrant ships' carrying more than twenty alien steerage passengers, it did not capitulate to the demands of the BBL and, in particular, it did nothing to prevent the immigration of the able bodied competitor whom the Brothers feared.[86] The whole debate surrounding the Royal Commission and alien immigration which finally resulted in the 1905 legislation makes no sense unless it is understood that a discussion was taking place primarily about *Jewish* immigration. But whatever was implicit in the situation, the fact remains that the legislation was aimed at aliens rather than specifically at Jews as Jews. In the circumstances of the time 'alien' was widely interpreted as 'Jew' and, whether implicitly or explicitly, they were discussed as if they were synonymous. Nevertheless, in its form, it is more appropriate to categorize the 1905 legislation as anti-alien rather than anti-semitic. There was nothing specifically in the legislation which discriminated against Jews as such.

So far we have concentrated essentially upon hostility directed towards Jewish newcomers arising out of specific local situations. But, at this point, reference might be made to the National League for Clean Government which directed its attention towards the Jewish plutocracy. The League was an offshoot of the *New Witness*, whose particular stamp of anti-semitism we have already considered[87] and while it was not overtly anti-semitic – this is something which needs to be stressed at the outset – some key members of the organization were hostile towards Jews and used the League as a vehicle for communicating their hostility in a way which gave it an anti-semitic flavour. Hilaire Belloc, G. K. Chesterton and Cecil Chesterton were members, as was the viciously anti-semitic F. Hugh O'Donnell. The League could also count upon the support of Rowland Hunt MP, Vivian Carter, editor of the *Bystander*, whose anti-semitism was condemned by the *Jewish Chronicle* in 1913. At more of a distance, it also had the sympathy of Leo Maxse, who had carried a series in the *National Review* in March 1913 on 'The Fight for Clean Government' and who spoke in glowing terms of the need for a movement such as the League.[88] In its broadest sense the organization reflected a disenchantment with the Liberal government and the party political system but it has to be recognized that within it there were forces which linked these problems with Jews and Jewish interests. For instance, at a meeting on 8 December 1913 Rowland Hunt complained bitterly about 'influence' and went on to spell out his objections: 'We are really in danger of being ruled by alien votes and foreign gold. . . . The aliens and foreign plutocrats are driving out British blood.'[89] This was a thinly disguised reference to Jewish financiers, and this element of the League's activity was referred to by David Low, the cartoonist, who attended one of its early meetings:

> The occasion had been a meeting at Chelsea Town Hall to expose the sale of honours and the corruption of the House of Lords. There was a full house, naturally, since there was in these subjects much matter for exposure. It did not see the light on that occasion. Nobody came down to cases and all the audience got was vague anti-semitism, which I found very irritating.[90]

The dual nature of the League – political reform mixing with anti-semitism – was apparent from the beginning. The initial plan, as expressed in the *New Witness*, was to hold a series of conferences in the hope and anticipation that they would become a weekly event. Consequent upon this the first meeting was held on 27 June 1913. The speaker was F. Hugh O'Donnell and his subject was 'The Meaning of the Marconi Scandal'. G. K. Chesterton was in the chair. Although O'Donnell claimed that corruption rather than race or religion was the issue, he was not entirely convincing and could not resist the temptation to attack Jews: 'When you catch an English pickpocket, he does not quote his church membership. When you catch a Jewish pickpocket, what right has he to scream out: "You are attacking my holy religion".'[91] This was O'Donnell running true to form and it was in this sort of atmosphere that a decision to form a non-party association to fight for clean government was taken.[92] Consequent upon this by the autumn a programme which referred to the reform of the party system of government, the importance of a free parliament, the removal of caucus control from politics, the need for purity in government and the exposure of corruption, the prevention of the sale of honours, and the need to secure parliamentary control over national expenditure, was being promulgated.[93] Furthermore, by this time, in addition to those already mentioned as associated with the League, it could count among its sympathizers Thomas Burt MP, the Lib-Lab MP for Morpeth, Lord Auckland,[94] Arnold White,[95] as well as F. W. Jowett, the Labour MP for the Bradford West constituency.

Throughout all this the 'Jewish factor' which was built into the origins of the movement continued to be emphasized in the columns of the *Witness*, as it did in the speeches which the dandified O'Donnell, who was chairman of the committee for the League, made at League meetings. But such emphases were not significant in the actual constituency battles in which the League became involved. From the autumn of 1913 into the spring of the following year it campaigned against corruption at by-elections in Reading, South Lanark, Bethnal Green, Leith, Poplar and Ipswich, where the tone of the opposition was more restrained. Nevertheless, such situations gave the *Witness* an opportunity to continue its attacks upon Judean money power.[96]

It might be assumed that the outbreak of war put the League out of business but, in fact, it did not go out of existence in 1914. It lived on until 1923, in its later years providing an outlet for the ideas and campaigns of G. K. Chesterton and the Distributists which involved in part an attack upon Jewish influences.[97] Its end came when the *New Witness*, whose life had often been financially precarious, finally succumbed. But by lasting until then the League had ensured that at least one bridge was built between the anti-semitism of the 'old' pre-war years and that of the 'new' post-war world.

7 Anti-semitism and society

How widespread was anti-semitism between 1876 and 1914? Whereas social scientists concerned with present-day issues are able to rely upon interview and questionnaire responses in their attempts to ascertain the distribution of anti-semitic attitudes, we cannot accurately reconstruct the past by such methods.[1] In this respect the historian works under particular disadvantages.[2]

But if we cannot measure the extent of anti-semitism, we are able to say that there were pressures at work in society which restricted its overt, public expression. This was well recognized by Arnold White, who, when referring to Jewish immigrants, told the 1903 Royal Commission on Alien Immigration:

> Whoever frames an indictment against the quality of some of these poor creatures is laid open to the dreaded charge of anti-semitism. Nobody can honestly do it without being called anti-semitic all over the world, thus gaining a reputation which in these days spells ruin to most people.[3]

This disreputability of anti-semitism was particularly strong in liberal circles because it was considered to involve a rejection of the historically evolved ideology of liberalism, two aspects of which assumed an importance in this respect. First of all, religious toleration was part of the liberal ideology and any attack upon the Jewish religion was frowned upon. Secondly, liberalism was the political creed of bourgeois capitalism. As such it was particularly tolerant towards those groups whose social behaviour was regarded as bolstering capitalism and this could encourage a defence of Jews, whether as hard-working immigrants or sophisticated traders. Such bald comment requires some gloss and it should be said first of all that toleration was not expressed in such materialist terms: instead, reference could be made to the assumption that all men were essentially the same. Secondly, toleration was not synonymous with acceptance. The liberal compromise offered emancipation in the expectation that Jews would cease to be Jewish and move closer to British society. Thirdly, although liberal ideas extended beyond the Liberal Party, not everybody upheld the principle of toleration towards Jews. Hence the anti-semitism with which we have been concerned. But the effectiveness of a principle does not depend necessarily upon a universal appeal and the toleration of Jews was widely accepted within the British power elite and consequently exercised a significant impact on the debates which took place between 1876 and 1914. Fourthly, it needs to be underlined that toleration was not always apparent in the treatment of minorities, as the German gypsies who entered Britain between 1904 and 1906 soon discovered. Toleration was a means of guaranteeing the smooth working and efficiency of a particular social system and it was not believed that all minorities had equal significance in this respect. Toleration was not, in fact, a self-acting agency; it often needed an appropriate push and those groups most likely to be tolerated were those which were well organized and which either directly or through sympathizers had access to the offices of the state and the other important agencies of public opinion. Consequently, the fact that there was down to 1914 an established, emancipated Jewish community which accepted the challenge of the liberal compromise, was not without significance. It was in the light of such principles and pressures that the predominant ideology in Britain between 1876 and 1914 presented a favourable image of Jews, that Jews were brought more closely into the service of the state and nation and the challenge of anti-semitism was opposed.[4]

As capitalism extended its sphere of influence in the course of the nineteenth century, the values of liberalism became increasingly pervasive, even though they were not unchallenged. The consequence was that many who opposed Jewish immigration tried to make it clear that they were not questioning these fundamental values; they had to do so in fact if they were to enlist support for their campaign. Hence the *Briton*, a paper which circulated briefly in the East End in 1887, carried a report of a meeting in the East End on 19 April 1887 at which Arnold White found it necessary to preface his speech about immigration with the remark:

> The question was not a religious question and they denied that the immigration of pauper foreigners was in any way to do with their creed.[5]

A similar concern was apparent in the statement put out by a section of the British Brothers' League:

> It is of no consequence whether a destitute immigrant believes in the Bible, the Talmud or the Koran.[6]

In brief, liberalism was associated with religious toleration: it was liberalism, after all, which had emancipated various religious minorities, including Jews, in the course of the nineteenth century and the efforts of those who opposed Jewish interests to show that they were not mounting an attack upon religious grounds is indicative of the strength of its influence. So, while there were some who found it difficult to oppose Jewish immigration because of the strength and influence of free trade opinions within the liberal creed and while there were others who were reluctant to press for the exclusion of refugees fleeing from the harsh barbarism of the Russian Bear, and those who welcomed them as a personification of liberal capitalism, a specific concern about Jewish immigrants as a religious group was also apparent throughout the immigration debate and hung like a persistent shadow over the whole proceedings.[7]

It has been argued that not only did these influences affect those at the centre of the campaign to restrict or prevent the process of Jewish immigration but that they also influenced the attitude of the Conservative Party (in power for most of the time that immigration was a matter of public debate) towards the introduction of restrictive legislation. 'Anti-semitism', it has been written, 'was not merely disreputable, but also possessed the same sort of reputation as witchcraft' and it was this kind of cultural pressure which seemed 'at least partially, to explain the curious and thoroughly ambivalent behaviour of the Conservative front bench' towards the immigration issue.[8] 'Dilatory verbiage' and procrastination governed Conservative policy; there was much talk but little action. The consequence was that in 1892–3, for instance, there was the suggestion of a government bill to control immigration but nothing appeared on the statute book. And this approach continued: it was only in 1905 when a general election seemed imminent that a revived interest was shown. It has to be said that it was not easy to frame legislation which would keep out pauper aliens, if only because it was notoriously difficult to define the category with any legislative certainty. But while this might have impeded legislative developments one should also be aware of the government's reluctance to become involved in any measure which seemed to involve a move against Jews as such. Hence the curious state of affairs in which government spokesmen studiously refrained from mentioning the word 'Jew' in the discussions and debates on the bill. Hence too, the warning which seems to have been given to those Conservative MPs who became associated with the British Brothers' League and who might, therefore have become tainted with anti-semitism.[9]

It was precisely because of the strength of liberal toleration and the aura of disapprobation which surrounded anti-semitism that Jewish interests could turn the threat of anti-semitism to their own advantage. This was brought home to the 1903 Royal Commission on Alien Immigration when A. T. Williams and Arnold White were giving their evidence. Williams, whose attitudes and connection with the British Brothers' League have already been noticed, commented that it was difficult to get witnesses before the Royal Commission in order to express an anti-alien case:

> From the very first, when there was an agitation started in the East End to press upon Parliament that these aliens should be kept out, the Jewish press has always endeavoured to persuade its readers that this was an anti-Jewish, and not an anti-alien question.[10]

In order to counteract this, Williams was encouraged to inform East Enders that, in his view, the immigration issue did not involve anti-semitism.[11] In his turn White made a number of similar emphases in the course of which he told the Commission:

> The disinclination of every Englishman worthy of the name to harass the persecuted Russian Hebrew, or to run counter to enlightened Jewish opinion by undertaking the invidious task of advocating restriction makes it difficult for a mere private person to obtain trustworthy evidence; and it has left the

> case for restriction in the hands of violent and unreasonable men, who neither appreciate the enormous weight of the reasons advanced for leaving things as they are, nor refrain from exaggerating the evils that exist, and who therefore weaken the case for restriction by exaggeration.[12]

In short, suggestions were made that the Jewish community used the fear which clearly existed of contamination with anti-semitism as a weapon against those who opposed alien immigration. It was in the interests of the community to do so, just as it was in that of Williams and White to play down the existence of anti-semitism and to complain bitterly of the exploitation of the issue by Jewish spokesmen.

But, while exploiting susceptibilities to the charge of anti-semitism, it was not totally in the interests of Jewish spokesmen to press these charges continuously and we can also find them denying that anti-semitism existed or, on other occasions, proclaiming that it had an 'artificial' quality to it.[13] The emancipation process urged upon the community the need for a low profile approach on such matters and this denial of anti-semitism was, in part, a corollary of the acceptance of such a position by Jewish leaders. But there were also other influences at work. Repeat often enough that anti-semitism did not exist and, with luck, some of this might sink home and help at least to counter the talk of probable outbreaks of hostility against Jews.[14]

At this point the broader responses of Jews in Britain to the immigration from Russian Poland might be mentioned, and it needs to be emphasized that 'no single policy or attitude consistently governed the attitude of the entire native Jewish community.'[15] Even so, a keen interest in the immigrants was evident within Anglo-Jewry: indeed it has been suggested that during the first decade and a half of immigration it was the Anglo-Jews who noticed and worried most over their arrival.[16] This concern gave rise to various attitudes. The dominant one was that taken by families such as Rothschild, Montefiore and Mocatta and was reflected through institutions like the Jewish Board of Guardians, the United Synagogue and the *Jewish Chronicle*. The opinion expressed in these quarters was that access to England should remain but no encouragement and as little aid as possible should be given to immigrants.[17] A further group, which centred upon Hermann Landau, Samuel Montagu, Herbert Bentwich and Leopold J. Greenberg, who took over the *Jewish Chronicle* in 1907, adopted a different line. 'These men's outlook did not advocate cordiality to immigrants', it has been written, 'but besides the open door it demanded a greater measure of aid and comfort.'[18] In addition to these groups there were immigration restrictionists within the Jewish community who regarded the existence of Jewish charity as an invitation to Jewish paupers to descend upon England.[19] The most vociferous voices of this kind belonged to the older generation of previous immigrants, the Dutch, Russian and Polish Jews, who perceived a threat to their own newly won positions in the arrival of the newcomers.[20] It was among these marginal Jews, insecure and uncertain about their own status, that the newcomers were viewed with suspicion.

Although the Jewish community presented no united front on the immigration issue, it has been claimed that its presence and various actions helped to case the path of the immigrants. It is likely that in general this did happen, although in a less clear cut and direct way than might be commonly understood. It has been suggested, for instance, that the existence of a settled community provided the immigrants with a 'working example' of the possibilities and desirability of 'assimilation' and, in so far as this encouraged the immigrants to foresake notions of separateness, it could help to ease their entry into British society.[21] But we need to be cautious in proposing this. Any 'change' from Jew to Englishman was regarded with suspicion or downright scepticism in some quarters and, as we have noticed, there were others who would have rejected the possibility of any Jew ever becoming an Englishman.[22] And no automatic reliance could be placed upon all Jewish Members of Parliament exercising a positive influence in the immigrants' favour.[23] Furthermore, Jewish institutional activity was susceptible to more than one interpretation. It was contended by some that the work of the Jewish Board of Guardians prevented immigrants coming on the rates and there was therefore no reason to assume that the newcomers constituted a financial burden to the receiving society. But there were other voices which argued that the existence of Jewish charity (as evidenced in the loan-granting activities of the Board) intensified competition in the labour market and in other respects acted as a magnet drawing supplies of immigrants westward from the Russian pale of settlement to Britain where, it was claimed, they knew they were assisted towards a life of relative comfort.[24]

Nevertheless, certain decisions probably succeeded in reducing the potential for the emergence of anti-semitism or a sustained campaign along those lines. In this respect steps which were undertaken to divert immigration to the United States and the influence which was exerted to persuade potential immigrants to stay in eastern Europe, while self interested and often callous and designed to keep Jews out of the limelight of public debate, helped to limit the build-up of pressure in the immigrant areas. Similarly, the activities of the Four Per Cent Industrial Dwellings Company and the East End Dwellings Company Limited, which were specifically designed to disperse Jewish immigrants and render them less 'visible', also helped to ease the way towards acceptance or toleration.[25] This latter activity was undertaken at a time when there was an atmosphere of distance and, in some cases, mutual disdain between native and immigrant Jews and it says something for an underlying strength of fellow feeling that even in these difficult days the sense of a single community was maintained. The achievement of this was the community's greatest triumph of the immigration years. Although tensions did develop within the power elite of Anglo-Jewry over the direction of policy, major splits, unbridgeable discords, and running battles might well have exposed it to attack and rendered it vulnerable. As it was, an underlying unity was maintained down to 1914 and the children of the immigrants began to assume control of Jewish communal affairs in the 1930s and 1940s.[26]

The toleration which officially attached itself to the Jewish community meant that there was nothing in terms of an official barrier which prevented

Jews obtaining positions in society – as was clearly illustrated in the elevation of Nathan de Rothschild to Lord Rothschild. In 1869 Gladstone had recommended the Queen to elevate his father, Lionel de Rothschild, but the request was refused. The Queen was of the opinion that such a move would not be well received in society and it would, in fact, harm the government. However, Gladstone's recommendation in 1885 was accepted 'without a murmur'.[27] Following this, others were raised. Henry de Worms became Lord Pirbright, Samuel Montagu became Lord Swaythling in 1907 and – an indication of the extent to which attitudes had changed in the half century following Gladstone's abortive proposal on behalf of Lionel Rothschild – the names of Sir Edgar Speyer, the Right Honourable Arthur Cohen, Sir A. D. Kleinwort, Henry Oppenheim, R. C. Lehmann and N. Seligmann were all considered as propective peers at the time of the 1913 constitutional crisis when discussions took place to pack the House of Lords.[28]

There were other indications, apart from these, that Jews could attain positions of influence. Indeed, 'persons of Jewish faith or descent attained high office on a scale unequalled and certainly unprecedented in a Western country in modern times'. In addition to Disraeli, politicians such as G. J. Goschen (who was chancellor of the exchequer between 1887 and 1892), Farrer Herschell (who was lord chancellor in 1886 and again in 1892–5), Sir George Jessel (solicitor-general between 1871–3 and master of the rolls and the first Jew to become a minister of the crown), Rufus Isaacs (who was solicitor-general in 1910, attorney-general between 1910 and 1913 and lord chief justice in 1913), Herbert Samuel (who held office before 1914 as chancellor of the Duchy of Lancaster and then as postmaster-general), and Edwin Montagu (under-secretary of state for India), were all members of British governments.[29]

These were also years when great fortunes were made by individual Jews, which in some cases heralded the start of new dynasties. And, since money has no smell, the piling up of wealth was often the key to obtaining respectability. and as we have already noticed, the *entrée* into official circles.[30] We can in fact go some way towards quantifying this financial success. Although the Jewish population never amounted to more than one per cent of the total population, between 1910 and 1919 23 per cent of the non-landed millionaires were Jewish and 16 per cent of all millionaires.[31] The emancipation process further guaranteed that there were no official restrictions upon the uses to which this wealth could be put. There were no barriers upon the ownership of land and property. There were no residential restrictions which required Jews to live in certain areas. There was no legally enshrined *numerus clausus* in existence to hinder the education of children from Jewish families, so that over time some significant contributions could be made to the arts and sciences as well as to government and business.[32] It was in such circumstances that in 1897, in the summer of Victoria's Diamond Jubilee year, the Chief Rabbi could dilate upon the successes which the community had achieved and the contribution it had made to many departments of the nation's life.[33] It was, furthermore, such evidence of success which led a later commentator to remark that the years between 1870 and 1914 'may well be described as the golden age of the Jewish people in Britain'.[34] But here, in the midst of optimism and satisfaction, is the place to remind ourselves of the other side of the coin.

So far we have been referring to the strand of toleration in British society and have stressed particular instances in which it worked favourably for individual members of the Jewish community and to the disadvantage of those who believed they had a case to present against Jews and Jewish influence in British society. But the warmth and comfort of the liberal womb should not encourage us to stay there. We need to emerge and take account of the world outside. And, once there, it becomes apparent that, while brilliant illustrations can be provided of Jewish successes, discrimination against Jews during these same years prevented some individuals exercising the full extent of their talents.

In Bethnal Green, for instance, the Liberal and Radical Club passed a resolution in 1901 'that, in future, no candidate will be accepted as a member if he be of the Jewish race.'[35] Two years later, the executive committee of the St George's and Wapping Liberal and Radical Association unanimously rejected one of the candidates put forward by the local Labour Party for a united ticket on the grounds that he was a Jew.[36] Eight years later it was the turn of the local Guardians in Bethnal Green to provide further evidence of discrimination against Jews in the course of their discussion of the half-yearly milk and poultry contracts, when it was made clear by certain individuals that Jews should not be favoured with these. In the former case a Jewish contractor had submitted the lowest tender while there were only two tenders, both at the same price, for the poultry contract. In neither case was the Jewish tradesman preferred. However, the following week it was reported that in the interval the milk award had been given to the Jewish contractor. But the discriminatory element in the initial decision was clearly evident.[37]

And it was not merely in London that such incidents took place. A local observer of the Leeds scene also reported that Jewish immigrants had to contend with the response 'no Jews need apply' in their efforts to find work and obtain a place to live and the immigration years also witnessed running fights between Jews and other residents in the Leylands area of the city, especially on 'pay day' when gangs of locals selected individual Jews or groups of Jews for their attention.[38]

It was not only in immigrant areas that the weapons of discrimination were in evidence. When Lewis Namier, the historian, applied for a Fellowship at All Souls in 1911, he found his origins held against him. A. F. Pollard, who was present at the election meeting, wrote to his parents about the circumstances:

> The meeting on Friday morning for the election of Fellows was lively and I was told the debate was the best on record, which perhaps I should not repeat as I had to take a considerable part in it. The lawyers could not conscientiously run a law candidate, so we had two for history. The best man by far in sheer intellect was a Balliol man of Polish-Jewish origin and I did my best for him, but the Warden and majority of Fellows shied at his race, and eventually we elected the two next best.[39]

There is evidence that this was not an isolated example, a unique aberration in academic life. Shortly afterwards, for instance, Woolfe Crammer, writing to the *Jewish Chronicle*, quoted a letter he had received from an Oxford don admitting that anti-semitism did exist in the area of scholastic appointments, although it did not assume significant proportions and in no way compared with the circumstances prevailing in Paris or Berlin.[40] Elsewhere, far away from dreaming spires, in the fashionable, frivolous world of London society, Jewish socialites encountered varying degrees of hostility, even though the accumulation of wealth and adherence to the rules of etiquette had given them some access to that small world devoted to its own lavish and conspicuous pleasures.[41] Claims that individuals or groups have been recipients of prejudice or discrimination are not always easy to verify, of course, and not all instances which have been adduced to illustrate the existence of anti-semitic discrimination are based on clear-cut evidence.[42] But sufficient accounts can be authenticated for it to be stated that discrimination against Jews did occur.

Such incidents and circumstances, individually and cumulatively, provide evidence that there were counter forces at work in society which were not restrained by the liberal tradition, as do the various anti-semitic attitudes which we have been able to identify. Immigrant Jews found themselves facing an opposition which derived its strength from a belief in the incompatibility of the newcomers with British society. And it was not only Jewish arrivals who were attacked on such grounds. Goldwin Smith could question the patriotism of strict Jews and the loyalty issue was also raised at the time of the Boer War. Furthermore, incidents such as the Swaythling will in 1911 provided grist to the mill of those who claimed that Jews could never be true patriots, that a homeless, rootless tradition guaranteed a first allegiance to other Jews and Judaism rather than to Britain.[43] In addition, the rich, acculturated Jewish element in British society – some belonging to long established Anglo-Jewish families, others of more recent vintage – found themselves facing charges that they were using their positions of power and influence to manipulate British society in their own sectional interests or in flagrant disregard of long established principles.[44]

There were occasions when hostility towards Jews did in fact become organized. We have referred to instances of discrimination against Jews as such and in the Creagh incident such treatment assumed an organized social form. In addition to this, movements such as the British Brothers' League and the National League for Clean Government formed focal points for group opposition to various Jewish interests and in south Wales crowd violence could be directed against Jews at a time of economic hardship. In none of this did the situation become as acute as it did in various parts of Europe and little of the hostility expressed in such incidents embraced all Jews within its scope. Most of it was expressed towards sections of Jewry: immigrant Jews and rich financiers were each endowed with a range of special qualities, derived from their experience as Jews, which were regarded as dangerous to British society.[45] And it was in such terms that organized group hostility towards Jews before 1914 was manifested.

If we stand back from all these various expressions and consider them, it becomes apparent that, whatever their causes – and these will be discussed later – hostility was expressed through two main images. One stress was upon Jews as aliens. This was made manifest in the debate at the time of the Russo-Turkish War in the emphasis placed upon Disraeli being an 'oriental', or a 'Hebrew of the Hebrews', someone who had the mental processes of a 'foreigner' and who was consequently incapable of understanding English policy.[46] It was also present in Goldwin Smith's doubt as to whether strict Jews could ever be patriots.[47] It was heard in the East End in the references which were made to 'Yiddish speaking aliens', 'Jew alien landlords', and in the critical remarks on 'traditions, usages and customs' which were highlighted by a Jewish separateness.[48] It also appeared in the *Witness* where comment was passed upon the vigour of Jewish exclusiveness.[49] It was present too in that debate which emphasized the physical consequences of Jewish immigration. Hence the references which could be made to strange diseases which even passed the understanding of doctors, to the 'Asiatic invaders', the 'alien immigration plague', 'Asiatic physiognomy', and to Jews as an oriental breed.[50] And it echoed through the debates about Jewish power and possible dominance of society and the Jewish capacity of 'fix' situations in their own interest. In this connection Jews could be referred to as agents of 'cosmopolitan and materialist influences fatal to the existence of the English nation' or, more directly, as 'cosmopolitan Jews most of whom had no patriotism and no country'. It comes as no surprise, therefore, that the Marconi scandal could be discussed in terms of members of 'this gifted Asiatic tribe' coming together to secure their interests while flouting convention and disregarding the interests of the British people.[51] Technically, of course, some Jews were aliens but the term was used in a wider sense than this. It was employed more generally to emphasize what was perceived as an essential incompatibility between Jews (or sections of Jews) and a variously defined British way of life.

The other powerful image which emerged was that which emphasized Jews in the capacity of Shylock, and as the personification of capitalism and materialism. In some instances their activity as moneylenders was specifically stressed as when, in a discussion of moneylending in East Anglia, Joel Ford could be referred to by a prominent campaigner as 'the Jew usurer'.[52] And a similar emphasis was present in the debate in 1900 on the Moneylenders' Bill, when comment was passed upon the exploitative activities of Isaac Gordon, whose name was synonymous in some quarters with all the worst evils which moneylending entailed.[53] And such an emphasis was possibly even more apparent in the abortive attempt by Lord Newton in 1913 to control what he chose to call 'the tribe of usurers' – a significant 'long hand' image. Throughout the debate on Newton's motion a stress was placed upon Blumberg becoming Burton, on Cohen becoming Curzon – indeed, on 'Moses and Aaron trading as Crewe and Lansdowne'. Newton's bill was intended to enforce the disclosure of the identity of those actually involved in moneylending and the debate turned heavily upon the assumption of English names by Jewish lenders.[54]

But the image is wider than this and more closely concerned with an associated link between Jews and various forms of capitalist endeavour and outlook. This was apparent in references made at the time of the immigration debate to a Jewish capacity for 'getting on', something for which Jews were described as having a 'deadly resolve', and which, together with their 'assiduity' and 'ambition', meant that to some commentators Jews were the personification of capitalist virtues.[55] As we have already argued, there were those who rejoiced at the injection of such qualities into British society, stumbling as it was in the face of world competition.[56] But equally there were those who did not exult at the presence of Shylock Smiles in Britain, perceived in many cases as moving rapidly from immigrant to businessman or financier, and this was reflected in opposition to rich Jews – the Augustus Melmottes of this world, who dominated Trollope's novel *The Way We Live Now* (1875). Such types could be portrayed as ruling the world through the 'sceptre of finance' or the 'engine of finance' as it was sometimes called, in their role as international financiers 'par excellence'. The consequence was, F. Hugh O'Donnell argued, that the Jewish financier, 'a living type of international capitalist', had become the king of the age, through controlling key sections of the economy and the press.[57]

Very few of all these charges were levelled against Jews as a whole. For the most part hostility was directed towards individual Jews or, more often, towards sections of Jews – immigrants from eastern Europe, rich Jews, Jewish financiers, international Jews – when a stress was placed upon the fact that the conflict involved Jews and this gave it its significance.[58] In some cases what we would now regard as racist expressions of hostility occurred when all Jews came under attack. But they are exceptions in a complicated situation which is best left for a fuller discussion elsewhere.[59]

Such images as we have been considering arose in the course of specific conflicts generated after 1876 but there is evidence of another stratum of hostility which also laid a stress upon Jews as essentially alien and as agents of an unwelcome materialism. It will be recalled that in the 1960s controversy developed over the dictionary definition of the word 'Jew', when reference was made to its popular association with cheating and dishonesty.[60] But this was not a recent development in definition. At the turn of the century, while we can find Jew being defined as 'a person of the Hebrew race, an Israelite', it was also observed that the word was in widespread use as a form of 'opprobium' or 'reprobation'. In this respect it was meant to convey 'a grasping or extortionate moneylender or usurer' or, alternatively, a trader who drove hard bargains or dealt 'craftily'.[61] As a verb the word was also in common use when it was synonymous with 'to cheat', 'to over-reach' and, to illustrate its point, in 1901 *A New English Dictionary* quoted the *Daily News* of 2 November 1891, which contained the telling remark, 'he'd take care he didn't "Jew" him again.'[62]

A further indication of the qualities which were generally regarded as attaching to Jews was provided in the depiction of characters in both popular and serious literature. It was once argued in this connection that as the century progressed the written word began to reflect the liberal tradition and that this was apparent in the increasingly sympathetic treatment of Jewish characters.[63] But this needs to be seriously questioned and it has been suggested instead that we need to take account of the 'massive durability' of the Jewish stereotype in literature and the continued perpetuation of Jews in the role of 'outsider' villains and materialists.[64] This is not to suggest, however, that all portrayals of Jews were hostile and malicious. How otherwise would we account for *Daniel Deronda*? But there was no inexorable victory for the sentiments of acceptance or tolerance – even among Jewish writers.[65] And what is particularly significant for the present discussion is that where hostile stereotypes did appear, in the case of both Jewish novelists and their non-Jewish contemporaries, there was a pronounced stress upon a Jewish obsession with money and materialism, with the cult of Mammon, and an equally pronounced thirst for social advancement.[66]

Furthermore, it was not only in literature that unflattering images could be found. A recent study of cartoons and caricatures of the Irish maintains that 'Victorian political cartoons were closely linked to popular prejudices about all manner of people and issues' and it is not without interest to consider the portrayal of Jews in *Punch*.[67] Jews were presented as 'visible' both in terms of physical appearance and use of language – both of which emphasized their alien qualities.[68] But, in addition, there was a prominent stress upon Jews as oblivious of any interest except that of material gain. In a cartoon drawn at the time of the Russo-Turkish War, under the title 'Professional View of the Situation', the following conversation appeared: 'Awful dem Rooshian atroshities – shtrippin' de poor creeturs naked! Von ting – ole clo's'll be sheap."[69] Alternatively, a number of drawings appeared which were intended to create an image of Jews as 'sharp boys'.[70] It was not merely Jewish 'sharpness' which was being emphasized in such drawings. The depictions also carried with them an implicit assumption that Jews lacked cultural finesse, that to them art was merely another trading commodity and this was further underlined when an artist by 'a mere alteration of titles' was depicted as achieving a sale of unmarketable pictures – to a plutocratic Jewish buyer, well built, dressed in astrakhan coat and flourishing an ample, ready cheque book.[71]

We need to know far more about such images, expressed outside the heat of the battle by those who do not figure as central characters in the history of anti-semitism. By presenting particular images of Jews, whether literary or verbal, writers and artists hoped to achieve an identification with their various audiences and it is through such sources rather than the writings of individuals such as White and Banister that we are able to obtain a glimpse of more general perceptions of Jews in British society. On examination of such material it is clear that Jews were commonly regarded as representatives of alien materialism and it is likely that a wider survey of popular attitudes – contemporary music hall material comes to mind – would confirm that such images did have a general currency.[72]

The time has now come to pull together the previous arguments and attempt to account for the hostility which Jews encountered in the forty or fifty years which preceded the First World War. First of all, it might be noticed that Jewish commentators have usually preferred to work within a scapegoat framework. 'The Gentile's misconception of the Jew', wrote Max Hunterberg in 1913, 'has for ages been the chief cause of the malady of Anti-Semitism, which, like a three-headed monster, so often appears in the form of fanaticism, hatred and persecution.'[73] And this opinion reflected a prominent strand of explanation at the time. 'If there be a Jewish question, except in the imagination of the enquirer, what is it?', a commentator asked in 1882, echoing Macaulay in the sentiment that 'the real difficulty in speaking in favour of the Jews [arises] from the circumstances of there being no valid arguments advanced against them.'[74] Shortly afterwards, in similar vein, it was stressed that anti-semitism had little to do with the activity of Jews but was basically a reaction, a despairing gesture, against the movement of history and was essentially an attack upon liberalism narrowed down to a convenient size.[75] Another could claim that every country had the Jews it deserved. The Jew was largely what the Christian had made him.[76]

Somewhat later, adopting a narrower approach, a contributor to the *Jewish Review* wrote that it was the pressure encountered by lower middle- and upper working-class groups in the face of Britain's declining competetiveness which lay behind anti-semitism, although no evidence was offered to support this explanation. Building upon this assumption, the writer went on to say that the 'vexation' accumulated in such circumstances was responsible for the hostility encountered by Jews, who were regarded as 'taking the bread out of the Englishman's mouth'. In the same literary breath, however, his readers were told that it was not necessary to consider whether or not such 'vexation' was justified.[77]

My own emphasis has been rather different. Before starting to analyse any of the evidence relating to the years between 1876 and 1914, I drew attention to the fact that there was a tradition of hostility towards Jews in British society, which ran parallel with the liberal tradition of toleration and which was likely to affect perceptions of Jews. Stereotypes which reflected earlier conflicts and clashes still survived and such 'mind set' images need to be considered in discussing the hostility which Jews in Britain encountered between 1876 and 1914. We know that once established such images possess considerable tenacity and durability and are capable of sustaining a life even in the absence of Jews.[78] In the case of the Jewish minority, its portrayal needs to be considered within the framework of a tradition, stretching back to the middle ages and kept alive through cultural transmission into more recent times, ready to play a part in directing and sustaining hostility in a variety of circumstances. Images of Jews as Shylock and an awareness of religious differences between Jew and Gentile had been present in non-Jewish culture for centuries and continued to exercise an influence over society. More recently, as mentioned earlier, the emancipation debate had witnessed an opposition to full Jewish participation in British society on the grounds of a continuing

Jewish foreignness and the low moral character of Jews arising out of a concentration upon financial gain.[79] The emancipation debate, which was protracted and difficult to resolve, kept these images before the public and problems relating to Jews as aliens and on account of their concentration in finance continued to be emphasized between 1876 and 1914.[80]

Once we move into the years between 1876 and 1914 additional pressures began to exercise an influence over Jew-Gentile relations. For the first time Jews had no official restrictions placed upon them and throughout the years down to the First World War careers were, theoretically, open to talent, although in practice life was not always the sister of the dream. And the hostility towards rich Jews after 1876 is made more understandable if it is kept in mind that it occurred within this changed context. When F. Hugh O'Donnell drew attention to the meteoric rise of Rufus Isaacs, when hostility was focused upon Jews in government office, when Fellows of All Souls could object to an appointment of a Polish-Jew, they were all, to a greater or lesser degree, finding it difficult to come to terms with the emancipation process.[81]

Furthermore, as we have shown at various points, the debates about the presence in Britain of poor Jews or rich Jews occurred against a background of anxiety about the state of the nation which was debated with increasing urgency after the mid-1870s. By then it was widely claimed and frequently emphasized that the days of Britain's greatness were over, that the growing industrial and political power of Germany and America was significantly in the process of altering world relationships. In this situation the feeling was aroused not only that Britain's pre-eminence was under threat, but that the Jewish presence encouraged this process. And it was in such circumstances that liberalism, the political ideology of bourgeois capitalism, came under scrutiny. Doubts about the continuing viability of the system raised questions about its dominant political creed.[82] Disillusioned or disgusted by the present, some people also retreated into a past golden age – a time when the problems which anxiously tormented their own day did not exist. It was against such a background that the debate over Jewish immigration took place and the role of rich Jews in British society was discussed. And it was within that kind of context, particularly between 1899 and 1914 in circumstances of social distress and uncertainty and a gathering nationalist sentiment, that immediate trigger factors sparked off the major hostility towards Jews which we have considered.[83]

What were these immediate trigger factors, these concrete tensions and face-to-face rivalries? In some instances it has been vital to take cognizance of the individual psychologies of anti-semites – Burton and Banister come to mind – but in general the emphasis has been elsewhere.[84] In fact, we are unlikely to make much sense of anti-semitism if we concentrate exclusively upon individual personalities and regard such hostility as a projection of personal problems and frustrations. It was suggested some time ago that even if we were familiar with the individual psychologies of all Germans between 1919 and 1939 it would not adequately explain the nature and evolution of German anti-semitism during these years and the remark has a general relevance.[85] In our own case attention has been concentrated upon specific situational tensions, arising from the processes of social interaction rather than abstract clashes of individual minds. It has been further argued that such tensions cannot be appreciated without reference to the attitudes, assumptions and behavioural patterns which attached to both sides in the conflict situations. The circumstances were those in which each party believed they had a reasonable point of view and reflected what have been called elsewhere 'irreducible irritations'.[86]

The anti-semitism expressed after 1876 cut across class and party boundaries, as individuals and groups encountered what they perceived as a conflict between their own and Jewish interests. In attempting to understand this it has been found necessary, therefore, to draw attention to issues such as the differences in social mores in the East End of London between Jewish immigrants and native East Enders, to the Jewish involvment in credit trading in south Wales at a time of social misery and tension, to the hostility which was created among court elements, when largesse and influence seemed to be moving in the direction of *arriviste* Jews, to the suspicion generated by the business connections and political activity of powerful Jews at the time of the Marconi and Indian silver scandals and when war between Germany and Britain was becoming increasingly unavoidable.[87] The outbreak of war or its threatened commencement acted generally as a powerful trigger drawing attention to the Jewish community – particularly to rich Jews. The fact that some individual Jews had international business links rebounded upon the community at the time of the Russo-Turkish War in 1877 as well as during the later prospect of hostilities against Germany. On both occasions such connections permitted the suggestion that there was an antithesis between certain Jewish and British interests. Furthermore, at the time of the Boer War, the involvement of prominent Jews in the development of southern Africa was an important element helping to sustain the view that the war was engineered mainly by Jewish gold to protect and extend Jewish interests.[88] But it has been suggested that the role of Jews in all such conflicts became simplified, distorted or exaggerated and it was through such a process that anti-semitism emerged. There were those like Banister who could create a frightening vision of the world, involving Jews, which related more to the holder's inner psyche than any observable reality. But this was rare and other simplifications and distortions occurred as part of the general process through which social situations are refined in order to be 'understood'.

At this stage, now that we have discussed the tension between toleration and hostility, a final comment might be made about the solutions to the Jewish question. There was no single response and little was as definite or as clear cut as the statement of Chief Procurator Pobedonostev in imperial Russia that one third of the Jews were to be made to emigrate, one third were to be destroyed and the remaining one third would be absorbed. Nevertheless, a number of suggestions and solutions became apparent in the course of the debate.[89]

A major emphasis among those who offered solutions made a virtue of exclusion in the belief that Jews, or sections of Jews, were unwanted and incompatible elements in British society. This was apparent in the debate over Jewish immigration when pressure mounted in certain quarters for some measure of immigration control. The need for legislation along these lines was contained in individual statements and was reflected in an organized sense in the activity of bodies such as the British Brothers' League and the Immigration Reform Association.[90] A similar type of exclusionist response, applicable not merely to recent immigrants, was present elsewhere in *The Jew, the Gypsy and El Islam* in which Richard Burton made it clear that he did not object to 'the restoration of Israel'. But he was also at pains to emphasize that Jews should be grateful that Russia stood in the way. If Jews did return and attempted to implement the philosophy decreed by their religion, he argued, the hand of society would be turned against them, and 'the "Chosen People" would once more be prostrate in their blood and be stamped out of the Holy Land.'[91]

Burton was not alone in referring to a territorial solution to the Jewish question. Arnold White also gave his support to schemes which would enable Jews to maintain a separate existence and could combine this with a plea for legislative control upon the entry of Jews into Britain. At one stage of his career he supported Baron de Hirsch's scheme to plant Jewish colonists in Argentina, and, in place of Zionism, he later proposed that a Jewish settlement should be founded in Turkish Armenia which would allow the prospect of surplus population moving into the Holy Land.[92] If some of this seems weird today, we should realize that it was being suggested at a time when some Zionist sources seriously considered the British government's proposal for settlement in Uganda.[93]

This is not the place to engage in a detailed study of attitudes towards Jewish settlement in the Middle East – or elsewhere – and to plot the history of the early Zionist movement. That is a specialist work best left to other hands. But it is important to make the point that down to 1914 a number of British anti-semites were easily reconciled to Zionist proposals which would divert Jews from Britain and provide for their recognized settlement elsewhere. David Hope Kyd, the prospective Conservative candidate for Whitechapel, was not alone when he made it clear that he was in favour of Israel Zangwill's territorial scheme of settlement in Uganda which, he emphasized, would divert pressure from east London.[94] And while there was no fiercer opponent of Jews than Joseph Banister, he could also view the prospect of Zionism with equanimity. To his bubbling imagination, it meant fewer grunting, itching, disease-laden oriental arrivals in Britain and opened up the prospect of a release from Jew-power if wealthy Jews had their interests diverted elsewhere.[95] Similarly, Major Evans-Gordon, who played a prominent role in organizing opposition to Jewish immigration, was sympathetic to a Jewish homeland in Palestine and, as an expedient measure, since this seemed likely to be long delayed, also supported Zangwill's Uganda ambitions.[96] Finally, shortly afterwards, Stephen Graham, in an article which amounted to an *apologia* for the Russian persecution of Jews – Russia was then a wartime ally – could reflect that there 'may be something in the possibility of the re-establishment of the Jews in Palestine as a nation'.[97]

Such suggestions envisaged the prospect of Jewish settlement outside Britain which would take some pressure off Britain's resources. But the most comprehensive avoidance solution was that put forward in the *Eye Witness* in 1911 when a series of arguments were presented which rejected emancipation as the solution to the Jewish question in favour of an 'apartheid' arrangement.

The main theme in this series of articles was that the Jew was a Jew, he would remain a Jew and this had to be legally recognized. Consequently, it was proposed that Jewish names should be registered and that 'special and definitely Jewish representation' should be provided in the councils of government.[98] It is difficult to avoid the conclusion that this solution, repeated by Hilaire Belloc in *The Jews*, would have led to a two-tier citizenship with all the implications that such a concept contains. Such was the solution presented in the *Witness* in its discussion of 'The Jewish Question' in 1911 but once war broke out in 1914, Cecil Chesterton, who had been keenly involved in the *Witness's* discussion of Jews and the Jewish question, envisaged how this solution could be linked to settlement in Palestine. The principal allies in the War had all suffered from a Jewish presence, he argued, or, in his own words, 'whether they have persecuted the Jews, or tolerated the Jews or submitted to the dictation of the Jews, they have equally found the omnipresence of this people an insoluble problem.'[99] However, the war presented an opportunity for overcoming such a problem. There was no reason, he believed, why an independent state should not be established in Palestine with the proviso that the Holy Places should be placed under international control. It would clearly not be possible for all Jews to return there. But, he argued, once the Jewish state existed with a Palestinian ambassador in every capital it would be appropriate to treat the resident Jews in every country as a foreign community with their proper privileges and proper disqualifications – just as the original scheme in the *Witness* had proposed.[100]

Solutions which advocated some form of exclusion would have allowed for the preservation of a Jewish culture outside Britain. By contrast, missionary work was specifically designed to undermine Judaism and this alternative approach to the Jewish question was also apparent in the years between 1876 and 1914 among those who still regarded the problem in sacred rather than secular terms. We have already referred to this kind of activity and also commented upon its lack of impact.[101] Most Jews had no particular taste for an assault upon their religion which, in different ways, provided them with a sense of identification.[102]

While there were those who tried desperately to save souls for Christ and procure the Jew's faith there were others who were more interested in his blood. The Conservative journal, the *Outlook*, commented in a review of Israel Cohen's book, *Jewish Life in Modern Times*, that anti-semitism was a 'perfectly natural' tendency and arose from the exclusiveness of Jews. Jews might provide different nations with good parents and children, and might have fine abilities and constitute a 'charitable', 'friendly' and 'cheerful' people but, according to the *Outlook*, they had to realize that what they gave the world was as nothing until they fearlessly gave themselves. Only in a state of their own would their separatist nature be acceptable.[103] Intermarriage was also proposed by Arnold White when, simplifying Britain's economic problems in an age of intense international competition to a simple dimension, he advocated the infusion 'of Jewish mind and thrift' into the Anglo-Saxon race as a means of regenerating the 'racial common sense' of the Anglo Saxon and counteracting 'racial thriftlessness'.[104]

In proposing solutions along more than one front, White was not alone, as was apparent from H. B. Marriott Watson's reflections which appeared in the *National Review*. 'The apparent hope of solving the problem resides either in the Zionist movement or in absorption', he wrote in 1905, 'and the latter seems almost an impossibility.' Nevertheless, if the Jew devoted himself to the 'task of peopling Palestine', the residue of this race 'could be left for absorption' which, he believed, could work to the benefit of the 'various national amalgams' among which the Jews resided.[105] Such a proposal of course reminded the Jew of the emancipation bargain – that in exile he should cease to be a separatist.

Part II

8 Anti-semitism in the First World War

Like other wars before it the First World War generated its own specific forms of nationalism and created allegiances and alliances which flourished best under wartime conditions. This became apparent almost at once. With the German attack on Belgium, Townsend in *Punch* could invite readers to identify with 'gallant little Belgium', defending itself against the German bully, and the Belgian refugees who streamed away from the hostilities and made their way to England were regarded, in the first flush of the war, as the innocent victims of a David and Goliath struggle. By contrast, Germans living in Britain became objects of suspicion, potential spies, agents of the Kaiser, and a viciousness was given to such feeling by the sinking of the unarmed Cunard liner, the *Lusitania*, by a German submarine on 7 May 1915. In the wake of this, Germans, some of them long standing residents, were subjected to physical assault in centres such as Liverpool and the East End of London. Elsewhere, more genteel but nevertheless damaging hostility was expressed in the Stock Exchange, where discrimination took place against members with German and Austrian origins. Such anti-German feeling could in fact reach into the highest echelons of society and, rather later, it was no accident that Lord Haldane, who had always been regarded as having close connections with Germany and German culture, was made a scapegoat in 1915 for the policy deficiencies of Asquith's government. In general, the war brought a close scrutiny of aliens so that as early as 5 August 1914 the Aliens Restriction Act was passed and was itself to be strengthened in 1918. During the space of these four years public opinion on such matters could shift quite remarkably, with the result that the Belgian refugees who were welcomed in 1914–15 stayed long enough to experience that sympathy give way to apathy or hostility. The kittens became unwanted cats. But if sympathy could be capricious, hostility towards 'things German' remained. We always hate our enemies with more consistency and thoroughness than we love our allies.[1]

Where did Jews stand in this kind of war situation? Their position was complicated in the sense that some of them were still aliens; they had not been naturalized and were still technically German or Russian citizens. Others who had been naturalized and had become part of the British social fabric were nevertheless widely known to have German origins and a number of prominent personalities fell into this category, among them Sir Felix Semon and Sir Ernest Cassel.[2] In addition to these well known figures, distinguished respectively in the worlds of medicine and finance, there were others who were associated with them, including Sir Edgar Speyer, the banker and financier,[3] and Sir Alfred Mond, the industrialist.[4]

In discussing the hostility which Jews undoubtedly encountered and concentrating initially upon that which involved rich Jews, we are at once faced with the question as to whether the opposition they faced was anti-alien, in most instances anti-German, or anti-semitic in character. We need to remind ourselves that it is only when we can detect hostility towards Jews as Jews that we can properly refer to anti-semitism.[5]

Situations are rarely simple, of course, and the dividing line between anti-alienism and anti-semitism – as argued earlier with reference to the Jewish immigrant – was not always easy to draw. In the case of the rich Jews, for instance, while a stress might be placed in public, particularly in 'respectable' circles, on anti-alienism, those who engaged in such talk could hardly have been unaware of the ethnic origin of those whom they attacked. When, after the first World War, Alfred Mond was greeted with cries of 'German Jew', it might be held that this was simply making explicit what had always been known and understood, even if forces of restraint had not encouraged its expression and emphasis.[6]

Nevertheless, throughout the tense atmosphere which developed in 1915, *The Times*, contrary to an assertion in the *Jewish Chronicle*, was very careful and restrained in its coverage and refrained from commenting upon Jewish origins. The claim in the *Chronicle* that 'The Thunderer' was using the words 'German' and 'Jew' interchangeably was an exaggeration based mainly, it would seem, upon two specific comments which followed the sinking of the *Lusitania*. Writing in *The Times* on 11 May 1915 Valentine Chirol, formerly director of the foreign department of the newspaper, referred to Albert Ballin, the German shipping magnate and head of the Hamburg-America Line, whose ships had been in competition with the *Lusitania*, as the 'Hof-Ozean-Jude'.[7] In addition, in the following issue reference was made to 'the unbridled joy of Hamburg, and of the Jewish financial press generally, at the destruction of so important a ship and so hated a rival'.[8] But there was no emphasis of this kind in the leader columns at the time of the 'loyalty letters'.

The loyalty issue was raised initially on the day following the report of the sinking of the *Lusitania*, when Sir Arthur Pinero, the playwright, whose dramatic reputation had been established since the staging of *The Second Mrs Tanqueray* in 1893, suggested in a letter to *The Times* that 'Germans who are naturalized British citizens holding prominent positions in this country' should raise their voices against Germany rather than sit 'on the gate'.[9] Consequent upon this *The Times* began to publish what have come to be known as 'loyalty letters' through which prominent German born individuals, including German born Jews, affirmed their loyalty to their adopted land. This resulted in correspondence from Felix Semon,[10] Ernest Cassel and a host of others who had been born into Jewish families in Germany but who had later become British citizens.

However, not everyone was prepared to affirm loyalty to Britain. Sir Edgar Speyer had come to London in 1887, had become naturalized in 1892, had involved himself in Liberal politics, and had been created a privy councillor in 1909. He had also emerged as a leading figure in the world of philanthropy and music. But in 1915 his origins were recalled to mind. Speyer reacted more aggressively than those who wrote their loyalty letters and on 17 May 1915 he offered to renounce his title and resign his membership of the Privy Council in view of the hostile pressures under which he found himself. But this was refused by Asquith, the prime minister. Consequently, an action was brought against Speyer and Cassel by a Scottish baronet, Sir George Makgill, which called on both of them to show by what authority they claimed to be privy councillors since they were not natural born British subjects.[11] The case lasted for five months before the action was judged to have failed.[12] Speyer, though, had had enough. He resigned all his offices and went to New York. The sequel to all this came in 1921 when his name was struck off the privy council list and his naturalization, together with that of his wife and three daughters, was revoked. A White Paper of January 1922 accused him of exchange arbitrage in 1915 knowing that it would involve traffic with Germany. The action taken against him and his family was justified by the authorities on these grounds.[13]

Throughout the issue of the loyalty letters the stress was upon the German and not the Jewish origins of those involved; in the action against Cassel and Speyer brought by Makgill, for instance, Cassel was described as 'born at Cologne of German parents'[14] and in the discussion in the House of Lords on Speyer's attitudes it was commented that they revealed a 'brutal and insolent German manner'; the lesson clearly was – 'once a German always a German'.[15] Similarly, Sir Almeric Fitzroy, who acted as clerk of the Privy Council between 1898 and 1923 and who was therefore in no doubt about the ethnic origins of Speyer and Cassel – in other instances he referred openly to them – made no mention of the Jewish connection in 1915.[16] A similar emphasis was also apparent towards the end of the war, as was illustrated by a question in the House from Mr Swift Macneill, in which he asked whether Felix Cassel KC, Sir Ernest's nephew, had resigned or intimated his intention of resigning from the position of judge advocate general. The question did not stress Cassel's Jewish origins; the issue was considered to turn upon his being of 'enemy alien birth'.[17]

With all this said, we need to remind ourselves once again that the distinction between anti-alien and anti-Jewish was not always easy to maintain. This became apparent during the first heady days of the war, in the columns of the *New Witness*. Its readers were warned in September 1914 about the dangers which aliens posed to the nation and this acted as a prelude to a discussion which placed an even greater emphasis upon such matters.[18] The putative theme was 'the predominance [within Britain] in the realms of finance and industry, and even of politics, of aliens whose allegiance, if they possess any allegiance, belongs to hostile states'.[19] This might be interpreted to mean a discussion about Germans but it is important to recall the earlier hostility of the *Witness* towards Jews and indeed it soon became apparent that the journal was essentially interested in people like Edgar Speyer and Felix Schuster, both of whom were Jewish.[20] These men were referred to as 'cosmopolitans, wanderers on the face of the earth, indiscriminate looters of the European nations', men who could rely upon the weight and intriguing influence of 'cosmopolitan finance' being thrown behind them.[21] Here, there is little doubt that we are in the midst of the language and imagery of an allusive anti-semitism.

On other occasions hesitancy was at a discount. In a discussion headed 'Schuster and Others', links were established with an inglorious past. 'Is it proper', it was asked, 'that Schuster should be allowed to remain at the head of a great banking Establishment while England is at war with his native country?' And then, as if to guarantee the reply, readers were reminded that 'at the time of the disgraceful business of the Indian loans and the Indian silver purchases it appeared that Schuster was in close touch with the Samuels.' Furthermore, 'he was financial adviser to the Indian Government when the Samuel who calls himself "Montagu" was Under-Secretary of India.'[22] The implication was: how could such a man remain in a position of influence? He was hopelessly compromised by his past. Here we can watch the *Witness* reviving the Indian silver scandal and, with it, memories of earlier campaigns against Jewish influence, and injecting them into the new debate. But then, after this, as if aware that a lack of balance had been exposed, attention was more generally directed to 'the whole group of German and German-Jewish financiers', all of whom it nevertheless recommended 'should be packed off into a concentration camp until the end of the war'.[23] In general, however, faithful readers of the *Witness* would have recognized the Jew as a special enemy.[24]

The difficulty in maintaining a distinction between anti-alien and anti-Jew which was evident in the *Witness* was further illustrated in the House of Commons debate in the summer of 1918 on the Trading with the Enemy (Amendment) Bill. Major J. R. P. Newman, the Unionist MP for Enfield, Middlesex, who displayed a keen interest in matters relating to aliens, had spoken about Shylock conducting business under a grand name but, in reality, being a one man concern working with his family and a mere handful of employees. On one level this could be construed as a hostile reference to Jewish moneymen – the term Shylock and the reference to a family orientated business might suggest this – but the meaning was not directly spelt out.[25] Later, when he moved an amendment which was concerned with taking action against commercial 'rings' which, while nationally based, could have an international influence, he told the House that in his opinion there was no danger from 'Germans with German names or obvious German names'. It was unlikely, he said, that they would set up business in Britain in the foreseeable future. But, he went on:

> What we shall have, undoubtedly, is the cosmopolitan financiers and money-lenders. We shall have a man whose father comes from Frankfurt-on-Main.

> He himself perhaps lived there as a boy. He and his father went from Frankfurt-on-Main to New York or Buenos Ayres and came to England or elsewhere.[26]

Now 'cosmopolitan' was, and still is, often synonymous with 'Jew' or 'Jewish' but it offers a degree of convenient ambiguity for those who use it. But consistency is an unusually testing virtue and Newman had to make it clear eventually that,

> To put it plainly, but not offensively, the majority of these cosmopolitan financiers are men of Jewish birth and origin.[27]

It had taken some time for this to emerge and it is indicative of the amount of trimming with which references to Jews could be surrounded.

If we now return to journalistic responses, apart from the *Witness* a considerable interest was taken in the activities of prominent rich aliens by Leo Maxse's *National Review*. We have already emphasized that well before 1914 Maxse was obsessed with German power and the threat it posed to British interests and with rich Jews and others who worked in the interests of Potsdam.[28] With the outbreak of the war, which Maxse had long prophesied, it was hardly likely that this theme would fade from interest. Indeed, the hostilities initially sharpened the conflict while also giving grounds for optimism that German influence in Britain would eventually be reduced or, as he expressed it, 'there should be a fair chance of relieving this unfortunate country of the German-Jewish yoke under which we have groaned for decades.'[29]

As before, when he made similar statements, Maxse did not regard such comments as being anti-semitic. He had no opposition, he claimed, towards Jews as Jews. It was just the German Jews who obsessed him, those who had not thrown in their lot with their adopted country but had remained 'Germans at heart', 'the ubiquitous German Jew', who had 'rigged the news, wirepulled the press, nobbled politicians and entrenched himself in the City'.[30] However, in reply to this it might be said that his stress was upon *German Jews* rather than *Germans*, which suggests that Jewishness was important, even though some of the individuals whom he attacked might have forgotten their ethnic origins.[31] In short, the war heightened Maxse's pre-war campaign and the fundamental emphases of these earlier conflicts were carried into the war years, as evidenced particularly by his attacks on German-Jewish press power and financial influence.[32] At first it was suggested that such power and influence was directed against Britain and her allies and it was emphasized that among such interests there was a reluctance to lend any support to Russia, the great dark persecutor of the Jews.[33] Later, by which time this exaggeration had been exposed, he began to accuse German-Jewish interests of scheming to bring about a premature peace in order to protect German interests.[34] In short, the war not only provided Maxse with an opportunity to continue his previous agitation against German Jews in what he regarded as the defence of British interests, but it also furnished him with further evidence of German-Jewish power and treachery.

Attitudes expressed elsewhere towards Jews displayed clear evidence of ethnic hostility, free from the trimming found at times in the *Witness* and the *National Review*. This was particularly apparent in opinion which developed towards recruitment at the beginning of the war. It was soon reported that a number of Jews had presented themselves at the recruiting station in Hackney and had been refused. The recruiting officer told the *Jewish Chronicle*:

> What happened was that we found a great deal of very strongly developed prejudice among a certain section – not the best – against the Jewish recruits. Generally they gave the Jews a rough handling in every possible way. They called them names, hustled them, distorted their foreign names and made things generally offensive. We therefore thought it best, in the interests of the Jews themselves, to refuse them.[35]

It would seem that there were a number of similar incidents in the early stages of the war when Jews were subjected to this kind of rough and ready treatment.[36] But as the war became prolonged, as casualties increased, as more blood congealed in the mud of the Western Front, as tensions and strains began to mount, a more serious situation began to emerge.

From the beginning of the war when voluntary enlistment was still official policy, Jews could be found enlisting in the ranks. Indeed, it should be stressed that Anglo-Jewry played its full part in the war effort. Isaac Rosenberg, the poet, who joined up in 1915, and was killed three years later on the Somme, on April Fool's Day, was not an isolated case.[37] But after conscription had been introduced in January 1916 a serious problem developed over the position of Russian Jews in Britain, who had entered Britain in the course of the immigration of the late nineteenth century and who had not taken out British citizenship. It was estimated in 1916 that 25 to 30 thousand individuals were in this category.[38] They were especially to be found in immigrant concentrations such as the East End of London and Leeds, both of which centres had expanded under the impact of this immigration and it was those alien Jews who showed a reluctance to fight who aroused the most serious anti-semitism during the war, although once generated the hostility was directed generally towards the Russian-Jewish population in Leeds and east London.[39]

With the introduction of conscription it could hardly be expected that aliens of allied powers should be allowed to remain in Britain without those of military age engaging in military service. Without such a step agitation against aliens was almost certain to occur. But, if such legislation were introduced, it was likely to meet with hostility from sections of the Russian-Jewish immigrant community, as a contemporary account of East End opinion by Vladimir Jabotinsky made clear:

> The most amazing thing about them was their blindness to everything that went on behind the imaginary wall which divided them (or so they thought) from the rest of England. 'Nobody interferes with us.'[40]

Behind such a wall there were those who were uninterested in the war because they preferred the lusher, safer pastures of civilian life. In Vladimir Jabotinsky's words, they preferred to 'entertain their girl friends and play billiards'.[41] But not far away from all immigrant minds were the memories and, in some cases, the scars of the pogroms. They, and representatives of other minorities oppressed by Russian power, had fled to avoid its arbitrary, authoritarian and persecuting influence, which before the war had extended to those exiles who had ventured to visit Russia. Why, some asked, should they now have to support the Tsarist state? There was, in addition, opposition of a different kind. Others in the recently formed communities, the Socialists among the ghetto dwellers – often 'professional' politicians who lived a precarious life of political agitation – joined with other Socialist elements in Britain – some of them fellow exiles from Russia – in declaring their opposition to any involvement in a capitalist war.[42]

By contrast, the Jewish establishment view as expressed in the *Jewish Chronicle* emphasized the need to support the patriotic cause. Consequently, 'printed avowals of loyalty to king and country', were prominently displayed on its pages, as were semi-humorous appeals to sentiment and custom' such as that exhibited in a barber's window: 'No Germans will be shaved here at any price. Frenchmen, Belgians and Russians will be welcome. God Save the King.'[43] Reference was also made to the enlistment of Jews,[44] declarations of patriotic loyalty by local communities[45] and prominence was given to Jewish war heroes.[46] But by 1916 the *Jewish Chronicle* had to recognize that the presence of Russian Jews in the so-called ghetto areas, who had little affinity with the establishment and who were not engaged in military service, was a major problem.

After the failure of a voluntary recruiting drive early in 1916, Herbert Samuel, the home secretary, announced that Russians of military age settled in Britain would be required to enlist in the British army unless they preferred to return for military service in Russia. Tribunals would be set up to deal with exemptions on principles similar to those which applied to British subjects. An assurance was provided that these tribunals should include persons specially qualified to deal with the cases of Jews who formed 'so large a proportion of the Russian immigrants'.[47] Precise details of the scheme were promised at a later date.

Such action on the part of the government was welcomed by the *Jewish Chronicle* and the Board of Deputies. The government, it was stated, would be assured of the 'cordial assent of the overwhelming majority of the Jews [in Britain]'.[48] At the same time, the *Chronicle* reiterated its opposition to the formation of a special Jewish Legion which was being advocated by Vladimir Jabotinsky.[49] However, in spite of this, and in the face of opposition not only from the British government but also from Zionist sources and Russian-Jewish Socialist groups in the immigrant areas, Jabotinsky persisted with his scheme. This was the situation in the summer of 1916.

The aims laid down by Samuel in June and then in more detail in July 1916 continued to form the basis of government policy towards Russian-Jewish aliens.[50] There was indeed little alternative to this policy in government opinion. Conscription had been introduced for British subjects in the previous January and agreements had been reached for the similar treatment of friendly aliens – such as the Belgian refugees –

and the government was not persuaded that Russian Jews should constitute a special case.[51] Russia was an ally in the war and this rather than the previous history of Russian persecution of Jews was held to be paramount, particularly since the government believed that the rights of political refugees who had entered Britain from Tsarist Russia could be safeguarded.[52] Furthermore the government's resolve was stengthened by its knowledge that earlier attempts at voluntary enlistment had proved to be a resounding and somewhat embarrassing failure. Herbert Samuel reminded the House on 24 July 1916 that the War Office had previously agreed to recruit a certain number of Russian aliens up to a limit of two per cent of the total establishment of the British army. Steps had also been taken to publicize this 'offer' – as Samuel liked to call it. Posters had been issued in Yiddish and English, leading figures of the Jewish community had been interviewed and a recruiting committee had been established at Lord Rothschild's offices. But, at the end of the day, the government had to confess that the 'offer' had led to 'very inadequate numerical results'.[53] Finally, the government's resolve to do something was strengthened by its awareness, on the basis of police and special branch reports, that discontent was growing among non-Jewish sections of the population in immigrant areas as a result of the continued exemption of Russian Jews from military service.[54]

But, facing opposition, the government delayed and it was not until 1917 that a military agreement was signed with the Russians. In July 1917 the Anglo-Russian Military Service Agreement was concluded and in August of the same year, by an Order in Council, Russian aliens were placed under the provisions of the Military Service (Conventions with Allied States). As a result, all Russian male subjects who chose to remain in Britain were to come within the operation of the Military Service Acts of 1916 and 1917, as if they were British subjects ordinarily resident in Great Britain. Alternatively, they could return to their own country for military service. Statutory provisions for exemption from service were allowed for – as they were in the case of British subjects. Such arrangements enlisted the approval of the Jewish authorities in Britain.[55]

Throughout the time when these matters were being debated and cemented, and also after they had been finalized, a persistent opposition could be heard to the idea of military service from sections of the Jewish community and their sympathizers and we need to be aware of this if we are to understand the outbreaks of hostility encountered in 1916 and 1917 by the Russian-Jewish populations in Leeds and east London. Official files indicate that opposition certainly existed in some Russian-Jewish circles to the government's conscription proposals and police reports provided the Home Office with a flow of detailed information on organizations and individuals hostile to its policies. In this respect the government was well informed about the Foreign Jews Protection Committee which was regarded by the police as stuffed with revolutionaries and anarchists.[56] It was also fully cognizant of the activities of Solly Abrahams alias Abraham Bezalel – or Belzebub, as he was dubbed by one Home Office official exasperated by his activities – who assumed a prominent role in challenging government policy.[57] Bezalel and the Foreign Jews Protection Committee, of which he was a leading light, were from the first opposed to Russian-Jewish participation in the war and, later, were understandably hostile to the Anglo-Russian military convention and tried to mobilize ghetto opinion against it.[58] As we shall discover, Bezalel also attempted to influence the Petrograd Soviet in its appreciation of wartime conditions in Britain but his message was intercepted by the authorities.[59]

In its campaign to counteract government policy in the East End the Foreign Jews Protection Committee rejected the suggestion that Russian-Jewish immigrants had robbed East Enders of their employment. On the contrary, it was argued in February 1917, they had built up businesses which added to local prosperity. They were doing all in their power to show their appreciation of the freedom they enjoyed, a freedom which was regarded 'not as a boon for which they must bow down as slaves but as a right freely and generously accorded by a free and generous people'. Now, as a result of government policy, the Committee contended, Jewish immigrants were threatened with deportation to the country from which they had fled to avoid persecution. They asked that the right of asylum should be preserved.[60] This was the kind of material which was issued in the immigrant areas. It stated a black and white propaganda case, which at times was closely if not absolutely repeated in the House by Joseph King, the Liberal MP for North Somerset. He acted as a spokesman for the Russian-Jewish cause and was reminded by Herbert Samuel, on one occasion when the home secretary was dealing with the complexities and guarantees in the government's policy, that he should not believe everything he was told by the parties whose interests he represented.[61]

This campaign against conscription by Russian-Jewish interests and those sympathetic to their cause persisted throughout the rest of the war. The Anglo-Russian agreement of 1917 had been designed to tighten the grip of the British government over Russian aliens but, in fact, it had disappointing results. The agreement had been concluded with the Provisional Government but the British soon found themselves having to treat with the Bolsheviks. This rapidly changing situation in Russia stiffened the resolve of the war dissenters and created complications for the British government. There was a suspicion that exemptions from military service were easily granted by the Russian authorities in London and, since the granting of immunity was the prerogative of the Russians, the British could not interfere.[62] And when the Bolsheviks came to power, and particularly after they had ended Russian participation in the war by signing the Peace of Brest Litovsk with the Germans on 3 March 1918, the convention became meaningless.[63] The result was that some Jews, particularly those from settled Anglo-Jewish families, contributed to the war effort either through enlistment or conscription, some Russian Jews living in Britain went back in the early days of the war to fight in the Tsar's army, some Jews fought in the Jewish Legion, which Jabotinsky finally secured in July 1917, and others were brought into service through the Anglo-Russian military convention. But for a variety of reasons this agreement never secured the services of all those for whom it was intended – although the government was never prepared during the war to state how many Russian Jews had been brought into the ranks.[64]

It is against this background that the disturbances against Jews in Leeds and east London took place. Those which occurred in Leeds have been either ignored or incompletely understood.[65] We have already commented that Leeds was an important area of Jewish immigrant settlement in the late nineteenth and early twentieth centuries, in the course of which the Leylands area of the city became a Jewish quarter. Those who settled there were part of that migration which also helped to build up the Jewish population in east London and, further afield, contributed to the swelling of the Jewish quarters in the teeming life of urban America. Although attempts were made by the established Jewish authorities in Britain to render the immigrants less visible than might otherwise have been the case, there was still a distinctive Russian-Jewish community in existence during the war. And an awareness that such communities might encounter hostility if they did not enlist was used by the government as one justification for the introduction of its conscription proposals. In the event, the opposition of some of the Russian-Jewish minority to accept such a policy led to the outbreak of trouble which the government had attempted to avoid.[66] As the stresses of the war mounted, as wartime propaganda worked its influence, after conscription was introduced, and against a local history of hostility towards Russian Jews in Leeds and east London, the complexities of the war situation were narrowed down to a manageable size: the obligation to fight was being avoided. And in the wake of such sentiments the general Russian-Jewish population in these areas was exposed.

The first official intimation of tension in Leeds came when the Home Office was informed of the situation by the chief constable in a letter of 4 June. 'I beg to inform you', he wrote, 'that during the past two or three days there have been disturbances between the English youths of this City and those of the Hebrew persuasion.' The Home Office had already received a telegram from Jewish sources in the city giving an account of the situation and it was in the light of this that the chief constable had written his report. It would appear that there had previously been disturbances in two areas of the city, in Briggate and Woodhouse Moor, which had been dealt with by the police and the local justices but the disturbances which had just occurred were more serious and attacks had been carried out on Jewish property. In an attempt to control the situation special constables had been placed on day and night duty and these services had been augmented by the regular police, as a result of which all rotary leave was cancelled for 5 June. The chief constable's opinion was that police arrangements were adequate to deal with the 'evil' and assistance from other police forces or the military was not required.[67]

According to the local press, the incidents constituted collectively one of the most serious outbreaks of violence the city had witnessed for a long time. More than one thousand men, youths and a sprinkling of women had been involved. The principal damage, it was stated, was done to shops in the lower part of Bridge Street. 'Here every Jewish shop window was smashed, and the street was littered with fragments of glass and the damaged remnants of goods' and 'in no case was a shop occupied by a British subject molested.'[68] Reporters were left in little doubt about the intensity of the feeling involved[69] while the selection of Jewish shops as targets and 'the unmistakable evidence of Jew-baiting'[70] clearly illustrated that Jews were a specially chosen target.[71] This was made further apparent when a dozen youths charged with disorderly conduct appeared before the stipendiary magistrate, where evidence confirmed the selection of Jewish shops as targets and police accounts of verbal abuse underlined that the hostility was aimed at Jews.[72]

More disturbances occurred as the chief constable was writing to the Home Office. On that day, 4 June, according to court evidence, there were at some points three thousand people involved in the disturbances and previously undamaged sections of the ghetto were attacked. As a result more offenders appeared in court and on this occasion not all of them were youths: four women, five boys and a number of older men as well as an assortment of youths were brought before the stipendiary magistrate.[73] However, by 5 June when the chief constable was once again in touch with the Home Office, matters had quietened down[74] and by 18 June he was able to write a report of the incidents and to make some attempt to ascertain causes.

In his assessment of the situation the chief constable had no doubt as to the main reason why the disturbances had occurred. He wrote:

> In my opinion, the chief cause of the feeling of the Christian people towards the Jewish population is brought about by the large number of alien Russian Jews of military age that we have in this city who can be constantly seen promenading about our principal streets and the various pleasure resorts, especially during evenings and weekends and members of the Christian population have been heard to ask why these men are not serving in the Army as the husbands, brothers and sons of the Christian population have had to do.

There were, he commented, about 1,400 alien Jews in Leeds, chiefly Russian Jews, who were of military age, and out of that number only twenty-six had joined the forces. Upwards of 200 Russian Jews who were British subjects had joined the British army, although it was difficult to give precise numbers. In addition to this information the chief constable said that the police were aware that 'a large number of Jews of military age' were believed to have gone to Ireland to avoid military service.[75]

In the face of the June disturbances there was mounting anxiety in the Jewish quarter. Many of the inhabitants must have wondered whether the Russian experience was to be repeated in a different setting and the public display of fear, anxiety and fury by 'a Jewish matron' who, we are told, had been 'hunted like a wild beast from Odessa', only to find havoc perpetrated on her home in faraway Leeds, was doubtless a private experience for many more.[76] It comes as no surprise, therefore, to learn that the Home Office received telegrams from Jews in Leeds. A student society communication of 4 June referred to 'mob riots on Leeds Jewish Quarters. Shops looted, many injured. Bigger ones threatened tonight . . . immediate action urgent'[77] while another telegram drew attention to

> serious rioting, looting attacks on women and Jewish populace taking place here. Police protection inadequate developing seriously anticipated damage to property tonight. More protection for public desperately required. Protest meeting. Synagogue Chambers, Belgrave Street, Leeds.[78]

We can detect in this the transparent fear which ran through many Jews but we should be wary about accepting the suggestion that police protection had been inadequate or insufficient. The press commented on the judicious use of the police and it would seem from the chief constable's letters that considerable police activity took place.[79] Indeed, this was well recognized by the Leeds Jewish Board of Guardians which expressed its appreciation to the police for the 'prompt and decisive steps' which had been taken to crush the 'riots' in the Jewish quarters. The Board appreciated that it was on account of such 'zeal and energy' that no greater damage was done.[80] Police activity was in fact crucial in controlling and stabilizing the situation during the tense wartime summer of 1917 in Leeds.

But 'reality' had more than one face. Abraham Bezalel (mentioned earlier in connection with agitation against the war and any Russian-Jewish participation in it) seems to have been in Leeds at the time of disturbances or to have gone there, and the Home Office files contain an intercepted telegram which Bezalel sent from Leeds to the National Council for Civil Liberties (NCCL). This communication, sent on 5 June, referred to 'most serious anti-semitic outbreaks, rioting, looting, attacks on helpless women and children', police apathy, indeed enjoyment of the affair, and went on to request the NCCL to have the matter raised in Parliament, with a view to getting a public enquiry and assurances regarding the protection of the Jewish community. 'Jews are terrified and helpless', he concluded.[81] The telegram was intercepted by the censor and the Home Office refused to be panicked when it came into its possession. In reaching this decision, the House Office could hardly have been unaware of Bezalel's purpose. It he could show that Britain displayed the same kind of anti-semitism as that found in Russia, his case that Russian Jews should not give their support to the war effort would have been strengthened. Since the government wanted something diametrically different, it was hardly surprising that it attempted to play down the seriousness of the disturbances and to make different emphases from Bezalel's.

The National Council for Civil Liberties was not the only organization which Bezalel tried to inform about the events in Leeds. He also attempted to communicate on 8 June 1917 with the Soviet in Petrograd and persuade it that the condition of Jews in England was a matter of concern; indeed, he was prepared to point out the similarities which existed in some respects between the treatment of Jews in England and their past experiences in Tsarist Russia. His telegram, which was cut off by the British government censor, who could hardly have failed to detect its attempt to encourage hostility to the government's conscription plans, ran as follows:

> The Foreign Jews Protection Committee against deportation and compulsion calls your attention dangerous position Russian Jews England while compulsory military service bill going through parliamentary stages. Programs [sic] on Jews taking place big industrial centre Leeds. Similar disgraceful scenes as witnessed under Russian old regime actively carried out in England today. No serious police portection [sic] provided for foreign Jews while English hooligans attacked them at Leeds Sunday and Monday last. We urge you to make instant representations to English Government and insist that adequate protection be provided for Russian and foreign Jews in England we implore you to act swiftly as danger similar outbreaks all over England imminent.[82]

Once the violence had occurred in Leeds it is clear from this that it was instantly worked into wartime propaganda and served to bolster pre-existing ideological positions. The likelihood that this would happen had been commented upon by a leading member of the local Jewish community at the time the disturbances were taking place. While Jews felt resentment at being attacked, he said they were also concerned about the consequences which the 'racial riots' would have on the national cause:

> It will seem from the exaggerated reports which will be published in the foreign and neutral press as if Jews in England are treated just as they have been in Russia under the old regime.[83]

The fear was justified since, in addition to the way in which Bezalel and his organization attempted to make use of the disturbances, they were also seized upon by the Germans to portray British society in an adverse light in neutral countries. The Foreign Office informed the Home Office that on 27 or 28 June a German wireless story on the Leeds disturbances was broadcast and a Wolff telegram sent it out to various neutral countries. The German report ran as follows:

> Berlin, 29th June – Wolff's Bureau states: The Jewish Bureau of Correspondence at the Hague states that a Jewish Pogrom has taken place at Leeds in England. The disorders began on the 3rd June and were continued on the following days. Thousands of youthful boys and girls assembled on the greens in front of the town and distributed themselves after a concerted plan throughout the Jewish quarters in Leeds.
>
> The window panes of the Jewish shops were broken, their stores plundered and their wares cast into the streets. All Jews who were seen were chased and thrown stones at. Only with the greatest difficulty did the Jews save themselves from the raging mobs. The police showed itself powerless on the Sunday and Monday afternoons. Only after the representatives of the Jews had pointed out to the authorities the seriousness of the situation and had emphasized the fact that the Jews would have to organize themselves for their own protection if the protection afforded by the authorities showed itself to be insufficient, were energetic measures taken.
>
> The Chief of the Police issued a proclamation warning the population against a continuation of the disorders, threatened severe punishment and promised the Jewish population compensation. The participants in the

> pogrom were punished with small fines. The Jewish population in England is seriously alarmed.
>
> The pogrom is no chance affair. It is a consequence of years of systematic incitement by the yellow press which governs Leeds. Already before the war there were disorders resembling pogroms both in England and Ireland. The question of the obligation to military service of the Russian Jews has been utilized for violent anti-Jewish propaganda. The Jews in Leeds have, however, given a higher percentage to the army than the rest of Leeds.[84]

A further attempt to exploit the Leeds disturbances came later after the riots against Jews in the East End, and on this occasion the outbreaks in Leeds and London were joined together with the intention of damaging the allied cause.[85]

Bezalel and the German propaganda authorities were clearly interested in exploiting the outbreaks in Leeds for their own political ends and for its part the British government, faced with this prospect, decided to adopt a restrained approach to such challenges. The director of public prosecutions advised against a prosecution of Bezalel for attempting to contact Petrograd on the grounds that even on the presumption that a conviction could be obtained it was not desirable to prejudice relations 'with our ally Russia'. He went on to say that the recent disturbances in Leeds were 'comparatively little known' to the public even in Britain and, moreover, they appeared to be at an end. Furthermore, a prosecution which might involve the publication of the telegram might have the effect of reviving the trouble in Leeds as well as 'conveying to the public in general and to Russia in particular, that their proportions were greatly in excess of the actual facts'. Thanks to the action of the censor no harm had been done. In addition, the director was not convinced that a prosecution would be successful since, although the statements made by Bezalel were exaggerated, it would be difficult to prove that the description of events in Leeds was false.[86] Similarly, the Foreign Office was advised by the Home Office that 'a complete and categorical contradiction' could not be given to the Wolff report and it was left to the Foreign Office to decide whether any action should be taken.[87] As far as can be ascertained no action was forthcoming.

This opposition to military service by some Russian Jews also led to disturbances in London. Hostility began to develop here in the course of 1916. Soon after Herbert Samuel's announcement to the House of his proposed treatment of Russian-Jewish aliens in the summer of 1916, the *East London Observer* was launching into an attack upon the Foreign Jews Protection Committee and denouncing its policy as 'shameless, barefaced and selfish'. According to such editorial opinion, it was nothing less than a 'desire to escape every burden of civilization' and there could be no excuse for holding out against military service when blood was flowing for the freedom of the world. The home secretary, it was stated, was right to assume that East End opinion was concerned about the issue: if the Russian Jews refused to obey the law of the land they should be sent back to Russia. It was concluded:

> If the Government show weakness in their determination and allow themselves to become victims of the 'political refugee' trick, we fear the consequences will be serious. The misbehaviour of any offensive foreign bounder, or the impertinence of a Whitechapel Jew boy, may light the smouldering fires of native feeling. To use a familiar colloquialism, East London is 'fed up'.[88]

Popular East End opinion was further expressed at a meeting held at Bethnal Green Town Hall on 23 January 1917, when emphasis was placed upon the serious situation which had developed over the question of allied and enemy aliens. The tenor of the meeting was apparent from the resolutions: they stressed that men were dying at the front while aliens of military age were allowed to strengthen their industrial position without any sacrifice; that this would create serious difficulty after the war; that there should be equal sacrifice; that the government should take steps of a compulsory nature to remedy the situation; and finally, that a conference of east London bodies should be held to discuss the prospects of sending a deputation to the secretary of state for war.[89]

Soon afterwards the *East London Observer* was carrying reports of a meeting held by the Foreign Jews Deportation Committee and also of a deputation to the House of Commons when various East End representatives met local MPs. At the former, great stress was placed upon vindicating the right of asylum, whereas at the House of Commons when they met their local MPs East End representatives placed greater emphasis upon the need to conscript Russian aliens. The mayor of Bethnal Green said that feeling on the question of immunity from military service was 'keen' – indeed, with the support of opinion from Poplar and Stepney, he believed it was 'almost keen enough to cause a revolt'. The deputation made it clear, to remove any doubt in Members' minds, that the issue which had brought it to the House was one of far reaching complexity. It was not merely a case of expressing concern that Russian Jews were allowed to remain in Britain without obligation to undertake military service; popular opinion was also inflamed by a belief that the Russian Jews were establishing themselves in the place of native labour which had gone to the war. Furthermore, it was claimed that through the mechanism of mock tribunals, aliens – on this occasion it could not be definitely stated that they were Russian Jews – were perfecting techniques which would help them to secure exemption from military service when they appeared before properly constituted local bodies.[90] Around the same time the government was receiving similar police advice, which stressed the potentially serious nature of discontent in the East End and advised that the bill to secure the conscription of alien Jews should be expedited and a declaration of intent should be made to this effect.[91] The government did of course obtain assent for its military convention with Russia in August 1917 but this did not prevent disturbances ocurring in the following month.

In early September there were clashes between Russian Jews and the local population around Euston as some Jews who had elected to go back to Russia were on the point of leaving.[92] But the major disturbances came shortly afterwards on 23 and 24 September 1917. The trouble started in Bethnal Green between 'several Englishmen and Russian Jews' in the late afternoon of 23 September, although the incident originated in a dispute between an 'Englishman and a Russian Jew', both apparently unknown, which took place in Bethnal Green on the previous evening. The Russian, it would seem, told a wounded soldier that he was a fool for having enlisted.[93] The parties met again the following day, the dispute was renewed, and this triggered off a more general disturbance in which a crowd of 5,000 people was soon involved.[94] It is clear from the police report that Jews were the targets of the crowd and of the damaged properties listed in the police report all were Jewish, and, with one exception, Russian-Jewish. It is also evident from the one arrest that was made for using insulting words that Jews were the focus of attention. Altogether 113 police officers were used to contain the operation. By 10 p.m. on 23 September the situation was regarded as under control.[95] But in a second report of 25 September, headed, 'Anti-Jewish Demonstration' it was indicated that damage was done on 24 September to the property of a Russian-born naturalized British subject, while attacks were also made on three Jewish soldiers.[96]

This was the East End's physical expression of discontent towards Russian-Jewish aliens over the military service issue and, as with the Leeds disturbances, the events were used – not surprisingly – by the German authorities for propaganda purposes.[97] Once again, as might have been expected, the official Home Office reaction was to pour water on inflammatory claims. The whole incident was dismissed as a street brawl rather than a pogrom; it was noted that only one person had been charged with insulting behaviour; there had been no continuation of the disturbances and indeed there had been nothing which could be properly called riots since the disturbances which followed the sinking of *Lusitania* in the spring of 1915.

The essential impetus behind the disturbances in Leeds and London was the same. Both had at their core a hostility towards Russian Jews over the military service issue at a time when Britain was 'holding on' in the war, when opposition to a continuation of the war for a 'knock out' victory was becoming increasingly evident and when the rest of the adult male population were liable for conscription. By 1917, when tragedies and unhappiness resulting from the war had been impressed upon many families, those who were perceived as avoiding their social obligations could expect little public sympathy; in both Leeds and London there were existing traditions of hostility which had emerged during the immigration years and this also served to direct hostility towards Jews and helped to guarantee that the tension which developed out of wartime irritations was directed generally towards the Russian-Jewish population rather than exclusively towards those who were avoiding military service.

In the case of Leeds we might also speculate whether a part was played in triggering off the enhanced interest in Russian Jews in 1917 by the holding of the Democratic Convention in the city on 3 June 1917.[98] The conference, inspired by the first Russian revolution, demanded the establishment in Britain of workers' and soldiers' councils and adopted the view that peace must be secured by negotiation rather than through a war of attrition. The pacifist tendencies of the conference, it has been argued recently, were stronger than its revolutionary sentiments.[99] The Russians, it was believed, were ready to come to terms with the Germans. And the conference stressed that such a move should encourage a similar response in Britain.[100] Did this support for what some would undoubtedly regard as Russian treachery turn attention towards the Russian Jews whose activities were also regarded by some as smacking of the same quality? Or were they the scapegoats for hostility which might otherwise have been directed against the Socialists? Such a suggestion has been made but no 'hard' evidence has been adduced in its support.[101]

The preceding discussion has emphasized that Jewish groups in Britain – both rich Jews and poor Jews – found themselves facing hostility in the course of the war and, in this respect, their history mirrored that of Jewish communities elsewhere. In some instances, as in the Russian war zone and in Russian occupied territory such as Galicia, where the harsh physical brutalities of the pre-war years continued to be perpetrated, such hostility was expressed with a persistent savagery which was not paralleled in Britain. We should be aware, however, that in the course of the war the situation in Russia itself assumed complicated dimensions. The overthrow of Tsarism and the establishment of the Provisional Government led on 3 April 1917 to Jews being granted equality, but the civil war and the Polish-Russian war created considerable chaos often with dire results for Jews.

If we take other situations it can be said that Jews in Britain had less to contend with than those in Germany where organized group anti-semitism began to increase from December 1915 onwards and by 1917 the ground was being prepared to make the Jewish community responsible for the difficulties encountered by the German war effort. In Austria too, when the problems faced by Jewish refugees from areas such as Galicia and Bukovina are considered along with the discriminatory provisions prevailing in the legal profession and in the medical faculty at the University of Vienna, it is apparent that there was here a willingness to initiate anti-Jewish measures of a kind which had no British comparison.[102] It is in fact evident that the situation of Jews in Russia, Germany, Austria and Palestine, where the war and eventual Turkish involvement in the war created a difficult situation, was far worse in terms of discrimination and organized hostility than it was in countries like Britain, France, 'which exhibited minor symptoms of anti-semitism' and America, where the main nativist hostility seems to have been directed at the German minority.[103]

In Britain – and elsewhere for that matter – this wartime anti-semitism was not divorced from what had gone before, nor was it without its significance for the future. It was no accident that violence over the conscription issue was located in Leeds and east London. These were, after all, the major centres of Russian-Jewish settlement, and, as already suggested, folk memories of earlier hostility survived and maintained an influence into the war years.[104] In this respect the wartime violence was linked with the earlier immigration and might be regarded as part of the "working out" process of that immigration. We cannot close the book on the movement from the Tsar's Empire in 1914, draw a line and estimate a profit and loss account. Professional expediency might encourage this but boundaries in history are less precise. And, just as the wartime hostility towards Russian-Jewish aliens had links with the past, it also carried implications for the future, in the sense that the campaign by the British Union of Fascists in east London in the 1930s involved political activity in an area which had, as a result of the experiences of the war years as well as the earlier immigration debate, a continuing tradition of anti-semitic hostility which could be tapped and wedded to later problems.

The rich German Jews who also found themselves facing hostility during the war were magnets of attention on account of their German birth and in some instances – Speyer comes to mind – because of their continuing German connections. But, in other respects it is also possible to consider this hostility (which, apart from its manifestation in 1914 and 1915, was also strongly in evidence in 1918 when the war showed signs of having an interminable life) as a continuation, in different circumstances, of the antipathy which had been manifested towards the 'Court Jews' and other rich Jews in Edwardian England.[105] So while wartime hostility was often expressed in terms of an undesirable alien presence and involved aliens other than Jews,[106] it embraced those Jews who had encountered the earlier suspicious hostility of certain court circles who were hardly likely to worry over the difficulties in which prominent Jews found themselves during the war. The exposed position of certain Jews after 1914 was also unlikely to enlist sympathy from the *New Witness* group or Maxse's *National Review*. Indeed, in both cases the war provided the occasion for a continuation and further flowering of their anti-semitic hostility which had already been in evidence before 1914. There could be no clearer additional evidence in support of this claim than G. K. Chesterton's open letter of 1918 to Rufus Isaacs, by then Lord Reading, expressing the fear that Reading would be involved in peace negotiations. On this occasion Chesterton wrote:

> Have you ever considered, in a moment of meditation, how curiously valuable you would have to be, that Englishmen should in comparison be careless of all the things you have corrupted, and indifferent to all the things that you may yet destroy? Are we to lose the War which we have already won? That and nothing else is involved in losing the full satisfaction of the national claim of Poland. Is there any man who doubts that the Jewish international is unsympathetic with that full national demand? And is there any man who doubts that you will be sympathetic with the Jewish International? ... Do you seriously imagine that those who know, that those who care, are so idolatrously infatuated with Rufus Daniel Isaacs as to tolerate such risk, let alone such ruin? Are we to set up as the standing representative of England a man who is a standing joke against England? That and nothing else is involved in setting up the Chief Marconi Minister as our Foreign Minister.[107]

Comment is made elsewhere how the memory of Marconi was revived after the war and Chesterton's letter shows that before then it was present in the peace discussions.[108]

In our discussion of pre-1914 hostility in the *Witness* and the *National Review* we noticed that there was a tendency for it to concentrate upon a drive towards Jewish dominance and thereby establish a link with later, more extreme expressions of conspiratorial anti-semitism. This take-off into the world of plot, conspiracy and intrigue developed rapidly after 1918, and individuals who were to assume a prominence in such later developments can be found flexing their mental capacities on the Jewish question during the war. For instance, in 1917 J. H. Clarke added *The Call of the Sword* to his already wide-ranging list of publications. Clarke, employed at the London Homoeopathic Hospital, turned his attention from medical matters and focused upon issues generated and highlighted by the war, which he described as descending upon a nation which had been overtaken by 'the cult of the coin', which had foolishly attempted to serve God and Mammon and which had degenerated under alien influences into 'a nation of moneylenders'.[109] Man, he proclaimed, could not serve God and Mammon; it was when he attempted to do so that 'the Sword appeared in the Nation's path.'[110] In order to safeguard its future Britain 'must be clear of Shylock's bond' and subject to no influence other than 'Britain's genius'.[111]

Clarke's book has disappeared into the fog of history and been lost even to avid searchers in pursuit of the roots of British anti-semitism. But it should be brought into the light since Clarke was that 'anonymous author' of *England Under the Heel of the Jew*, published in the following year, in which the threat of Jewish power and domination was raised yet again and it was he who was one of the founding members of the Britons and a leading member of that organization from its origins until 1931.[112] Since Clarke's ideas and activities were at their most significant in the inter-war years they are more fully referred to later on but some reference is appropriate at this juncture, as it is to the work of Ian Colvin.[113]

Colvin was associated in the war with the *National Review* and it was the *National Review* office which published his propaganda work, *The Germans in England. 1066–1598* in 1915. Apart from this Colvin also wrote *The Unseen Hand in English History*, which appeared in 1917. In this he argued that men and nations had first of all to live and while actions could be rationalized in terms of 'faith' or 'virtue', the basic pressure influencing social behaviour was 'interest'. Indeed, history was made by what he called 'the unseen hand of organized interest', or men coming together to guarantee their 'livelihood'. The most a nation could hope for was that the 'unseen hand' which guided human activity should be in national rather than alien hands. England, he claimed, was 'most happy' when the government and the national interest worked together and 'least happy' when the government was 'controlled by the unseen hand of the foreigner'.[114] The way to the future was clear: 'We must return to a national system founded upon production. We must protect British industries and agriculture with a British tariff in order to recover our security, our strength and our economic independence.'[115]

But, as at times in the past, there was a stumbling block. Colvin's historical work had resulted in his writing about an earlier Britain suffering 'under the thumb of the Hanseatic League'[116] and in his own day he was anxious about the strength of international economic forces which could dominate national interests. This was made particularly apparent in 1915 and 1916 in two crucial articles he wrote for the *National Review*, in which he concentrated upon the international economic power of German interests. These forces were, in fact, mainly German-Jewish, although there was no particular stress upon this.[117] Such writing about the 'German bacillus'[118] fitted in well, of course, with the existing traditions of the *National Review*. But, in turning his attention towards contemporary manifestations of organized international forces operating against national interests, he was also building a bridge towards his contribution to the eighteen articles on the Judeo-Masonic conspiracy which appeared in the *Morning Post* in the summer of 1920, shortly after the first publication in Britain of *The Protocols of the Elders of Zion*, or *The Jewish Peril*, as it was called, where similar although more extreme claims were systematically and elaborately stated.[119]

Through their wartime writings both Clarke and Colvin pointed the way to the future. Their fears, their views, their expressions, were central to the colour and texture of British anti-semitism in the inter-war years and it is to this we might now turn our attention, bearing in mind that the Russian Revolution of 1917, in itself precipitated by the war, was to act as a powerful lever upon such thinking, just as another incident associated with the war, the issue of the Balfour Declaration on 2 November 1917 was, over time, to add yet another hostile shaft to the changing armoury of anti-semitism.[120]

Part III

9 *The Protocols* and the Britons

The anti-semitism of the years immediately following the First World War not only pointed the way to the future but also had its roots in the past. There could be no greater mistake, in fact, than to discuss the anti-semitism of the 1920s without reference to certain specific developments which manifested themselves before these years. The history of anti-semitism, like all history, bears the signs of being a seamless garment.

The immediate post-war years witnessed a marked increase in anti-semitic discussion. It was at this time that *The Protocols of the Elders of Zion* first appeared in Britain, when *The Cause of World Unrest* was published and the Britons first came into prominence. All these developments have received some attention, even if it has been for the most part sparse, inadequate or misleading and they necessarily form the centrepiece of any discussion of anti-semitism in the early inter-war years. But, while dealing in the new, anti-semites also referred to what had gone before. In these circles, memories of Richard Burton's work remained very much alive.[1] Attention was still being drawn to the South African War and 'the filthy and murderous means by which the Jew-power . . . acquired the Lordship of South Africa'.[2] Furthermore, the Marconi scandal lived on and the involvement of Rufus Isaacs and Lloyd George in that murky transaction remained for some a vivid memory.[3]

More recent incidents also exercised an influence over what was said and printed and prominent in this respect were a number of developments associated with the recently ended war. In particular, the events in Russia were given considerable coverage, and hostile comment on what was happening there was clearly apparent in the *Morning Post* which was then under the vigorous editorship of H. A. Gwynne.[4] The paper, which acted as a repository of High Toryism, was not initially downcast at the collapse of Tsardom. When V. E. Marsden, its correspondent in Petrograd, described the old regime as disappearing under 'an elemental tidal wave', a leader, probably written by I. D. Colvin, could debate upon 'the great events' and 'thrilling news' coming in from Russia and could assure readers that there was now a force in Russia working for 'the freedom and orderly progress of a great nation'.[5] But this was to change. Under Marsden's influence – but not only, one suspects, on that account – the Revolution came to be portrayed in a different light. By October 1917 there was an emphasis upon the state falling to pieces and the growing influence, at the Provisional Government's expense, of the Petrograd Soviet which, it was also emphasized, was heavily influenced by men of German birth or who were 'friends of Germany by predilection'.[6] Soon, a stress was being placed upon a Jewish involvement in the Soviet or, more precisely, upon 'Russian Jews of German extraction' who were working for a German peace.[7] This became a prominent aspect of Marsden's reports from Petrograd and his conviction, once the Bolsheviks had seized power, that Lenin and Trotsky were working for Germany, was confirmed for him by the Russian capitulation to the Germans in March 1918 in the Treaty of Brest Litovsk. Once news of possible developments of this kind were known, Marsden felt compelled to write:

> so far as external appearances go, Russia is under the Government of Jewry, and . . . it is the Jew spokesmen who have contrived publicly before the whole world to degrade Russia to such depths of natural debasement as have never been reached before by this absurd affair of peace proposals proferred to the contemptuous German.[8]

Marsden's despatches and the work he published later illustrate quite clearly that he regarded Jews in Russia as a dangerous force. He was further convinced that the power of international Jewry, working on the side of Germany, had to be faced and combatted before such elements destroyed the fabric of Christian civilization.[9]

It was not only the *Morning Post* which was prominent in drawing attention to the association of Jews with Bolshevism and attacking the government of Jewry which was considered to be in charge of Russia's destiny. Another important avenue through which such views were channelled was *The Times* and, in particular, the columns of Robert Wilton, its correspondent in Petrograd.[10] Wilton was in sympathy with the Tsarist dynasty and his reports were remarkable for the hostility which he displayed towards those who replaced the Romanoffs. From the beginning of the war Wilton identified Jews as working in the German interest, or being sympathetic to German aims, and he was critical of them on that account.[11] Such hostility continued in an undisguised form, becoming particularly apparent after the fall of the Tsar, and the consequence was that Wilton's work was the subject of complaint by such different bedfellows as Abraham Bezalel of the Foreign Jews Protection Committee, whose activities have already been commented upon, and the British Foreign Office.[12] It was also objected to in Russia where, in his agitation against Jews, Wilton was regarded as imitating 'the old practice of our reactionaries by trying to set one section of the population against the other'.[13] Well before this there had been friction between Wilton and New Printing House Square over other matters but it was not until 1921 that the two parted company, by which time Wilton's major analyses of developments in Russia had already appeared.[14]

But it was not merely newspaper correspondents writing in the heady, uncertain, far off atmosphere of Russia who drew the link between Jews and Bolshevism. There was, for instance, a quite extensive correspondence involving claim and counter-claim on this score in *The Times*,[15] in addition to which the Foreign Office collection of reports on Bolshevism in Russia which also appeared in 1919 contained a number of testimonies from eye witnesses in Russia, or those in receipt of such evidence, that there was a pronounced Jewish involvement in Bolshevism.[16] It was, furthermore, a stress which appeared in Mentor's column in the *Jewish Chronicle*. In this the unknown consequences of Bolshevism were fully allowed for: 'Bolshevism', it was written, 'is at once the most serious menace to, and the best hope of, Civilization.' It pulled down existing society, it was 'a political disease, an economic infliction, a social disaster'. And yet, whatever excesses were perpetrated, Bolshevism was an attack upon social iniquities and inequalities and offered men the prospect of a fuller, richer life. And, it was believed, 'there is much in the fact of Bolshevism itself, in the fact that so many Jews are Bolshevists, in the fact that the ideals of Bolshevism at many points are consonant with the finest ideals of Judaism' that thoughtful Jews had cause to ponder such things.[17] However, while Mentor could reflect on a happy conjunction between Jews and Bolshevism, a different tone and one which was more in line with the other impressions we have been considering, was present in Winston Churchill's reflections on Zionism and Bolshevism. Here, the former was urged upon Jews to provide an antidote to a rampant Bolshevism, run by atheistical and international Jews, which was, in effect, a 'world wide conspiracy for the overthrow of civilization and for the reconstitution of society on the basis of arrested development, of envious malevolence and impossible equality'.[18]

The Bolshevik Revolution was a major historical event which could hardly have failed to spark fierce and divergent passions and the importance of the revolution as a stimulus to Fascism and anti-semitism in Germany has already become widely accepted. But in Britain too, the events in Russia were followed with interest and, as we have just shown, the association of Jews with Bolshevism was openly discussed. The precise relationship is a complicated matter. It involves a decision whether to count apostate Jews as Jews. It requires an awareness of the important participation of Jews in anti-Bolshevik groups, as well as an appreciation of the hostility shown by some Jews towards the revolution and a recognition that allegiances could change over time. But, given all that, a considered opinion is possible that Jews were important within the ranks of Bolshevism, particularly in the lower levels of the party machinery and to a greater extent after the revolution than before it. Of course none of this allows the claim to be sustained that Bolshevism was Jewish and essentially alien to the Russian people and that those Jews involved in Bolshevism were working for Jewish ends but it does enable us to consider the discussion within its appropriate context.[19] But propaganda has little concern for accurate niceties of this kind and the cry of Jewish Bolshevism not only generated a hostility towards Jews in the first flush of the revolution, it was a theme which, as we shall discover, echoed in anti-semitic circles throughout the 1920s and 1930s.

The war highlighted other problems which were added to this threat of an overpowering Jewish internationalism. The conflicting loyalties experienced by certain German Jews in the course of the war were still emphasized.[20] It was, in fact, in connection with alleged irregularities of this kind concerning the allotment of shares to Germans by Sir Alfred Mond during the war, that H. H. Beamish, who was to play a key role in international anti-semitism during the inter-war years, first came into public prominence. For engaging in publicity over this alleged action by Mond, in 1919 Beamish and Commander H. M. Fraser were taken to court by Mond who sought 'an injunction to restrain them from printing, publishing or exhibiting any poster or advertisement alleging that he was a traitor or from publishing any similar libel affecting him in his profession and office'.[21] Beamish exploited the court situation to the full to drive home the message of Jews as a separate race whose loyalty could not be guaranteed. 'A man can't be both a Jew and a German', he claimed and later emphasized that 'A man can't be both English and Jew'. At this point, 'there was some applause at the back of the Court.'[22] Mond was awarded £5,000 damages by Mr Justice Darling but Beamish, who according to evidence in court was starting to organize the Britons, gave notice that 'he was about to take a sea voyage for the benefit of his health' and promptly removed himself to South Africa without paying the fine.[23]

Other issues grew out of the war, a number of which appeared in *Plain English*, a journal started by Lord Alfred Douglas in July 1920.[24] It was on the basis of reports in this particular journal, in fact, that four years after the Mond libel the courts were hearing the case of Churchill versus Douglas.[25] The action centred upon an alleged defamatory libel of Churchill by Douglas in a pamphlet called *The Murder of Lord Kitchener and the Truth about the Battle of Jutland and the Jews*. Although this particular attack was made in pamphlet form, the claims had first appeared in *Plain English* in 1921. The accusations had also been referred to in an action which Douglas brought against the *Morning Post* in the summer of 1923.[26] Encouraged by the outcome, Douglas summarized his articles in pamphlet form. Churchill's action over this was intended to counteract the claim that Churchill and Sir Ernest Cassel, with whom Churchill had a close relationship, had conspired to issue a false statement about the Battle of Jutland in order to bring about fluctuations in British government stock from which, it was alleged, Cassel and other Jewish financiers were major beneficiaries and Churchill received an appropriate consideration. The whole case turned upon unsubstantiated gossip and revealed that Douglas was influenced in his reports by a version of events given to him by Captain Harold Sherwood Spencer, an ex-officer of questionable sanity, who mixed religious obscurantism with a pronounced anti-semitism.[27] The consequence for Douglas of listening to social tittle-tattle was six months' imprisonment and a financial obligation to keep the peace and be of good behaviour.[28]

The Churchill libel indicated how events of the war could be drawn upon in the anti-semitism of the 1920s and the Jutland affair was not an isolated example. *Plain English*, for instance, ran a series of articles which were critical of Jewish behaviour during the war and, in the same pamphlet in which Douglas attacked Churchill over the Jutland issue, the charge was also advanced that Jewish interests were responsible for the murder of Lord Kitchener. Douglas accused them of arranging the sinking of the *Hampshire* as it steamed towards Russia so that Kitchener would be unable to nip Jewish Bolshevism in the bud.[29]

There were also attacks from a number of sources upon the participation or, more accurately, what was regarded as the undue influence of Jews in the Versailles Conference which ended the war. Among the unofficial groups in Paris were Jewish delegations from the United States, Britain, France and eastern Europe and it was from such quarters that pressure was exerted to preserve the rights of minorities (including Jewish minorities) and to further the interests of Jewish settlement in Palestine following the 1917 Balfour Declaration. But it was not merely this lobbying which attracted attention. The influence of individual Jews over particular delegations was also alleged. It was emphasized that Lord Reading (Rufus Isaacs) remained close to Lloyd George and it was claimed that Bernard Baruch shared with Colonel House the position of Woodrow Wilson's most confidential adviser.[30]

The League of Nations, born out of the Versailles Settlement, was the object of much hostility among British anti-semitic groups throughout the 1920s and later. The presence of Jews at Versailles, the appointment of individual Jews to official positions within the League, the assumption by it of the Palestine Mandate and fears that Jewish influence in Palestine was growing at the expense of the Arabs and creating a base for international intrigue, provided the background to the charge that the League was a vehicle for Jewish interests.[31] And, as the message of *The Protocols* became known, as conspiratorial theories took root, such developments could be portrayed as part of a plan of Jewish conquest which could have serious repercussions for Britain's world role exercised through the Empire.[32] It was out of the convergence of elements of reality relating to Versailles and the League, the myth of *The Protocols* and a passionate patriotism that an anti-semitism developed which lived on throughout the 1920s and 1930s, gathering sustenance en route from other developments.

While anti-semitism in Britain drew strength from such developments connected with the First World War, as the nation took stock of its position,[33] anti-semitic comment in Britain was also triggered off by a number of post-war events, particularly in the field of government appointments. For instance, the choice of Herbert Samuel as high commissioner for Palestine in July 1920 provoked hostility on ethnic grounds. How could such a man represent *British* interests, it was asked? And, drawing upon their own tradition, opponents were anxious to draw the Marconi incident into the discussion. Hence it was claimed that the 'Jew-alition Government' had 'a Marconi Premier in Lloyd George' as well as 'a Marconi Lord Chief Justice in Rufus Isaacs'. It was this same administration, it was emphasized, which had appointed Samuel to Palestine. Godfrey Isaacs, through his Marconi interests, was 'Chief over all messages in the Empire' and 'cousin Edwin Samuel alias Montagu', as secretary of state for India, was presiding over the destinies of the eastern Empire. In other words, 'From East to West and West to East' there was 'Jewry ueber Alles'.[34]

The appointment of Lord Reading to the viceroyship of India in 1921 also encountered opposition on account of his being a Jew[35] and comment in *Blackwood's Magazine* was especially sharp. There were a number of reasons, it was stated, why Lord Reading, 'a lawyer of alien blood', should not be appointed viceroy but the chief of these was that his race should incapacitate him from holding the post. 'By blood and breeding' he was a foreigner and *Blackwood's* contended that it was quite inappropriate that he should represent British interests in its vast eastern sub-continent.[36] But the danger did not lie solely in this one appointment. The real issue according to *Blackwood's*, was that it added 'to the many Jews who [were] taking part in the government of her Empire'.[37] Indeed, it was claimed that Jewish influence was such that an inscription had been placed over the door at 10 Downing Street proclaiming, 'None but Hebrews may apply.' However, the journal was confident that some day this would be replaced by 'the ancient and worthier legend: "Greater Britain for the Britons"'.[38]

Samuel in Palestine and Reading in India were two major government appointments which provoked hostility and earlier incidents in the careers of both men were turned against them. Opposition towards them and to Edwin Montagu as secretary of state for India – the three of them were collectively described as 'holding the gorgeous East in fee'[39] – was joined by hostility towards the appointment of Sir Alfred Mond, another old enemy of the anti-semites, as president of the Board of Works. In each case it was claimed that 'their Semitic blood and connections' had provided them with 'a secret advantage'.[40]

Underpinning this opposition to Jews were the troubles and dissatisfaction which faced the country in the years following the First World War. The promise of a 'fit country for heroes to live in' was soon forgotten and some of those who had experienced the *union sacrée* of the trenches and had hoped for a better future became permanently disillusioned. Some undoubtedly sank into a trough of apathy and disillusion. Others, however, channelled their discontent into political action and with 'the failure of social reform' between 1918 and 1920, there were many who would have answered H. H. Beamish's question, 'was this country now a place for heroes to live in?', with a resounding 'no'.[41] In such circumstances an appeal to patriotism and national regeneration was possible. It was this kind of sentiment which, as we shall discover shortly, was tapped by the Britons and it was a source of political strength which was later drawn upon by the British Union of Fascists.[42] In such circumstances, minorities were exposed. The Liverpool race riots of 1919 provided one indication of this just after the war, as did the 1919 Aliens Act, a child of a lingering wartime xenophobia and post-war uncertainty, and the hostility which we have already noticed being directed against Jews was further evidence of the trend.[43]

While some worried about 'the failure of social reform', the inability to implement social legislation to guarantee a more equitable society, there were others who, in the context of the same social circumstances, were exercised by different matters.[44] Survivors of the First World War have displayed a tendency to refer to it as a watershed and to regard their later lives as some kind of unexpected epilogue. Similarly, those anxious to preserve the social *status quo* in British society also regarded the war as a turning point which unleashed new and terrifying dangers. It was believed that the old stability of the pre-war days had gone. Now society was portrayed as having to face the growth of labour – the Labour Party was the largest opposition party after the 1918 election – and the threat of Bolshevism. Strikes, particularly in the coal industry in October 1920 and April 1921, the troubles in Ireland, as well as discontent in India and Egypt, also created disquiet and posed a cumulative threat to a well-ordered world.[45] In such circumstances High Tory groups were particularly anxious and it was among those keen to preserve society against change that anti-semitism took hold. The cry was for Britain and Britons first, and in such circumstances ethnic origins were recalled to mind.

It was in this atmosphere that Hilaire Belloc wrote *The Jews*.[46] But the publications which crucially directed attention towards the activity of Jews in these difficult times were *The Jewish Peril* and *The Cause of World Unrest*. Both books are consequently deserving of some attention. The former, which appeared early in 1920, was an English language version of *The Protocols of the Elders of Zion*. This particular work had been published in Russia in 1903, and its message, transmitted to readers in a particularly unattractive style, was that there was a Jewish plot to dominate the world. It came to be revealed in 1921 that the work was closely modelled, with appropriate amendments, on a book by Maurice Joly called *Dialogues aux enfers entre Machiavel et Montesquieu* which had been published in Brussels in 1864 and which constituted a political attack upon the absolutism of Napoleon III. The fabricators of *The Protocols* – almost certainly attached to the Tsarist secret police in Paris – amended the work to suit Russian conditions. And in the disturbed years which followed the war, aided by astute propaganda on the part of emigré Russians, *The Protocols* was regarded in some circles as having a more universal message.[47] With that in mind we might consider the launching and reception of *The Jewish Peril* in Britain.[48] The work was published in February 1920, having been privately printed by Eyre and Spottiswoode, and until recently very little has been known about the circumstances which led to the publication.[49] It was suggested in one source that the translation was undertaken by George Shanks[50] and the version of *The Protocols* which is currently issued by the Britons refers to Shanks in this connection. New evidence confirms that Shanks was indeed involved but it reveals a good deal more besides.

H. A. Gwynne, the editor of the *Morning Post*, was around this time taking a keen interest in conspiratorial explanations of social developments and information was placed into his hands which indicated quite clearly that it was Shanks who had translated *The Protocols* into English. After the *Morning Post* had reviewed *The Jewish Peril*, Gwynne received a letter from Robert Cust which said that Shanks, 'son of a well-known and highly respected English merchant till recently established in Moscow', was the actual translator of the work. Shanks's mother, it was reported, was of French extraction. 'Of course', the letter continued, 'the entire family are now ruined and refugees in London.' Cust's information on all this came via Major Edward G. G. Burdon of the Northumberland Fusiliers, 'a most accomplished linguist', who had shown Cust the manuscript of *The Jewish Peril* in November 1919 and asked for his help in securing its publication. According to Cust he did in fact provide help in this matter.[51] Clearly, it was not only German society which owed its introduction to *The Protocols* to the activities of refugees from Russia.[52]

Gwynne took a great interest in the publication and considerable activity went on in the offices of the *Morning Post*, in the British Museum and the Bibliothèque Nationale to establish whether or not any credence could be placed upon the claim that a Jewish conspiracy was at work in society. According to the *Morning Post* review, *The Jewish Peril* was 'a very remarkable book' and one which could not be dismissed as 'mere anti-semitic propaganda'. However, the reviewer was not convinced that it was genuine; even so, it was a work which could not be ignored, 'since it may affect the safety of the nation'.[53] But if the mouthpiece of High Toryism had its reservations, the Britons, founded in 1919, in the first issue of their journal, *Jewry ueber Alles*, were less restrained. According to this source there was nothing new in the message; it was noted that the activity of Jews and their plans had always been evident but, even so, *The Jewish Peril* was noteworthy for its 'diabolical cruelty and cold blooded calculation' and readers were urged to obtain a copy.[54] Elsewhere, response was less than ecstatic. For instance, the *Nation* could wonder why 'this kind of nauseating outpouring of perverted religiosity should be foisted on the British public' and a similar tone was adopted by the *Jewish Guardian*, which argued that the innocence of the average Englishman in matters of anti-semitism provided anti-semites with an opportunity for exploitation.[55]

The Times did not receive a copy of the 'singular little book' but Wickham Steed urged the establishment of an "impartial enquiry' into it. Nothing could be gained from 'a shrug of the shoulders' except an accusation from anti-semitic sources that there was 'a conspiracy of silence' and, in any case, it was important to know whether by straining every nerve to escape a 'Pax Germanica' the danger of a 'Pax Judaica' had been missed.[56] Steed's unsigned article led to a fair amount of correspondence, indicative of the interest in such matters, including a perceptive letter from Aylmer Maude, who neatly isolated – in general terms – the origins and function of the work.[57]

In contrast to Steed's hesitancies, the *Spectator*, which turned to the matter in the following week, dismissed the work as a piece of 'malignant lunacy'; in it were 'bottlefuls of the most dangerous poison distilled by a lunatic of genius and prescribed by a panic-stricken Muscovite of the old *régime*'. And, continuing the imagery, it was claimed that 'if swallowed by the unthinking' it could do 'enormous harm'.[58] The paper did not dismiss the important role of conspiracies in history and it believed that there was a Jewish problem. But it did not accept that it was the same as that outlined in *The Jewish Peril* – a pamphlet which was 'brilliant in its moral perversity and intellectual depravity' but, ultimately, unconvincing.[59]

By the early summer of 1920 it is clear that *The Jewish Peril* had had a number of question marks placed against it and, apart from support among the Britons, there was no outright acceptance of its message. However, as 1920 wore on the situation became more involved.

At this juncture, in the early summer of 1920, the *Morning Post* published a series of articles on the theme of world unrest which took the debate a stage further. We have already remarked that H. A. Gwynne, the editor, had taken a keen interest in *The Protocols* and the articles, which were published between 12 and 29 July, and which later appeared in book form with the title *The Cause of World Unrest*, were written in the belief that there had been 'for centuries a hidden conspiracy, chiefly Jewish, whose objects have been and are to produce revolution, communism, and anarchy, by means of which they hope to arrive at the hegemony of the world by establishing some sort of despotic rule'.[60] Once again no final seal of approval was given to *The Protocols*, although the importance of the work for an understanding of recent events in Russia and other international developments was openly acknowledged. And, in order to give credence to suggestions that conspiracies were important, conspiratorial activity was discussed within an historical dimension.[61] At the same time, an attempt was made to give greater weight to the claims concerning Jewish activity by stating that to accuse all Jews of engaging in work on behalf of the Jewish interests would be 'downright wicked'.[62] 'It is necessary', Gwynne wrote, 'to distinguish . . . between those Jews who have definitely adopted a single nationality and those to whom the Jewish nationality is the only one that counts.'[63] And it was crucial that Jews should explain where they stood on this issue. In short, an attempt was made to reduce what might be regarded as the flights of fancy attached to *The Protocols* while preserving essential elements of its message.

Until recently there has been no firm indication of who was responsible for the articles in the *Morning Post* and *The Cause of World Unrest*. Ian Colvin's name has been mentioned in this connection but other opinion would have it that H. A. Gwynne and V. E. Marsden were the authors.[64] However, it is now possible to dispel any doubts and clear away existing uncertainties. It is clear that, in fact, the work came from a number of hands associated with the *Morning Post*; the bulk of it was written by Ian Colvin, although he refused to allow it to appear under his name, while other sections were contributed by H. A. Gwynne, Nesta Webster and a number of journalists associated with the paper. Not everyone on the staff was happy with the decision to publish the articles and it is clear that they went ahead at Gwynne's insistence.[65]

By the summer of 1920, therefore, *The Jewish Peril* had appeared and had been followed by *The Cause of World Unrest* and between them they raised fundamental issues about Jews and Jewish activity. In such circumstances it was hardly surprising that Jewish interests should engage in countermeasures. According to H. A. Gwynne, Jews bought up the Spottiswoode copyright and all the remaining issues of *The Jewish Peril*[66] and a correspondent in the *Morning Post* complained that certain influences seemed to be at work with the intention of preventing the circulation of the publication.[67] Later in the same year, with the support of the Board of Deputies, Lucien Wolf attacked *The Jewish Peril* in his publication *The Jewish Bogey and the Forged Protocols of the Learned Elders of Zion.* This essay, which also censured the 'demonology' of the *Morning Post* for its articles on 'The Cause of World Unrest', was an attempt to deflate the impact of *The Jewish Peril* and related theories by locating their origins within the musings of German anti-semites. It was claimed that the collection of protocols originated in the writings of the German novelist, Herman Goedsche, adapted to the circumstances of the Russian Revolution in 1905. Wolf not only attempted to reduce the appeal of the book by referring to its origins; he also played down the links between Jews and Bolshevism.[68]

By contrast there were those such as the Britons who gave publicity to any development which seemed to support the message of *The Protocols*[69] and additional support came from Lord Alfred Douglas's journal, *Plain English* which, contrary to what might be expected, offered far more than a drawing-room, 'arty' type of anti-semitism. In it the *Morning Post* articles on 'The Cause of World Unrest' were described as 'admirable' and, in addition and more significantly, on 21 August 1920 a series of articles began to appear which spun a confused and tangled web of theories about 'The Jewish Peril' which, readers were assured, was essentially to do with the threat of Bolshevism. It has already been noticed that *The Jewish Peril* was a translation from the Russian made by one fugitive from the Russian Revolution, George Shanks, and in the columns of *Plain English* we encounter yet another emigré influence in the shape of Major General Count Cherep-Spiridovitch. To *Plain English* he was 'a prophet', a sage with 'preter-natural intuition' who had accurately forecast events of the First World War. He was also described as an enthusiastic supporter of Great Britain which he claimed as the last of the great Christian empires. It was through the medium of his musings that *Plain English* continued the task of exposing world unrest.[70] It has been claimed that Spiridovitch's work needs to be read to be believed but it might equally be said that it had to be believed in order to be read. Like the racing tipster he had so many forecasts up his sleeve that something was likely to turn out to be true and his staggering capacity for projection enabled him to explain anything and everything in conspiratorial terms.[71] As a supplement to activity of this kind the Britons also managed in a direct way to keep *The Protocols* before the public by soon assuming responsibility for its future publication.[72]

In the light of developments in 1920, in the autumn of that year the *Spectator* called for a royal commission to enquire whether or not a revolutionary conspiracy involving Jews could be detected in society. If there were such an involvement the *Spectator* had no doubt that it arose on account of the past persecution of Jews but that, it was claimed, was not currently the issue at stake. It was necessary to stop persecuting Jews but, at the same time, 'great caution' should be exercised in admitting Jews to full citizenship if the game of subversion was being played.[73] While the *Spectator* could exercise a degree of discretion on such matters this quality was less apparent in *Blackwood's Magazine*. Here it was written that wherever there was a rebellion there was 'a Jewish organization to strengthen and support it' and it was claimed that an appreciation of this gave understanding and insight to the problems which faced Britain and the Empire, underlined the threat from Bolshevism, and gave significance to *The Cause of World Unrest* and *The Jewish Peril*.[74]

In short, in the course of 1920 certain groups in British society were able to identify the causes of unrest and instability in an uncertain post-war world. Among the extreme anti-semites all Jews were the agents of disruption. Hence in a journal like *Jewry Ueber Alles*, put out by the Britons, readers were informed that, 'with Jewry the tribe is the unit. With white people every adult is a responsible individual: a Jew is not an individual – he is only a bit of his tribe.'[75] By contrast, in the *Morning Post* attacks were restricted to sections of the Jewish community.[76] But, whatever its forms, hostility towards Jews drew upon certain post-war developments, problems recalled from the First World War and upon memories of an even older anti-semitism, all of which now tended to be refracted through some kind of conspiratorial view of the world.

If there are details surrounding the context and publication of *The Protocols* which deserve some comment, there is considerably more to say about the exposé of the publication in *The Times* which restricted its use after 1920 to the extremist fringe of political life. We know that the exposé of *The Protocols* appeared in *The Times* in August 1921 and that it was contributed by Philip Graves who was then the paper's correspondent in Turkey. We know that Graves had acquired a volume from a Russian emigré acquaintance, and that it was this same Russian who told Graves that such a volume formed the basis of *The Protocols*. But until recently, the actual developments whereby *The Protocols* was demonstrated to be a plagiarism have never been fully documented, even though the process forms an indispensable element in the history of the publication.[77]

It all began on 12 July 1921 just over a year after *The Protocols* appeared in Britain when Philip Graves, then in Constantinople, received a communication in which the writer claimed that he was

> en possession d'un preuve irréfutable que le livre des soitdisant 'Protocols' ou procès-verbaux des sages d'Israel . . . n'est qu'un plagiat audacieux d'un livre francais, edité il y a une soixantaine d'années, mais évidemment complettement oublié par les bibliographes de nos jours.

After tempting Graves along these lines the writer provided him with further details:

> C'est un petit traité de politique générale que les auteurs du plagiat avaient approprié à leurs vues antisémitiques mais d'un manière si superficielle, que

> des passages entiers des 'Protocols' se retrouvent facilement dans le texte original, qui n'a été qu'à peine remanié.

He concluded by making an offer to Graves:

> Croyant, que la révélation d'une mystification si prodigieuse serait d'un intérêt vraiment mondial, je m'adresse à vous pour me renseigner: ne voudriez-vous pas acquérir l'exemplaire, que je possède du susdit livre et quelles seraient dans ce cas là vos conditions?

The writer concluded with the comment that he was able to meet Graves that evening at the Club de Constantinople. The letter was signed by M. S. Raslovleff.[78]

The meeting took place and was followed by further correspondence. In a letter on 13 July Raslovleff sent a collection of material to Graves which enabled him to ascertain that *The Protocols* was based upon a work with a Geneva preface of 1864 which consisted of a series of dialogues between Machiavelli and Montesquieu and the motives which led Raslovleff to offer such information to Graves were spelt out for the first time. He wrote:

> I would like to make it clear that I don't consider this as a purely business transaction; had it been so, I would have certainly applied to one of the Jewish (Sionistic [sic] or other) organizations of C-ple who, no doubt, have greater interest than the ,Times' in purchasing the ,Dialogues' and using them as a weapon against certain people and newspapers.
>
> But, as I have already told, it is not a matter of pure, unpolitical business: I would not like to give a weapon of any kind to the Jews whos [sic] special friend I never have been. Moreover, I kept for a long time the secret of my discovery (for *it is* a discovery!) in the hope of using it one day or other as a proof of impartiality of the political group to which I belong. And it is only a very urgent need of money that persuaded me to change my mind.[79]

The picture begins to emerge of someone who was not pro-Jewish and whose circumstances had become straitened as a result of the Bolshevik revolution to which he was ideologically opposed. More information about the informant was provided in the postscript to a letter which Graves despatched to Wickham Steed, the editor of *The Times*, on 13 July 1921, where it was stated that Raslovleff was a nephew of Prince Volkonsky and a member of a monarchist group.[80]

Raslovleff's correspondence with Graves stressed the financial difficulties he was encountering. Consequently, he queried whether, in return for the information he provided about *The Protocols*, he could be loaned £300 'from some establishment which would not require them back ... until the settling of civil peace in Russia'. After all he was, he told Graves, the landowner of two estates in Russia and the proprietor of a town house. He was also anxious to conclude a deal as soon as possible:

> The amount I immediately need, of the forementioned sum is 200 Ltqs [Turkish liras]. If you can lend me that sum at once, I can wait for two or three weeks for the answer from London, but if you cannot, or if you consider my conditions impossible for the ,Times' I will be forced to apply to the Agence Havas or any other place which would advance me the necessary money without delay. In that case I trust you as a gentleman to forget *all about the book*, which I will come to fetch this evening at the Club at 7 o'clock.[81]

Faced with this situation Graves lost no time. He explained the situation to his editor, noting that there were 'scores' of resemblances between *The Protocols* and the book now in his possession, a great many of which were 'extraordinary'. He was also keen to emphasize that there were 'the elements of a scoop' in the situation. As for Raslovleff, Graves informed Steed that he wanted 'to make something out of it' and that on his own responsibility he had advanced money to Raslovleff so as to secure a hold on the story. Graves reiterated the nature of the journalistic coup (noting that his information improved upon that provided by Lucien Wolf's work on *The Protocols*) and stressed the need for urgent haste in the whole matter.[82]

The Times saw the potential which existed in the situation and, very soon, a frantic correspondence was taking place between London and Constantinople, a correspondence which indicated Graves's sense of anxiety and anticipation.[83] The upshot of all this was an agreement on 2 August 1921 between Graves acting for and on behalf of *The Times*, its editors and proprietors and M.S.M. Raslovleff. The latter received a loan of £337 for the information he supplied. The loan was to be for five years and was guaranteed by Raslovleff's property in the *Gouvernement* of Saratoff. By way of consideration the copy of the book was also handed over to *The Times*. It was agreed that *The Times* should have exclusive publication rights over the contents of the book and become owners of all rights therein, including copyright for five years. It was further agreed that on the full repayment of the loan at the end of five years the book should be returned to Raslovleff, together with all copyright. It was also agreed that no interest should be charged on the loan or any part of it and finally, that Raslovleff should not make use of the book either in whole or part during the following five years, without the permission of *The Times*. All this was drawn up and witnessed by Henry E. Pears, a barrister-at-law in the office of the British High Commission at Constantinople.[84]

Shortly afterwards Graves was informed that his articles based upon the information supplied by Raslovleff had appeared in print, by which time it had been ascertained by *The Times* in London that the book which had come into its possession was the *Dialogue aux Enfers entre Machiavel et Montesquieu*, written by Maurice Joly and first published in Brussels in 1864.[85]

Two later developments related to the 1921 scoop deserve some mention. In 1924 Raslovleff, who was then living in Paris, enquired whether his book could be returned if he repaid at once the loan of £337.[86] *The Times* had no objection to this but it wanted assurances as to the bona fides of the claimant.[87] Nothing happened about the repayment at this stage. In 1927 the newspaper took the initiative and pointed out to its Paris representative that the repayment of the Raslovleff loan was due and it was requested that Raslovleff should be informed of this fact.[88] Raslovleff's reply came from Charenton. He was anxious to point out that the situation had changed since 1921 when he thought the Russian régime would not last and his line of defence in 1927 was that the continued existence of

Bolshevik rule meant a prolongation of his financial difficulties. In the circumstances he saw only two ways of settling the matter: either *The Times* entered into definitive possession of his book and gave him a quietus for the amount of the loan or it renewed the loan for a further five to ten years, keeping the volume at Raslovleff's disposal in the event of his property in Russia being returned to him.[89] In the event it would seem that *The Times* wrote off the loan and took possession of the book.

Graves had undoubtedly secured an important coup, and *The Times* was able to capitalize on this by publishing *The Truth about 'The Protocols'. A Literary Forgery*, which reprinted Graves's articles in pamphlet form, but relations between Graves and the newspaper over the matter were not always easy. This became evident in the course of the Berne trial in 1935 and the subsequent appeal in 1937 when the Jewish community of Berne and the united Jewish communities of Switzerland, in an attempt to show up the spurious nature of the publication, took action against Swiss anti-semites who had been distributing *The Protocols*. In the course of the 1935 action an attack was made upon Graves. It was suggested that *The Times* had been deceived by him or had shared in the deception. It was also claimed that the copy of the book held by *The Times* did not exist. In view of this Graves thought it desirable to provide the Swiss court with documentary evidence which would substantiate the exposé – although he was not in favour of revealing the name of his Russian informant 'whose very name I cannot now spell'. He was also anxious about the situation because if it were suggested that he had faked the evidence on *The Protocols* this could have an adverse effect upon his relatives in Germany whose connections with him were known to the Nazi authorities.[90] *The Times* did in fact provide the Board of Deputies of British Jews with information which could be used in the Berne trial, although it was emphasized that the Russian informant's name should not be revealed – a condition which Neville Laski, on behalf of the Board, was prepared to accept.[91] A request from the court at Berne to use all the material contained in the archives of *The Times* was refused.[92]

Two years later in 1937 a further request for information came from Jewish authorities in Britain and Switzerland. In a memorandum to the manager of *The Times* Graves said that the Jewish authorities were anxious to know the name of the Russian informant. Graves was of the opinion that the name could be revealed. 'Most of the leading communists', he claimed, 'have been killed or are doing hard labour, and it is very likely that the present Russian government would not show any hostility to a man because he had formerly been cooperating with me for a short spell.' Consequently he was in favour of giving the name, on condition that assurances could be obtained from the Russian embassy that the informant, if living in Russia, would not be treated with hostility on account of his past association with *The Times*. In his memorandum Graves also made it clear that he would be grateful if a fuller disclosure could be made than in 1935 and particularly if it could be revealed that the correspondent of *The Times* in Constantinople in 1921 was not a Jew. This, he believed, might help his relatives in Germany, whose connections with him, he stressed yet again, were known to the authorities.[93]

Graves's advice was not taken. This is evident from a communication which passed between Neville Laski and the manager of *The Times* which made it clear that *The Times* was prepared to allow the full use of the material in the Swiss trial, 'save and except for the name of Mr Graves' informant'. The only conditions on which this name could be revealed were either if it were found that the informant was no longer living, or with the informant's consent, if he were still alive.[94] As for Graves's anxieties about his relatives in Germany, neither in 1935 nor 1937 did such a consideration weigh heavily in the calculations and decisions of *The Times*. Graves might have obtained a coup for the paper – indeed he never ceased to remind its representatives of it – but *The Times* had full rights over writings published in its columns and it was not slow to remind Graves of this fact.[95]

From this correspondence in the archives of *The Times* we can trace for the first time the details of the journalistic coup. We can identify the Russian emigré who had no love for the Jews.[96] We can trace the anxiety of Graves who was eager for a scoop. It was this rather than a sentiment of philo-semitism which guided his actions. Indeed, there is evidence that Graves like Raslovleff, was not totally sympathetic to Jewish interests. His cryptic reference in correspondence to the tendency of the Jews to have ears in many places and his eventual opposition to political Zionism expressed both in published work and correspondence hardly allow his enlistment as an unqualified champion of Jewish interests.[97] Finally, the archival material enables us to appreciate the correct, businesslike approach of *The Times* throughout the whole affair.[98]

So far we have discussed the background to the appearance of *The Protocols*, as well as its actual publication and the exposé which followed soon afterwards. At this point we ought to make some reference to the life of *The Protocols* after the appearance of Graves's articles. After 1921 we have been told that 'so far as Britain was concerned it was in effect their end.' After that the work appealed only to 'isolated eccentrics' and it was not to become part of the ideological armoury of British Union of Fascists in the 1930s.[99] Such conclusions are generally sound.

Among individuals whose faith remained unshaken, the main argument used by Baron Sydenham of Combe was one which emphasized that the origins of *The Protocols* were of less significance than its message.[100] Just as the Christian could continue to believe in the message of the First Book of Genesis even after the various sources which lay behind its compilation could be traced, so those who found themselves in a crumbling world could continue to believe in the intrinsic message which *The Protocols* presented.[101] Among others, Nesta Webster, who firmly believed in a conspiratorial interpretation of history, never committed herself firmly to a belief in the authenticity of the document, but salvaged what she could from the situation by claiming that, "whether genuine or not, *The Protocols* do represent the programme of world revolution.' She also suggested that, 'in view of their prophetic nature and of their extraordinary resemblance to the protocols of certain secret societies in the past they were either the work of some such society' or alternatively, 'of someone profoundly versed in the lore of secret societies'.[102] Also, appropriately enough for a conspiratorialist, Mrs Webster believed that not everything had been found out about *The Protocols*: 'Much yet remains to be discovered concerning this mysterious affair.'[103] Such defences of the publication occurred in the 1920s. Years later, after the Second World War, it was still possible to find *The Protocols* being granted a significance by individuals who had played a prominent role in combating Jewish influence.[104] Indeed, a belief in its fantasies sustained the political career of Arnold Leese from the 1920s until his death in 1953.[105]

But it was not merely among individuals that a continuing significance was given to *The Protocols*. After *The Times* exposé, journals committed to an anti-semitic position continued to assert their importance. For example, in *Blackwood's Magazine*, still concerned about the Bolshevik threat, *The Protocols* could be defended as a devastating insight into the Jewish-Bolshevik way to power and its implications for the world.[106] And to *Plain English*, which had concentrated upon popularizing the message of *The Protocols* through the agency of a mythical John Brown, the claims of *The Times* were dismissed as 'preposterous'. It was alleged that events in Russia subsequent to the publication of *The Protocols* showed that the author 'was a prophet unequalled by any prophet born since the beginning of the world'. Indeed, it was said that no person outside a lunatic asylum could read the book and remain unconvinced that it was a document 'of astounding value' which 'may yet save Christian civilization from destruction'.[107] There were echoes too, of a continuing affirmation of faith in *The Protocols* elsewhere. This was evident in a publication of the British Fascists[108] and it was also present over ten years later among the Militant Christian Patriots.[109] In addition, the *Patriot*, the journal started by the duke of Northumberland in 1922, continued to inject *The Protocols* into its discussion of the Jewish question and it also made a brief excursion into the pages of the *National Citizen* in 1937.[110]

In contrast to this it has been claimed that the British Union of Fascists did not feel it could make use of such an anti-semitic source.[111] But this is to simplify too much. The BUF sometimes distributed *The Protocols* at street corner meetings and there is evidence that it did not scorn the publication.[112] For instance, in 1937 *Action* contained an advertisement for 'The Most Astounding Book ever published, *The Protocols of Zion*'. According to this, the work predicted 'a universal economic crisis' which would throw European workers out of employment. 'Every Fascist should read "The Protocols"', it was urged, 'it's terrific'. Copies were available at a cost of 1*s*. 3*d*. from the Blackshirt bookshop or, it was claimed, any newsagent.[113] Moreover, it should not be forgotten that a main theme in BUF propaganda concerned the international machinations of Jewry, in the course of which the imagery and arguments of *The Protocols* were used in speeches and publications even if they were not openly sealed with its own inexorable 'logic'.

But the major organization associated with *The Protocols* is the Britons, which was founded in 1919 by Henry Hamilton Beamish. An important part of the group's activity occurred in the field of publishing which was carried out at first through the Judaic Publishing Company, which was founded in 1919 and which became the Britons Publishing Company in 1922. As a political organization the effective end of the Britons came in 1925 with the cessation of its journals but it was not until February 1932 that a major reconstruction occurred. After the death of Dr J. H. Clarke, who had been a guiding force in its affairs, a separation took place between the Britons and the Britons Publishing Society, after which point the former was concerned with propaganda, appeals, subscriptions and membership and the latter with the sale of literature and publications.[114]

The basic elements of the message transmitted in the inter-war years by the Britons and the associated publishing companies are not difficult to discern, since they were repeated with a pronounced degree of consistency and regularity. At the core was a continuous concern for British interests and a reciprocal hostility towards Jews which assumed certain well defined forms.[115] It was alleged that Jews were separated off from other aliens and it was considered had distinct qualities which made them a special object of concern.[116] Jews were discussed in fact as a distinct racial category, bound together by their special characteristics and possessing a culture which was totally incompatible with and inimical to British as well as other national interests.[117] Consequently, it was an imperative task to isolate the Jews and, on the basis of such a belief, it was suggested that Jews should be excluded from British society and settled in Palestine, Madagascar or Australia.[118] The establishment of a distinct, self-contained Jewish settlement, absorbing all not just a selected number of Jews, would enable Britain to become once more a national home for Britons and no longer a close preserve of Jewish interests.[119] In addition, the desirability of extermination was raised.[120] But any developments along these lines were for the future and had to be fought for.

Reality as it appeared to the Britons was somewhat different. Jews in Britain were described as holding influential political positions.[121] They were said to be prominent in the press and in finance and consequently in a position to exercise a profound indirect influence over society.[122] And, since it was impossible to be a Jew and an Englishman, it was claimed that such Jews were working essentially in the interests of Jewry and laying siege to the economic, political and even sexual life of the nation.[123] This was regarded as a continuation of a historical struggle. It was alleged, for example, that the First World War had been fought to enlarge the interests of Jewry in the sense that Jews had used the German army and navy in an attempt to extend their own interests[124] and after the war it was believed that Jewish ambitions were being promoted by the agencies of Bolshevism and the League of Nations.[125] Jewish power was generally regarded as increasing through discontent and it was claimed that, unless Britons were vigilant, a fostered disruption would enable Jewry to mount an attack upon 'the established divine order of things,' in other words the moral superiority and consequent world responsibility of the British. There was, it was stated, a 'fundamental necessity for the British Race, in the interests of the whole world and especially of the Christian Church, to keep itself pure by casting out from its councils and counsels this asiatic race'.[126] It was in short, a mixture of opposition based on race and religion which was directed towards Jews in an attempt to defend the old values which, it was believed, had built the Empire and added to Britain's world prestige.

In support of such a philosophy – described at first by those who presented it as pro-British rather than anti-semitic – constant reference was made to certain intellectual sources, including the works of Disraeli,[127] the discredited teaching of August Röhling,[128] the writings of Werner Sombart, particularly *The Jews and Modern Capitalism*,[129] the philosophy of Houston Stewart Chamberlain,[130] and Oscar Levy's preface to George Pitt-Rivers's *The World Significance of the Russian Revolution*.[131] By contrast, the conspiratorial views of Nesta Webster, although admirable in parts, were regarded as regrettably lacking in their appreciation of the Jewish question.[132] But such intellectual supports were props, used to strengthen the central core of the Briton's philosophy, which was revealed through a persistent reference to *The Protocols*. It was, as we have noticed, the Britons Publishing Company which took over the publication of *The Jewish Peril* from Eyre and Spottiswoode.[133] It was the same company which later published its own translation of *The Protocols* by V. E. Marsden and which was prepared to do this in defiance of the exposé in *The Times*.[134]

At this point, having discussed the launching of *The Protocols* in Britain – at a time when the work was being widely published[135] – and having considered the substantial elements of its history in Britain in the inter-war years, a number of concluding comments might be made.

It should be said first of all that the history and impact of *The Protocols* cannot be discussed exclusively in terms of post-war developments. For some time before the outbreak of hostilities between Germany and Britain there had been expressions of concern about the power of rich Jews in society and the threatened or actual domination of Britain by Jews. It was, as we remarked in our discussion of the problem, a fear generated by a number of social pressures in the nineteenth century. Furthermore, as the war approached, the activity of certain prominent German Jews in striving for peace between the two countries led to the charge that there were in Britain German Jews who were engaged in plotting and planning against Britain in the furtherance of German and ultimately Jewish interests. It was allegations such as these which provided an atmosphere against which later more sophisticated arguments about Jewish power and influence could be listened to.[136] In this connection a crucial linking role was played by H. H. Beamish's *The Jews' Who's Who*, which provided great detail on the role of Jews in Britain, particularly in finance and the press. This work clearly drew upon this pre-war tradition of hostility and provided the kind of detailed evidence on the role of Jews which was lacking in *The Jewish Peril*. Both publications appeared in 1920 and complemented each other.

But if there was a pre-history of a particular strand of anti-semitism which needs to be considered when we discuss the appeal of *The Protocols*, it also has to be recognized that a number of preconditioning factors exercised their influence over events. The involvement of Jews in the early history of the Bolshevik Revolution and in Communist experiments elsewhere, the activities of some individual Jews and delegations representing Jewish interests at the Versailles Peace Conference and certain aspects of the work of the League of Nations all provided grist to the mill of anti-semitism. Together with the prominence of individual Jews in journalism and finance they allowed generalized, exaggerated claims to be made which attempted to give credence to the prophecies of *The Protocols*.[137]

In addition to these influences, the time and trouble spent over *The Protocols* needs to be considered against the post-war problems which Britain faced, when conflict was present between those who wanted to make Britain a society fit for heroes to live in and those who were more interested in securing and furthering the plutocratic gains of the war years, when Britain faced trouble in Ireland and the Empire, when the country encountered severe internal industrial strife, when, in short, Britain's pre-war society and her significance as a world power, were under threat and challenge, when explanations were being sought for this state of affairs and when what could be considered as rival world influences to Britain and her Empire were the subject of hostile scrutiny.[138]

It was in the light of such developments and in pursuit of the reasons for them that conspiratorial theories were accepted by certain individuals and groups in British society and, once accepted, provided their own version of reality. Full acceptance of the message which expressed itself within a racist, conspiratorial framework, in the sense that all Jews were considered to be participating in the grand design of *The Protocols*, was never common. It seems to have been confined to certain fringe elements in British society.[139] Of potentially greater significance was the more considered analysis suggested by *The Cause of World Unrest* and in the *Spectator*.[140] This cut away some of the excesses of *The Protocols* and was therefore less exposed to attack. At the same time, however, those who presented such views were unlikely to be worried by any influence which the more extreme message of *The Protocols* might have had.[141]

Although 1920 seemed to offer promise to such forces, after 1921 there was a decline in the support given to *The Protocols* which was undoubtedly related to the exposé in *The Times*. From that time onwards it was difficult for 'respectable' opinion to espouse a belief in the publication and it was left to the outsiders in British political life to keep *The Protocols* alive.[142] In itself such a reaction is a testimony to the power of rationality and enlightenment which could assert itself in the midst of so much talk of plot and intrigue. The exposé in *The Times* could in fact be fed into the tradition which rendered anti-semitism socially disreputable and, at the same time, it helped to strengthen such a tradition.[143] The consequence was that while social-economic problems remained acute throughout most of the inter-war years and Britain's place in the world continued to be a matter of concern, respectable, established opinion did not turn to *The Protocols* to account for Britain's national plight and, for a variety of complex social reasons, those who might have invoked such explanations never assumed political power.[144]

This analysis of *The Protocols* has emphasized the importance of social tension and change for an understanding of the reasons why the message of *The Protocols* could exercise an appeal. There is, however, an additional dimension to the discussion surrounding *The Protocols* which calls for comment. It has been suggested in a recent work that those who believe in the conspiracy theory of anti-semitism find in it an answer to deep, individual, emotional needs and its attraction is to those who have an abnormal degree of fear and hatred of the father figure. This, it has been further remarked, becomes transferred and focused on the Jew. In this sense it is possible to describe conspiratorial anti-semitism as a form of paranoid schizophrenia. Individuals and groups who adopt the myth of the Jewish conspiracy operate in the grip of a delusion; their anti-semitism is the hostility of madmen; their world is a lunatic phantasmagoria.[145] If it is assumed that conspiratorial anti-semitism does indeed reside in the anti-semite's personality and if it is further believed that it was the conspiracy theory of anti-semitism which led to genocide, it would certainly be true that the deadliest form of anti-semitism had little to do with real conflict between living people.[146]

If we turn from the general and abstract to the particular and consider the case of British anti-semites it might well be that personality traits need to be considered in explaining the persistently affirmed belief in *The Protocols* displayed by individuals such as H. H. Beamish and Arnold Leese, as well as the extravagantly bizarre view of society held by the Conservators of the Privileges of the Realm.[147] And it could well be that the lifelong conspiratorial analyses of Nesta Webster also fulfilled a personality need.[148] But we simply do not have the evidence to comment in detail on such matters and, in any case, we should not lose sight of the importance of the social context which encourages or restricts the expression of ideas.[149] Consequently, the primary intention of this present discussion has been to identify those social tensions and pressures which lay behind the changing fortunes of *The Protocols* in Britain between 1920 and 1939, which added yet another strand to its strange and mysterious history.

10 Other anti-semitic worlds

The Britons did not possess a monopoly of anti-semitism in Britain in the inter-war years. Although Oswald Mosley's British Union of Fascists was the major Fascist group to appear on the political scene,[1] there were a number of other manifestations of Fascism at this time and anti-semitism was present among them as it was also within the ranks of patriotic, anti-semitic, organizations.[2] In the present chapter attention is restricted to three such groups and the centrepiece of the discussion is concerned with the ideas of Arnold Leese and the Imperial Fascist League.

Leese was born in 1878 at Lytham into what was apparently a middle-class family but when he was fifteen his father's death left the family in straightened circumstances and Leese had to leave boarding school. Eventually, with some financial assistance from his grandfather, he went to the Royal College of Veterinary Surgeons in Camden Town, where he qualified in 1903. After taking a further course of study he accepted a post, which he held for six years, in the Indian Civil Veterinary Department. After this he was employed by the East African government in Kenya, where his service was interrupted by the First World War, throughout which he served in the Royal Army Veterinary Corps. After his discharge he settled in Stamford in Lincolnshire where he continued his veterinary work. He retired in 1928 and allowed an ex-serviceman to take over his practice.[3]

Leese commenced his political career in March 1924 when he founded the Stamford branch of the British Fascisti and was elected its president.[4] The British Fascists had been founded in May 1923 by Miss R. L. Lintorn-Orman but her influence was soon removed and R. B. D. Blakeney, a former serving officer, assumed the presidency of the association and anglicized its name. The organization stressed the need to defend the constitution, the social status quo, and the British way of life, all of which involved it in a reciprocal hostility towards the 'alien menace', 'international finance', and everything which was perceived as a threat to British values. An analysis of its membership revealed that it was 'composed of retired military officers, right-wing Conservatives, obscure peers and "public spirited" women'. It was such a group which maintained an existence for almost twelve years, until 1935, when the effective membership went over to the BUF and it was to the Fascisti that Leese first committed his allegiance.[5] But just as he found it far from easy to 'get on' with colleagues in the colonial service, he also found it difficult to continue in the British Fascists and in 1927 he broke away to form the Fascist League.

By this time he had already become aware of anti-semitic sources. In Stamford he had met Arthur Kitson, a local industrialist and economist, who like many monetary reformers before and since was also anti-semitic, and it was Kitson who launched Leese upon his anti-semitic career by introducing him to *The Protocols of the Elders of Zion* and the address of the Britons.[6] An enquiry from Leese resulted in a visit from H. H. Beamish who gave Leese all the details regarding the 'Jewish Menace'. Beamish was openly acknowledged by Leese as his mentor in anti-semitism and the agent who awakened him to the 'Jewish menace'.[7]

In 1928 Leese moved to Guildford and it was from this base that the IFL, his main political vehicle, was founded, apparently in mid-1928. It would appear that he formed the organization with the help of other dissatisfied elements in the British Fascists and it seems likely that he assumed control soon after its foundation. After six months he was made director-general[8] and by 1931 was exercising unquestioned control over the formulation of policy and expressing his ideas mainly through his monthly newspaper, the *Fascist*. An indication of how generally important he was to the movement is the way it floundered in 1936–7 while Leese was serving a prison sentence for an article which had appeared in the June 1936 issue of the *Fascist*. With his release the organization recovered its poise and, according to the most detailed account we have of its history, the IFL 'probably reached its greatest strength and viability as a political group', in the years immediately preceding the Second World War. Indeed, it has been claimed the movement 'was at a peak when the onset of war terminated its further growth'.[9]

During the period of the 'phoney war' up to May 1940, Leese and the IFL joined other groups in campaigning for peace. The *Fascist* was not published after September 1939 but Leese had a channel of communication in *Weekly Angles*, published by the northwest London group of the IFL which the authorities still allowed to appear. However, in November 1940 after the government had introduced its defence regulations, Leese was arrested and taken into custody. He was to remain interned until February 1944.

At the end of the war Leese soon recommenced his activities. On 22 June 1945 he began to issue *Gothic Ripples*, which became his main line of communication, and he also wrote *The Jewish War of Survival*, in which he put forward the view that the war had been fought solely for Jewish interests.[10] But, in spite of this quick return to political activity, he did not achieve even his pre-war success, sparse though that had been, with membership of the IFL never exceeding a few hundred. His efforts after 1945 centred almost exclusively upon the production of *Gothic Ripples* and the struggle to keep alive the idea of anti-semitism. It was basically a one-man campaign which he was now leading, although he called his organization, somewhat grandly, the Anti-Jewish Interest and

Information Bureau. However, some support for his work came in 1948 from Beamish, his mentor in anti-semitism, who in his will in March of that year provided Leese with funds to continue the fight against what they both regarded as the Jewish enemy.[11] Even so, although he had funds at his disposal, Leese found it difficult to generate anti-semitic groups and by 1951 had turned his attention to the Britons. By 1955 he had spent half of Beamish's legacy on them. Leese died on 18 January 1956, leaving behind him a long list of publications which have often been reprinted after his death and an estate of £18,000, all of which went to his wife.[12]

After considering the man we might now turn to an examination of his ideas. We have been told recently that for Oswald Mosley the Jewish issue was merely an adjunct to a much wider view of politics, but Leese was someone for whom after 1930 racial ideas and philosophies were central and paramount. This is not to suggest that they were expressed in a sophisticated or systematic fashion; they appeared rather as derived and vulgar generalizations from the work of others, but whatever their source and form, they dominated Leese's view of the world. His writings assumed that different genetic endowment between races was a self evident truth and a distinction which had profound consequences. 'Heredity always seemed to me to be a far more important factor in the basic character formation of the individual than mere environment', he wrote in his autobiography.[13] In Leese's work, divisions between races were made broadly on the basis of skin colour and then refined by making use of other variables such as head shape, hair colour, stature, lip form and nose form. He believed that these specific endowments accumulated by a race were passed on to succeeding generations in accordance with the genetic rules of heredity. Racial integrity was therefore of paramount importance if each race were to maintain its attributes and, thereby, its position in the world. Consequently, the worst possible sin was marriage across racial divisions.[14] To engage in such activity was to fail one's race.

Starting from this base Leese developed the belief that the Aryan race alone – sometimes referred to by him as the Nordic or Gothic race – had a singular ability to create a worthwhile civilization and this placed it at the apex of the racial hierarchy. And, from the assumption that 'race' was 'the true basis for politics', he went on to develop a concept of the Aryan ideal and achievement.[15] It was the Aryan race, he claimed, which was actively spreading the benefits of civilization.[16] But, opposed to the Aryans were the Jews, and the relationship between the two was presented by him as one of clear conflict.[17] In dealing with the Jews one was not involved with Europeans or indeed with a race as such but with

> a mongrel conglomeration of Hither Asiatics, indigenous to Asia Minor and Armenia, Hamitic and Negroid blood from Egypt, and East Baltic, Inner Asiatic, Mongoloid and Alpine strains from the Khazar Empire.[18]

The 'plague' which resulted from such crossings had a physical appearance which was repulsive to Aryans,[19] it was incapable of mental innovation and was parasitic upon Aryans for its ideas, which were then adopted by Jews for their own use.[20] It was also criminal in a direct sense.[21]

In addition to these qualities Leese stressed that Jews had an inherently sadistic nature and proceeded to base another part of his hostility towards them on that account. He believed that such traits arose from the processes of Jewish history, noting that many Ashkenazi Jews came from southern Russia, in the area around the Crimea where the Khazar Empire existed from the mid seventh to the tenth century. Leese claimed that the conversion of the Khazars to Judaism in the eighth century had led to the mixture of oriental blood and Jewish blood which, he believed, resulted in the transmission to the Jews of many deplorable characteristics, the chief of which was cruelty allied to sadism.[22] In addition the Hither Asiatic background of the Jews led to a love of blood and suffering. Hence the indulgence in circumcision, the involvement in bloody sacrifices, and the mutilation of enemies captured in war.[23] There were in fact certain instances of so-called Jewish cruelty which Leese was especially keen to emphasize. In this connection he not only referred to ritual murder, but was also concerned to draw attention to *shechita*, the Jewish method of animal slaughter.[24]

The charge against the Jews of committing ritual murder, often known as the blood libel, was not new: as we have already noticed, it had its roots in ancient and medieval society and had indeed been revived in the course of the late nineteenth century.[25] But an accusation of this kind in the 1930s was uncommon. Nevertheless, it was an allegation which Leese was prepared to make.[26] Two years after Julius Streicher had devoted the May 1934 issue of *Der Stürmer* to the blood libel, Leese repeated the charge in the *Fascist* in July 1936, and, on account of this and other attacks upon Jews in the same issue, Leese found himself in court. Although he was found not guilty of seditious libel, he was nevertheless sent to prison for six months on his refusal to pay a fine after being found guilty of conspiring to effect a public mischief and of effecting a public mischief. The publisher of the *Fascist*, Walter Whitehead, was fined £20.[27]

Leese claimed that it was possible to identify two main types of ritual murder, separately associated with the Jewish feasts of Purim and Passover. In both cases murder was carried out with singular brutality and was usually accompanied by some form of mutilation. Victims of murders carried out around Purim were usually adults and the blood which was obtained was used in the triangular feast cakes, although some dried blood might be left over for the following Passover. The victims of murders associated with Passover were generally under seven years of age. In these instances the blood was used in the preparation of the unleavened Passover bread. Adult victims tended to be subjected to straightforward sadistic murder but Leese claimed that in the case of children the ritual involved crucifixion and the complete draining of blood from the child's body.[28]

The reasons why Jews became involved in such activity, it was suggested, related to their racial background, which produced a 'physical manifestation of a desire for bloody sacrifices'.[29] In addition, Leese believed that ritual murder was a feature of Jewish religious thinking and suggested that the Chassidim sect was primarily responsible for the dissemination of such teachings among Jews, although he never substantiated his contention that Judaism sanctioned ritual murder by reference to any concrete proofs.[30] He admitted, in fact, that no evidence urging the need for ritual murder could be found in any of the Jewish religious books but claimed that certain esoteric teachings were known only to Jews.[31]

References to ritual murder did not form a major element in the canon of Leese's anti-semitism. His major stress and concentration was upon a Jewish conspiracy to achieve world hegemony and domination. In other words his analysis was tied to the message of *The Protocols*. In line with this he saw the Aryan race building up civilization only to see the fruit of its labour being infiltrated and dominated by the Jews, whose values were 'inevitably antagonistic to the character and ideals of Nordic civilization'.[32] In short, Leese saw a struggle for world domination taking place, a struggle rooted in race, expressed in terms of a conflict in which Aryan/Nordic/Gothic forces were ranged against a Jewish enemy, a struggle in which the former was the creative, building force and the latter the destructive, infiltrating agent.[33] That was the essence of his analysis to which he proceeded to add a variety of supportive evidence.

Leese regarded world control by Jews as a long term aim which would be achieved over time through a series of national dominations. These activities were thought to be directed by a secret governing body which would eventually consolidate these local conquests. This agency was identified as the World Zionist Congress.[34] But if this were the central organization what were the forces which operated at a local or national level?

In discussing this Leese argued that the most important step towards obtaining global control occurred with the creation of the Soviet Union, which was taken to be nothing less than a vehicle for Jewish influence.[35] Indeed, Bolshevism was defined as, 'state capitalism run by Jews in the Jewish interests'.[36] As it had developed it had nothing in common with the theories of Communism but had become a method of subjugating 'a herd of Gentile serfs' to Jewish domination.[37] This was a process which, he argued, had been facilitated by the racial composition of the Russian people who were incapable of raising themselves above the level of barbarism and were therefore prone to Communism since it relieved them of the necessity to display political initiative.[38]

Such an argument could not be universally applied: it was unsuited to the British situation, for instance, where a quite different racial situation existed. But Leese had arguments to hand to explain what was happening here. The reason why Jewish power could increase outside Russia, in a country such as Britain, was related to the existence of democratic systems of government. Or, as Leese chose to express it, 'Jews like Democracy: it delivers the people into their hands.'[39] 'Democracy', he wrote, 'works out as the Dictatorship of Organized Money Power and that is a Dictatorship of the Jew.'[40] Starting from this base he found it necessary to substantiate his case by showing the extent to which, in his opinion, Jewish power had increased and was continuing to increase within the body of British democracy. This, he argued, could be shown by reference to politics and business. Consequently, an emphasis was laid upon MPs with Jewish connections,[41] as well as upon Jewish personnel in government and government departments.[42]

On the basis of evidence he accumulated on such matters Leese concluded that Britain had been the prey of the Jews[43] and that a major consequence of such influence was an ascendancy exercised by Jews in foreign affairs. He believed that a similar type of influence was present in other societies and also regarded supranational institutions as a particularly happy hunting ground for Jews. He was consequently suspicious of all attempts at world cooperation. The Versailles Conference of 1919 was, in his opinion, 'a Kosher conference' yielding 'Kosher results', one of which was the League of Nations[44] and it is possible to trace in his work a reiterated hostility to this 1919 settlement,[45] the League of Nations[46] and, after the Second World War, to the United Nations Organization.[47] His conclusion was that these were forums where Jews could arrange matters to their own satisfaction and force their decisions on the rest of the world. In the inter-war years he believed that with Jewish control being exercised in Russia, and with the democratic nations rapidly falling a prey to Jewish conquest, and with Jews at work in international bodies only Hitler's Germany stood out against Jewish hegemony. It was hardly surprising, therefore, to Leese, that Jewish interests engineered the Second World War with the specific intention of breaking the power of Hitler's Reich and thereby, in his view, increasing Jewish power.[48]

But it would be a mistake to assume that Leese was concerned only with Jewish political power. He emphasized that Jewish economic influence, particularly in the field of finance, provided a base for the exercise of such power. Before the collapse of the Gold Standard in the 1930s Leese claimed that Jews controlled the supplies of gold and argued that it was this which underwrote their financial and hence political influence.[49] After the Gold Standard ceased to be important, Leese argued that a crucial agency of Jewish power could be found in the banking system. The availability of finance derived ultimately from the banks and he firmly believed that these, particularly those of an international character, were in the hands of the Jews,[50] with the consequence that Jews could impose their will upon government,[51] industry[52] and individuals,[53] in all cases in the furtherance of Jewish interests.[54] In brief, he saw 'unproductive' capitalist activity or 'destructive' activity (that is, finance) working for Jewish ends.[55]

According to Leese, Jewish control was also exercised over sectors of the economy outside finance and was particularly apparent in the media industries. Hence his reference to 'Jewish control of the Press, the Cinema and Films, [and] the Broadcasting Company'.[56] Indeed, it was claimed that the press was subject to Jewish control 'to such an extent that hardly anything unfavourable to the Jewish interest [was] allowed to appear'.[57] Apart from such charges, his work also emphasized the influence of Jews over the popular music industry[58] and their responsibility for much of modern art – which he disliked.[59] In short, in common with many of his contemporaries who were hostile towards Jews, he mounted an attack on Jews as the agents of modern popular culture as well as on what he regarded as their disproportionate power in British economic life.

Leese believed that it was this accumulated influence in the world of finance and communications which provided Jews with powerful agencies of social control. But there were other channels of Jewish influence. According to Leese, Freemasonry was a subversive organization under Jewish domination. In fact, Freemasonry was 'Jewish from start to finish'[60] a movement which had fertilized and bred Socialism[61] and which, by promoting the idea of universal brotherhood, posed an antithesis to Leese's own philosophy that the world was divided into higher and lower races. The promotion of Freemasonry, he claimed, had led people to forget their hereditary instincts of racial preservation and purity with the result that they could be subverted by debased and debasing Jewish ideas.[62]

As if all such forces were cumulatively insufficient, Leese added a final agency to account for the influence exercised by Jews. He devoted some attention to the destruction of Gentile society – as he saw it – through intermarriage, concentrating particularly upon the movement of Jews into the aristocratic families. This was a process which, in his opinion, destroyed the heritage of the race, which it was a duty to protect.[63] On several occasions in the course of discussions on this problem he compiled lists of individuals and families who were associated with Jews and were therefore regarded by him as having fallen under Jewish control.[64] Even more disturbing to him than traceable intermarriage was his belief that there was an element of the population with Jewish origins which even he, with all his research assuidity, was unable to uncover. In claiming this he referred to a process by which Jews had paid poor Gentile families to raise illegitimate Jewish children, thereby guaranteeing a disguised Jewish infiltration of society. He believed that the only possible method by which this type of transaction could be revealed was through the sudden enrichment of a Gentile family or the abrupt rise of an individual Gentile, 'men whose features and characters [were] Jewish but whose official pedigrees [were] unblemished Aryan'.[65] On the assumption that there was in existence a subterranean Jewish world of this kind, Jews who could 'pass' as Gentiles, Leese estimated that there were at least 2·5 million Jews in Britain.[66] In order to place this in perspective, a generally accepted estimate of the size of the Jewish population at the outbreak of the Second World War would be around 370,000.[67]

Leese also suggested ways in which the Jewish question could be solved. At first he had no defined policy but he soon devoted some attention to the problems involved and, in one significant comment, could assert that that there were

> only three possible ways in which the Jewish menace can end. The first is in their extermination; the second their assimilation, which no decent Nordic man or woman could seriously consider; and the third is their compulsory segregation.[68]

In addition, some attention was given to sterilization as a solution to the Jewish problem, but in the event the two milder solutions of assimilation and sterilization were specifically rejected. Assimilation, as Leese indicated from the moment the idea came under consideration, was unacceptable: basing himself upon his racist view of the world, he believed that such a policy would have resulted in the destruction of the Aryan race and its eventual domination by Jews. The idea of sterilization, first mentioned in connection with mental defectives, received little support or amplification.[69] Leese believed that the administrative difficulties surrounding the implementation of the policy would have been too great and, since Jews would not have been removed from Britain by such a policy, it would have a dangerous incompleteness. Consequently, it was not regarded ultimately as an alternative, although it was realized that it could be useful in dealing with the problem of Jewish quadroons and octroons, once the main body of Jews had been dealt with by other means.[70]

But what other means? Leese gave a great deal of consideration to the idea of segregation or exclusion which he regarded as the most feasible solution and in advocating this he was once more indebted to Beamish.[71] The suggestion was that Jews should be sent to Madagascar. In the first mention of segregation among the Britons, Palestine was suggested as a possible destination.[72] But shortly afterwards Beamish proposed that Madagascar was more suitable as a home for Jews on the grounds that Palestine was already occupied and could not hold 'a tithe of the Jews of the world'.[73] In essence the policies advocated by Leese, basing himself upon the Britons, were similar to those developed by the Nazis when they studied the Plan in 1940.[74] It was believed that an island was the most effective camp for the Jews but it had to be large enough to contain all the Jews while having a density of population which would allow for the possibility of their economic absorption. Madagascar was regarded as fulfilling these criteria.[75] It was an island which could be divided into northern and southern halves, with the latter being allocated to the Jews who would have to pay compensation to France and the native population for the 'privilege' of their new National Home. The area would be patrolled, at Jewish expense, by some future league of Nordic nations which would have to guard the east-west land frontier across Madagascar and would be expected to encircle the island to prevent escape. The problem of how best to treat those Jews with diluted blood was difficult, but it was suggested that half castes should be included in the enforced emigration. However, quadroons and octroons would be exempt from the scheme if they were sterilized and on condition that they were barred from holding certain posts of responsibility.[76]

The remaining alternative solution was extermination and Leese was certainly prepared to give some consideration to such a proposal, thereby providing a genocidal link with the Britons.[77] As early as 1931 Leese gave the first intimation that extermination might be considered as a feasible solution and, although the theme was not developed, the idea was openly mentioned.[78]

> It must be admitted that the most certain and permanent way of disposing of the Jews would be to exterminate them by some humane method such as the lethal chamber. It is quite practicable but (some will say unfortunately), in our time it is unlikely the world will demand the adoption of the drastic procedure.[79]

Leese was, therefore, an early advocate of the possibility of extermination and it was a constant feature of his discussions during the 1930s even though exclusion in the form of Madagascar was always regarded as the most effective solution.[80] After the war, however, in an age when extermination was the unspeakable crime, Leese swam against the tide and, while he still referred to the Madagascar plan, he was prepared to give greater emphasis to an exterminatory solution to the Jewish question.[81]

Now that we have discussed Leese's anti-semitism we might briefly consider the attitudes of other fringe societies on the right wing of British politics, starting with the British Fascists which, in May 1923, under its original name of the British Fascisti, was the first distinctively Fascist organization to be formed in Britain. In the fullest account we have of its political evolution it has been suggested that in the first instance the organization was little more than a militant anti-Communist group, that in its second phase it was concerned to offer solutions for what it regarded as shortcomings in the economy and government and that finally, in the 1930s, it adopted a straightforward Fascist policy modelled on Italy.[82] However, whatever shifts of emphasis were present, from the earliest days an opposition towards Communism and aliens as dangers to the nation was built into the programme of the organization and throughout its brief existence a hostility towards Jews can be detected as part of its patriotic reflex.[83] This was particularly apparent in the early 1930s, as the staider members of the organization faded away and as events in Europe made an increasing impression upon the remaining membership. It was against this background that its anti-semitism became more pronounced.[84]

At no point does its anti-semitism create an element of surprise in the sense that its main emphases were also present in the writings of Fascist and High Tory anti-semitism in the 1920s. Reference was made in the early days of the movement to Jewish Bolshevism, to the 'Junta of Jews' who had seized control in Russia and whom, it was proclaimed, 'a super pogrom' would send to their final account.[85] And, towards the end of its life, this hostility still remained. Russia was portrayed as 'dying under the Jewish yoke'. Under 'the true rule of Israel', life in the country was described as a living nightmare and 'the Jewish World Revolutionaries' were claimed to be intent upon transforming the whole of the globe into a hell ruled by Judaism.[86] On other occasions the connection of Jews with international finance which worked against national interests was also noticed.[87] Indeed, the internationalism of Jews highlighted by an involvement in Socialism and Communism and international finance was regarded as lying at the centre of Fascist opposition towards Jews. 'Internationalism', it was proclaimed, 'is Jewish Imperialism.'[88] Jews were Jews by race and their own interests reigned paramount among them 'notwithstanding the fact that they may assume "British" citizen rights'.[89] Such international ambitions ran counter to British interests and consequently it was believed that the Jew should be declared an alien by nationality and should be denied the privilege of British citizenship.[90]

The IFL and the British Fascists were self confessed Fascist organizations which had anti-semitism built into their programmes. In the former case, Leese's anti-semitism was the axis on which the movement revolved; in the latter it became a more important feature in the early 1930s. But it has already been shown in our earlier discussion of the 1920s that anti-semitism was not the prerogative of Fascism and after considering its expression within two early Fascist bodies we might now turn to its manifestation within the context of religion and patriotism.

The organizations which we have so far considered were children of the 1920s but it was not until September 1935 that the association called the Militant Christian Patriots was formed.[91] 'The programme of the MCP', it was stated in a leading article, 'which, broadly speaking, is to wage a militant campaign for the triumph of Christian principles in everyday life is divided into two parts – political and moral'. And, in extension of this, it was explained that MCP members would 'endeavour to expose all subversive movements' and fight against any plan which threatened individual freedom and attempted to destroy 'Patriotism, Nationalism and the Welfare of the British Empire'. In the moral sphere members of the organization would 'expose and militantly oppose all movements subversive of Christain faith and ideals'.[92] It was from this ideological base that the MCP operated and it is within this context that its anti-semitism should be considered. From the beginning this hostility was expressed in terms of a racial difference manifesting itself in differing cultures and was referred to as a re-enactment of the old battle between Judaism and Christianity in modern garb. Hence reference could be made to Jews as a threat to an Aryan-Christian civilization.[93]

From this base there is no doubt that down to 1939 – its activities folded with the war[94] – the MCP displayed a clear hostility towards Jews and what it described as Jewish interests. British society was portrayed as under siege from agencies and pressures reflecting Jewish interests and the MCP considered that it was part of its task to point out this threat. It also undertook to coordinate the opposition to such perceived developments and, in view of this, its anti-semitism brought it closer into touch with Fascist groups and placed anti-semitic hostility more towards the centre of its life than was the case with a patriotic association such as the Boswell Publishing Company.[95] It was in line with this kind of thinking that it could attempt 'in this year of Grace, 1936' to awaken Britain to the fact that, 'a decisive battle must be fought against the enslavers of our race whose power is concentrated in Zionism.'[96]

Jews were described as a race without a country. They were everywhere sojourners and deficient therefore in patriotism.[97] And throughout the 1930s the MCP was concerned to pinpoint the organizations through which Jewish interests were allegedly promoted and the particular ways in which it was believed that Jews were undermining the patriotism, nationalism and welfare of the British Empire, the bulwark of Christian civilization.[98] One assault upon such values was perceived in the promotion of Zionism. Through such an ideology it was claimed that Zionists expressed an allegiance to the 'Jewish race', to the Jewish religion, or to Jewish nationalism, in preference to an allegiance to Britons, to Christianity and the British Empire.[99] Zionism was in fact regarded as nothing less than a Jewish attempt at world conquest and the League of Nations was referred to as the vehicle for such a design.[100] But Zionism was not the only international influence working on behalf of Jews which was considered to threaten British interests. An anti-British, anti-Christian threat was also present in Jewish Bolshevism which, it was believed, not only threatened the political life of the British Empire but also posed a challenge to the Christian basis of civilization.[101]

While international agencies threatened British interests it was also claimed that the country was being undermined from within. With its strong belief in the value of laissez-faire – 'capitalism has not failed'[102], the *Free Press* proclaimed in its first issue – the MCP was suspicious of economic planning at a time when such a tendency was becoming increasingly fashionable in the wake of international economic problems. In particular, the MCP was hostile to Political and Economic Planning (PEP), which was founded in 1931 'as an anonymous group of civil servants, businessmen and academic and professional people interested in politics and economics' who devoted themselves to the impartial study of the problems of industry.[103] The suspicions of the MCP were heightened by the fact that Israel Sieff of Marks and Spencer acted as PEP's president.[104] Apart from what it considered to be the undermining influences of PEP, with its emphasis on 'Socialist' planning, the organization also expressed concern at Jewish immigration into Britain, particularly the influx of doctors, and psychoanalysts who were regarded as carrying on a profession which was subversive of Christian ideals.[105] In addition, anxiety existed about the role of Jews in education, particularly higher education, where the minds and ideals of youth could be corrupted.[106]

There was a degree of urgency in the writings of the MCP, and through its account of the various machinations of Zionism and Bolshevism, not to mention Freemasonry, as well as PEP, a picture was presented of subversive developments intent upon wrecking Britain and the Empire and its historically evolved values and ideals.[107] In such circumstances it was considered necessary to isolate the Jews, to restrict the damage they could inflict and the harm they could do. It was with this policy of exclusion in mind that the MCP could suggest, with a magnificent, opaque vagueness, that Jews should combine resources and buy a National Home for all Jews.[108] Settlement in Palestine was no answer. The MCP like the Britons and Leese was hostile to a solution which, it was believed, could work only at the expense of the Arabs and was also opposed to any plan which did not guarantee the removal of all Jews from the societies in which they happened to reside. But, in practical terms, what could be done? Apart from its suggestion that Jews should combine their resources, the MCP had little new to offer except for the exotic suggestion that support should be given to the Soviet homeland for Jews in Biro-Bidjan.[109]

If we stand back from all these expressions of anti-semitism, there is little in them of a surprising or unexpected nature. There was a reiterated stress upon the existence of a Jewish conspiracy, upon the dangers of Jewish Bolshevism, upon the anti-British activities of allegedly Jew-dominated international bodies, upon the social and economic power exercised by Jews in their own interests, as well as upon the additional dangers which British society was creating for itself by the liberal immigration policies which swelled the number of Jews in the country. Most of this complemented the message of the Britons. However, these were some distinctive features. Leese's emphasis upon ritual murder, and the MCP stress upon the desirability of a free market economy rather than what it called Fabian-Zionist planning, come to mind. And, in terms of a solution to the Jewish question, while references to a possible settlement in Madagascar clearly derived from the Britons and Leese's discussion of extermination also found an echo among the Britons,[110] reference by the MCP to an isolation of Jews in Biro-Bidjan seems to have been a unique suggestion among British anti-semites.

So much for the ideas which were expressed on the Jewish question. Why, it might be asked, did they arise? Can we explain their manifestation in terms of individual psychologies? In discussing conspiratorial theories it was suggested that, in the case of H. H. Beamish and Nesta Webster, it might well be necessary to take account of personality mechanisms in order to understand their persistent adherence to such explanations of social change and development.[111] And it has been claimed that Leese's anti-semitism, his view of the world through the window of *The Protocols*, was a reflection of his personality structure.[112] Throughout his career there was a quest for 'definiteness' a need to separate 'the good' from 'the bad', so that in his analysis of the Aryan-Jewish struggle and in his later hostility towards blacks, when as early as 1952 he coined the phrase 'Keep Britain White', Leese saw the world in dichotomous terms.[113]

In view of this it has been suggested that his social philosophy can best be categorized as paranoid and, in this instance, emerging from a clinically paranoid personality.[114] Leese did not involve himself in his anti-semitic political career until he was about fifty years of age and it has been estimated that this is the median age for the onset of paranoia in men.[115] Why his character should have developed in this way is difficult to say. Psychiatric evidence suggests that such behaviour results from intra-family relationships. But we cannot say anything significant about the possible struggles and repressions of Leese's childhood and no purpose is served by speculation. But, whatever the causes, Leese displayed a paranoid fear of Jews and, like the clinical paranoiac, maintained his belief in all circumstances. We have been told that

> The sufferer is keyed up all the time. Even public disapproval, ridicule, exposure or jail do not deter him. Although he may stop short of inciting his hearers to violence he has an intensity, a humourlessness and aggressiveness that nothing can shake. Neither argument nor experience will change his views.[116]

This fits Leese exactly. However, even in the case of Leese the influence of the social dimension on the expression of anti-semitism can hardly be ignored, just as we are unable to overlook its significance for other anti-semitic opinions. Developments such as Bolshevism, Zionism and the League of Nations which were closely associated with the recently ended war form the background to the hostility shown by the IFL (essentially Leese), the British Fascists and the MCP.[118] In addition, there were more immediate pressures such as the unrest and uncertainty of the post-war years and the difficult times which followed the world crisis and depression of 1929–31. It was in such circumstances that pronounced forms of nationalism were manifested, conflicting with the various international developments of the time. All this provides the general backcloth to the hostility shown towards Jews.[119]

As for expressions of opposition on political grounds, all the groups we have been discussing were sensitive to issues such as Bolshevism, Zionism and the League of Nations, since their world was viewed through *The Protocols*, itself a product of the disturbed years of the early twentieth century. It was through the message of *The Protocols* that they made sense of the crises of their time. The 'revelations' which the publication contained appealed not only to the clinically paranoid but also to many individuals in the bodies we have been considering, who adopted a paranoid style as they perceived a culture, a nation under attack. Its view of the world provided a mirror through which all these developments could be perceived and hostility towards Jews could be rationalized and justified. To those who accepted its message Jews automatically worked for Jewish ends and all movements and organizations with which Jews were associated, or which became involved with a Jewish cause, were viewed as agencies of Jewish Domination. To the BF the IFL and the MCP, Bolshevism was suspect on these grounds and the hostility shown towards Zionism and the League of Nations needs to be considered in this context.[120] It was out of the interaction of such pressures that hostility arose, in the course of which reference could also be made, in supportive fashion, to the traditions of anti-semitism which were present in British society.[121]

We have shown that such political hostility towards Jews was complemented by attacks upon Jewish economic activity and against that general background of the inter-war years, which has already been discussed, the specific reasons for directing economic hostility towards Jews should now be mentioned. The attacks upon Jews in finance have to be set not only against the prominence of certain Jews in international finance, but also within the context of a general hostility among the IFL, the BF and and the MCP to money making as opposed to wealth creating activity. It also has to be considered against a shared belief among them that there could be serious implications for the nation arising from Jews wielding an influence in finance. All such considerations ultimately derived from the warning sounded in *The Protocols* that the mechanism of international finance was one agency through which Jewish world influence would be attained.[122] Similarly, it might be suggested that interpretations of national loyalty and the importance of the message in *The Protocols* concerning the power of the press help us to understand why the well worn emphasis upon Jewish press influence was maintained and attention could become focused upon any instances of Jews involved in press affairs as well as other parts of the modern communications industry.[123]

Finally, the hostility towards Jews participating in the rationalization of British industry, economic planning and monopoly, and the implications for the scale of operations in industry and commerce, have to be considered in relation to two factors – first, the support given by the IFL and the MCP to the small businessman in whom it was believed the spirit of enterprise rested, and in the case of the IFL, the veneration of agriculture rather than industry or commerce; and, secondly, the fear that any increase in scale could be interpreted as a step towards internationalism, which, it was believed, could work in the interests of an international minority group rather than in the interests of the British people. This was inevitably a powerful consideration for groups working under the influence of *The Protocols*.

Such were the influences which played upon Leese, the British Fascists, and the MCP – just three examples from a corner of the political world which possessed more insignificant shades who have disappeared even more rapidly into the thickets of the past, only to be temporarily rescued, examined and then placed back into their surrounding obscurity by the most tenacious chroniclers and persistent enquirers into the by-ways of British anti-semitism.[125]

11 The BUF and anti-semitism

Fascist anti-semitism in Britain in the inter-war years is commonly associated in the public mind with Oswald Mosley and the British Union of Fascists (BUF), the organization which Mosley founded in 1932 after an earlier career in both the Conservative and Labour Parties and a transient period as founder member and leader of the New Party.[1] In the sense that Mosley dominated the BUF, an analysis of its anti-semitism might appropriately take as its centrepiece the ideas and attitudes of a man who has been variously regarded as Peter Pan, Lucifer, Colonel Blimp, the British Julius Caesar, the dandy of politics, Faust and Don Quixote and build a wider picture around such a base.[2]

It might be of interest first to consider earlier opinions expressed on Mosley, the BUF and the question of anti-semitism. Over recent years a number of works have appeared in which the issue is discussed and the general verdict is that Mosley and the BUF – or at least, sections of it – did reveal themselves as anti-semitic. As might be expected this was apparent in Frederick Mullally's *Fascism inside England*, published just after the end of the Second World War, at a time when Mosley could expect little sympathy, particularly on the left, and this trend continues in more recent work.[3] A conviction that Mosley was an anti-semite and that the BUF adopted and projected an anti-semitic philosophy and programme was present in Colin Cross's account of the Fascists in Britain,[4] and a similar judgment appeared in Benewick.[5] All these studies were concerned with Fascism rather than specifically with anti-semitism, but when a work did appear which addressed itself directly to the issue of the BUF and anti-semitism, there was no change in the basic conclusion reached. It was considered that Mosley revealed himself as an anti-semite and the movement, it was suggested, propagated anti-semitic ideas and, at a particular stage in its history, translated these ideas into action.[6] This might be called the 'classic' point of view.

But, by implicit definition, a 'classic' view does not exist in isolation and over the past few years this assessment has come under attack or qualification. The process began with the publication of Mosley's autobiography. In the course of this he argued that he was not an anti-semite since he did not attack the Jews for what they were but for what they did and, as he had always been prepared to argue, there was nothing which made the Jews above criticism.[7] When the reviewer in *The Times* found this 'convincing' a flood of correspondence descended on the newspaper, almost all of it hostile to Mosley.[8]

Following this, Skidelsky's long awaited biography of Mosley spends some time, as part of a wider study, considering the attitudes towards Jews adopted by Mosley and the BUF. And, on the basis of this analysis, while Skidelsky is prepared to admit that Mosley was anti-semitic, that such anti-semitism was the 'greatest blemish on his whole career', and an instance of 'intellectual and moral carelessness', he argues that Mosley's own anti-semitism, unlike that of some in the BUF, was not a significant feature of his personal philosophy.[9] 'To him the Jew was a metaphor rather than a belief, a word added to a pre-existing structure of thought to sharpen the propaganda line.'[10] As for the BUF, while it undoubtedly emphasized the existence of a Jewish question, some of its hostility towards Jews was a response to violence initiated by Jews and in this sense Mosley and the BUF were as much sinned against as sinning. Such conclusions have not been universally welcomed.[11]

What can we make of this? Is it possible to offer any further assessment of the problem in the light of what has already been said? I think it is, in terms of answering the following questions: what was the essential nature of Mosley's attitudes towards Jews? How did his attitudes compare with those held by others within the ranks of the BUF? and why did such ideas take hold?

There are a number of key speeches and statements made by Mosley which help to provide us with the essence of his responses towards Jews. A start might be made by considering his remarks of 29 September 1934 delivered at Belle Vue, Manchester. This was not the first occasion on which he had launched into an attack upon Jews – in common with others in the BUF he had attacked Jews in late 1933 – but it marked a significant development in his position.[12] Hitherto he had attempted to restrain the burgeoning anti-semitism within the BUF both in mid-1933[13] and in early 1934, at which latter time it seemed possible that an 'alliance' might be forged with the press baron Lord Rothermere, an association which would doubtless have proved politically advantageous to the BUF. However, pressure within the movement made such containment difficult and the Rothermere-Mosley alliance ran into the sands in July 1934 with anti-semitism counting for one of the disruptive factors. Rothermere wrote: 'I have . . . made it quite clear in my conversations with you that I never could support any movement with an anti-semitic bias.'[14] It was in the wake of this loss of Rothermere's support and in an atmosphere of growing anti-semitism in the BUF, reflected in the issues of *Blackshirt*, the movement's own paper, that the Manchester speech occurred in late 1934.

The meeting was a second anniversary rally at which Mosley encountered considerable interruption. At a certain point, when he had clearly had enough of this, he lashed his hecklers with the accusation that they were the 'sweepings of the continental ghettos hired by Jewish financiers'. In the course of his retaliation he attacked 'these Jewish rascals', and launched into an indictment of Jewish influence, with reference to 'this little crowd brought here by Jewish money'. He also referred to the 'yelping of a Yiddish mob', 'alien Yiddish finance', and the 'alien faces' in his audience. 'Jewish finance' came in for particular hostility, in the course of which he claimed:

> What they call today the will of the people is nothing but the organized corruption of Press, cinema and Parliament, which is called democracy but which is ruled by alien Jewish finance – the same finance which has hired alien mobs to yell here tonight.[15]

The speech at Manchester might be regarded as a temporary aberration – an exchange of insults delivered when under pressure – and in this sense hardly indicative of Mosley's real position. But the same could not be said about the next major occasion when Jews were discussed at the Albert Hall on 28 October 1934. This was regarded as an important meeting and Mosley used it to deal with the Jewish question and to issue a challenge to the Jewish community. According to recent opinion, 'it marked the end of the sparring with the issue, and the beginning of the real fighting.'[16]

He told his audience first of all:

> I have encountered things in this country which, quite frankly, I did not believe existed. And one of these is the power of organized Jewry, which is today mobilized against Fascism. . . . They seek to howl over the length and breadth of the land that we are bent on racial and religious persecution. That charge is utterly untrue, and I can prove it, again and again, from documents issued in the early days of the Movement, absolutely forbidding any form of attack upon Jews. . . . And today we do not attack Jews on racial or religious grounds.

He went on to give his reasons for opposing Jews. They had engaged in attacks on Fascists. Jewish employers had victimized Fascist employees and 'big Jews', through advertising and business pressure, had dissuaded potential Fascist support. It was these 'big Jews' who were a particular menace, more so than the 'sweepings of foreign ghettos' whom the pre-war Liberal government had allowed to enter Britain. Between the BUF and the rich Jews, who exercised control over the press and the cinema, there was no prospect of compromise. Indeed, the BUF was especially selected for attack by the 'big Jews' because it stood out against 'international usury', which provided the base of their influence. Furthermore, the BUF was an intensely national organization, whereas it was claimed that Jews had no national allegiances. The BUF was also opposed to intervention in Germany which was what Jews wanted. Finally, he assured his audience that despite Jewish power, its physical attacks and its exercise of insidious pressures, the BUF would win the battle and a new Britain would be built.[17] In the light of such sentiments it has been claimed that the speech marked a turning point:

> 'A new phase [had] entered the history of Fascism'. . . . Henceforth the BUF would fight against 'organized Jewry, representing an unclean, alien influence in our national and imperial life'.[18]

What Mosley said in the Albert Hall about a Jewish power at work in society, a power which worked against Fascist, and therefore, in the opinion of Mosley and the BUF, against British interests, was to become a major obsessive theme in his references to Jews. He returned to it, for instance in a speech at the Albert Hall on 24 March 1935: 'We see the enemy and foe, sweating the East and ruining the West, destroying the Indian masses and filling the unemployment queues of Lancashire... grasping British government and Parliament, grasping the puppets of Westminster.... There is the enemy which Fascism alone dares to challenge, international Jewish finance'. He was prepared, in fact, to expand on this. The enemy was

> that nameless, homeless and all powerful force which stretches its greedy fingers from the shelter of England to throttle the trade and menace the peace of the world. This is the force which holds us to internationalism, which ruins agriculture, which ruins Lancashire and Yorkshire, which challenges Germany and our European neighbours with chatter and menaces of war, using the power of the Press and cinema to insult and to provoke the new world force of Fascism.[19]

The theme of Jewish power also appeared in a further speech at the Albert Hall on 22 March 1936 when, at the same time, he threatened to smash its very existence.[20]

Some attention should also be given to Mosley's statements on the Jewish issue. Here we can find a more restrained although still hostile tone. In 1934 for instance, after the break with Rothermere, he stated:

> We have given our pledge that no racial or religious persecution will occur under Fascism in Britain, but we shall require the Jews, like everyone else to put the interest of 'Britain First'.
>
> We do not admit Jews to membership of our Movement because (a) they have bitterly attacked us (b) they have organized as an international movement, setting their racial interests above their national interests, and are, therefore, unacceptable as members of a national movement which aims at national organization and revival.
>
> We are certainly not prepared to relax our attitude towards Jews, in view of the fact that in the last year 80 per cent of the convictions for physical attacks on Fascists were pronounced on Jews, while the Jewish community represents only 0·6 per cent of the population.[21]

Here was an attempt at a reasoned case against Jews and later in *Blackshirt*, on 3 October 1936, he warned against making statements 'which appear... so violent or so foolish that [the public] are made to regard the Jews as a wronged and persecuted people'.[22]

The emphasis so far in a consideration of his speeches and statements has been upon the difficulties which a Jewish presence created. It might fairly be asked on the basis of these how such problems were going to be resolved. Here the evidence is less plentiful. But Mosley clearly believed the BUF was under an obligation to preserve the British character and tradition, even though this was left undefined, and it was in line with such thinking that he proposed to deport Jews for anti-British conduct. Although such a statement was vague, it has been underlined that the majority of Jews in Britain would have been included and the minority against whom no such charge could be directed would have been deprived of the rights of British citizenship. The ultimate solution to the Jewish question was conceived in terms of the resettlement of the Jews in one of the waste areas of the world (excluding Palestine or the British Empire) possessing great potential fertility, where the Jews could recover the status of nationhood.[23]

In his own assessment of his views on the nature and solution of 'the Jewish question', Mosley has argued that there is nothing to justify a charge of anti-semitism. The reasoning behind this advanced in *My Life* and reflected in statements in the early days of the BUF rests on the argument that religious and racial toleration was part of the Fascist creed and, if Jews were attacked, it was on objective grounds. 'We attack Jews for what they do not for what they are. . . . No Jew could be attacked on ground of race or religion only for political opinion or action.'[24] In reply to this it has to be said that Mosley did not make it a practice to attack Jews in racist fashion. And, as will be argued later, the conflict between the BUF and Jewish interests certainly needs to be set within the wider context of BUF ideology and the social structure of the Jewish community, even if the nature of the clash came to transcend such circumstances. But, having said that, it also needs to be recognized that while Mosley might not have exhibited the kind of racist anti-semitism present in the Britons and Leese, which started from race as the true basis for political beliefs and action, he was nevertheless prepared to refer to Jews in categorical rather than *ad hoc* terms. In other words, his analyses tended towards determinism, even if the ascription of qualities was not tied to a genetic base.[25] We need to develop these points.

It is perfectly true that while he could perceive Jews in an unsystematic way as a race, Mosley did not often base his attacks upon Jews on a racist framework. In other words we do not find him attacking all Jews, arguing that there was some quality in the genetic endowment of Jews which made it necessary and inevitable for them to engage in particular forms of social behaviour. Nor do we find him basing his hostility directly upon certain perceived inferior Jewish physical characteristics. However, heated references such as 'stronger even than the stink of oil rises the stink of the Jew'[26] indicate that traces of an implicit emotive racism were present in Mosley's thought. But no attempt will be made here to argue that these were in any sense significant or substantial.[27]

The stress in Mosley's utterances lies elsewhere. If we scrutinize them we can detect that his opposition was to 'alien Jewish finance'; 'organized Jewry'; 'the organized corruption of Press, cinema and Parliament, which is called democracy but which is ruled by Jewish finance'; 'big Jews', that is, 'international usury'; 'Jewish international finance' – 'the nameless, homeless and all powerful force which stretches its greedy fingers from the shelter of England to throttle the trade and menace the peace of the world'; Jews 'setting their racial interests above their national interests'; Jews attacking Fascists.[28] This was the nature of his opposition at the time when the 'Jewish question' was a central feature in BUF activity and, as the Second World War edged nearer, he reiterated a charge which had been present in the BUF since its early days, that this Jewish power was the force which was driving Britain into a war in response to pressure from Jewish interests.[29]

In other words, his attitudes revealed a hostility towards Jews which was expressed within an ethnocentric and conspiratorial framework. The former dimension was apparent in his opposition to the Jews organizing as a minority within a nation, in his hostility to German Jewish refugees taking jobs from Englishmen,[30] and in his charge that Jews had no national allegiances.[31] But in these attempts to put 'Britain first' his ethnocentrism became closely allied to and difficult to disentangle from his assault upon Jewish internationalism, as a consequence of which his hostility assumed conspiratorial tones. Hence his references to the enemy and foe sweating the east to ruin the west, destroying the Indians and filling the unemployment queues of Lancashire; his opposition to 'the nameless, homeless and all powerful force' which throttled the trade and menaced the peace of the world;[32] his hostility towards Jews on account of their organizing 'an international movement, setting their racial interests above their national interests'.[33] Contrary to his later protestation, in pursuit of the Jewish enemy Mosley's thought clearly did assume a conspiratorial form.[34]

For the most part it was a hostility expressed in relatively restrained and sophisticated terms. As one commentator has written: 'Mosley was intelligent enough to realize that . . . extravagant abuse coming from him did little good. . . . On the whole he tended to see himself as a rational anti-semite.'[35] While there might be some hesitation about using the word 'rational' in this context the general point can be taken. But those who regard Mosley as a reasoning politician miss another darker side to his nature. 'In fact', it has been written, 'there are (and perhaps always have been) two sides to Mosley's personality.[36] And both sides of his character were revealed in his references to Jews. In his set speeches and public statements the approach was a reasoned explanation of the matter in hand, but he could show when angered the other side of his personality, shedding the persona of reason and becoming 'the black knight'.

At this point, having commented upon Mosley's thought, we might ask whether anything similar was expressed elsewhere in the BUF. Special consideration will be given to the attitudes of William Joyce and A. K. Chesterton, both of whom have been regarded as central to the anti-semitism manifested within the BUF,[37] although other views will be mentioned in order to provide a rounded picture.

There is no need to engage in an account of Joyce's life and career since this has been covered elsewhere, except to say that his Fascist career began in December 1923 when at the age of seventeen he joined the British Fascisti.[38] He began his association with BUF in 1933 and stayed until the 1937 'purge' when together with John Beckett, the ex-Labour MP who had also been removed from the BUF by Mosley in the 1937 reorganization, he founded the National Socialist League.[39] A few days before war broke out Joyce slipped out of Britain to Germany where he remained during the war, engaging in his now notorious propaganda work for which he was executed by the British in 1946.

During his time in the BUF Joyce's most extensive treatment of the Jewish question was given in *Fascism and Jewry* which appeared in 1936. In this he devoted himself to a range of issues involving Jews and the pamphlet provides a clear guide to the nature of his anti-semitism. In some respects there were striking similarities with Mosley's own analysis, as in his insistence that Jewry was responsible for instigating attacks upon Fascism, using as its rationalization the charge that Fascism threatened religious and racial persecution.[40] It was a charge which Joyce rejected. Fascism, he claimed, recognized religious liberty and its belief in a racially diverse empire made nonsense of the idea that a persecution on racial grounds was contemplated.[41] The reason why Fascists attacked Jews, Joyce argued, lay elsewhere: 'This movement does not attack Jews by reason of what they are, it resists them by reason of what they do'[42] – an argument which Mosley echoed.[43].

What did they do? In what sense were Jews a threat? According to Joyce they held a disproportionate responsibility for attacks upon Fascists; Jewish employers engaged in victimization of Fascist employees; and, more importantly, Jews were intent upon drawing Britain into a war with Germany thereby pushing a policy based on racial rather than national interests. All this mirrored Mosley's own analysis.[44] Joyce's pamphlet also argued that there was an international Jewish force at work through the agencies of finance and Bolshevism, and this was echoed in Mosley's own references to the machinations of international Jewry, which were a feature of his speeches in the 1930s but which, as already mentioned, he no longer finds convincing.[45] In the main sets of arguments of the two men we can therefore detect similar emphases.

But there was an important difference in expression. In Joyce's case we have been told that he wrote as he talked[46] and, whereas Mosley was concerned to engage in a reasoned argument against Jewry, Joyce knew no such restraint.[47] The consequences of this were readily apparent. For instance, describing Jewish opposition at Fascist meetings, an opposition which, he said, enjoyed police protection, Joyce referred to 'a mass of bestial Jewish faces contorted into hideous and obscene grimaces' and shortly afterwards he could refer to such opposition as 'Jewish sub-men'.[48] In fact, he had a considerable stock of choice phrases to throw at the opposition, describing Jews on one occasion as 'Simians with prehensile toes', 'crawling vermin', and, when the mood took him, 'lousy semi-orientals'.[49]

Furthermore, whereas Mosley's hostility did not carry a clear racist emphasis, Joyce persistently referred to Jews as 'Orientals' and drew a sharp distinction between them and 'white people' and asserted that differences in race were reflected in undesirable Jewish cultural characteristics.[50] This was particularly apparent in *Twilight over England*, written after he had left the BUF. 'We must consider the Jewish character', he wrote. 'It must moreover be considered in relation to race and not religion. Whether the Jew is orthodox, atheist or Christian, he remains a Jew'. Everywhere, in fact, the Jew carried with him 'his racial consciousness, his racial character, his racial purpose and his monstrous materialism'. Elsewhere in that work the system of government in Britain could be described as 'Jewish in purpose', reference could be made to 'typically Jewish greed', and critical comment could be passed upon 'Hebrew enterprise' and 'Jewish corruption'.[51]

Let us now turn to A. K. Chesterton (1899–1973), a second cousin of G. K. Chesterton. Chesterton was born in South Africa and educated in that country and in England. He served in the First World War with distinction and after a period in journalism in South Africa and some involvement in politics out there, he resumed his journalistic career in Britain, after which he worked as a public relations officer at the Shakespeare Memorial Theatre. He joined the BUF in 1933 to begin a Fascist career which spread over forty years and which was to take him through the BUF and the League of Empire Loyalists and eventually into the National Front. In the course of this journey he wrote a good deal – on Mosley, his split with 'the Leader' and persistently and obsessively about Jewish power. A restless soul, he has been described as the BUF's 'best polemicist'.[52]

In his references to Jews Chesterton's hostility was capable of being expressed in vicious terms which often assumed an implicit racist imagery.[53] To him Jews were 'positively anointed with semitic grease';[54] alternatively they were 'ape-like thugs';[55] 'vultures';[56] 'cowardly rats';[57] 'financial sharks'.[58] The Jew was also portrayed as being parasitical and sucking the life blood from western civilization.[59] Chesterton's work in the years before 1939 also displayed a more explicit racism and in concentrating upon such expressions of hostility he separated himself from Mosley's manifestations of anti-semitism and aligned himself alongside those like Joyce. Chesterton believed in a Jewish 'race consciousness', and was convinced that Jews had a 'natural gift to purvey trash' and undermine the values of society.[60] Indeed, 'every vitiating and demoralizing factor in our national life was Jew-ridden where it was not Jew-controlled', he wrote in 1937 in his biography of Mosley.[61] 'The Jews who murdered Christ', he wrote elsewhere, 'and who throughout the ages have murdered the Christ spirit chuckle inwardly as they rake in the Christian shekels'.[62] He did, however, anticipate a day when 'the Yiddish St George' and 'his foul values of profit, exploitation and decay' would be removed from influence and the people of England would 'regain possession of England and assert once more their ancient values of patriotism and service and square dealing among men'.[63] In addition, Chesterton's hostility assumed conspiratorial forms in the sense that in common with a multitude of Fascist contemporaries he saw danger arising from the siamese twins of 'International Jewish Finance' and 'International Jewish Bolshevism' which he regarded as intent upon securing 'the ruination of the world'.[64]

In both Joyce and Chesterton we can therefore detect an opaque emphasis upon racist hostility towards Jews – what Mosley himself would regard as real anti-semitism[65] – as well as a tendency to engage in more violent imagery than Mosley was inclined to use. This violence of expression, incidentally, was apparent not only in the attitudes of Joyce and Chesterton, who were closely associated with the BUF at the centre, but also among those leaders who were thrown up in the East End, such as E. G. 'Mick' Clarke. This was clearly shown in a speech in which Clarke attacked the decision, supposedly taken under Jewish pressure, to ban a projected Fascist march in east London. In the course of this he told his audience:

> One of them thought that on July 4th we intended to have an unofficial pogrom in East London and persecute the undesirables from our midst and drive them down to the docks. Just fancy, a few British people, born in the East End of London, wanting to have a little walk round; and then they want to wind up in Trafalgar Square and hear the voice of a white man . . . to hear a white man speak and put forward a policy for the British people.
>
> I read that the Jews were going to demonstrate to the Commissioner and the Home Secretary with a view to getting the march banned and apparently they succeeded very well. . . . But I don't want people to be led away with the idea that it is our desire to walk through the land of the waving palm, because we can do that any night of the week we jolly well choose. . . . For my part I have no desire to mingle with them whatsoever. The only time when I would visit the land of the waving palm is when gas masks are issued.
>
> In the meantime boys, I have been trying to ascertain what part of this London of ours belongs to Englishmen. What part of England is Jew-land? You know, like the swine of the earth, the kangaroos are scattered far and wide, and now we find that Wobbly Willie[66] has ticked it off very graciously in order that we can see the area of the East End of London which belongs to the Jews. . . . Gradually we are seeing the big drive of Jewish international financiers from the top of the tree down to the stalls and shops in our own local markets. We gradually see the boards of Smith and Brown taken away. In place of Smith and Brown we see another name [inaudible]. Moreover, underneath we see kosher signs and 'Hot Salt Beef sold here'. Silently do we see the Englishman driven from his stall because Jews have become real Englishmen and have got our birthright.[67]

It was a speech which led to Clarke being bound over to keep the peace for the next twelve months, a conviction which was quashed on appeal. In addition to what has been given here, it would seem that Clarke, who worked in the furniture trade, and was one of the ablest of Mosley's recruits, had referred to Jews as 'greasy scum', 'lice of the earth', and 'untouchables.'.[68] Here was someone who clearly revelled in insults and, unlike Mosley, required little provocation to engage in crude verbal assaults.

Among the major figures in the BUF Joyce and Chesterton were both prepared to indulge in unambiguous racist expressions of hostility towards Jews. In the Fascist press similar assumptions tended to be expressed though racist imagery rather than in a direct sense and images involving slime, grease and oil were not uncommon.[69] Such nuances were particularly apparent in a series on political natural history, in which 'the She-Neelouse' was described. It was revealed to *Blackshirt* readers as a 'parasite with a large hook-beaked protuberance and vile smell', and could also be recognized on account of 'its flat bloated appearance' and the 'slimy oil trail' it left behind as it crawled its way through life.[70]

The conspiratorial strain of anti-semitism which has been noted in all the 'major' thinkers referred to in the present chapter was also apparent among other Fascists. The theme of Jewish financial power dominated A. Raven Thomson's *Break the Chains that Bind Us. Our Financial Masters*, and elsewhere political parties were described as 'completely Jew-ridden'.[71] On a wider scale, an emphasis was placed upon international Jewish business power in discussions of the New Deal which was frequently referred to as 'the Jew Deal',[72] while Jews were seen as owning Czechoslovakia,[73] having Poland in their grip,[74] running Stalin's Russia,[75] as well as fostering and sustaining an alliance between the Jews of the Kremlin, the Avenue du Bois, Park Lane and Park Avenue, to make the world safe for Communism and international Jewry.[76]

General evidence of the ethnocentric hostility which was central to Mosley's responses can also be detected in the Fascist press. This was particularly evident in the references to immigration, where a belief in British rights and British interests was clearly apparent. 'Britain for the British', 'The Alien Menace',[77] 'Refugees to have *your* boys' jobs',[78] 'Aliens or Britons? Shall British money go to Jews while Britons starve?'[79] and 'Help Unemployed First'[80] were headlines which gave a clear indication of ethnocentrism, and many of these ideas were repeated in the leaflet *The Simple Jewish Worker* in which 'Britons true' were enjoined, with heavy sarcasm,

> So grasp the Jewish worker by his hard and horny hand. And think of how he works for us and for our dear Homeland.

The overall message was clearly summed up in the anonymous BUF pamphlet on *Britain and Jewry:*

> As the Jews insist upon putting JEWRY FIRST we reply by demanding that we, as a nation, put BRITAIN FIRST and reserve BRITAIN for those who are truly BRITISH.[81]

As a final stage in this analysis, bearing in mind the guidelines suggested earlier on, we need to ask about the motivation of Mosley and the BUF for their involvement in anti-semitism. Those who have already written about the BUF have provided us with their interpretations and we might begin by mentioning these. At one stage of his discussion Benewick adopted a scapegoat approach, seeking an explanation by concentrating on the needs of the BUF for a new dynamic; but eventually he seemed to throw up his hands in despair at the problem with the comment, 'whatever the motivation. . .'.[82] Soon afterwards Mandle, while admitting that Jews might have helped to stimulate the hostility, ultimately concentrated on political and personal pressures within the BUF encouraging it to engage in a policy which had proved its political value elsewhere.[83] Mosley, of course, in *My Life* denied in 1968 that he ever became involved in anti-semitism; he put forward the view that his attacks were directed against Jews not for what they were but for what they did.[84] We have already argued that this defence is unconvincing. Skidelsky has suggested more recently that anti-semitism was present both in Mosley's thought and more widely within the BUF and has offered a convergence type of explanation, which takes account of pressures within the BUF as well as the activities of a Jewish opposition, but this has in no way ended the debate.[85]

If we take it that Mosley and the BUF did engage in hostility towards Jews along the lines already presented in their speeches and statements, as well as involving themselves in action against Jews – which is referred to later – how can we account for it? It has been suggested in two recent discussions that to answer this we need to understand individual psychologies.[86] It was nevertheless admitted by one of the writers that such an approach would be hazardous, as indeed it would, if only because psychohistory is 'a delicate and insufficiently formulated subject' and, as yet, unable to lead us very far. However, the importance of personality psychology ought not to be ignored.[87] We know, from contemporary testing that some anti-semitism is related to personality disturbance and it can be tentatively suggested that this might be relevant to William Joyce. Joyce built up a view of Jewish hostility towards himself which, in fact, had no basis in reality. His accusation that his scarred face resulted from a razor slash by a Jewish Communist cannot be substantiated, nor can the claim that his university research career was ruined when 'a Jewish woman tutor' appropriated his research notes. Indeed, in this latter instance the suggestion can be disproved.[88] It could well be that a rounded explanation of Joyce's anti-semitism would need to delve into the history and structure of his personality. But we need to be wary of explaining anti-semitism in terms of individual personalities without reference to the social context within which an individual has to express himself. Or, as it has been stated elsewhere:

> From our point of view, personality is best conceived not as a collection of traits, not as a static system . . . but as a process. . . . The process of carrying out the functions of a shop steward in a union, superintendent of schools, or 'courteous customer' does not allow full individual variation to come into play. The roles themselves have some compulsions that influence which of the various tendencies the individual will express.[89]

In short, we should resist the temptation to explain racial and ethnic conflict as if it emanated solely from the recesses of the mind and exclusively from within the individual personality.[90]

The appropriate starting point if we are to gain an understanding of the clash is at the social rather than the individual level and through a consideration of the individual as a social being. If we accept this we need to go deeper than to suggest, as one commentator has recently done, that the anti-semitism of Mosley and the BUF grew out of an anti-semitic culture in which they were merely carrying coals to Newcastle.[91] But it has to be recognized that the BUF in its campaign could tap the anti-semitic sentiments which were present in Britain, just as it had to face the powerful forces ranged against anti-semitism.[92]

But there were other forces at work. There were, first of all, features of BUF policy which predisposed it towards a concentration upon Jews. In common with other British Fascist groups the BUF placed a stress upon Britain for the British. This was a prominent feature of the movement's response to 'the crisis', as it called the economic, social and political upheavals of 1929–31 which had led to its birth. This message was clearly spelt out in speeches[93] and also in *The Greater Britain*, where Mosley commented:

> We work to organize the Modern Movement in this country by British methods in a form which is suitable to the characteristics of Great Britain. We are essentially a national movement, and if our policy could be summarized in two words, they would be 'Britain First'.[94]

In short Fascism was presented as within the mainstream of British interests and tradition. A similar theme was apparent in many aspects of BUF literature, such as *Britain and Jewry* and F. D. Hill's *'Gainst Trust and Monopoly*.[95] It is not impossible, of course, for Jews like many other minorities to identify themselves with a policy of 'Britain First' – as indeed they have with 'Germany First'. The insecurity of some minority racial and ethnic groups can make them more royalist than the king, more nationalistic than the nationals, but the tendency displayed by some sections of Jewish communities in the Diaspora to retain their own distinctive culture and forms of social organization has served at times as a magnetizing factor in attracting the attention of nationalistic groups and created complications for some sections of Jews in terms of ultimate loyalties. For instance, Fascist hostility to the projected Jewish boycott of German goods in the 1930s has to be considered in this kind of context.[96] Jews, as members of a democratic society, had a perfect right to exert pressures for such a boycott.[97] But it is equally true that Fascists had an equivalent right to oppose such policies if they ran counter to their political outlook and what they interpreted as the nation's interest. And it is easy to grasp how this issue could be used to question Jewish loyalties. Accepting this, however, does not justify the violence towards Jews by means of which this policy conflict was partly expressed.[98]

There was another powerful strand of BUF policy which would incline the BUF into conflict with Jews against the general background of the world crisis and depression. This was the movement's opposition to finance capital. Hostility towards the City and a suspicion of finance which featured in the thought of many economic reformers, as well as in other sections of British Fascism,[99] were outstanding characteristics of Mosley's economic thinking from the early 1920s and he continued to refer during his Fascist years to an antithesis between productive and financial capital. In his opinion, many of the activities of the City of London were disastrous to national interests:

> In every struggle between producer and financial interest in recent years, the latter power has been triumphant to the detriment of the national interest. In fact, we have within the nation a power, largely controlled by alien elements, which arrogates to itself a power above the State, and has used that influence to drive flaccid governments of all parties along the high road to

> national disaster. No state can tolerate within its body the irresponsible superiority of such a power, nor the policy inimical to every productive interest which it has pursued.[100]

This was a point of view reflected in other BUF publications by, among others, Raven Thomson,[101] William Joyce[102] and the anonymous author of *Britain and Jewry*.[103] It was present in Fascist groups outside the BUF as well as in High Tory patriotic circles.[104] This finance power was characterized with greater or lesser degrees of directness as Jewish and such an accusation could attain a specious reality on account of the prominence of certain Jews in liquidity occupations and, more particularly, the historical constellation of Jewish interests within merchant banking and related activities.[105] In common with others who raised this fear, concern was also expressed that this financial power spilled over into the press and other media interests which, it was further argued, were employed against national interests and indeed, were actively involved in undermining the nation's strength.[106]

In short, it is possible to argue that the clash between the Fascists and Jews, which was present as early as 1933, although it was repressed at times for political convenience, possessed an interacting social dimension which a concentration upon the psychological make-up of certain anti-semites should not be allowed to obscure. But such pressures by themselves do not explain the BUF's significant involvement in anti-semitism. It is important to stress that anti-semitism was present in the BUF from the beginning. It was part of its nationalist, patriotic response to the world crisis and depression. But from 1934 it became a more significant element, although between then and 1939 its importance was subject to variation. In accounting for its elevation within the BUF programme we need to take account of a complex situation. As the economy began to stabilize, the BUF started to place less weight on the economic aspects of its programme and to emphasize other related issues. And this was taking place at a time when there was a growing German influence over the movement which was particularly apparent in foreign policy matters, as a result of which the BUF could argue for an alignment with Germany in the face of oriental Bolshevism and international finance. It was out of this combination of circumstances that anti-semitism was given greater prominence.[107]

With this general background in mind attention might now be turned to an explanation of why the BUF chose to launch its anti-semitic crusade in the East End. A common interpretation of this move is that Mosley sought out the East End and used the tactic of anti-semitism in order to boost his flagging movement.[108] Both nuances are suspect. Apart from the fact that, as just mentioned, the drive towards anti-semitism generally possessed more positive features, it needs to be emphasized that sections of the East End also reached out for Mosley.[109] The East End was not in fact some kind of inert mass waiting to be picked up and moulded by Mosley; what developed was a symbiotic relationship between the two. Why, we might ask, did this occur?

In considering this we need to recognize not only the forces already referred to but additionally those factors which were special to the East End. This area was still characterized by the existence of major social problems. We know that the industrial depression of the early 1930s was particularly acute in east London and unemployment and short time working had forced earnings in some trades below the poverty line. This was particularly the case in tailoring, furriery and cabinet making.[110] But it was not simply that the economic depression had struck hard in east London. The East End also had the ambience of a forgotten land, a slab of urban neglect, whose inhabitants exerted little power and influence. This was nothing new. We have already noticed that the social problems discovered at the heart of the Empire in the late Victorian and Edwardian years encouraged young social reformers to interest themselves in the East End, just as guilt-ridden, well brought up young Americans involved themselves in 'the negro question' in the 1960s. But flesh is grass and commitment can be transient and, in the case of east London, reformers had come and gone but life seemed little changed.[111] People faced the future because they had survived an existence in the past. In place of all this, as an answer to their frustration, Mosley offered them the BUF, and a concern for their social problems: it was an offer which had an undoubted appeal to certain sections of East society. It was, of course, never intended as an appeal to disadvantaged Jews in the East End, those who had failed to 'make it' to the gilded ghettos of London. They were counted among the enemy.

Mosley also involved himself with more than a depressed and neglected part of the capital when he raised his standard in the East End. He was moving into the old area of Jewish immigration where there were still folk memories of past campaigns against Jews.[112] Indeed, he was moving into an East End which was still in some quarters visibly Jewish. 'It was as if a piece of Jewish East Europe had been torn up and put down again in the middle of East London,'[113] and a glimpse of the situation in some areas can be obtained from the comments of Dr Harry Roberts, a well respected medical practitioner, who had lived in the East End for almost thirty years. In 1936 he wrote:

> Mile End, in which I live, differs in many important respects from most of its neighbouring districts. Its peculiar relevance to recent disturbances – sufficiently exciting to gain considerable newspaper notoriety – lies in the fact that its population is made up of members of two very different races, in numbers fairly evenly balanced. . . . Steadily the Jews have spread eastwards; and I have seen street after street in Mile End which were, even twenty or so years ago, almost wholly occupied by 'Gentiles', progressively occupied by Jews until almost every house in the street, including every little corner shop has come to be in Jewish occupation. The Jews are much more clannish than the natives whom they have so largely replaced; what they want to buy, they prefer to buy from Jews; when they have a post to fill they prefer to fill it with a Jew. Exclusiveness and nationalism are not peculiar to Aryans; indeed, in matters of intermarriage with neighbours of a different 'faith', the Jews have set an example which the Hitlerites have imitated. Few of us worry about whether we have a drop of German or Dutch or Scandinavian blood in our veins, and few English people mind a substantial streak of

> Semitism or other orientalism in their make-up. But the orthodox Jew will have none of it. What endless interviews and arguments I have devoted to Jewish parents in an effort to induce them to see that their cosmopolitan-minded daughters have not committed the ultimate sin against the Semitic equivalent of the Holy Ghost in falling in love with a worthy young Gentile clerk with whom they work in some City Office! Even when I have sought and obtained the sympathetic collaboration of an intelligent rabbi, my efforts have ended in failure. If one is to understand the present situation and the recent outbreaks of insult and violence, it is necessary to bear in mind these circumstances.[114]

Magnitude of numbers is not significant in this context: the concentration within specific areas is a more powerful force and, although the East End Jewish population had declined in size since the high peak of immigration from Russia, resentment at what was perceived as a takeover of certain areas clearly existed as a result of a Jewish concentration in particular parts of the East End and the BUF tapped this.[115]

The economic concentration and separateness of Jews also needs to be considered alongside these cultural-geographical forces. Jewish workers tended to be employed by Jewish employers in small scale concerns and the fact that the Jewish proletariat was exploited by Jewish capitalists did not automatically create a link with other East End labour. Complaints about Jewish sweating and undercutting which had been heard at the time of immigration from the Russian Empire were still being made, and there was a tendency to stereotype Jewish employers as being intent upon the ruin of British businesses.[116] It has been written that 'the complaints about Jewish competition show surprisingly little variation over time,'[117] and issues raised during the immigration years were certainly present again in the 1930s in tailoring, the furniture trade and the grocery business.[118]

So where does all this lead us? Anti-semitism was certainly a useful tactical weapon; by stressing its opposition to the world force of Jewry the BUF could increase its own importance; by putting the Jew in the forefront of capitalism the anti-capitalist sting of the BUF was removed and there was more prospect of it drawing support from right and left; finally, by concentrating upon the foreignness of the Jew the BUF could try to overcome the foreignness of its own ideology.[119] But the situation was more complex than this and requires us to take notice of both individual psychologies and social structure and indeed the interaction between these two forces.[120] It is almost certainly true that some individuals in the BUF became involved in anti-semitism because a hatred of Jews was central to the functioning of their personality and the particular social and political circumstances of their time encouraged the expression of their hostility. In short, we need to acknowledge that there were individuals within the BUF whose psychological make-up was probably similar to that of other anti-semites such as H. H. Beamish, Leese, and that early Jew-hater, Joseph Banister.[121]

But an explanation also needs to recognize the general importance of social pressures. Consequently, in referring to the BUF's campaign against Jews we have tried to suggest that an understanding of the movement's anti-semitism needs to take account of an existing tradition of anti-semitism in Britain. This was particularly important in the case of the East End campaign. But added to this was the predisposition towards anti-semitism which was present within the BUF as a result of the ideology it evolved in response to the crisis of 1929–31, which was likely to bring it into conflict with certain Jewish interests in the East End and elsewhere. The significance of these sets of pressures grew in importance and became openly manifest after 1934. However, in the course of the intensified anti-semitic campaign mounted by the BUF after that date this base of the conflict, which contained an identifiable core of grievances, gave rise to a 'superstructure' which had a more tenuous relation to reality. As the German influence got to work the illusions of those who were severely prejudiced against Jews, individuals like Joyce and Chesterton, began to weave their own idiosyncratic patterns, with the result that other elements, in some instances 'pathological fantasies disguised as ideas', became injected into the conflict.[122] In Joyce's case, for instance, the whole East End problem was related to Jewry.[123] And even the rational Mosley erected an edifice of spurious accusations – the assertion that international finance was Jewish; that charge that Jews were driving Britain to war;[124] the claim that Jews were the power behind the political system. In short, a set of identifiable issues was transcended and a veritable Pandora's box of fantasies was opened up.[125] And what this might have produced, in different circumstances, can be gleaned from a discussion of the solution to the Jewish question. The BUF never basically solved the question of how the Jews should be treated. Although Mosley could allude to the exclusion of Jews from Britain, he made little reference to a solution of the Jewish question. However, for others this was regarded as 'a matter of life and death for our people'.[126] And against that kind of background, anti-semitism could be treated as a natural biological urge:

> Anti-semitism is intrinsically a normal reaction to the anti-social activities habitually practised by the alien.... Exactly as the human blood stream, infected by a poisonous bacillus, responds by mustering devourers to attack and eliminate the invader, so does a race conscious community at once mobilize its forces to fight the alien influences which instinct teaches would imperil its very existence.[127]

These sentiments and imagery convey their own message – and where they could have led in different historical circumstances requires no great leap of the imagination.

12 Attack and counter-attack

So far our attention has been concentrated upon anti-semitic thought and the background which encouraged and sustained it. But if we accept that thought can be translated into action, that those who philosophize about the world can also attempt to change it or preserve it in their own image, we need to consider the possibility of aggressive action being directed against Jews as well as the emergence of an organized opposition to such forces.

Since Mosley's movement made the most significant attempt to convert anti-semitic thought into action, the activity of the BUF is singled out for analysis. Physical attacks upon Jews became a prominent feature of British anti-semitism in the 1930s and social violence increased considerably in 1936 when the BUF started its campaign in east London.[1] Leeds and Manchester were also chosen as target areas but neither received the attention which was lavished upon the East End and consequently an emphasis will be placed upon what happened there, as the area 'become a spasmodically used but nevertheless active battleground'.[2] Mosley's campaign in the East End reflected an increasing interest in anti-semitism by the BUF, as a result of which it was brought closer to the centre of British political life. Consequently, after discussing the events in east London an attempt will be made to explain why organized anti-semitism was contained and did not prove to be an avenue to political power. Finally, the reactions of the Jewish community to this growing menace to its own position will be considered, concentrating particularly upon the counter-attack planned under the aegis of the Board of Deputies.

Once the BUF moved towards anti-semitism, for reasons we have already discussed, the East End was a potentially fertile area for its activities. Some reference to these local pressures has also been made but at this point the main stresses might be repeated.[3] There was, first of all, a tradition of hostility which had developed during the immigration years and the First World War.[4] But there were more immediate influences. Almost one third of Britain's Jewish population lived in the East End and a pronounced Jewish culture was present there. The Jewish inhabitants of the area 'were mainly foreign immigrants who had come in about the turn of the century and who remained largely unassimilated.... There were Yiddish newspapers, Yiddish shops, a Yiddish theatre.'[5] In addition, there were housing and unemployment problems which, in much popular opinion, could not be disentangled easily from the Jewish presence in the area. Although improvements had occurred since the late nineteenth century, particularly in the housing sector, complaints about Jews buying up property, raising rents and forcing native East Enders into overcrowded conditions were still prevalent. A pronounced concept of rootedness was held by many working class East Enders and, in their view their sense of neighbourhood stability had been threatened by the influx of Jews.[6] Complaints about unemployment also echoed those of the immigration years and the image of the situation perceived by those who were hostile to Jews was something along these lines:

> On the one side there is the native artisan or merchant, not very bright or enterprising perhaps, but solid, hard-working and competent (on his own valuation). On the other side, there is the pushful Jew, who comes in and steals the business by superior cunning and flagrant disregard of custom and etiquette, soliciting trade instead of waiting patiently for it to come to him, entrapping his customers by slick advertising patter, dealing with all forms of merchandise instead of sticking to one line, price cutting shamelessly, and perhaps above all, 'sticking together' – at any rate until the Gentile has been driven out.[7]

These sentiments were an almost precise echo of what had been heard in the East End at the time of the great immigration, thirty, forty or fifty years earlier.

Once the BUF started its campaign it succeeded in attracting support and it has been underlined that attempts to dismiss this as nothing more than 'a function of psychological disturbance in the individuals concerned'[8] or as the loutish activities of a *lumpen proletariat* 'are not convincing'.[9] The *Jewish Chronicle* and the East End Communists were both aware that the Fascists could collect support because they offered some hope to sections of the East End which considered that they were socially disadvantaged.[10] In this sense the BUF and sections of the East End came together: each saw a usefulness in the other. But this still leaves unanswered the question: why should the union of the BUF and East End have assumed a dimension of violence? From the beginning there was within the BUF an element which found in violence an outlet for its sadism[11] and it is quite possible that the failure of the orthodox campaign – evidenced by the reaction to the 1934 Olympia meeting and the inability in the same year to maintain Lord Rothermere's support – encouraged this strain of hostility. In order to understand why such an approach could find support in the East End we need to remember that group violence often occurs when conflict has not been resolved through non-violent and institutionalized channels.[12] This is of direct relevance to the East End situation. A view of east London as a neglected area was certainly present at the time of the immigration from Russia[13] and we have recently been reminded that the area's social and economic problems during the inter-war years, 'had their roots in inadequate social control'.[14] No one in authority seemed to care consistently about the area's problems. In these circumstances it was possible for the East Ender to feel that he was 'a forgotten man'.[15] Might it not also encourage some to believe that if improvements in their lives could not be obtained through conventional channels there was nevertheless a chance that unorthodox pressures against what was to them an identifiable source of their problems, that is the Jews in east London, might be more successful?

Whereas the reasons for the appeal of violence to some East Enders still require further consideration, the Fascists' responsibility for this episode in social aggression has received much more attention. In the three years following 1935 'stories repeatedly appeared of Fascist atrocities, numerous delegations called on the home secretary imploring him to take action, and Jews were described as living in a state of panic and hysteria.' All this was referred to in the press as the 'Fascist terror' and has provided a fulcrum around which historical accounts have been based.[16] More recently, however, an attempt has been made to modify the stresses present in earlier analyses. The Metropolitan Police archives provide evidence of Jew baiting activities from January 1936 onwards and, on the basis of these, it has been argued that Fascists and Jews engaged in assaults on each other and traffic in violence was certainly not all in one direction.[17] In other words, it has been suggested that the East End struggle needs to be considered within an interactionist or convergence perspective.

It is apparent from police reports that some of the violence was basically nothing more than 'brawls between groups of teenagers' catharsisizing the frustrations of youth.[18] But a flashpoint of more socially significant violence came at the time of Fascist meetings and processions. These were attended by Jews and other anti-Fascists with the distinct object of disrupting the proceedings. Hence it has been written:

> Of the 1,075 people arrested in the East End between January 1936 and December 1938 for disturbances arising out of meetings and processions, 352 were Fascists and 723 were anti-Fascists. The vast majority of the disturbances leading to these arrests took place at Fascist meetings and processions. On the other hand, at only a very few anti-Fascist meetings was there any interruption of any importance by Fascists or their sympathizers. This was not because Fascists lacked support or sympathy in the East End . . . but because breaking up opponents' meetings was not a tactic of the BU, whereas it was of the Communist Party.[19]

It was not simply that the Fascists incited violence by their undoubtedly provocative speeches – considerable abuse could be uttered without a technical break of the law – but also that young intellectuals hostile to Fascism, groups associated with the Communist Party and a number of Jewish organizations, such as the Jewish People's Council against Fascism and Anti-Semitism, a Communist front organization, were dedicated to silencing the BUF at a time when the Board of Deputies preferred to fight Fascism by quieter means.[20]

The most publicized disruption of Fascist activity occurred on the occasion of the march culminating in what has become known as the Battle of Cable Street on 4 October 1936. The march was intended to assert Fascist ideas and policy in London, particularly in the East End, along a route which took in Shoreditch, Limehouse, Bow and Bethnal Green. The erection of barricades in Cable Street in Stepney and the inability of the police to clear a way for Mosley's men have often been referred to and there is no need to go over the ground again. It is sufficient to say that the incident has been variously proclaimed as a victory over Fascism and intolerance, or from the Fascist point of view, as a failure by the state to deal with 'Jewish rabble' in the streets of London.[21]

In meetings and processions, therefore, the BUF confronted opposing forces in the East End and irreconcilable differences were proclaimed on either side. Such confrontations between Fascists and their political opponents were not of course confined to the East End even if the best known took place there. Oxford, Manchester, Hull, Leeds and Sheffield all witnessed violent meetings. In the East End, however, the Jewish factor was never far from the centre of the BUF's campaigning activity and this became further apparent in the 1937 municipal elections. The electioneering began in February 1937. Alexander Raven-Thomson and E. G. 'Mick' Clarke stood in Bethnal Green North East; Anne Brock Griggs and Charles Wegg Prosser were the candidates in Limehouse and William Joyce and Jim Bailey put up for Shoreditch. All these seats were Labour held and the BUF managed to win none of them. Even so, in the March elections it captured 23 per cent of the votes in Bethnal Green, 19 per cent in Limehouse and 14 per cent in Shoreditch and it must be remembered that many of Mosley's young supporters would not be householders and would therefore have been ineligible for the vote.[22] In the course of the campaign some of the candidates ensured that a strong anti-semitic flavour was injected into the proceedings. According to Special Branch observers, who had been busy compiling reports of Fascist speeches and activity since 1936 as well as infiltrating Mosley's organization, the theme of the British Union campaign was 'to attack semitism, international financiers (alleged to be Jews), Jewish landlordism in the East End, shopkeepers, employers of labour, and Jewish members of the LCC'.[23] In many instances, in fact, the campaign was cast along the lines: who controls the East End, the Britons or the Jews? This is not to suggest that anti-semitism eclipsed every other issue. Attacks were made on Labour's housing record and there were deliberate attempts to capture the Catholic vote. All this spelt defeat for William Joyce who would have couched the campaign in entirely anti-semitic terms but even so the BUF programme 'was based primarily on anti-semitism'.[24] It was an appeal which took votes mainly from the Liberals and anti-socialists rather than from Labour, which could be translated to mean that however much popularity Mosley might have had in the East End, at this stage it was clearly insufficient to effect a transformation or significant shift in traditional working-class political allegiances. Whether or not this would have been remedied in 1940 is impossible to say; the municipal elections of that year never took place. By then east London had wider issues on its mind.[25]

This activity, it has been emphasized, was part of the growing involvement of the BUF in anti-semitism and we might now try to explain why the BUF's general campaign did not bring the political fruits which were anticipated. In an existing analysis two major stresses have been brought forward to explain this. First of all, it has been contended that in Britain 'a distressed or tension-ridden situation' was absent.[26] Secondly, it has been suggested that some consideration needs to be given to the actions of the police and the government. In other words, in contrast to what happened in other countries, the law was not abandoned in the face of Fascist challenges.[27]

What are we to make of these claims? There was considerable economic distress in the inter-war years, particularly following the world crisis and depression of 1929–31 and the fact that it was localized and concentrated in the old areas of Britain's industrial strength should not allow us to forget it. But, although there was distress in this sense, Britain survived the crisis of the 1930s without making any structural changes. Indeed, the National Government symbolized a willingness at the level of power politics to close ranks in the preservation of the social-political system.[28] In Britain there was a long history of parliamentary democracy which, over time, had displayed a degree of flexibility and a capacity for absorption which had guaranteed its self-preservation and continuity.[29] And this system continued to show its resilience in the inter-war years. The contrast, in this respect, between Britain and Germany during the years 1929–33 is a sharp one and it is worth remembering that the extent of the economic problem in Germany in terms of the percentage rate of unemployment was roughly the same as in Britain, although the descent into it was more rapid and tension was aggravated by its more even geographical spread and memories of the war years and their immediate consequences.[30] This stability of British society assumed an importance since anti-semitism in the 1920s and 1930s was associated with a threat to existing structures and it was the durability of the system which enabled pressures to be brought to bear upon those who challenged the state through the agency of anti-semitism.[31] And, after the mid-1930s of course, the National Government was operating in a context of rising living standards for those in work, recovery in the new light-industrial sector and some revival in the old staple industries. In other words, the economy began to move in the government's favour – although localized unemployment remained significant – and the converse of this was that the BUF was working against a generally unfavourable background as anti-semitism became a more central feature of policy. Consequently, although Mosley continued to believe in a crisis which would bring him to power, like an irritating mirage it kept disappearing from view.

In this sense Mandle has rightly emphasized: 'The times were against Mosley.'[32] In extending this argument in support of the claim that a tension-ridden situation was absent in Britain, he proceeds to argue that we should recognize not only the existence of a stable political structure in Britain but also that mysterious entity, national character. This too, it is asserted, worked against Mosley. But we should be wary of attempts to discuss historical issues in terms of a 'cultural tradition' as if we are all heirs to some kind of homogeneous conditioning process in the course of which, like Pavlov's dogs, we learn the correct responses. There is a powerful strand of thought in the liberal social sciences which would assume of imply something along these lines and which remarks on the emergence of inner anxiety and public embarrassment when these norms are knowingly contravened.[33] But there is no such thing as a monolithic cultural tradition, in this instance one which proclaims a belief in toleration towards minorities. For instance, the cultural assumptions held by sections of the working class at any time are often at variance with those which guide the behaviour of the middle-class 'opinion makers'. On close examination, in fact, the concept of a national culture, a cultural tradition, disintegrates into different traditions. Thus in the East End little restraint was shown by BUF leaders like Mick Clarke who found it easy to operate outside the conventions of contemporary politics,[34] whereas by contrast, Mosley, a calculating politician, versed in the system even if he rebelled against it, could display more self-restraint and allowed only an occasional raw emotional streak of anti-semitism to appear.[35]

What is significant in this context, however, is the fact that although some individuals within the power elite shared the general non-theoretical hostility towards Jews which was present in Britain, the mainstream tradition in British society rejected the public expression of anti-semitism and those in power showed no inclination to base policy on it.[36] Both before the First World War and afterwards such circumstances helped to restrict or limit the influence of anti-semitism in Britain. In short, there was a tradition, deriving from the historical development of liberalism, which placed limits upon the expression and influence of anti-semitism, but it would be unwise to assume that it was universally accepted and dangerous to discuss it as some kind of autonomous, universal force inhering within the nation. In fact, it needs to be considered as a product of a particular set of social circumstances and ultimately open to the prospect of change, even if possessed of considerable resilience and durability.[37] If, for instance, the BUF had assumed power there would soon have been a different tradition in existence. But the nature of the crisis in Britain and the strength of the historically evolved social-political system withstood the Fascist assault whether from the BUF or other groups and, as already mentioned, one consequence of this was that the central authorities played a positive role in combating the BUF's anti-semitism.

This leads into the second stage of the discussion relating to the containment of organized anti-semitism in Britain. Work on the relative levels of violence in race relations in Britain and the United States has clearly demonstrated that the role of the central authorities can be of crucial significance in preventing social tension being translated into violence and this has an undoubted relevance to the BUF's campaign both inside and outside the East End.[38] But what was the attitude of the authorities? A Home Office view was that democratic rights could extend to the opponents of democracy. As long as they did not break the law, Fascists were to be accorded the same scope for action as any other political movement. However, a sense of urgency was displayed by the commissioner of the Metropolitan Police who, from an early date, pressed for government action to control Fascist activities. But it was not until July 1936 that the police received instructions to deal with Fascist and anti-Fascist agitation in general and anti-Jewish agitation in particular.[39] And, once in possession of such powers, the police tended to use their authority mainly against the anti-Fascists, since it was they who were responsible for stirring up agitation against the well organized Fascists, and their activity often contravened the framework of the law, whereas Fascists could pursue their political tactics at this stage without much legal restraint. In addition, there is evidence that the police not only permitted a great deal of anti-semitic propaganda to go unchallenged but also engaged in unnecessary violence against anti-Fascists.[40] There must be a suspicion, indeed, that among certain officers there was some sympathy towards the Fascists, although in understanding police behaviour it also has to be recognized that resources were stretched to the limit and they were having to cope with a new type of situation. Nevertheless, in spite of some shortcomings the police almost certainly helped to control the East End situation and they were backed in this by government legislation.

Under pressure, particularly after the Battle of Cable Street, the government took action and decided in 1936 to introduce the Public Order Act in an attempt to defend the conventional liberal order against those who abused its openness. The Battle of Cable Street took place on 4 October 1936, the Public Order Bill was introduced into Parliament on 10 November and it became law in the following month. In its details the Act enabled the authorities to take action against the wearing of uniforms for political purposes, it proscribed quasi-military organizations and it gave the police power to ban processions for up to three months with the consent of the home secretary. A person who acted in a disorderly fashion at a lawful public meeting was made liable to arrest, the possession of offensive weapons at public meetings and processions was prohibited and the law against insulting or abusive language likely to lead to a breach of the peace was restated.[41]

The Public Order Act signalled the intention of the authorities to defend the traditional concept of law and order against any attempt to challenge the right of the state to have a monopoly over force and, in the process, victimize one section of the population. And the authorities were prepared to do this even if some civil liberties had to be curtailed. The Act did not prevent the outbreak of disorder as a matter of course, nor did it halt Fascist or anti-Fascist activities. And, of course, it did nothing specifically to stop the anti-semitic agitation by the Fascists which had been occupying police officers before the Act was passed. What it did do, however, was to take away the Fascist uniforms without which the BUF seemed less impressively organized. In addition, and of crucial significance, the BUF was denied the right to engage in their provocative marches through the East End by means of which local resentment could be channelled towards Jews and anti-semitism could be kept on the boil. The consequence was that while there seems to have been a bias against the left within the police and, among certain ranks, some sympathy with the Fascists, it was the latter who felt the major weight of the 1936 Act. Almost all prosecutions brought under it were directed against members of the BUF.[42]

What made control over BUF anti-semitism more effective than it might otherwise have been was a willingness in certain Fascist circles to work within the law. While exploiting the political situation, it is clear that some forces within the BUF were prepared to adhere to the letter of the law.[43] On the specific question of attacks upon Jews similar evidence of restraint was also apparent. In July 1936, for instance, great care was being taken not to overstep the mark in making anti-Jewish comments and an even greater caution was present in August, possibly on account of the presence of Special Branch shorthand writers implementing the surveillance instructions which the police had just been given. But, in addition to these influences, other pressures were at work. The impending trial at the Central Criminal Court of Arnold Leese for statements in the *Fascist* relating to Jews exercised an effect and it was in such circumstances that it was remarked:

> The British Union of Fascists [Sir Oswald Mosley] has given a definite warning to its speakers to refrain from attacking the Jews at public meetings, it being emphasized that arrests of its members for Jew baiting is likely to do the Fascist movement in this country more harm than good.[44]

However, such a policy could not be absolutely maintained. At this time there were sections within the BUF which were anxious to raise the level of tension between Jews and non-Jews in the East End, even though BUF headquarters was opposed to this.[45] It was, of course, forces of the former kind which became prominent within the movement at the time of the 1937 municipal elections in the East End when, as already noticed, the BUF campaign assumed an anti-semitic flavour. In these circumstances rabid firebrands like 'Mick' Clarke and William Joyce were particularly difficult to restrain.[46] Control over such factions was not easily achieved and it was equally impossible to prevent hooligan elements deriving inspiration from Fascist activity and engaging in their own brands of anti-semitism, ranging from graffiti to physcial assault.[47] Ultimately, of course, responsibility for such developments within the BUF leads back to the leadership, just as it remains accountable for the anti-semitism of its press.[48]

In addition to these general forces which have already been mentioned as restricting the BUF's anti-semitic campaign certain local elements need to be considered. Like most of the other variables under consideration they should be regarded as helping to account for the lack of success of Fascism as well as explaining the more specific issue of why the political anti-semitism of the BUF was successfully contained. Significant in this connection in the East End was the activity of the Stepney Communist Party under the leadership of Phil Piratin.[49] We have already commented upon the BUF's tactic in capitalizing upon the East Ender as a forgotten man.[50] Piratin's reply was to remove the bait and, in line with this strategy, the Stepney Tenants' Defence League was formed to combat the difficulties which the BUF exploited. One of its activities was to organize rent strikes and, although the organization obtained support from Jews, Jewish landlords were among those selected as targets in the campaign. On another front Mosley's attempt to capitalize upon the unemployment situation was counteracted by transferring a branch of the National Unemployed Workers' Movement into the area. In short, the social grievances which Mosley could exploit and turn against Jews began to be tackled by these rival forces.[51]

Action of this kind was merely one instance of opposition within the East End to combat Fascism. In 1936, for instance, the Council of Citizens of East London was formed and the same year witnessed the formation of the East London Anti-Fascist United Committee. But, if we return to Piratin's activity, this particular strand of opposition has to be considered within the context of the broader reaction of the Communist Party towards Fascism. And in discussing this it needs to be stressed that while the Communists could pose as champions of Jewish interests, in effect the party was less concerned with the Jews than with the principle of attacking Fascism. It so happened that an attack upon one coincided with a defence of the interests of the other. But throughout the Fascist offensive the CP never forgot that the wider interests of the working class took precedence over those of ethnic interests. The real union was that of all the exploited, irrespective of ethnic origin, against all the exploiters, whoever they might be – hence the attack upon Jewish landlords by the Stepney Tenants' Defence League.[52]

On the basis of the evidence so far it might be suggested that the reasons why organized anti-semitism did not take root in Britain in the 1930s reflected a number of interacting social pressures. Vague reference to a cultural tradition, to the essential civility of the British, as if such a quality hung sanctimoniously over the land, leads nowhere. Britain did not have an exemplary record in its treatment of all the ethnic and racial minorities living under its government and the official toleration of Jews was quite compatible with the gross exploitation and dehumanization of other ethnic and racial groups, particularly external subordinate groups. Indeed, it might be asked, although no firm evidence is forthcoming, whether the transfer of aggression into colonial territories – after all, as Orwell suggested, niggers did not count – might have reduced ethnic tensions in Britain. But to return to firmer ground. The major influence in the inter-war years which restricted the impact of organized anti-semitism was the fact that the state did not fall apart in the wake of the world economic crisis. Consequently in Britain, which by the 1930s had a long official tradition of hostility towards Jews, the state was able to turn its power against those who raised the challenge of anti-semitism as part of a threat to its continued existence. Special Branch surveillance, the general deployment of the police and the passing of the 1936 Public Order Act were major devices used by what Mosley called the old gang, the exhausted volcanoes of the twentieth century, in their task of combating Fascism and Fascist anti-semitism. And support for such a policy was forthcoming from groups in society which had their own quarrels with Fascism, organizations such as the CP, the Jewish People's Council and the Council of Citizens of East London, all of which helped, in varying degrees, to control anti-semitism in the East End.

Mention of the Jewish People's Council is a reminder that the BUF's drive towards anti-semitism created far more of a potential problem for the Jewish community than the activities of any of the marginal Fascist groups in Britain and it was in this kind of situation that Anglo-Jewry began to organize itself officially to combat the threat of anti-semitism. The Board of Deputies established a defence committee in July 1936 which, while anxious about East End developments, conceived its role as defending Jewish interests on a broader, more general front. As a body, the defence committee had to face the opposition of the more militant defenders of Jewish interests and, in its turn, was constantly trying to undermine the work of the Jewish People's Council, which was active in the East End, and establish itself as the sole mouthpiece of the Jewish community.[53] The Board's activity might be regarded as representing the policy of the Jewish establishment and, in conjunction with the other forces we have been considering, it helped in the general containment of the anti-semitic campaign of the 1930s. With these prefatory remarks we might begin to discuss the role of the Board of Deputies in such developments.

The Board had been slow to move in the face of the threat of Fascist anti-semitism and, throughout, it never lost its faith in the capacity of the state authorities to deal with the problem. Its own role was conceived in terms of striking a nice balance between Jewish and national interests and an indication of the delicate situation in which the defence committee believed it had to operate was provided in the report prepared by its ex-secretary, Sidney Salomon.[54] In this it is possible to detect the wish of the Board not to place Jewish above national interests and its simultaneous intention to expose the Fascist threat as involving more than Jews.[55] Against such a background the Board operated on four fronts. It exercised indirect pressure on government officials and others; it sponsored apologetics; it involved itself in self-criticism to reduce the objective causes of anti-semitism; and, finally, it engaged in urgent appeals to Jews to avoid getting caught up in disorders.

Its greatest efforts were centred upon the publication of apologetics, which were full of a faith in reason and a belief that it was possible to tap what it regarded as the essential toleration of the British.[56] Donations of books on aspects of Jewish life were made to the churches and, apart from this, the actual publication of material was undertaken, articles were placed in the press, books which combated anti-semitism were distributed and the defence committee gave financial backing to certain publications. For instance, it supported Louis Golding's *The Jewish Problem* as well as *The Folly of Anti-Semitism* by Sidney Dark and Herbert Sidebotham. It purchased and distributed James Parkes's *The Jew and His Neighbour* and John Gwyer's attack on *The Protocols* which appeared as *Portraits of Mean Men*. In addition, the publications sub-committee reproduced and distributed George Lansbury's article on 'Anti-Semitism in the East End' which was written originally for the *Spectator*, and was generally responsible for a long list of publications which defended Jews against anti-semitic charges and simultaneously stressed the Jewish contribution to British life.[57]

Other avenues of communication were exploited. The BBC undertook to submit scripts of any programme on Jewish interests to the defence committee and the working relationship between the Corporation and the committee was such that Sidney Salomon commented that there was 'an almost complete elimination of anything unsatisfactory or objectionable in BBC programmes'.[58] The defence committee also attempted to ensure that there was no representation of anti-semitism on the stage and, on a more positive note, help was given to pro-Jewish productions such as *Jerusalem* by I. Masade which was put on at the Playhouse Theatre, London, under a financial guarantee from the trustees of the Board of Deputies.[59] In addition, speakers were organized by the Board to combat Fascist attacks and schooled in the techniques of political oratory and crowd management, in order that they could effectively present the Jewish case.[60]

While engaging in this activity the Board exerted pressure to prevent the dissemination of anti-semitic ideas in the press. Consequently, apart from trying unsuccessfully to persuade the *Jewish Chronicle* to give less prominence to the opinions expressed in *Blackshirt*, the Board became concerned about the *Catholic Times* and *Truth*, believing that both of them engaged in anti-semitism. The former was regarded as exhibiting sympathy for Nazi ideals in its editorial and correspondence columns and generally displaying an attitude of hostility towards Jews. The defence committee tried to combat this. 'We felt it right', Salomon wrote, 'after having made every reasonable effort to persuade it to change its attitude, to approach the Catholic authorities on this subject.' Consequently, under the cover of an organization called the Kulturkampf which was concerned with fighting the Nazi attack on religion, a deputation on which the defence committee was represented was received by the private secretary to Cardinal Hinsley, Cardinal Archbishop of Westminster, in January 1938. It was pointed out by Hinsley that censorship of the Catholic press did not take place except in relation to matters involving faith and morals. But after the meeting the defence committee received a letter from the cardinal's private secretary to the effect that steps had been taken which, it was hoped, would modify attitudes along the lines desired by the deputation. After this the view of the defence committee was that the paper was no longer characterized by a hostility towards Jews.[61]

But the defence committee did not win all its battles and no satisfaction was expressed over its efforts to reduce the anti-semitism appearing in *Truth*.[62] However, it was successful in preventing the *National Citizen* from falling under the influence of H. H. Beamish and changing from a patriotic Conservative journal into an anti-semitic one, as appeared to be happening in 1937. At this point the journal was making references to the ideals of Bolshevism being consonant with those of Judaism. It was publishing Lientenant Colonel A. H. Lane's reflections on 'Alien Penetration' which displayed a clear anti-Jewish bias and advertising anti-semitic literature, including publications of the Imperial Fascist League.[63] And this was followed in May 1937 by a block advertisement outlining the programme of the Britons.[64] Furthermore, in the following month Meriel Buchanan, a regular columnist, wrote in support of *The Protocols*. Sceptics might scoff, she asserted, 'but can even the most unbelieving among them deny that the resolutions laid down therein have not been most thoroughly – we might almost say miraculously – carried out.'[65] It was this kind of development which worried the defence committee. In view of such tendencies the secretary wrote: 'We made contact with certain members of the National Citizens' Union including the Duchess of Atholl with the final result that the extremist group was defeated and the National Citizens' Union returned to its original allegiance.'[66]

As a supplement to such activity the Board, through the defence committee, engaged in disseminating information on individuals who were regarded as anti-semitic. It did this in the South Peebles constituency of Captain A. H. M. Ramsay and also passed information on him to the Home Office and Special Branch.[67] The Home Office and police were also provided with reports from informers acting for the defence committee who managed to infiltrate the BUF, the Militant Christian Patriots and the Nordic League.[68] By its nature, of course, none of this work could be readily apparent to Jews living in east London.[69]

The other aspect of the Board's work involved attempts to improve the image of the Jewish community either through self criticism or influences upon personal behaviour. It was such considerations which resulted in attention being given to the question of 'bad' Jewish employers, Jewish involvement in price cutting and the activities of Jewish property racketeers.[70] But it would be a mistake to regard the pressures encouraging this response as being purely internal: we know that others, outside the community, urged upon Jewish leaders, who were willing to accept such advice, the paramount need for more than a hundred per cent correct conduct, as if Jews had some special obligation towards society.[71] In addition to this kind of activity, the defence committee made efforts to influence the behaviour of Jewish refugees and with this in mind published *While you are in England. Helpful Information and Guidance for Every Refugee*, which gave advice on practical matters and provided the refugees with a code of conduct which, it was hoped, would help to reduce their 'visibility'.[72]

And there, on a note urging Jews to become Englishmen as soon as possible, which was itself an echo from the immigration years, we might leave these incidents in Britain between Fascist forces and those who opposed them. But not before reminding ourselves that Fascism and organized anti-semitic groups did not have monopoly rights over anti-semitism in the inter-war years. We might now turn, in fact, to expressions of hostility towards Jews from other sections of British society.

13 Anti-semitism and society 1919–39

'If this volume offers any moral for the Jews', H. S. Ashton wrote in 1933, it is perhaps that they should fail to look upon themselves as Palestinian expatriates and that they should cast off their ancient dogmas.' All of which was followed by the comment, 'if there is any moral for the Gentile he had better seek it for himself.'[1] Ashton's work was stimulated by the fact that 'the Jews are in the news', in other words by the anti-semitism of the inter-war years and it was one of the many works which attempted to place the Jewish question in perspective. After a similar exercise Lewis Browne, having traced his way through it all, could conclude that the only solution to the problem was to 'redeem the Jew and remake the Gentiles'. 'The ultimate need', he suggested, was for 'a quickening of intellect and a cleansing of soul among the Gentiles'.[2]

Vagueness of this order was not uncommon. Hence another analysis could conclude with the suggestion that Gentiles and Jews must be prepared to meet each other half way, each must shed prejudice and sentiment, and leave the grooves in which their minds had run for two thousand years.[3] Similarly, Wyndham Lewis, the novelist, envisaged a need to reverse the past, to 'make an end of this silly nightmare once and for all, and turn our backs upon this dark chapter of our history'. In his view, this meant that 'Anglo-Saxons and other Europeans' had to reform themselves and liquidate the 'Jewish Problem'. Such a problem was not inherent in the nature of Jews but resided in the character of the Christian nations and their attitudes towards Jews.[4] For others, after an analysis 'to discover the essential cause of the disease and, if possible, to indicate the cure', the solution to anti-semitism was suggested in socialism, the de-judaising of the Jew and his merging into a socialist society.[5]

Commentaries such as these appeared during a major international wave of anti-semitism and openly reflected such developments in Britain and elsewhere. In considering the British background which encouraged their publication, it is necessary to survey a wider front than has so far been covered. Although Fascist anti-semitism and that of firmly committed anti-semitic groups provided an obvious focus of attention for such studies, anti-semitism was present outside these circles. In order to present a rounded survey of hostility towards Jews in the inter-war years, we must take account of this and devote some attention to discriminatory action which Jews encountered as Jews as well as to the manifestations of anti-semitic attitudes outside Fascism and organized anti-semitic groups. We have already noticed some of these expressions when referring to the *Morning Post* and *National Review* in discussing the atmosphere of the immediate post-war years.[6]

From time to time the *Jewish Chronicle* picked up reports of clear discrimination against Jews, or 'anti-Jewish differentiation' as it preferred to call it. One issue drew attention to an advertisement in the *Daily Telegraph* which stipulated that 'no Jewesses' need apply for a typing vacancy and an announcement in the *Hackney Gazette* which offered unfurnished rooms but insisted that 'no children or Jews' would be accepted.[7] An advertisement inserted by a boarding house keeper in the official guide to Shanklin in the Isle of Wight which said 'no Jews catered for' was also noted, as was the lengthy discussion in the town council, after which a majority of the councillors decided in favour of allowing the advertisement to stand.[8] The column 'Jewry: Week by Week' also discovered with 'mingled astonishment and regret' that Middlesbrough Motor Club was refusing new applications by Jews for membership. Out of the 400 members it seemed that six were Jews and a local interviewer was told by an official of the club that, in their opinion, they had sufficient Jewish members. 'If this is not Hitlerism', the *Jewish Chronicle* contended, 'then black is not black, or white white.'[9] Discrimination in the provision of services was also commented upon in relation to the case of a Belfast garage proprietor who was prosecuted for allowing a person who was presumably Jewish to use a car without the driver being insured against third party risks. The insurance certificate issued on the car stated that it did not extend to cover Jews, who were thereby bracketed with other categories such as music hall artists, theatrical agents, bookmakers and foreigners. The *Chronicle* argued for insurance assessment in terms of personal record.[10]

The Board of Deputies, as a custodian of the community's interests, was called upon to combat such developments and it devoted some attention to apparent discrimination in the fields of housing and employment. In the 1930s for instance, some discussion took place regarding an LCC regulation of 1923 which affected housing policy. In clause (a), it was stated that a register should be kept of all persons of the working class displaced by the council, and such persons 'shall if possible have the first refusal of a tenancy in any of the Council's dwellings'. Clause (b) stated that in the letting of accommodation on the several housing estates of the council preference 'shall be given to British subjects, subject to clause (a) of this regulation'. There was some discussion within the Board as to whether this constituted discrimination against Jewish aliens. There were a number of Jewish immigrants, mainly from Russian Poland, who had never taken out British nationality and the Board was anxious that they should not be discriminated against. Counsel's opinion was sought on this and the Board was advised by E. M. Trustram Eve on 28 April 1933 that the management and control of housing was given to the county council by statute and therefore had to be exercised in a reasonable way. Counsel went on to say: 'It is difficult to advise with any certainty upon the present regulations but, upon the whole, I am of opinion that the Courts would hold that the present Regulation was within the discretion given by Parliament to the County Council.' On the receipt of such advice that particular matter was allowed to rest. There was, in addition, some discussion about possible discrimination against Jews in the Glasgow housing market and also by the marquess of Northampton's trust, but nothing substantial emerged from this.[11]

The Board of Deputies also considered discrimination in employment. Certain well authenticated cases in which Jews were singled out for special treatment in this respect came to light:

> We are sorry that you have sent a Jewish demonstrator to this Exhibition and must ask you to be good enough to make other arrangement for Gravesend, Hastings and Reigate as we decline to have Jews demonstrating at our exhibition under any circumstances. . . .
>
> We have no complaint to make against this man as he has carried out his duties satisfactorily. It is, however, on account of assurances made to our promoters in the respective towns, that this stipulation be carried out.[12]

It was in such terms that a firm called Official Exhibitions wrote to Roboway Sales of Blackpool. But, on other occasions, it was difficult for the Board to decide whether individuals had in fact been discriminated against as Jews or whether there were other substantial grounds for action against them.[13]

If we leave action and turn to attitudes, we might make a start by considering anti-semitism which developed out of face to face tensions. One indication of the kind of hostility which could emerge outside Fascist and organized anti-semitic circles was provided by the debate over Jewish traders in The *Grocer*. In the course of this correspondence, which provided a later version of the kind of controversy which had arisen at the time of Jewish immigration in the late nineteenth century, there were correspondents who praised the achievements of Jews in the retail trade and who emphasized that larger stores meant more substantial orders for salesmen and cheaper goods for consumers.[14] By contrast, there were those with different interests who believed that the influence of Jews in the retail trade had become too pronounced,[15] that cheapness was unacceptable if it were achieved at the expense of others in the trade and who believed that an awareness of such matters was encouraging the growth of a strong feeling against Jews.[16] In addition, there were Jewish traders who protested that price cutting was not a Jewish monopoly and that Jews themselves could be badly affected in its operation.[17] There were, finally, manufacturers who seized upon the debate to make allegations regarding the 'rascality' of Jewish traders and the prevalence of unsavoury bankruptcies among them.[18]

The arguments put forward by those hostile towards Jews described them as pushing and aggressive and a threat to their British counterparts who were interested in fair dealing and fair competition. Added to such moral economy assumptions was a strand of belief that, even if they were less efficient, British traders should have their livelihoods safeguarded.[19]

As at the time of opposition to Jewish immigration in the late nineteenth, early twentieth century, hostility developed out of a complicated set of social circumstances in which the industry concerned was undergoing a period of significant change. Reckless price cutting, the growth of chain stores and the development of the co-operatives all created tensions and strains within the distributive trades and the opposition we have been considering – which was naturally utilized to the full by groups such as the BUF – needs to be set against that background.[20]

Opposition towards Jews on account of their competition was not confined to the retail sector. It was also present in professional circles in relation to the German-Jewish refugee immigration of the 1930s. The history of the German-Jewish refugees who fled to safety from Hitlerite persecution has been told elsewhere and there is no need here for a detailed recapitulation of it.[21] The background is straightforward. In Germany the National Socialist government gradually placed increasing pressure on Jews and burdened the Jewish community with considerable disabilities. The reaction in Britain to such developments, as displayed in press reports, was ambivalent. On the one hand there were expressions of sympathy towards the refugees who began to leave Germany but some anxiety was also manifested about protecting the interests of the British population who might be affected by such an immigration.[22]

When opposition towards the immigration of the 1930s did arise it was particularly strong in the medical profession. As early as 1933 concern was being expressed about the 'inundation' of the country by foreign practitioners and an associated plea was being entered for the safeguarding of British interests.[23] Against this point of view it was claimed that no inundation was taking place and that medicine was international in character.[24] But, even so, the protective, patriotic opposition to the influx did not lie down.[25] And the shots fired in this encounter were not an isolated salvo. Concern came to a head over the admission of Austrian doctors, which encouraged the British Medical Association to set up its own committee to advise the home secretary on the conditions under which such refugees were to be permitted to come to Britain. In 1938 the committee was able to report that it had succeeded in securing a severe limitation on the number of refugees to be admitted. Each applicant would be subject to careful scrutiny and would be required to undertake at least two years' clinical study before being allowed to practice.[26] This kind of opposition was not being argued upon anti-semitic lines; the emphasis was upon a defence of the employment of British subjects which was, arguably, threatened by those was happened to be Jewish. But this kind of stress was not universally evident and in the popular press such matters could be discussed in much less restrained terms.[27] There, attacks were not mounted upon all Jewish doctors: a distinction was drawn between British Jews and alien Jews and opposition of an ethnocentic kind, stressing the alien Jewish background of those attacked, was directed towards the latter. In concluding this survey it should be emphasized that medicine was not the only profession where tensions of this kind existed and the cry of 'Britons first' was uttered.

Opposition based on similar grounds was present among architects and also in the academic world.[28]

Not all opposition to this particular immigration was based upon employment fears. Outside the professions hostility could arise from those who objected to what they perceived as the introduction of objectionable un-British standards and behaviour into the sturdy life of the nation.[29] And this serves as a reminder that apart from face to face hostility towards Jews, it is also possible to find anti-semitism at more of a distance, within groups or associations which took a keen interest in the social, economic and political problems of the inter-war years. Most of the well known themes of anti-semitism were present, for instance, in the works issued by the Boswell Publishing Company founded in 1921 by the duke of Northumberland and they also appeared between 1922 and 1940 in the associated journal, the *Patriot*, the aim of which was to reveal details of a perceived conspiracy against the British Empire.[30] It was in the troubled years following the First World War, which encouraged the attention given to the Jewish question by the *Morning Post* and Henry Page Croft's National Party, that the Boswell Company and the *Patriot* were born and down to the Second World War the two latter sources displayed a persistent interest in the Jewish question[31] which needs to be set against the general advocacy of a High Tory, patriotic philosophy and a pronounced hatred of Socialism in any form.[32] This was the message which was transmitted through the Boswell Company's journal and books, and which was also presumably on offer to those who approached its enquiry centre.[33]

From the beginning the *Patriot* made it clear that it intended to publish news which was omitted by other sections of the press but which was 'of vital importance to the proper understanding of movements and tendencies below the surface of events'.[34] And, since its first issue also showed that Sydenham of Combe and Nesta Webster were prepared to write for it, it comes as no surprise to find that the influence of Jews was stressed as one of the forces vital to an understanding of contemporary society. The cultural tradition of anti-semitism in the form of the Indian silver scandal could be referred to when Sydenham of Combe attacked Edwin Montagu's administration in India,[35] and Ian Colvin could recall in verse form memories of Lloyd George's involvement with the Marconi scandal[36] and refer scathingly to his penchant for the company of Jews. But it was with circumstances of the day that the *Patriot* was essentially concerned and here certain predominant themes emerged in its pages and in the work of those published by the Boswell Company.

In common with the Britons, a central stress was placed upon Britain and the British Empire as the repositories of Christian civilization and it was this system which was believed to be under attack from Jewish influences.[37] It was claimed that a coordinated action was taking place against Christian civilization and, while the expression of this fear varied to some extent according to the writer, it was often linked with a Jewish involvement in Bolshevism.[38] In the course of such discussions, Bolshevism – which like any other form of Socialism was regarded as an alien creed – could be described as nothing less than an attempt to gain world primacy in line with the prophecies contained in *The Protocols*.[39] Consequently, an attempt was made to portray Bolshevism as run in the interests of Jews rather than of the proletariat. Indeed, nothing good for any section of the British people, it was believed, could come out of Moscow.[40]

While this was one fear, another related concern emphasized Jewish separateness. Jews were referred to as a nation within a nation and possessing an allegiance above all else to other Jews in other countries.[41] Such an outlook was regarded as irreconcilable with true patriotism. It was, of course, a familiar argument which had been heard with great frequency in other circles.[42] And, since it was believed that a Jewish patriotic allegiance could not be guaranteed, it was regarded as particularly undesirable that Jews should play a prominent role in national institutions such as the City and the press. It was queried whether men of such allegiance could be relied upon to support Britain's interests.[43] Concern was also expressed about Jewish political power and the continued immigration of Jews into Britain.[44]

In making these comments it has to be admitted that within the ranks of writers sponsored by Boswell there was often an attempt to restrict the nature of their opposition towards Jews. In this respect the anti-semitism in the *Patriot* and the Boswell publications had less rigidity than that encountered among the Britons and Leese and was more akin to that shown in the *Morning Post*.[45] It was pointed out, for instance, in one article in the *Patriot* that Jews could not be discussed as a social entity. Some were simple nationals, other viewed themselves as members of a racial minority and others regarded themselves as a sovereign race with a home in Palestine.[46] It was also stressed at times that opposition was not being expressed against all Jews but only towards sections of the Jewish community, those involved in what was considered to be undesirable political activity and those who insisted on being members of a nation within a nation. And, since opposition was not expressed towards all Jews, on racial or religious grounds, for no reason whatsoever, it was further asserted that the *Patriot* could not be regarded as anti-semitic.[47]

Such neat compartmentalization was not always easy to maintain and in some instances, was not even attempted. Even when it was, the defence against anti-semitism was specious, since although hostility might be reserved for a section of Jews, it was not uncommon in such cases for a stress to be placed upon Jewish origins as a key to an understanding of the conflict situation.[48] But it could hardly be expected that the Boswell group would accept its own anti-semitism. Those involved in it were aware of the effects this might have upon its work and acutely conscious of the traditions of toleration which it was not good form to cross.[49] Hence its constant defence of its position on such matters, and its chiding of the Jewish press which was urged to campaign against 'undesirable' Jews as a means of bringing about a solution to the Jewish question. Such pressure, it was claimed, would remove the necessity of journals such as the *Patriot* involving themselves in these matters.[50]

The Boswell group was concerned to highlight a perceived threat to Britain and the Empire and, simultaneously, to proclaim the need to combat the crisis. And other groups also identified Jews with the causes of Britain's problems following the First World War. The Social Credit Movement, under the driving force of Major C. H. Douglas, placed a stress upon a total reform of the financial system and in the course of presenting such a programme showed a clear hostility to Jews.[51] Social credit philosophy, one of the many panaceas which have emerged to cure the problems of capitalism, hinged upon the belief that there was a permanent deficiency in consumers' aggregate incomes compared with the aggregate price of productive output and Douglas's suggestion was that this should be remedied by making periodic monetary distributions to citizens by way of a social dividend. In the established economic system, where there was a constant deficiency between aggregate incomes and aggregate prices, Douglas argued that the continuance of economic activity depended upon the supply of credit, which gave considerable power to financiers. Starting from this position Douglas began to think in terms of a power seeking conspiracy and this was soon articulated as 'a very deeply laid and well considered plot of enslaving the industrial world to the German-American-Jewish financiers'. However, 'it was not long before the German-American element faded into the background, leaving the Jews as the real villains of the piece.'[52]

Douglas acknowledged that the persecution of Jews would mean an irreparable loss to the rest of the world but he summed up the reasons for his hostility as follows. Organization, he believed, was a Jewish speciality; the Jews were 'a splendidly organized race'. But it was a special type of organization in which they excelled. The most important characteristic he attributed to Jews was their exclusiveness. This, he contended, had resulted in the breeding of a race which was far more homogenous than any other and which tended to think in an overall way. This meant that the Jewish community was an ideal vehicle through which those seeking power could achieve their ends. And Douglas regarded the Jews as part of a system to which he was opposed. On the one side there was an 'Inductive, Democratic, Baconian, Realistic, Christian, Love of Freedom, Organic Growth' system in existence and its opposite was the 'Deductive, Totalitarian, Machiavellian, Idealistic, Jewish, Love of Power, Planned Economy' system. In this sense it has been suggested that his anti-semitism was 'merely an extreme form of religiophilosophic propaganda'.[53] But whatever the form in which it was expressed, Douglas believed that unless and until Jews gave up their Messianism, their belief that they should be 'the dominating race', they would remain a menace to any organization in which they were allowed to acquire a vested interest.[54]

Among the avenues through which social credit ideas were transmitted was the journal, the *New Age*, which throughout the 1920s and 1930s, down to its closure in 1938, turned its attention towards high finance which, it was frequently stressed, worked only for the benefit of a small elite of financiers. At times it proved difficult to prevent such discussions assuming anti-semitic dimensions, so that in 1924 a correspondent complained about the journal's Judaeophobia – a charge which the editor denied.[55] A defence of the cartoon, 'The Inspector of Weights and Measures' which appeared later that year might well have created more of a problem.[56] And, two years afterwards, a more extensive correspondence took place over the accusation that the New Economics (social credit) was being tinged with anti-semitism.[57] It is clear, in fact, that while the journal could dismiss *The Protocols*[58] and the *New Witness* could be advised to decide whether its concern was with 'the monopoly of high finance' or a 'narrow anti-semitism', in practice it was difficult at times to restrain anti-semitic sentiments in the *New Age* itself.[59] Consequently, not only could hostile woodcuts by Haydn Mackey appear; a poem on 'The Slaughter of the Innocents' could direct hostility towards Jews;[60] publicity could be given to Joseph Banister, whose anti-semitism we have already considered in some detail;[61] interest in the Marconi scandal could be revived[62] and in hostile discussions of Jews considerable use could be made of Werner Sombart's *The Jews and Modern Capitalism*.[63] All this made it difficult for Jews who believed in the New Economics to grant the movement unqualified support.[64]

At this point, in commenting on reform movements which displayed hostility towards Jews, we might turn once again to Chesterbelloc. We have already noticed the activities of G. K. Chesterton and Hilaire Belloc in discussing anti-semitism in Britain before the First World War when the *Eye Witness*, the *New Witness* and the National League for Clean Government campaigned against political corruption. In analysing these themes it was mentioned that the League did not die until 1923 and, in this respect, the activity of Chesterbelloc formed a link between pre-war and post-war hostility towards Jews.[65] With the demise of the *New Witness* in 1923 it fell to *G. K.'s Weekly*, which first appeared in March 1925, to carry the Chesterbelloc message for the reform of society, which during these later years assumed the form of Distributism.[66] In addition to using this channel for their comments on Jews, both Chesterton and Belloc produced individually important works.

Chesterton's book *The New Jerusalem* made it clear that in his opinion Jews were Jews: they were not 'Russians or Roumanians or Italians or Frenchmen or Englishmen'. Jews were Orientals and had to be recognized and treated as such.[67] Ideally, 'so far as possible', he believed that Jews should live in a society of Jews, should be judged by Jews and ruled by Jews. Hence, at this stage, it was possible to support Zionism.[68] But this did not lead Chesterton to advocate the abrogation of civil equality in mixed societies: 'Let all liberal legislation stand, let all liberal and legal civic equality stand; let a Jew occupy any political or social position which he can gain in open competition; let us not listen for a moment to any suggestions of reactionary restrictions or racial privilege,' he wrote.[69] But every Jew must be clearly designated and identifiable through dress as a Jew. 'The point is', he wrote, 'that we should know where we are; and he would know where he is, which is in a foreign land.'[70] For Chesterton such measures were necessary because he could not accept that Jews, with their international connections, as members of a family 'generally divided among the nations', could know the meaning of patriotism and national loyalty.[71] Rich Jews, particularly those engaged in money lending, gave him especial concern.[72]

Turning now to Belloc, it has been suggested that there was a difference between his pre-war and post-war attitudes towards Jews, that 'when he was an older man, Belloc adopted civilized (though always utterly unrealistic) ideas about Jews.'[73] If reference is intended here to his work *The Jews*, in which Belloc's major comment appeared, it should be said straight away that this was in many respects a repetition of the views he had expressed before the war in the *Eye Witness*. In short, there was a continuity between pre-war and post-war thought, between the young and the old Belloc. The question posed in both circumstances was: is it possible for Jews to be fully accepted by English society? This, it might be noted, was also the theme – conceived on a more modest scale – which characterized Galsworthy's play, *Loyalties*, which opened at the St Martin's Theatre in London around the time Belloc's book was published. In both the book and the play the answer was 'no'. In Belloc's work because of qualities attaching to Jews, in Galsworthy's because of the loyalties of the upper-class English, who were quite prepared to close ranks to protect one of their guilty kind against the charges of De Levis, the Jew. In the *Eye Witness* before the war Belloc claimed that Jews were aliens, whose presence had always created friction with the 'host nation'. This theme was also present in the first chapter of the book. In 1911 and 1912 there was a stress upon the inevitability of this conflict, which society was generally reluctant to recognize. This also appeared in the second chapter which was called 'The Denial of the Problem'. In short, the opening arguments in the articles and the book were the same and a similar correlation was apparent throughout. References to Jewish power, the threat which Jews posed to non-Jewish interests and their alleged addiction to secrecy, all of which appeared in the articles were also present in chapters 4 and 5 of the book. Similarly, the solution which Belloc posed to 'the Jewish problem' in *The Jews*, with its suggested recognition of the separate nationality of the Jews and the establishment of separate Jewish institutions, reflected what had been written eleven years earlier in the *Eye Witness*.[74]

In a comment upon Chesterbelloc, it has been written that Belloc did not consider that his own sense of nationality, divided between France and Britain – he had been born in France in 1870 – was parallel to the dual nationality with which he challenged Jews.[75] But this is not really surprising. We know that marginal men, the product of two environments, can exhibit fiercely nationalistic tendencies while denying the possibility of this in others. While such a force might partially explain Belloc's attitudes, there were other important pressures which help to account for the Chesterbelloc hostility towards Jews. Both men, it should be realized, were exponents of a romantic, conservative Christianity which drew inspiration from an idealized medieval Christendom. Viewed from that standpoint Jews were cultural antagonists, a separate racial-religious group which posed a potential threat to the essential philosophy and organic Christian structure of British society.[76] Moreover, there was built into the philosophies of both men a related rejection of modern capitalist society which, it was claimed, was founded upon usury to which they were opposed and this led to a concentration upon Jews as symbols, as agents of finance power, or what they called usury. In place of this type of socio-economic organization Chesterton and Belloc praised the virtues of Distributism, which involved the widest possible distribution of private property. It was a system advocated in Leo XIII's encyclical *Rerum Novarum* in 1891 and repeated forty years later by Pius XI in *Quadragesimo Anno*.[77]

In advocating such ideas Belloc and Chesterton devoted some of their energies in the inter-war years to *G. K.'s Weekly* in the course of which they continued to assert their hostility to Jews, repeating their distrust of Jewish separateness, describing Jews as a 'parasitic organism',[78] claiming that it was 'the fate of the Jew to be parasitical' and owing to 'the peculiar qualities of his race' that he had been able to both preserve his identity and exercise a deep effect upon the nations he had 'penetrated'.[79] Such remarks came from Chesterton and, by way of an ultimate solution to the Jewish problem, he advocated the separation of Jew and Gentile and the fostering of a separate Jewish settlement.[80] At one stage hope along these lines had been placed in Zionism but this had become tarnished as a result of troubles in Palestine and the disabilities which he believed had resulted for the Arab population from continued Jewish settlement.[81] Belloc had less faith in plans for a Jewish settlement whether in Palestine or elsewhere since he doubted whether the 'influential cosmopolitan Jew' could be induced to contemplate residence along such lines. 'Privilege' remained Belloc's solution. In other words, 'the recognition of the Jew as a man of a special kind with rights and privileges of his own'. If that were accepted, 'the bestial cruelty periodically inflicted upon perfectly innocent people would cease to disgrace the world, and the peril arising from the actions of an alien culture would be minimized.'[82] Thus wrote Belloc five years after the advent of Hitler.

An account of the ideas of Belloc and Chesterton, the two outstanding Catholic novelists of their day, provides a springboard for the next two stages of the present discussion. First of all, some attention might be given to the continuation during the inter-war years of the long running battle between sections of Catholic opinion and the Jewish community. From time to time attitudes in sections of the Catholic press caused disquiet among the Jewish authorities and the Board of Deputies found itself involved in making a number of protests about such matters. For instance, from 1924 down to 1940 the *Catholic Herald* was regarded by the Board as an irritant in the life of the Jewish community. Concern was expressed on the one hand about references which appeared in the paper to the ethnic origins of Jews who had become involved in criminal activity,[83] and protests were also made about the tendency to refer to Jewish Bolshevism and the remarks which were carried on *The Protocols*.[84]

Other sections of the Catholic press, such as the *Catholic News* and *Catholic Gazette*, also found themselves coming to the Board's attention on account of their reporting of Jewish affairs.[85] In addition, a battle was fought with the *Catholic Times* over charges that Jews were responsible for the murder, among others, of the Holy Child of La Guardia and Father Thomas of Damascus. In this instance the Board enlisted the help of Cecil Roth as an expert in historical matters of this kind and an approach was also made to Cardinal Bourne at Westminster, who was moved to act in the matter.[86] In this issue, and the others just considered, we can detect a battle taking place between certain sections of the Catholic population and representatives of the Jewish community, a battle which, whether fought on historical or contemporary issues, reflected a longstanding hostility between those who regarded themselves as the guardians of the Christian faith and the Chosen People. Out of this clash a historical tradition of enmity had been created, whose echoes were clearly still present in the 1920s and 1930s.

Historical traditions of enmity were reflected in a different source – and once again the preceding discussion of Chesterbelloc provides an *entrée* to this – to the extent that they were to be found in the expression of literary attitudes. Here we can discover the image of the Jew as the agent of a regrettable modernism which had brought society to chaos, along with stock images of Jews in terms of speech and physical appearance. Although new elements, reflecting current pressures and tension could also be found, the well worn Jewish stereotype clearly possessed considerable durability.[87] In order to gain an understanding of such matters, some reference, however selective, is necessary not only to 'serious' literature but also to its more 'popular' equivalent. A certain amount of attention has in fact already been given to the presence of anti-semitism in literature and T. S. Eliot's work in particular has come under close scrutiny on several occasions.[88] The problem in approaching Eliot – and other writers, too – is not in accumulating examples of what they wrote about Jews but in assessing and categorizing such evidence. More precisely, we need to decide whether remarks which appeared in novels or poetry were intended to convey characterization or whether they reflected the author's own attitudes. In either case, the written word has a significance but we need to tread carefully in this particular area.

In Eliot's case it has been suggested that in his verse and prose there were too many hostile references to Jews for this to be accounted for in terms of characterization.[89] And it has been claimed that for him Jews symbolized the threat to civilization. Eliot's ideal was that of a classical world which could be protected only through an awareness felt by an elite of educated and sensitive men. Such a world was contrasted with a cultureless, traditionless mass society symbolized by those of rootless, cosmopolitan origins. And the Jew, whether the property owner 'spawned in some estaminet of Antwerp', or Bleistein, 'the Chicago Semite Viennese', reflected everything that Eliot hated and encapsulated his fear of the destruction of Western civilization and the Catholic religion.[90] In short, these references – we are told, incidentally, that the anti-Jewish bias in his work disappeared over time – need to be considered within the framework of his rejection of societies 'worm eaten with Liberalism' and his veneration of an earlier, settled classical civilization.[91]

Like Eliot, D. H. Lawrence yearned for a different order of society from that under which he had to live. In fact, 'Lawrence . . . was horrified by the twentieth century, by mass society.'[92] And, not surprisingly, in his work too, we can detect expressions of hostility towards Jews. In *Kangaroo*, for instance, published in 1923, Richard Lovat Somers, generally taken to be Lawrence himself, could equate democracy with the rule of Jewish financiers and 'gradually came to believe that all Jews and all Celts even whilst they espoused the cause of England, subtly lived to bring about the last humiliation of the great old England.' The whole of the liberal democratic tradition was, in fact, 'essentially Jewish in nature'.[93] Later, in 1930, Lawrence was also capable of portraying his Jewess in *The Virgin and the Gipsy* in stereotyped terms.[94] Here it should be said that references to Jews were not common in Lawrence's work but, whether through endowing characters with what might be considered appropriate social attitudes or, as in *The Virgin and the Gipsy*, through the descriptions given by the author as storyteller, Lawrence was able to present his readers with hostile images of Jews. Once written, of course, Lawrence could not control the responses to the sentiments and characterization which were present in his work.

Examples of popular literature should also be considered for it was a product written to sell in quantity and was aimed to strike an immediate chord among its readers. And in this pulp world it is possible to find pronounced stereotypes of all foreigners, including Jews. This was particularly apparent in the best selling novels of John Buchan where there was a persistent emphasis upon Jews as negative, subversive elements and a threat to society.[95] But there are issues which need to be kept in mind in assessing Buchan's work. As with other authors we have to be careful in ascribing views to the author on the basis of his novels. And, as for his readers, we might reflect whether Buchan's work was popular not so much because they could recognize the negative images attached to all those other than God's Englishman or whether the popularity of his books was related more to an identification with Buchan's heroes. The question is necessary, even if the answer is likely to remain elusive.[96]

Elsewhere in the popular field it has been argued that similar traits to those found in Buchan's work were present in the novels of Sapper and Dornford Yates, in both of which clearly upper class English types battled against an assortment of pernicious alien, including Jewish, influences in a gallant attempt to fend off the destruction of the country's social fabric.[97] In the detective story, too, negative Jewish stereotypes were sometimes in evidence as in the work of Dorothy L. Sayers, so that we have been told, 'only *The Unpleasantness at the Bellona Club* and *The Nine Tailors* have no perjorative remarks about Jews.'[98] In discussing this it has been claimed by some critics that such remarks appeared because they were appropriate to particular characters and did not reflect the author's personal views, but the most recent analysis of Miss Sayers's work is unimpressed by this. The way in which Jews were unnecessarily introduced into stories and her treatment of them, it is claimed, suggest the reverse.[99]

Such anti-semitism as we have been discussing did not emerge in a social vacuum. Like the remorseless anti-semitism of the Britons and the Imperial Fascist League and the pronounced anti-semitism within the BUF it has to be considered against the fear, anxiety and uncertainty of the inter-war years. Against this general background the hostility in certain trades and professions was triggered by the pressures of face to face competition from Jews at times of rapid change or employment insecurity. In such circumstances there was a cry of 'Britain first'; and in that situation Jews in the retail trade and immigrant Jews in the professions were exposed and could encounter hostility and discrimination. At the same time, Fascists who played upon such tensions could gain support.[100]

In High Tory circles, and elsewhere, it was insecurity on a wider scale which made its presence felt. The loss of Britain's prestige and influence after the First World War and discontent within the Empire played upon such groups.[101] New international tendencies were regarded as a threat to Britain's former worldwide influence and it was in such circumstances that the Bolshevik Revolution assumed such prominence. Here, it could be believed, was a direct threat to Britain's position and, from that base, it could soon be asserted that all Socialism was antipathetic to Britain's interests. The involvement of Jews in the revolution also led to the claim that Socialism in whatever form was Jewish and was therefore doubly alien and dangerous to Britain. Such fears, underlined for some through the agency of *The Protocols*, provided a powerful dynamic in driving believers towards anti-semitism.

In addition to such micro- and macro-social tensions, there were older influences, stimulated and sustained by the pressures of the inter-war years, which exerted an effect over the anti-semitism of this period. The hostility of Belloc and Chesterton was essentially a continuation, in different circumstances, of that which they were expressing towards Jews before the First World War. The antagonism towards Jewish finance in the social credit movement was a reflection of the general opposition which this movement displayed towards finance capital and to which Jews, because of their role as financial middlemen, had been traditionally exposed. In the case of the *New Age* the antipathy went back to the Marconi scandal.[102] In the Catholic press hostility towards Jews reflected long-standing religious differences, although an acceptance of *The Protocols* could add to the armoury of opposition and lead to the positing of an international conflict between Catholic and Jewish interests. As for the literary responses in which Jews were portrayed as alien, undesirable social agents, these reflected the amorphous, historical tradition that Jews were not quite acceptable which, in fact, forms the background to all these expressions of hostility we are now considering.[103]

In the course of the conflicts which emerged in such circumstances impressions became distorted. The role of Jews in the grocery trade became exaggerated; the impact of Jewish immigrants upon the professions became overdrawn; *The Patriot* and sections of the Catholic press exaggerated the link between Jews and Bolshevism; the social credit movement and the *New Age* presented well-worn stereotypes of Jews in the world of finance; Chesterbelloc continued to offer an overdrawn image of Jewish separateness; in literature Jews became used by some serious and popular writers as a shorthand for liberalism. In short, specific grievances and irritations gave rise to expressions which distorted reality, even if in part they reflected it.

In this respect, as well as in the specific themes which were emphasized there were similarities between this anti-semitism and that manifested by the Fascists, and organized anti-semitic groups like the Britons and the Militant Christian Patriots, whose programmes turned upon anti-semitism. Of course not all the messages which had a common currency in Fascist and organized anti-semitic circles were repeated outside them so that, for instance, Jewish moneylenders could find defenders,[104] Disraeli, an arch enemy of many extreme anti-semites, could avoid condemnation,[105] suggestions of a Jewish controlled press could be met with scepticism[106] and an emphasis upon the Jewish revolutionary bogey, as portrayed in *The Cause of World Unrest*, could be dismissed by Hilaire Belloc as 'lunatic'.[107] More significantly, a racist opposition towards all Jews and a proposed genocidal solution to the question of a Jewish presence did not exercise a general appeal.[108]

But to consider similarities. Hostile references to the role of Jews in the First World War, to their activity at the Versailles Peace Conference, their involvement in Bolshevism and other forms of collectivism were not confined to Fascist and organized anti-semitic groups.[109] Moreover, the stress we noticed earlier in such groups upon the economic dangers of Jewish immigration, the problem of Jewish undercutting and the threat, underlined by *The Protocols*, of an ultimate Jewish dominance of Britain had a more general currency.[110] References to Jewish control over the world of finance,[111] Jewish influence within the communications industry[112] and, more generally, the role of Jews as agents of modernism,[113] as well as the image of Jews sapping the strength of Britain and weakening it in the interests of a group which had its own allegiances and loyalty – to Jews elsewhere rather than to the nation – were to be found outside Fascist circles and groups such as the Britons and the Militant Christian Patriots.[114]

Linkages of a different kind can also be traced. Comments, reflections and information, once made public, become common currency and material often reappeared in sources quite different from the original. A classic example of this came with the publication of Karl Pearson's work on Jewish immigration.[115] Pearson's findings appeared in 1925–6 in the *Annals of Eugenics*, which carried on its title page Charles Darwin's comment, 'I have no faith in anything short of actual Measurement and the Rule of Three' and a statement from Francis Galton in defence of statistical enquiry and 'cold blooded verification'. Immigration was given a central significance by Pearson: what was the point he asked, 'in endeavouring to legislate for a superior breed of men' if, at any moment, society could be 'swamped by the influx of immigrants of an inferior race'.[116] Basing himself upon children at the Jews' Free School, Pearson concluded: 'Taken on average and regarding both sexes, this alien Jewish population is somewhat inferior physically and mentally to the native population.' The difference was not so marked as some who wished to stop all immigration were inclined to claim and indeed it had to be accepted that some children of alien Jews had distinguished themselves academically; but, Pearson emphasized: 'No breeder of cattle . . . would purchase an entire herd because he anticipated finding one or two fine specimens included in it: still less would he do it if his byres and pastures were already full.'[117] The law of patriotism for a crowded country, it was stressed, was to admit only those who provided the country either physically or mentally with what it lacked or possessed only in limited quantity.[118] As for Jewish immigrants it was suggested that they should be settled in Palestine or some similar area, far away from the overcrowded cities of western Europe.[119]

Before the article appeared, Pearson had presented some of his research conclusions, including comments on Jewish cleanliness and intelligence, to the Union of Jewish Literary Societies at University College, London on 7 May 1922 and he thereby provided the Britons with ammunition which they were hardly slow to use. They might never have seized hold of an article in the *Annals of Eugenics* but the University of London talk was reported in the *Jewish Guardian* in which the Britons took an interest and in their hands Pearson's work was used to attack the concept of the chosen people and the alleged racial superiority of Jews. 'The verminous uncleanness of the Jewish masses', it was written, 'is all of a piece with the spiritual uncleanness of the mentality of the race' and it was hoped that the home secretary would take note of Pearson's work.[120] There could be no clearer indication of the political uses which could be made of scientific enquiry.[121]

In continued pursuit of linkages and differences, we have noticed in our discussion of the BUF that Mosley was, for the most part, the 'rational' opponent of Jews, whereas individuals like William Joyce, A. K. Chesterton and 'Mick' Clarke displayed less restraint. Similar differences, it should now be said, can be discerned in the expressions of anti-semitism with which we are currently concerned. For instance, while Belloc and Chesterton were clearly hostile towards Jews, they presented that hostility in carefully worded and sophisticated terms. Others were less subtle as 'Ipso Facta's' letters in the *Grocer* clearly show.[122] There was, in addition, a viciousness in T. W. H. Crosland's *The Fine Old Hebrew Gentleman*, revealed in its reference to 'nasal protuberance', 'shent per shent', 'Yids' and 'bithness' and in Keith Williams's instructional book, *Money Sense*, which was not matched in the Chesterbelloc or in *Britain's Jewish Problem*, appearing under the pseudonym of M. G. Murchin.[123] Others, like Douglas Reed, back in London after years working for *The Times* in central Europe, occupied a place somewhere in between either extreme.[124]

On an individual level these differences in expression might well have reflected personality variations but it is also possible that they were related to that social tradition which inhibited the discussion of anti-semitism and encouraged limits on what could be publicly expressed in literary and political debates about Jews.[125] Evidence that this disreputability of anti-semitism still existed was clearly shown in the attempts made to disguise the authorship of works which attacked Jews or analysed the Jewish question. Ian Colvin was probably affected by such motives, hence his reluctance to be linked directly with *The Cause of World Unrest*, and it is significant that the author of *Jews and the Jews of England*, even though he was 'widely learned in his subject' and 'able to give an objective account on which to form a judgement', decided to remain anonymous.[126] And this preference was also exercised by M. G. Murchin, which obscured the identity of the 'well known Fleet Street journalist' who wrote *Britain's Jewish Problem*. Similarly, the pen-name of H. S. Ashton, author of *The Jew at Bay*, hid the name of 'a writer of wide political and journalistic experience, an adviser of Governments, a friend of Cabinet Ministers and himself no mean judge of political matters'.[127]

These cultural restrictions on the overt expression of anti-semitism were fortified after 1933 with the emergence of Hitlerite persecution, even though developments in Germany were not universally condemned. We have already noticed that Arnold Leese and the Imperial Fascist League could indulge in obeisance to Streicher, whose vicious brand of anti-semitism had few equals even in Germany, and other Fascists could welcome the assault upon Jewry which the National Socialists proceeded to launch.[128] But the events in Germany did have a significant impact elsewhere. For instance, although Lord Alfred Douglas had been to the forefront of British anti-semitism in the early 1920s, he was quite unable to come to terms with the vicious racist anti-semitism in Germany.[129]

A problem was also created for G. K. Chesterton who, in a tortured piece in *G. K.'s Weekly*, tried desperately to minimize his own anti-semitism, attack Hitler's treatment of Jews and, at the same time, complain that whereas his own anti-semitism had been condemned, Hitler was allowed 'to cross Jews' with impunity.[130] However, it might be noticed that Belloc displayed a more complicated response. The persecution in Germany was described as 'abominable' and he could not support the 'brutal measures' of the Reich, but while passing such judgements he could write that it was desirable for the Jewish question to be brought into the open and could also claim that the apprehensions which led to anti-semitic persecution in Germany were not absent from the minds of other governments.[131] It is clear that Belloc more than Chesterton found it difficult to know what to believe and where he stood in relation to such matters.[132]

Well before Hitler came to dominate Germany, and before the National Socialists had the chance to implement their anti-semitic programme which raised such issues, Max Aitken, in writing about the situation in England, had asked: 'Why is there such a marked recrudescence of feeling against the Jews?'[133] Somewhat later, another commentator, referring to the 1930s could recall: 'Anti-semitism was in the air: an unmistakeable tang.'[134] And, even more recently, it has been suggested that a complex discussion about the reasons behind Oswald Mosley's adoption of anti-semitism was unnecessary. He was, after all, taking coals to Newcastle.[135] But we cannot be precise about the extent of anti-semitism in any form in British society between 1876 and 1939.[136] In the inter-war years we can certainly discover many traces of individual anti-semitism and some of this must be taken to reflect the opinions of the groups which such individuals represented. It has also been suggested that hostile literary stereotypes of Jews were unlikely to have been presented if readers were unable to identify with them. Faced with this, and adding to it the clear support for anti-semitism which was present in middle class professional organizations, as well as in Fascist and various nationalist circles. and considering all this alongside evidence of social discrimination against Jews, it would clearly be dangerous to underestimate the appeal which anti-semitism in various forms exercised in the inter-war years. But this does not allow us to assert: 'There is no doubt that at least nine tenths of the inhabitants of the British Isles think the worse of a man when they are told he is a Jew.'[137] Furthermore, it is significant in fact that, although hostile attitudes were generated in the inter-war years, Jews did not find themselves the targets of special discriminatory legislation. The 1919 Aliens Act was not aimed specifically against Jews, even though an anti-semitic tone was present in the debate,[138] and the reluctance of the British authorities to accept refugees from Nazi Germany did not turn upon the ethnic origins of the refugees, even if, as we have discovered, this worried certain groups in the British society.[139] More generally, no legal moves were undertaken to restrict the activities of Jews. And, on account of a number of interacting pressures, organized anti-semitism did not emerge as a serious force.[140] Elsewhere, circumstances were different and thought could be translated into action at an official level with frightening social consequences.[141]

14 The balance sheet

The time has now come to place anti-semitism in Britain between 1876 and 1939 within a wider context and to draw out the more important general conclusions suggested by this and the foregoing analysis.

We might ask first of all how the conflict between Jews and non-Jews during this period compared with hostility towards Jews in Britain at other times. And in this respect it has to be said that in general, as far as discriminatory legislation and physical violence are concerned, Jews lived easier lives between 1876 and 1939 than they did in earlier years. Violence certainly manifested itself in the East End at the time of the great Jewish immigration, in south Wales in 1911, during the First World War and as Fascist Blackshirts marched through east London – but Jews did not have to contend with the perpetration of a centrally organized pogrom such as that which disfigured the medieval history of York.[1] And nothing emerged in official policy which was as drastic as the expulsion order of 1290. The hopes entertained by some that Jews might be deported or encouraged to leave the country were never acted upon.[2] In so far as legislation was passed which affected the mobility of Jews, it was designed to exclude undesirable immigrants. But even here it has to be stressed that such legislation was not aimed specifically at Jews, nor was it ever intended to keep out the able-bodied immigrants who might benefit the country.[3] As for those Jews who were in Britain, no official action was undertaken to restrict their social and economic life. Medieval restrictions and the later problems of naturalization which sparked off the riots over the 1753 Jew Bill and the prolonged debate over emancipation in the nineteenth century were all reminders that Jews were not easily tolerated in Britain.[4] But, nevertheless, emancipation was achieved and the process was not reversed.

And yet, anti-semitic tension was present in Britain and the expression of hostile attitudes towards Jews was not uncommon between 1876 and 1939. In some respects old patterns of hostility in the form of religious opposition still persisted, and the themes which dominated the emancipation debate in the long golden afternoon of mid-Victorian England also echoed into the later, more troubled years of the century. And there was an increasing concern about Jewish power and a threatened or actually perceived dominance of Britain by Jews as the legal framework of emancipation allowed certain Jews to occupy important official positions.[5] As time passed, other new and powerful dynamics came to be added to the armoury of anti-semitism. Opposition of a racist kind was faintly heard in the late nineteenth century and became a more marked feature of the inter-war years[6] and this genus of anti-semitism possessed an inflexibility which older forms of opposition, separated from a racist base, did not possess. To those who held such beliefs no symbiosis was possible between Jew and non-Jew. This was the most important new development in anti-semitic thought which took hold between 1876 and 1939. In particular the emergence and acceptance of a conspiratorial expression of hostility based upon race contributed a significant new dynamic which helped to separate the post-war years from those before 1914. Even before the First World War opposition had developed towards the accumulation of Jewish power and influence, and rich and powerful Jews, the Sampson Levis of this world, could be accused of manipulating society in their own sectional interests. This provided a step towards later conspiratorial theories, but to argue that Jews as a racial entity, were engaged in such activity was a significant extension of anti-semitic hostility.[7]

Such hostile attitudes did not emerge without facing their own opposition. But in important respects conditions were more favourable for the expression of anti-semitism between 1876 and 1939 than in the years which followed. As the barbarism of the Holocaust became known, the disreputability of anti-semitism was powerfully reinforced and its public expression was driven further to the fringes of political life. And, while anti-semitism might find a surreptitious outlet, countervailing forces had a powerful, additional influence which could be used to protect the interests of Anglo-Jewry. Furthermore, whereas both before the First World War and in the inter-war years there were episodes of Jewish immigration which helped to focus attention upon Jews, the most prominent movement into Britain since the end of the Second World War has involved newcomers of West Indian and Indo-Pakistani origin. And, while this has helped to set up British Fascism in more recent years, it has also diverted some Fascist hostility away from Anglo-Jewry and directed it towards a more visible enemy.[8] In short, the climate for Jews has improved. However, economic and social circumstances and pressures are constantly changing and with the emergence of the National Front as a third political force in some constituencies, and the questioning which has also appeared concerning the central themes of the Holocaust and the reliability and accuracy of its history, the future is less certain than one might have been tempted to believe a few years ago.[9]

Apart from a consideration of anti-semitic thought and action in Britain between 1876 and 1939 some attention ought to be given at this point to a comparison between this total experience and the situation which prevailed elsewhere. In all the major European countries, as well as in America, it is possible to find evidence of anti-semitic thought and action between 1876 and 1939. Indeed, these years were of particular significance in the history of anti-semitism.[10] Even so, the intensity of opposition towards Jews displayed noticeable variations.

Russia was the country with the largest Jewish population before 1914 and the experience of Jews in the Tsar's Empire compared unfavourably with their history elsewhere. Jews in Russia had not been emancipated – this was not to occur until the 1917 Revolution – and the majority of them were confined to the pale of settlement, stretching between the Black Sea and the Baltic on the western boundaries of Russia.[11] Disabilities of this kind did not operate in Britain. Restrictions upon the participation by Jews in British life had been lifted in the course of the nineteenth century and Anglo-Jewry had to face none of the legal hindrances which continued to dominate the lives of Jews in Russia.[12] In this respect, of course, the lives of Russia's Jews compared unfavourably with those living in other major countries. In America Jews found themselves freed from legal restrictions in the late eighteenth century; in France emancipation came when men's horizons were extended by the 1789 Revolution; in Austria it was granted in 1867; in Germany it was written into the constitution of the German Empire.

Circumstances in Britain were sharply different from those in Russia in another sense. In common with other minorities and political opponents of the Tsar's government, Jews in Russia were subordinated through a policy of violence. In 1870, 1881–2, 1890, 1893 and 1904–6 Jews, or rather sections of the Jewish population in Russia, found themselves the victims of organized physical opposition. And although Jews in Britain had to face violence – in the East End, in Limerick and in south Wales – none of it equalled the viciousness and ferocity of the pogroms in the Russian Empire. Indeed, the barbarity of the Russian treatment of its Jewish subjects before the Revolution would be difficult to find paralleled elsewhere during these years.[13]

In the years after 1918 Anglo-Jewry never had to contend with clogging and dehumanizing legal restrictions which the National Socialists placed upon Jews in Germany, culminating in their exclusion as citizens of the state in 1935–6.[14] Neither did it have to face the severity of physical violence – whether promiscuous or organized – which characterized the lives of Jews in Austria and Germany.

Furthermore, at no time between 1876 and 1939 did Jews in Britain witness a major show trial. In France the Dreyfus Case was a prolonged issue which split French public opinion over the course of ten years. In America the Leo Frank affair which dragged on over two years between 1913 and 1915 acted as a cynosure for a number of issues affecting the lives of Jews in America. And in Russia the Beiliss trial, which had Mendel Beiliss accused of ritual murder, was yet another instance of a decaying Tsardom fighting a desperate, savage, yet losing struggle against the future and attacking its Jewish minority as the agents and symbols of what it feared, in the full light of world opinion.[15]

There were, of course, similarities between anti-semitism in Britain and elsewhere. As in Germany and America before 1914 concern was manifested about the impact of Jewish immigration. As in the Third French Republic doubts could be entertained about Jewish loyalty to the nation. As in Russia, Germany, Austria and America sections of society were concerned about the social advancement of Jews before 1914. As in most other countries after 1918 *The Protocols* came to feature in the opposition which was mounted against Jews and British Fascists echoed their European counterparts in attacking the internationalism of the Jews. Also, in Britain as elsewhere, some could propose an exclusionist solution to the Jewish question and urge the removal of Jews beyond national boundaries – whether to Palestine, Uganda or Madagascar – and others could tentatively discuss the prospect of extermination. But, it has been suggested, there were significant differences, too, between reactions in Britain and those manifested by sections of society in other major countries.

The major divergences in the historical experience of anti-semitism relate to Russia before 1914 and to Germany in the later years and as a prelude to a discussion of why these experiences were different from the British, it is necessary to indicate the dynamics of anti-semitism in both countries. In neither case will it be argued that the absolute number of Jews in the country was of great significance. The concentration of Jews, however, both geographically and occupationally was far more significant since either or both, together with the international links of Jews, could present an impression of Jewish power and influence. As for actual power, in both Tsarist Russia and twentieth-century Germany the social role of Jews assumed an importance out of proportion to their numbers. In Russia they were a crucial element powering forward the growth of capitalism, although industrialization left many Jews chronically poor and, for some sections of the community, created additional poverty. In Weimar Germany the influence of Jews, particularly in economic and cultural fields, although it did not outstrip that of 'Aryans', and an exaggerated emphasis could be developed by anti-semites on the basis of Jewish influence in centres such as Berlin, was also commonly acknowledged. Indeed, one sometimes hears it said that there was a fundamental difference between the role of Jews and Jewish influence in such countries and their impact on British society, and it is this which helps to account for a relatively muted form of anti-semitism in Britain. In considering this it should be said that my own work has argued throughout that in order to understand anti-semitic hostility we need to recognize the characteristics of the Jewish minority. But we need to tread carefully in discussing Jewish power and claiming that Jewish influence in Britain was less than it was elsewhere. We know very little about the economic and social history of Anglo-Jewry between 1876 and 1939 and the influence which could be attendant upon economic power. Statistics on Jewish occupations are hard to come by and there has probably been a tendency to play down the influence of Jews in British society and their contribution to national life. Evidence on such matters is fuller elsewhere. What can be said with greater certainty is that in any case, in both Russia and Weimar Germany anti-semitism had a many sided complexity which went beyond such considerations.[16]

In Russia, where the church and state were one and where the ruling ideology stressed the importance of the organic state, life had always been difficult for religious minorities in the Empire of all the Tsars. Furthermore, in the late nineteenth century, as industrialization got under way, a government of this kind, which also had its pillars in a rural peasantry, found itself facing major problems resulting from industrial growth and Jews became targets for tensions resulting from the policies of change. In this the state could count upon support from those sections of Russian society which encountered economic competition from Jewish businessmen or workers and those embittered groups whose hostility towards exploitative middlemen was often fastened upon Jews, whose own historical experience led to their concentration upon the role of middlemen. From this base anti-semitism developed, particularly at times of socio-economic unrest or political crisis and in such circumstances, conflict could derive support from other developments. Opposition towards individual Jews could become converted into a generalized hostility and, as part of this process of interaction, Jews could return the hostility from the regime by joining the ranks of political forces, such as the Mensheviks, Bolsheviks or the Jewish Bund. In its turn this could generate more hostility with Jews being automatically associated as dissidents and revolutionaries. It was in such circumstances that agitators on the make, the Osman Beys, the Jacob Brafmanns of this world, could earn a living and achieve a transient prominence as purveyors of anti-semitism.[17]

In Hitler's Germany, there was a long tradition of anti-semitism from which anti-semites could draw strength[18] and a combination of circumstances consequent upon the First World War guaranteed that the Jewish question assumed a social importance. To the nationalist groups, smarting under Germany's defeat in the war and groaning under the weight of reparations and the national humiliation which followed,[19] the Jew was perceived as an internal enemy. The involvement of Jews in the early history of the Bolshevik Revolution and the prominence of individual Jews within German Socialism encouraged the belief in nationalist circles – and it was assiduously fostered by White Russian emigrés – that Socialism was Jewish and therefore doubly dangerous. Such hostility was a reflection of a wider fear, a dislike of the present. The Weimar Republic in which Jews had the right to hold high public office – and some did – was a symbol of that present which the nationalists rejected. And, rejecting what they dubbed the 'Jews' Republic', they held Jews to be responsible for the catalogue of disasters which they believed had led to its existence, including Germany's defeat in the war. Such anxieties were kept on the boil until 1933 by the strength of the German Communist Party, which held the prospect of an unwanted Socialism before the nationalists' eyes, and by the social and economic disequilibrium arising from the war which Germany experienced in the early 1920s but whose consequences were long remembered. Added to such pressures were those resulting from the world crisis and depression of 1929–31 which hit Germany with considerable vengeance. In such circumstances anti-semitism could become a major weapon of self-interest, in the sense that Jews could be attacked as a means of removing potential or actual economic competition and it was such a background which the National Socialists could tap for political purposes. But, as will be explained below, anti-semitism arising out of these social circumstances could soon transcend them.[20]

But if these were the basic dynamics behind anti-semitism in Russia and Germany, what were the factors which enabled it to assume more severe and savage forms than it did in Britain? And why did it attain greater social significance? Before 1914 it might be suggested yet again that the most vicious anti-semitism in terms of action against Jews was witnessed in Russia where there was no significant tradition of liberalism.[21] The government which ruled Russia until the Revolution was autocratic and, as we have argued, found itself at odds with its Jewish minority at a number of points. Such conflict was heightened in the course of the late nineteenth century owing to the policy of modernization which was being pursued in Russia. As a result of this policy the Russian state was in the grip of a profound contradiction.[22] In order to survive in the world it had to be transformed. Yet, by changing, the Tsar's autocratic rule would also have to be modified. There were those within the ruling hierarchy who accepted the need for this but there were others who were hostile to it. It was in this kind of situation, where the whole concept of Tsardom itself was faced with the prospect of challenge and the need for essential change, when modernization was threatening to undermine the foundations of the state, that Jews, who were among the agents of change, were selected as targets by the state and the seriousness of the situation for the Tsarist authorities encouraged the savagery of its response. In such circumstances, although there were forces in Russian which opposed the anti-semitic policy of the authorities, they were unable to restrain it.

During the post-war years, as everybody knows, Germany assumed the role of being the arch persecutor of Jews and the significant turning point here came with the breakdown of the republic under social and economic pressures and the advent of the National Socialists. Whereas the British political system survived the world crisis, that of Germany succumbed to it. In 1933 Germany became controlled by a party which, it might be emphasized again, although it did not gain power because of its anti-semitism, contained anti-semites who believed that they and the Jews were locked together in a Manichean, life and death struggle, in the course of which Jews could be projected as the source of all evil. It also possessed leaders, some of whom shared these beliefs, and who were intent upon smashing liberalism and all its moral values. It was in such circumstances that anti-semitism took off in a new and frightening direction which transformed German anti-semitism, so that within ten years it could pursue a policy which reduced human beings with hearts, minds, emotions, hopes and aspirations into unbelievable heaps of drooping and anonymous corpses.[23]

Such an analysis suggests that the major instances of anti-semitic hostility between 1876 and 1939 – but not all manifestations of anti-semitism – grew out of economic and social dislocation when it could be believed that the social system was being undermined. But it was not such influences alone which generated the major outbreaks of anti-semitism. In Russia and Germany there was an accompanying ideological conflict taking place which assumed nationalist forms and it was out of this total combination of circumstances that attention was turned upon minorities[24] and it has already been emphasized that there were particular reasons why Jews became centrally involved in the conflict in both countries.[25] Furthermore, in both pre-revolutionary Russia and National Socialist Germany, anti-semitism could assume a more serious dimension that in, say, Britain or America, because those who held power at these time did not consider themselves committed to the fostering of emancipation. In both Russia and Germany, indeed, there were committed anti-semites at influential points in the political structure.[26] As such, circumstances were quite different from those prevailing in Britain, where anti-semitism never secured a major policy foothold within the political establishment and where the forces of a stable social-political system could be deployed against those who threatened to make anti-semitism a major issue.[27] The consequence of this difference was that in both Russia and Germany anti-semitism could become an orthodoxy and assume tragic proportions.

After this brief excursion into the arena of comparative anti-semitism the time has come to draw together the main conclusions which emerge from the whole of the foregoing discussion. However, before that, it might be emphasized yet again that an analysis of anti-semitism of the kind attempted here or indeed any discussion of Jews can easily set up tensions.[28] Partly as a consequence there has been some reluctance to engage in a tough, sinewy discussion of anti-semitism and a good deal of work has come from the hands of apologists. Such circumstances hardly encourage historical progress – as a well known Jewish scholar has recently reminded us.[29] Where the field has been cultivated it has also often been with the Holocaust experience in mind. A searing tragedy of this kind, involving Jews and non-Jews, has inevitably burnt itself into the souls of those who remain and has conditioned responses to the world. All this is understandable, but there is a serious danger of distortion if all modern hostility towards Jews is approached from that vantage point and the study of German anti-semitism has certainly suffered in this respect.[30] We need to consider earlier episodes of anti-semitism within their own context rather than project into them the qualities of a later period. In fact, this is merely one part of a wider problem, which has afflicted the history of minorities other than Jews, in the sense that there has been a pronounced tendency to discuss historical comments and attitudes on race in the light of later orthodoxies. The specific social environment in which such ideas emerged has been discounted at the cost of considerable distortion and in attempts to classify ideas there has been a corresponding increase in the lax, injudicious use of terms such as prejudice.[31]

This is not to suggest that such developments are unusual or restricted only to studies of race and ethnicity. Similar distortions, although for different reasons, have appeared in the history of the English working-class movement so that battles have been judged in the light of later developments rather than in their appropriate contemporary context. Hence E. P. Thompson's courageous and influential attempt to rescue the history of the English working class from the enormous condescension of posterity.[32] But if we return to the main theme, that the Holocaust has acted as a distorting agency, we might add to the preceding discussion by suggesting that the sheer magnitude and horror of what happened have also encouraged explanations of anti-semitism in terms of madness and directed attention towards psychopathological manifestations of anti-semitism, sometimes at the expense of the social context in which hostility was generated.[33] It has also, understandably, built up a tide of moral indignation with the consequence that the dividing line between historical research and moral tract has not always been easy to maintain. In passing, it might be noticed that a similar distortion, deriving from its own historical roots, has affected a considerable amount of writing on 'black' history. My own study has tried to avoid these particular pitfalls.

Anti-semitism has been defined broadly as a hostility towards Jews as such – towards individuals, a section of Jewry or, in some cases, all Jews, when a stress was placed on the Jewish origins of those who were being attacked. To the anti-semite, it was the involvement of Jews in particular issues which added significance to what was happening. It is such hostility, rather than every attack, literary, verbal or physical which involved Jews between 1876 and 1939, which we have been discussing. At times it has not been easy to do this since anti-semitism frequently lurks behind a different persona, but evidence of it can be found and, on examination, it is apparent that anti-semitism assumed various forms and carried a variety of emphases.[34]

At no point between 1876 and 1939 was there evidence of official governmental anti-semitism in Britain and in this respect the experience of Jews in Britain provided a sharp contrast with that in other countries such as Russia before 1919 and Germany and Poland after the First World War.[35] But if official hostility towards Jews was not pursued in Britain, various strands of oppositional anti-semitism were certainly present between 1876 and 1939.

Before 1919 a non-theoretical form of anti-semitic social discrimination in Britain was apparent, not only in various examples of discrimination against Jews which we noticed in the East End but also in the quiet genteel atmosphere of Oxford in the conclaves of All Souls.[36] None of this turned upon a highly sophisticated theory of anti-semitism; it was an in group – out group conflict which found parallels in the tension between English and German clerks or between British sailors and their Chinese contemporaries.[37] Similar behaviour has also been traced in the inter-war years.[38]

But it was not merely a non-theoretical social discrimination towards Jews which can be detected in Britain: there was abundant evidence of an attitudinal hostility towards Jews which assumed different forms. Before 1919 some of this developed a racist dimension – the writings of J. T. Sinclair, Joseph Banister and Frank Hugh O'Donnell come to mind[39] – and after the First World War such hostility became more pronounced. It was opaquely evident in the literature and attitudes of the Britons, it dominated Arnold Leese's hostility towards Jews, indeed it overshadowed his whole political philosophy, it appeared in the writings of A. K. Chesterton[40] and, wherever it was found, it regarded the Jew as the causal element in society's problems. Little of this was particularly sophisticated or systematic but it did attempt to theorize about the Jews' position in society. At a much lower level, an implied racism was also present in the fascist press.[41] But it should be stressed that racism was not the prerogative of Fascism: it was displayed elsewhere in theoretical, philosophical discussions of the Jewish question on the political right[42] and was also present in Belloc's work.[43]

But, as it was expressed, not all opposition towards Jews assumed a racist quality.[44] A rich strain of hostility in Britain before 1919 was directed towards sections of the Jewish community. This was to be found in the criticisms expressed by Goldwin Smith towards strict Jews at the time of the Russo-Turkish War when he argued that such individuals inevitably found themselves faced with problems of ultimate loyalties.[45] It was also present in the religious based opposition to Jews which was still manifested in the post – Darwinian age.[46] It was also evident in the hostility which manifested itself in the East End towards Jewish immigrants, and it was also present in the writings in which Leo Maxse attacked the German Jews. On a much more sophisticated level it was present in H. A. Gwynne's cautious if hostile approach to 'the Jewish Peril'.[47]

We should be quite clear about the kind of categorization suggested here. The racists mentioned above are those who subscribed to 'the doctrine that a man's behaviour [was] determined by stable inherited characters deriving from separate racial stocks having distinctive attributes and usually considered to stand to one another in relations of superiority and inferiority'.[48] They might not have articulated their beliefs in this way but this was the essence of their position. Such hostility could assume the form of a direct reference to genetic endowment, or alternatively it could take the form of an attack upon what was perceived as a biologically rooted culture. Both could be implied through the use of animal imagery.

Some have suggested that it was this dynamic which gave a new force to anti-semitism from the late nineteenth century.[49] Henceforth, it has been claimed, the Jewish question could not be solved in terms of conversion. Indeed, it has been asserted that racist anti-semitism encouraged the belief that no symbiosis was possible between Jew and non-Jew. But, it should be emphasized, racist anti-semitism was not prevalent in Britain before 1914 and there may be a divergence here between British and European experiences. Racist anti-semitism flowered essentially after the war but even then in conjunction with older forms of hostility. What was commoner in Britain before 1914 was a diffuse conception of race which could produce its own generalizations. It has been remarked that no major figure in the social sciences between 1860 and 1890 escaped the influences of race and Darwinism.[50] And one suspects that in many cases this arose partly because of the influence of neo-Lamarckian philosophy, in other words because of the widespread belief that acquired characteristics could be inherited.[51] Individuals like Arnold White,[52] and Beatrice Potter[53] could refer to Jewish immigrants having particular racial qualities which arose out of their cumulative historical experiences. But they did not then proceed to generalize about all Jews having such characteristics. Opposition of this kind turned upon race but could not be called racist in the sense in which it has been used here.

What further complicates analysis before 1914 is that the term 'race' was used in an even more general fashion, in the sense that it was sometimes used to refer to a group sharing a community of cultural interests.[54] This, together with the influence of neo-Lamarckianism means that any discussion of race and racism before 1914 takes place in a minefield and we need to be constantly aware of such difficulties. There is, finally, an additional problem which should be kept in mind. Even if hostility is not expressed in a racist form – as first defined – this does not necessarily mean that racism is not present. For example, by the 1920s and 1930s it was hardly respectable to be a racist anti-semite and this became more pronounced with Hitler's rise to power. Consequently, it could well be possible that certain individuals who might genuinely have held racist assumptions would not express them in that way but would restrict their attacks or proclaim their hostility without reference to genetic influences. Some of the hostility expressed towards Jews in the BUF campaign, for instance, categorized Jews although without reference to a genetic base. In other words, it hinted at a form of determinism even if it did not openly embrace it.[55]

Both before 1914 and afterwards there was a tendency for some of this hostility towards Jews in Britain to manifest itself within a conspiratorial framework. Before the war this was present in a non-systematic fashion in the attacks aimed at the rich Jews who were considered to be gaining an undue influence in British society. As we have noticed, it was evident at the time of the South African War, during the Marconi and Indian silver scandals and in the discussions about the alleged activities of German Jews just before 1914.[56] Such hostility grew out of the spectacle of individual wealth and influence and, in some cases, was strengthened because of suspicions which could arise from the position of Jews as an international minority.[57] In some instances after the war conspiratorial hostility assumed a more systematic character in the sense that certain individuals drew their beliefs from *The Protocols*, on the basis of which it could be emphasized that there was a Jewish plot to dominate the world. In Britain very few accepted this message in its most extreme form but a diluted version of it undoubtedly exercised an influence and added to the work's international influence. And its impact, it might be underlined yet again, was not unrelated to an existing tradition of hostility in Britain towards influential Jews which had earlier raised the spectre of Jewish power developing for Jewish ends. This old fear formed an important bridge leading towards the later, more sophisticated theories of Jewish domination and to ignore this is to overlook a vital link in the history of *The Protocols* in Britain.

There is an additional emphasis worth making in this categorization of thought patterns. In the course of analysing the nature of the Jewish question we noticed the various solutions which were put forward and the full range of these might now be referred to. Some of the opposition towards Jews which we have discussed limited itself to complaints about Jews and Jewish influence. But in others a wider approach was taken and solutions were offered. In the late nineteenth century there were still those who were anxious for the conversion of the Jews and, even later, G. K. Chesterton admitted that for him a mass conversion to Catholicism would have solved the problem but he acknowledged that such a prospect was not even a remote possibility.[59] But by the late nineteenth century it was possible to find reference being made in discussions of the Jewish question to the essential incompatibility of Jewish and national interests. At one point Arnold White could float ideas about intermarriage as a possible solution, believing that this would have a positive effect upon both parties but he also advocated the need to consider exclusion in the form of Jewish settlement in Turkish Armenia.[60] Joseph Banister could also argue in favour of exclusion,[61] and after the First World War this solution received increasing emphasis. The Britons, Mosley and the Militant Christian Patriots as well as Chesterton all advocated it and Palestine, Madagascar, Australia as well as Biro-Bidjan were all considered as settlement centres.[62] In the midst of such discussion a separate Jewish existence of a different kind – he called it 'privilege' – was advocated before 1914 by Belloc in the *Eye Witness* and again in 1922 in *The Jews*, in what was possibly the most intellectualized discussion of the solution to the Jewish question to appear in Britain between 1876 and 1939.[63] Last of all, there were tentative voices which raised the question of extermination. But these should not be exaggerated. 'Angulus' in the *Hidden Hand* and Leese could move in this direction and hints were dropped elsewhere.[64] But it was often a case of one step forward two steps back with those who mentioned such measures. The issue could be raised but usually with reference to the impossibility or impracticability of carrying out such a policy, thereby indicating yet again the strength of the forces which opposed anti-semitism in Britain.[65]

If we are able to identify these various forms of anti-semitism in Britain between 1876 and 1939, we are further required to account for their emergence and there is no shortage of theories which would attempt to do this. It was suggested earlier that it has become fashionable to discuss anti-semitism as some form of disease or madness and this has led inevitably to a concentration upon the personal psychologies of anti-semites. Such claims transcend those which would argue that adherence to any political creed is generally related to individual personalities[66] and extend as far as claiming that those who support anti-semitism are reflecting a degree of personality disturbance.[67] To those who believe this, the clue to an understanding of anti-semitism lies in comprehending the mind of the anti-semite. In some instances there would seem to be support for the view that individual personalities assume a significance although it should be stressed that the nature of the evidence would hardly allow even a specialist to offer a precise diagnosis. But it might be asked whether Joseph Banister's anti-semitism can be fully understood outside a reference to personality factors. His obsession with disease, his emphasis upon the dangers of skin afflictions derived from Jews, the viciousness of his language and his unvarying hostility towards Jews spread over almost thirty years, raise this kind of question. But we have very little hard evidence on which competent analysts could base an assessment of Banister's problems. However, it might be surmised – one could hardly make it any stronger – that here was someone whose hostility towards Jews, maintained in defiance of all convention and evidence, was central to the efficient functioning of his personality.[68]

It might also be suggested that H. H. Beamish, the founder of the Britons, possessed a similar need for his anti-semitic creed so that any 'evidence' against Jews was sought for and exploited by him throughout his long political life. As the judge in the Grahamstown trial in 1934 explained, here was a man who was prepared to believe everything of an adverse nature he was told against the Jews – such was his need for that kind of information.[69] In addition, it has been argued that Arnold Leese's anti-semitism had a similar inexorability to it and that this was also related to his personality structure. Even the Holocaust experience which caused many to mask or reduce the virulence of their anti-semitism did not shake him, nor did it affect William Joyce.[70] Personal factors of a less severe kind have also been brought forward in discussing the hostility towards Jews shown by Richard Burton.[71]

But even a detailed knowledge of the psychologies of all those whom we have encountered in the course of this analysis – and such information eludes us – would not adequately explain the anti-semitism of these years. This can be understood only within its appropriate social context and even those who were disturbed, the 'hard' anti-semites, were scarcely immune to the influence of this social dimension.[72] It is this which explains why Jews magnetized their attention and accounts for whatever influence they came to possess. In writing about this context of anti-semitism an emphasis has been placed upon the importance of immediate pressures, such as social competition and national loyalty. The former became a particularly acute issue at times of distress and uncertainty, as between 1899 and 1914, in the early 1920s and at the time of the world crisis and depression following 1929. In such circumstances considerations of national loyalty also became built into the discussion, when a stress was laid upon Britain for the British. In a different context national sentiments also became a major issue in times of war, or as war threatened, as in 1877, 1899–1902, 1914–18 and in the late 1930s, when voices were raised which questioned the loyalty of Jews to the nation.[73] It was at such times that the major manifestations of anti-semitism occurred, when individuals and groups perceived a clash between their own and Jewish interests. But it has also been stressed throughout that such conflict occurred within a social context in which images of Jews had already been constructed as a result of previous and, in some cases, ongoing social conflict.[74] This total interaction of circumstances needs to be acknowledged and in taking account of all such influences it has been suggested that the roles and activities of both agents within the conflict situation must be considered. In other words, the analysis has flowed mainly in an interactionist direction.[75] An emphasis has not been laid solely upon the activities of the anti-semites. The role of Jews and the social structure of the Jewish community have been treated as important for an understanding of the emerging conflict.[76] At the same time, it has been recognized that the behaviour and structure of the minority must be regarded as assuming more significance at certain times than others.[77] Indeed, on occasions the grain of truth is small, and even when it assumes a greater size concentration should not be placed upon it alone as an explanation of circumstances leading to anti-semitism.[78] Generalizations about Jews abound from particular cases and tensions arising from specific circumstances magnified and exaggerated the role of Jews working for Jewish ends.[79] There is no reason to assume that for the most part such distortions arose because those who adhered to anti-semitism had disturbed personalities and created a world peopled by their inner demons. Anti-semitism reflected the fact that reality is complex and difficult to grasp in its interconnectedness. It is, of course, the historian's task to penetrate this complex maze.[80]

In pursuing such an analysis of various types of anti-semitic hostility it became clear that it cut across party and class barriers. Socialist circles could become anti-semitic in their discussions of the power of finance capital before 1914. Liberals could hunt the Jew premier in 1877 and Jewish financiers at the time of the Boer War. Right wing papers such as the *National Review* and the *Throne* could use the Marconi and Indian silver scandals as opportunities to emphasize the Jewish origins of certain public figures and then proceed to beat them on that account and Maxse could be particularly hostile towards international Jews. None of this was characterized by a doctrinaire racism: that was to come later with the emergence of Fascist and patriotic groups in the 1920s and 1930s[81] but all attacks emphasized Jewish origins or a perceived Jewishness as a causal quality in the appropriate conflict situation. And, just as hostility towards Jews cut across party, so it transcended class. Sections of the East End proletariat became involved in anti-semitism in the immigration years, during the First World War and again in the 1930s. The pressure group around the *Witness* was one reflection of middle-class and professional hostility towards Jews; the stereotypes in English literature which reflected the tastes and predilections of this class were another; and the direct professional opposition to Jewish refugees in the 1930s was a further indication of this. In upper-class circles private comment both before and after the war indicated that anti-semitism had its lodging place here too.[82] Once again very little of this turned upon any theory of anti-semitism but it did reflect the perception of ethnic differences.

In tracing such developments we should not lose sight of the fact that Jews were not the only minority group in British society to encounter hostility between 1876 and 1939. A wide variety of racial and ethnic minorities, such as German clerks,[83] Polish miners,[84] Chinese seamen[85] and Britain's black community[86] faced opposition when they were perceived as competitors for society's scarce resources. Furthermore, the Chinese,[87] the Irish[88] and the blacks,[89] among others all ran into problems since they were regarded by some as possessing cultural values of various kinds which were inimical to those of the British. In addition, the Jews were not alone in discovering that hostile attitudes could become converted into social violence. There was public and private violence against the German gypsies between 1904 and 1906 leading to their eventual deportation.[90] There were disturbances involving the Chinese in south Wales in the summer of 1911[91] and also there were race riots in Liverpool and elsewhere in 1919.[92]

The paucity of research into most of these other minorities necessarily makes any generalized comparative comment about the treatment of Jews a potentially hazardous exercise[93] but it would appear that the Jews were better able to cope with the hostility they encountered than certain other groups. In contrast to the gypsies and the blacks, for example, they had evolved an organizational structure which, however reluctantly and slowly it moved in the immigration years and in the 1930s, could come to their aid, smooth the process of Jewish adjustment to British society and defend the interests of the community. In that respect Jews had some defence against the forces which opposed them. But there was a need for such support since the Jewish community did not have the kind of accommodative arrangement with British society which a number of other groups possessed. For the most part minorities can be tolerated within a licensed preserve.[94] The accommodative structure might be breached at times but a brake is generally placed upon the prospect of social tension even if it is unlikely to prevent grumbles about outsiders.[95] But Jews did not have a licensed preserve. Hence the influence of Jews – particularly after emancipation – could be felt at a number of different points in society. Partly because of this, partly because their historically evolved social structure created tensions with sections of non-Jewish society and partly because of a deep seated cultural opposition towards Jews which Britain shared with other countries, Jews found themselves facing a wide range of hostility. And some of it, we have noticed, led to action being directed towards the Jewish community or sections of it. More than any other minority in Britain, the Jews were asked to justify themselves and their actions in the balance sheet of the nation's activity.[96]

Nevertheless, although Jews in Britain faced a wider challenge than other racial and ethnic minorities it has been argued that, for a variety of reasons, anti-semitism was of a less severe and intense kind than that which manifested itself in certain other countries.[97] But this does not allow us to say that it did not exist in Britain or was insignificant.[98] Throughout the years 1876 to 1939 we have been able to trace a tradition of anti-semitism in Britain. It is true that anti-semitism as an organized political weapon, used in a bid for power and expressions of what we would now regard as racist anti-semitism were related essentially to the inter-war years, but at the same time it does not pay to neglect elements of continuity. In the course of our analysis we have found commentators drawing attention to earlier battles against Jews, using the arguments thrown up during those conflicts and thereby guaranteeing the continuance of a hostile tradition.[99] In some instances there was also a continuity of personnel engaged in hostility towards Jews.[100]

And yet anti-semitism was never a vehicle for political success in British society and those who drew from European experience and attempted to inject it into British political life were to be frustrated and disappointed by the results. Some anti-semitic sentiment did in fact come to Britain *via* these with an experience or awareness of European developments. The impressionable Arnold White was clearly influenced, although not totally seduced, by what he saw in Russia,[101] Frank Hugh O'Donnell was also affected by this European experiences[102] and Belloc grew up in the shadow of French anti-semitism.[103] Later, in the 1920s it was the Russian influence in the form of *The Protocols* which exercised a brief hold over anti-semitism in Britain.[104] And in the 1930s the various Fascist movements were clearly smitten by developments in Germany whether, like Leese, it was in the form of the vicious anti-semitism of *Der Stūrmer* or whether it was a more general influence of developments in Germany which made its presence felt.[105] Such currents found themselves facing powerful, resistive influences. However, the strength of the forces opposed to anti-semitism should not encourage us to dismiss the attitudes and actions which challenged them, whether directly, indirectly, subtly or with crude vigour.[106] To do so would be to lose a sense of historical perspective, just as a refusal or unwillingness to seek the causes of such a challenge would be a neglect of the historian's duty and to simplify its essence and expression would be nothing less than a cruel deception.[107]

Notes

Abbreviations

DNB	*Dictionary of National Biography*
FO	Foreign Office
HO	Home Office
MEPOL	Metropolitan Police
RC	*Royal Commission on Alien Immigration*, British Parliamentary Papers IX (1903)
TJHSE	*Transactions of the Jewish Historical Society of England*

Chapter 1

1 C. P. Snow, 'Family Ritual', *Financial Times*, 24 February 1972.

2 W. Laqueur in *Commentary* XLIV (July 1967), p. 84.

3 Lord Blake in the *Sunday Times*, 6 April 1975.

4 See B. Zawadzki, 'Limitations of the Scapegoat Theory of Prejudice', *Journal of Abnormal and Social Psychology* XLIII (1948), pp. 136–7 for a specific comment on this.

5 Based upon J. H. Robb, *Working Class Anti-Semite* (London, 1954), p. 11. See also L. Kushnick, 'Negroes versus Jews: Anti-semitism is Denied', *Patterns of Prejudice* III (March-April 1969), pp. 13–15. B. D. Weinryb, 'Antisemitism in Soviet Russia', in L. Kochan (ed.), *Jews in Russia since 1917* (2nd edn, Oxford, 1972), pp. 287–93, illustrates the problems of definition.

6 B. Glassman, *Anti-Semitic Stereotypes without Jews: the Images of Jews in England, 1290–1700* (Detroit, 1975).

7 L. Hyman, *The Jews of Ireland* (London/Jerusalem, 1972), p. 3; *Encylopaedia Judaica* XIV (Jerusalem, 1971), p. 1035; and *ibid.* XVI p. 250 provide bare details.

8 P. Hyams, 'The Jewish Minority in Mediaeval England, 1066–1290', *Journal of Jewish Studies* XXV (1974), p. 271. Well known works on the history of Jews in medieval England include H. G. Richardson, *The English Jewry under Angevin Kings* (Oxford, 1959), and C. Roth, *A History of the Jews in England* (Oxford, 1964). Hyams, *op. cit.* refers to a number of later sources.

9 Roth, *op. cit.*, p. 132.

10 J. Parkes, 'The History of the Anglo-Jewish Community', in M. Freedman (ed.), *A Minority in Britain* (London, 1955), p. 12.

11 W. De Archenhollz, *A Picture of England: containing a description of the laws, customs and manners of England. Interspersed with curious and interesting anecdotes of many eminent persons* (London, 1797), p. 177.

12 V. D. Lipman, *Social History of the Jews in England 1850–1950* (London, 1954), p. 66. This immigration has captured much attention recently but the earlier immigration from Russian Poland has been neglected. On the latter see A. R. Rollin, 'Russo-Jewish Immigrants in England before 1881', *TJHSE* XXI (1962–7), pp. 202–13.
13 J. A. Garrard, *The English and Immigration 1880–1910* (London, 1971), appendix 1, pp. 213–16 discusses the question of numbers.
14 C. Bermant, *The Cousinhood* (London, 1971), deals with this mainly Ashkenazi elite.
15 A. J. Sherman, *Island Refuge. Britain and the Refugees from the Third Reich 1933–1939* (London, 1973). The 'strange country' phrase is Freud's and relates to his discovery that in Britain only lords could properly sign their letters with a surname. See E. L. Freud (ed.), *The Letters of Sigmund Freud and Arnold Zweig* (London, 1970), p. 164 and a letter of 28 June 1928.
16 Lipman, *op. cit.*, p. 2; Freedman, *op. cit.*, p. 62.
17 Roth, *op. cit.*, p. 91; Perry, *op. cit.*, p. 5.
18 Freedman, *op. cit.*, p. 262 gives a figure of 385,000 for 1940. Of these perhaps 56,000 were refugees from Nazi persecution. See Sherman, *op. cit.*, p. 271.
19 These figures are based upon statistics for the Jewish population in Great Britain given in Freedman, *op. cit.*, pp. 260–62 and mid-year population figures for Britain are from B. R. Mitchell and P. Deane, *Abstract of British Historical Statistics* (Cambridge, 1962), pp. 8–10.
20 Perry, *op. cit.*, p. 5.
21 P. G. J. Pulzer, *The Rise of Political Anti-Semitism in Germany and Austria* (New York, 1964), p. 9.
22 Hyams, *op. cit.*, pp. 271, 273.
23 Perry, *op. cit.*, p. 7.
24 Lipman, *op. cit.*, pp. 18–27 and his article, "The Rise of Jewish Suburbia", *TJHSE* XXI (1962–7), pp. 78–104 and C. Roth, *The Rise of Provincial Jewry* (London, 1950), are concerned with these developments. The best study of a local community outside London is B. Williams, *The Making of Manchester Jewry 1740–1875* (Manchester, 1976).
25 *RC* I, p. 14 and appendix, p. 42.
26 L. Gartner, *The Jewish Immigrant in England* (Detroit, 1960), p. 142 referring to the East End. A second edition of this work appeared in 1973.
27 Freedman, *op. cit.*, pp. 66, 74–5.
28 A point referred to in R. Skidelsky, *Oswald Mosley* (London, 1975), p. 393.
29 Hyams, *op. cit.*, p. 273.
30 Lipman, *op. cit.*, p. 34.
31 Freedman, *op. cit.*, p. 47.
32 Lipman, *op. cit.*, pp. 78–9; Freedman, *op. cit.*, p. 47.
33 Freedman, *op. cit.*, pp. 222–3.
34 Lipman, *op. cit.*, p. 174.
35 Freedman, *op. cit.*, p. 221.
36 S. Aris, *The Jews in Business* (Harmondsworth, 1973), p. 7. See also Lipman, *History*, p. 172 and J. Gould and S. Esh (eds), *Jewish Life in Modern Britain* (London, 1964), p. 27 for comments about difficulties inherent in any discussion of Jewish occupational structure.
37 Roth, *History*, p. 9. Unlike accusations on the Continent no suggestion was apparently made that blood was required for ritual purposes. Details on the blood accusation are given in the *Universal Jewish Encyclopaedia* (New York, 1948) II, pp. 407–10 and *Encyclopaedia Judaica* IV (Jerusalem, 1971), pp. 1119–31. See also J. Trachtenberg, *The Devil and the Jews* (New York, 1966), and Hyams, *op. cit.*, pp. 280–83.

38 Perry, *op. cit.*, p. 1.
39 *ibid.* is a comprehensive account of the issue. More generally, U. R. Q. Henriques, *Religious Toleration in England 1787–1833* (London, 1961), is useful on such matters.
40 Freedman, *op. cit.*, p. 39. And, as Macaulay emphasized long before, wealthy Jews enjoyed power even though they were debarred from official office. Lord Macaulay, *Essay and Speech on Jewish Disabilities* (Edinburgh, 1909 edn), pp. 22–4.
41 Roth, *Jews in England*, p. 265. In 1890 emancipation was effectively completed when it was decided that no special legislation was required for a Jew to become lord chancellor or lord lieutenant of Ireland.
42 U. R. Q. Henriques, 'The Jewish Emancipation Controversy in Nineteenth Century Britain', *Past and Present*, no. 40 (1968), pp. 139–40.
43 L. S. Dawidowicz, 'Can Anti-Semitism Be Measured?', *Commentary* L (July 1970), pp. 36–43.
44 E. Bonacich, 'A Theory of Middleman Minorities', *American Sociological Review* XXXVIII (1973), pp. 583–94 is generally useful on the experience of Jewish and other minorities in relation to such matters.
45 See below chapter 7 for the full discussion of the nature of anti-semitic conflict in Britain between 1876 and 1914. See below p. 315, for evidence that an anti-semitic tradition was present in Britain, in the sense that specific conflicts encouraged references to earlier battles against Jews. G. E. Simpson and J. M. Yinger, *Racial and Cultural Minorities* (4th edn, New York, 1972), chapter 5 discusses in general fashion the importance of prior perceptions in conflict situations. In more concrete terms it should be said that we still need to know more about the images of Jews, the processes through which they were transmitted and their subsequent influence. See I. Shachar, 'Studies in the Emergence and Dissemination of the Modern Jewish Stereotype in Western Europe', unpublished PhD thesis, University of London, 1967, for some discussion of this. For observations on major problems connected with the processes of cultural transmission see the paper by Alan J. Lee delivered at the Society for the Study of Labour History Conference, May 1978.

Chapter 2

1 J. Picciotto, *Sketches of Anglo Jewish History* (London, 1875), p. 414, illustrates the confident approach to the position of Jews in British society.
2 Sir John Skelton's description of Disraeli in 1867. Quoted in H. Arendt, *The Origins of Totalitarianism* (2nd edn, London, 1958), p. 68.
3 R. Blake, *Disraeli* (London, 1966), p. 167. The whole issue is treated in R. T. Shannon, *Gladstone and the Bulgarian Agitation, 1876* (London, 1963; reprinted 1975). A recent detailed analysis of certain aspects is in H. Cunningham, 'Jingoism in 1877–78', *Victorian Studies* XIV (1971), pp. 429–53.
4 On Smith, see *DNB* second supplement III (London, 1912), p. 337. There is a recent biography: E. Wallace, *Goldwin Smith, Victorian Liberal* (Toronto, 1957).
5 Wallace, *op. cit.*, p. 11.
6 *Parliamentary Debates*, House of Commons CLXIX (1863), col. 96.
7 Wallace, *op. cit.*, p. 184 comments on this.
8 *The Times*, 9 June 1870. For further comment on the exchange, see W. F. Monypenny and G. E. Buckle, *The Life of Benjamin Disraeli, Earl of Beaconsfield* (2 vols, new and rev. edn, London, 1929) II, pp. 505–6.
9 *DNB*, pp. 334–5.
10 G. Smith, *Reminiscences*, edited by A. Haultain (New York, 1911), p. 183.

11 *ibid.*, p. 181.
12 A. Haultain, *A Selection from Goldwin Smith's Correspondence* (London, n.d.), p. 296.
13 Shannon, *op. cit.*, p. 300.
14 G. Smith, 'England's Abandonment of the Protectorate of Turkey', *Contemporary Review* XXI (1877–8), p. 617.
15 Shannon, *op. cit.*, pp. 25, 190. See also D. C. Blaisdell, *European Financial Control in the Ottoman Empire* (New York, 1929), pp. 37, 84.
16 Shannon, *op. cit.*, pp. 13–23 is concerned with 'The Spirit of British Eastern Policy'.
17 Smith, 'England's Abandonment', etc., pp. 617–18. Much later Hamilton Fyfe in 'The Alien and the Empire', *Nineteenth Century* LIV (1903), p. 419 was to argue that in every country where there was active anti-semitism it arose from the feeling that Jews put their original nationality before their adopted nationality. Two years later, H. B. Marriott Watson in 'The Jew and his Destiny', *National Review* XLVI (1905), p. 522, contended that Jews could never display patriotism 'of the same quality as . . . those whose blood thrills at the dipping of the Union Jack'.
18 H. Adler, 'Can Jews be Patriots?', *Nineteenth Century* III (1878), pp. 637, 646.
19 G. Smith, 'Can Jews be Patriots?', *ibid.*, p. 875. He also believed that Catholics were suspect in this respect.
20 Smith repeated these charges in his discussions of the Jewish question in Russia, in the course of which he claimed that Jews, because of their tribal exclusiveness, were incapable of 'an undivided attention to the national interest'. G. Smith, 'The Jewish Question', *Nineteenth Century* X (1881), p. 495. He admitted that there were some Jews to whom his criticisms did not apply but these individuals who had sloughed off their Judaism were not regarded by him as Jews. *ibid.*, pp. 495–6.
21 *Church Times*, 25 August 1876, p. 426, quoted in Shannon, *op. cit.*, p. 201.
22 Quoted in R. W. Seton-Watson, *Disraeli, Gladstone and the Eastern Question* (London, 1935), p. 281.
23 T. P. O'Connor, *Lord Beaconsfield: a Biography* (London, 1884 edn), pp. 613, 611. See below chapter 4 and p. 292 for further evidence of antisemitic hostility directed towards Disraeli.
24 The phrase is from Blake, *op. cit.*, p. 167.
25 *ibid.* Freeman's attitude towards Disraeli is also referred to in W. R. W. Stephens (ed.), *The Life and Letters of Edward A. Freeman* (2 vols, London, 1895) II, p. 126. Stephens remarks that the term 'the Jew', which frequently appeared in Freeman's letters, was his 'jocular designation' of Disraeli, in reference partly to his Jewish extraction, partly to his oriental sympathies. Such a defence would hardly justify Freeman's remark in a letter of 24 December 1876 that 'still they [the Tories] need not lie, but I suppose with a Jew at their head they really cannot help it'; *ibid.*, p. 143. For another clear example of anti-semitism see *ibid.*, p. 152.
26 Arendt, *op. cit.*, pp. 197–8.
27 It has been remarked that while most of the Uitlanders were English, 'more than a sprinkling' came from Riga, Kiev, Frankfurt, Rotterdam and San Francisco. C. de Kiewiet, *A History of South Africa, Social and Economic* (Oxford, 1941), p. 119. A number of writers have referred specifically to the Jewish role in the development of southern Africa. These include: Marcus Arkin's article 'The Jewish Share in South African Economic Development: a review article', *South African Journal of Economics* XXIV (1956), pp. 135–43 and his more popular work on 'The German Jewish Refugees in South Africa:

their Integration and Impact', *Jewish Affairs* XXI (June 1966), pp. 17–22 and 'Jewish Personages in South Africa's Hall of Fame', *ibid.* XXIV (September, 1969), pp. 14–17. See also D. M. Krikler, 'The Pioneering Jews of Rhodesia', *Wiener Library Bulletin* XXII (1973–4), pp. 19–24. In addition, G. Saron and L. Hotz, *The Jews in South Africa* (London, 1955), is a generally useful history of Jews in this part of the world.

28 See my chapter on 'J. A. Hobson and the Jews', in C. Holmes (ed.), *Immigrants and Minorities in British Society* (London, 1978), pp. 136–40. R. Price, *An Imperial War and the British Working Class* (London, 1972), is a recent example in a long line of publications to emphasize this stress among Radicals and Socialists.

29 *Labour Leaders and the War*, issued by the Birmingham South Africa Conciliation Committee and quoted in J. S. Galbraith, 'The Pamphlet Campaign on the Boer War', *Journal of Modern History* XXIV (1952), pp. 120–21.

30 See below chapter 5.

31 L. Gartner, *The Jewish Immigrant in England, 1870–1914* (London, 1960); J. A. Garrard, *The English and Immigration, 1880–1910* (London, 1971), and B. Gainer, *The Alien Invasion* (London, 1972), are the fullest accounts of the immigration.

32 See above pp. 5–6 for additional details.

33 See above p. 5

34 G. Stedman Jones, *Outcast London* (Oxford, 1971), p. 152.

35 *Eastern Argus*, 6 August 1887.

36 See below p. 32 for my comment on the charges.

37 The *Argus* continued to be exercised by undercutting at a time when this concern had been generally replaced by the housing situation. Its tone was still anti-alien rather than anti-semitic. *East End Argus*, 3 March 1888.

38 *East London Advertiser*, 3 March 1888.

39 *Eastern Post and City Chronicle*, 19 March 1887.

40 J. J. Bennett's Sheffield MA thesis is concerned with all the matters discussed in this paragraph. However, his arguments are based upon a much wider range of East End newspapers.

41 *East London Advertiser*, 26 November 1898.

42 *ibid.*, 10 January 1903.

43 *ibid.*, 20 January 1900.

44 *Jewish Chronicle*, 12 and 19 June 1901 contain comments from an anti-immigration standpoint by H. S. Samuel on the importance of overcrowding in generating tension over immigration. Gartner, *op. cit.*, pp. 155–6 refers to the activity of the companies. J. W. Carrier, 'The Four Per Cent Industrial Dwellings Company Limited', *East London Papers* II (1968), pp. 40–46 is concerned with the social composition of shareholders.

45 *RC* appendix, tables XLIX, L and LI are useful for statistics on overcrowding and changes which were taking place between 1891 and 1901.

46 J. J. Bennett, unpublished MS. on the *Eastern Argus*.

47 Garrard, *op. cit.*, p. 111 refers to the improvement in overcrowding. See also *East London Observer*, 8 June and 3 August 1907 for references to unlet properties and falling rents.

48 By the Jewish establishment as well as the East End. See W. J. Fishman, *East End Jewish Radicals, 1875–1914* (London, 1975), pp. 68–9.

49 *East London Advertiser*, 6 May 1899.

50 *ibid.*, 17 January 1903 and 20 September 1902. See also 30 August 1902 and 20 August 1904.

51 *East London Observer*, 23 May 1891 and 4 June 1898.

52 *RC* II, pp. 298 and 178.
53 *ibid.*, p. 286.
54 *East London Observer*, 25 August 1900. See also *ibid.*, 10 July 1897; 18 and 29 December 1900; 5 January 1901 and 12 December 1901. The August report was based upon G. A. Wade, 'Israel in London. How the Jew lives in Whitechapel', *English Illustrated Magazine* XXIII (1900), p. 406.
55 *Eastern Post and City Chronicle*, 22 November 1884.
56 *Eastern Post and City Chronicle*, 8 February 1902; *East London Advertiser*, 29 December 1901 and 18 January 1902; *Jewish Chronicle*, 24 January 1902 and *RC* II, p. 105. Even so the *East London Observer*, 1 March 1902 was not convinced about such protestations.
57 For a discussion of the issues involved, see below pp. 31–4.
58 Comments drawn from the 1902 meeting of the British Brothers' League. See evidence given before the *RC* II, pp. 286–90 and 292 and opinion reported in the *Eastern Post and City Chronicle*, 18 January 1902.
59 *East London Advertiser*, 30 May 1891.
60 *RC* II, p. 299.
61 Garrard, *op. cit.*, p. 73.
62 J. H. Robb, *Working Class Anti-Semite* (London, 1954), p. 210 and Fishman, *op. cit.*, p. 87.
63 See below chapter 5.
64 See below chapter 6.
65 See Garrard, *op. cit.*, p.. 95–102 for a number of arguments of this kind.
66 Charles Rolleston, in the *New Liberal Review* (March 1904), pp. 236–7.
67 B. Potter, 'East London Labour', *Nineteenth Century* XXIV (1888), pp. 176–7.
68 B. Potter, 'The Jewish Community' in Charles Booth (ed.), *Labour and Life of the People* (London, 1889) I, p. 590.
69 As referred to in Fishman, *op. cit.*
70 See the letters in *Encounter* starting in March 1976.
71 See below pp. 228–9 for more discussion of these matters.
72 Hobson, *op. cit.*, pp. 58–9. For similar remarks see Ben Tillett's comments in *Labour Leader*, 29 December 1894.
73 Hobson, *op. cit.*, p. 60.
74 Garrard, *op. cit.*, p. 71 and B. C. Roberts, *The Trades Union Congress 1868–1921* (London, 1958), pp. 182–3.
75 Garrard, *op. cit.*, p. 158 quotes a number of sources which illustrate this.
76 S. Lerner, 'The Impact of the Jewish Immigration of 1880–1914 on the London Clothing Industry and Trade Unions', *Society for the Study of Labour History Bulletin* XII (summer 1966), p. 14 gives an outline of changes in the unionization of London Jewish clothing workers.
77 This is particularly true of E. Silberner, 'British Socialism and the Jews', *Historia Judaica* XIV (1952), pp. 27–52 and in his book *Sozialisten zur Judenfrage* (Berlin, 1962). A recent study of Socialist attitudes is P. D. Colbenson, 'British Socialism and Anti-semitism 1884–1914', unpublished PhD thesis, Georgia State University, 1977.
78 The phrase is from *Commonweal*, 5 May 1888.
79 *ibid.*
80 As in *ibid.*, 19 May 1888.
81 *Justice*, 1 March 1902, 20 March 1902 and 6 May 1905. And argued specifically in relation to the housing question in 'The Jews in East London' by 'One of Them' in the *Social Democrat*, February 1903, pp. 80–81.
82 J. Bruce Glasier, 'Socialism and the Anti-Alien Sentiment', *Labour Leader*, 30 April 1904; J. Havelock Wilson's speech in *Parliamentary Debates*, House

of Commons, VIII (1893), cols 1156, 1171–74. H. Snell, *The Foreigner in England* (London, 1903), provide a cross section of opinion.

83 *Clarion*, 9 January 1892. On Blatchford and the *Clarion*, see L. W. J. Barrow, 'The Socialism of Robert Blatchford and the *Clarion* 1889–1918', unpublished PhD thesis, University of London, 1975.

84 *Clarion*, 12 October 1895.

85 *ibid.*, 22 June 1906.

86 *ibid.*, 13 July 1906.

87 *Justice*, 7 July 1906.

88 Silberner, *Historia Judaica*, p. 34. It might be stressed here that our concern is with the Fabians as a corporate body. The thought of prominent individual Fabians is referred to elsewhere. See above pp. 19–20.

89 E. J. Hobsbawm, 'Fabianism and the Fabians 1884–1914', unpublished PhD thesis, University of Cambridge, 1948, p. 38.

90 *Fabian News* XV, June 1905, pp. 29–30.

91 See above pp. 19–20 for Beatrice Potter's remarks.

92 Garrard, *op. cit.*, pp. 188–9.

93 *Parliamentary Debates*, House of Commons, CXXXIII (1904), col. 1149 contains a speech by John Burns in this vein; Garrard, *op. cit.*, p. 192 points out that *Reynolds's News* discussed the prospect of immigration legislation along related lines. Pete Curran could also turn a similar discussion into a forum for an attack on rich Jews – see *Labour Leader*, 27 January 1905 – as could Harry Snell in *The Foreigner in England* etc., p. 1. See below pp. 68–70 for socialist hostility of a conspiratorial kind towards rich Jews.

94 See, for instance, W. H. Chaloner and W. O. Henderson, 'Marx, Engels and Racism', *Encounter* XLV (July 1975), pp. 18–23, after which a debate, with wild and patronising overtones, began in the same magazine in March 1976 on Beatrice Webb's attitudes towards Jews. This was followed by G. Watson, 'Race and the Socialists. On the Progressive Principle of Revolutionary Extermination', *Encounter* XLVII (December 1976), pp. 15–23.

95 Details of White are given in *Who Was Who, 1916–1928* (London, 1929), p. 1116.

96 A. White, 'The Invasion of Pauper Foreigners', *Nineteenth Century* XXIII (1888), pp. 414–15, 419; his evidence before the *House of Lords Select Committee on the Sweating System*, British Parliamentary Papers XX (1888), p. 44, and the *Select Committee on Emigration and Immigration (Foreigners)*, British Parliamentary Papers XI (1888), p. 86, as well as his memorandum of the immigration question in H.O. 45 10062/B2386/8, collectively provide evidence on these matters.

97 White, 'Pauper Foreigners', pp. 418–19.

98 *House of Lords Select Committee on the Sweating System*, p. 46–7.

99 White, 'Pauper Foreigners', p. 418.

100 *Jewish Chronicle*, 3 February 1888.

101 A. White, *For Efficiency*, etc. (London, 1902), p. 164; and in his articles, 'Kishineff and after', *Living Age*, 26 September 1903, p. 809 and 'The Jewish Question: How to solve it', *North American Review* CLXXVIII (1904), p. 18, all discuss this.

102 The imagery is from H. Frederic, *The New Exodus* (London, 1892), p. 151.

103 On the Hirsch scheme see S. Joseph, *History of the Baron de Hirsch Fund* (Philadelphia, 1935), and *The Universal Jewish Encyclopaedia* V (New York, 1948), pp. 375–7. For some comments by White see 'Jewish Colonization and the Russian Peasants' *New Review* (1891), pp. 97–105 and *The Modern Jew* (London, 1899), pp. 131–5 and 294–301. His comment about the image of

the Jew is in *The Modern Jew*, p. 57. See also his article 'The Truth about the Russian Jew', *Contemporary Review* LXI (1892), pp. 699–700 and a letter from White to Hirsch, 27 June 1891 at the JCA in London.

104 White, *The Modern Jew*, pp. 39–40. See also his article 'Europe and the Jews', *Contemporary Review* XXII (1897), p. 738.

105 *RC* II, p. 15.

106 *ibid.*

107 *ibid.*, pp. 16 and 49–50.

108 *Modern Jew*, pp. xii, xiii, 144. White's arguments in this connection assumed a conspiratorial tone and are consequently discussed below in chapter 5.

109 *Pall Mall Gazette*, 3 November 1897.

110 White, *The Modern Jew*, p. 275.

111 *ibid.*, pp. 49–50.

112 See his evidence in *RC* II, p. 15.

113 See his views on the 'redemption' of the Jewish personality through contact with the soil which he expressed in *The Modern Jew*.

114 See A. White, *The English Democracy* (London, 1894), pp. 154, 165 for a discussion of this.

115 Gainer, *op. cit.*, p. 127.

116 HO 45 10063/B2840/A35; HO 45 10063/B2840/A36; HO 45 10063/B2840/A47, which have never been considered in any study of Jewish immigration, indicate how closely the government could consider his views. Interestingly enough, Beatrice Potter saw through him. B. Webb, *Diaries* XII, November 1887 to December 1888, entry for 27 November 1887, p. 12.

117 A. White, *The Problems of a Great City* (London, 1895); his book *The Modern Jew*, his article, 'The Jewish Question: How to solve it', *North American Review* CLXXVIII (1904), pp. 10–24 and his assorted ideas in *The Views of Vanoc* (London, 1913), are a useful guide to his attitudes. Gainer, *op. cit.*, pp. 121–7 is the best attempt we have to pull his wandering ideas into shape. See also S. G. Bayme, 'Jewish Leadership and Anti-Semitism in Britain 1898–1918', unpublished PhD thesis, Columbia University, 1977, pp. 136–56.

118 See below p. 92.

119 For biographical details see *Who Was Who, 1897–1916* (London, 1920), p. 284. For a sympathetic cameo picture see C. Weizmann, *Trial and Error* (London, 1950), pp. 118–20.

120 W. E. Evans-Gordon, *The Alien Immigrant* (London, 1903), p. 10. The pale of settlement was the territory in the west of Russia stretching from the Black Sea to the Baltic in which Jews, except those officially exempted, were obliged to reside by decree of the authorities.

121 *ibid.*, p. 247 provides additional information on this.

122 *RC* II, p. 69.

123 *ibid.*

124 *ibid.*, p. 95; see below p. 92 for additional references to Silver's position.

125 J. Banister, *England under the Jews* (3rd edn, London, 1907), p. 23. Banister's attitudes are extensively discussed below, pp. 39–42.

126 *East London Observer*, 27 June 1903; see below pp. 89–95 for references to Shaw and the BBL.

127 *Morning Advertiser*, 9 January 1906 in D. Hope Kyd press cuttings. For comment see the *Jewish Chronicle*, 12 January 1906.

128 See *Who Was Who, 1916–28*, p. 193 and A. Chesterton, *The Chestertons* (London, 1941).

129 D. Barker, *G. K. Chesterton* (London, 1973), pp. 210–11.

130 See below pp. 70–79 and for a discussion of the *Witness* and the Marconi

scandal and the National League for Clean Government.
131 'The Jewish Question', in the *Eye Witness*, 7 September 1911, p. 365.
132 *ibid.*
133 *ibid.*
134 *ibid.*, 28 September 1911, p. 459.
135 *ibid.*
136 *ibid.*
137 *ibid.*, 5 October 1911, p. 489.
138 *ibid.*, 12 October 1911, p. 522.
139 *ibid.*, 19 October 1911, p. 555.
140 *ibid.*, 26 October 1911, p. 589.
141 *ibid.*
142 The essential outline of the arguments was repeated by Cecil Chesterton in 'Israel A Nation', *British Review* (May 1913) pp. 161–9 and in the *New Witness*, 26 June 1913, pp. 240–41.
143 Fishman's phrase in *op. cit.*, p. 30.
144 Mundella to R. Leader, 4 May 1877 (A. J. Mundella papers, University of Sheffield Library). See also note 15 above.
145 Shannon, *op. cit.*, p. 200, quoting the *Jewish Chronicle*, 18 August 1876.
146 *ibid.*
147 S. Mendelssohn, *Jewish Pioneers of South Africa* (London, 1912), and, more recently, Emden, *op. cit.*
148 In the issue of 1 April 1904. The subjunctive irony in this clearly went over the heads of the editorial staff.
149 Arendt, *op. cit.*, pp. 202–3. For a further discussion of this matter see below pp. 68–70, 79, 81.
150 See below pp. 228–9.
151 See Garrard, *op. cit.*, pp. 95–102 for Liberal images of the 'Jewish economic man'.
152 Fishman, *op. cit.*, p. 49.
153 *ibid.*, p. 50. See also Lewis, *op. cit.*, pp. 83–4.
154 Garrard, *op. cit.*, p. 159.
155 Fishman, *op. cit.*, p. 79 brings perspective to this.
156 E. Bonacich, 'A Theory of Ethnic Antagonism: the Split Labor Market', *American Sociological Review* XXXVII (1972), pp. 547–59 is generally useful on immigrant labour and such matters.
157 *RC* II, pp. 19–20 refers generally to the impact upon British labour; Fishman *op. cit.*, p. 83 notices that the effect upon tradesmen could be variable.
158 Gartner, *op. cit.*, p. 147.
159 *Jewish Chronicle*, 28 September 1888. See also *ibid.*, 12 August 1881, 'they bring Poland to England and retain it while they stay here.'
160 Fishman, *op. cit.*, p. 54 and C. Lewis, *A Soho Address* (London, 1965).
161 Fishman, *op. cit.*, p. 69.
162 *ibid.*, p. 72. Even Arnold White acknowledge this. See *RC* II, p. 18.
163 J. A. Hobson, *Problems of Poverty* (London, 1891). p. 59.
164 Gartner, *op. cit.*, p. 152; *Lancet*, 3 May 1884, pp. 317–18 has comment on the hygiene problem; William Catmur in the *East London Observer*, 6 January 1906 provides a classic statement about the East End as a neglected area.
165 See above p. 28.
166 See his contribution in A. White (ed.), *The Destitute Alien in Great Britain* (London, 1892), pp. 87–92.
167 Fishman, *op. cit.*, pp. 83–6. M. J. Landa, 'The Economic Aspect of Alien Labour', *Economic Review* XVI (1906), pp. 43–55 is a contemporary pro-alien

assessment of the economic impact of Jewish immigrants.

168 See below pp. 64, 95.

169 See particularly H. B. Marriott Watson, 'The Jew and his Destiny', etc., pp. 518ff.

170 See above p. 29.

171 P. C. P. Siu, 'The Sojourner', *American Journal of Sociology* LVIII (1952), pp. 34–44 and E. Bonacich, 'A Theory of Middleman Minorities', *American Sociological Review* XXXVIII (1973), pp. 583–94 are useful here.

172 C. Roth, *The Sassoon Dynasty* (London, 1941), p. 229.

173 *ibid.*, p. 230. R. R. James, *Rosebery* (London, 1963), pp. 81, 84. In a comment which in itself is revealing in a number of different ways, Rosebery's brother wrote: 'Archie is to marry Miss Hannah Rothschild and her millions! I really believe the young woman has annually 80,000 £ worth of hard cash! I think that is enough to buy the consent of a whole tribe – were it even of Levi – I cannot conceal from myself that this marriage will be a great blow to my mother – whose house has hitherto stood out against an infusion of Jewish society – and whose sentiments even on the report were expressed with force.' For a more open view among the aristocracy see Eighth Duke of Argyll, *Autobiography and Memoirs* (2 vols, London, 1906) I, p. 279.

174 Sir A. Fitzroy, *Memoirs* (6th edn, 2 vols, London, n.d.) I, p. 102; *DNB 1912–21* (London, 1927), p. 99.

175 As is evident from a reading of C. Bermant, *The Cousinhood* (London, 1971).

176 See the details in *The Times* 6 March 1911. See also below p. 256 for further discussion of the matter.

177 J. Higham, 'Anti-Semitism in the Gilded Age', *Mississippi Valley Historical Review* XLIII (1956–7), p. 566 and the same author's *Strangers in the Land. Patterns of American Nativism 1860–1925* (New York, 1963), p. 402 are useful on this issue.

Chapter 3

1 K. Pearson, *National Life from the Standpoint of Science* (London, 1905), pp. 54, 104–5.

2 See below pp. 216–17.

3 Rentoul's death at the age of seventy in 1925 was noticed in the *Liverpool Daily Post and Mercury*, 5 September 1925 and there was an obituary in the *British Medical Journal*, 3 October 1925, p. 630.

4 R. J. Halliday, 'Social Darwinism: a Definition', *Victorian Studies* XIV (1971), p. 401.

5 R. R. Rentoul, *Race Culture*; *or*, *Race Suicide* (London, 1906), pp. xii, 1.

6 The quotation is from R. R. Rentoul, *The Undesirable Alien from the Medical Standpoint* (Liverpool, 1905), p. 5.

7 *RC* II, p. 128. Rentoul wrote a pamphlet on *Trachoma in Immigrants* which seems to have been lost without trace.

8 RC II, p. 165.

9 *ibid.*, pp. 135, 152, 197.

10 The series ran from 2 to 19 January 1905. J. A. Garrard, *The English and Immigration 1880–1910* (London, 1971), p. 62 is mistaken in thinking that it ended on 14 January.

11 *ibid.* The *Jewish Chronicle*, 13 and 20 January 1905 and 10 February 1905 have details of the correspondence.

12 The *Standard*, 5 January 1905.
13 *ibid.* See also 6 January 1905.
14 J. Higham, *Strangers in the Land. Patterns of American Nativism 1860–1925* (New York, 1963), refers to American legislation of 1882, 1885, 1887, 1891 and 1893. See pp. 43–4, 48–9, 99–100.
15 *The Standard*, 19 January 1905.
16 See below pp. 228–9.
17 For further details of his career see *Who Was Who, 1929–40* (London, 1941), p. 477.
18 *Yorkshire Post*, 21 April 1903.
19 *ibid.*, 25 April 1903.
20 *ibid.*, 25 April and 1 May 1905.
21 *ibid.*, 21 April 1903.
22 *ibid.*, 25 April 1903.
23 *Sunday Chronicle*, 5 January 1908.
24 J. Buckman, 'The Economic and Social History of Alien Immigration to Leeds, 1880–1914', unpublished PhD thesis, University of Strathclyde, 1968, pp. 454–9.
25 Hence it is discussed below in chapter 5.
26 J. Banister, *England under the Jews* (3rd edn, London, 1907), pp. 81, 21. The fullest discussion of Banister's thought is in my article, 'Joseph Banister's Anti-semitism', *Patterns of Prejudice* IV (July–August 1970), pp. 29–32.
27 Banister, *op. cit.*, pp. 57–8.
28 *ibid.*, p. 59.
29 *ibid.*, p. 61.
30 *ibid.*, p. 61. Lupus is a tuberculous skin disease; trachoma is a contagious eye disease; favus is a skin disease of the scalp.
31 *ibid.*, p. 64. Language of a similar kind directed against aliens appeared in the *Pall Mall Gazette* at the time of the smallpox scare in 1901. See Garrard, *op. cit.*, p. 61. A more balanced view and a corrective to the *Gazette*'s 'grunting' and 'itching' imagery is present in the discussion of the smallpox epidemic in the *East London Observer*, 28 September 1901.
32 J. Banister, *Hints to London Editors* (London, 1934), pp. 1, 7.
33 Banister, *England under the Jews*, p. 45.
34 Garrard, *op. cit.*, p. 57 raises the issue of the disreputability of anti-semitism.
35 J. Higham, 'Anti-Semitism in the Gilded Age. A Reinterpretation', *Mississippi Valley Historical Review* XLIII (1956–7), p. 563.
36 See Banister, *England under the Jews*, pp. 78–80; on mixed stereotypes see my discussion of Hobson's thought in C. Holmes (ed.), *Immigrants and Minorities in British Society* (London, 1978), pp. 142–3.
37 B. Bettelheim and M. Janowitz, *The Dynamics of Prejudice* (New York, 1950), pp. 37–8.
38 L. Lowenthal and N. Guterman, *Prophets of Deceit* (New York, 1949), p. 55.
39 *ibid.* In fact germs are not animals but this does not significantly diminish the point they are trying to make.
40 Banister, *England under the Jews*, pp. 19–20, 22–3, 64, 98, 155, 177.
41 Attention is restricted at this juncture to Banister's remarks before 1914 but it might be said that such imagery was also a feature of his later work. In *Our Judaeo-Irish Labour Party* (London, 1923), p. 56, he wrote, in crude, associative fashion: 'There are, in Russia, typhus, cholera, scarlet fever, bugs, beetles, lice, ticks (and 7 million of Trotsky's tribesmen).'
42 See below pp. 156–8 for a discussion of the Britons. Banister's work has sur-

vived in surprising number – perhaps he sedulously distributed them to leading libraries.

43 N. Cohn, *Warrant for Genocide* (London, 1967), p. 18.

44 Banister, *England under the Jews*, pp. 1–2. None of us is entirely alone, however. In the 1907 edition of *England under the Jews* which is to be found in the LSE library, the Jew-hater, C. W. Smith, wrote in 1909 that every word in the book was true and the Jews would yet be the ruin of 'Old England'.

45 See Vincent's evidence in *RC* II, pp. 820–23. His career is discussed in S. H. Jeyes, *The Life of Sir Howard Vincent* (London 1912). Anderson's views are recorded in Sir R. Anderson, 'The Problem of the Criminal Alien', *Nineteenth Century*, no. 408 (February 1911), pp. 217–25. The relations between police and aliens during these years are discussed in J. J. Tobias, 'Police-Immigrant Relations in England 1880–1910', *New Community* III (summer 1974), pp. 211–14.

46 *RC* appendix. Tables 64–70 provide certain statistical details and M. J. Landa, *The Alien Problem and Its Remedy* (London, 1911), pp. 153–68 discusses trends down to 1914.

47 B. Gainer, *The Alien Invasion* (London, 1972), pp. 203–6 provides a general view of these years. D. Rumbelow, *The Houndsditch Murders* (London, 1973), is useful on the 1909 Tottenham outrages, the Houndsditch robbery and the 1911 siege. See also my article, 'In Search of Sidney Street', *Bulletin of the Society for the Study of Labour History* XXIX (autumn 1974), pp. 70–77 for a review of the literature and evidence on Sidney Street. Mr Colin Rogers has another book on these themes which is awaiting an adventurous publisher.

48 Gainer, *op. cit.*, p. 100.

49 *ibid.*, p. 101. L. Gartner, *The Jewish Immigrant in England* (Detroit, 1960), chapter 4 *passim* discusses such matters and the world of Jewish radicals is lovingly recreated in W. J. Fishman, *East End Jewish Radicals 1875–1914* (London, 1975).

50 W. H. Wilkins, *The Alien Invasion* (London, 1892), p. 48.

51 Letter to Salisbury, 5 July 1894, in Salisbury's papers. Quoted in Gainer, *op. cit.*, p. 104.

52 Gainer, *op. cit.*, p. 105. On Sherard's reports see pp. 37–8 above.

53 S. H. Jeyes, 'Foreign Pauper Immigration', in A. White (ed.), *The Destitute Alien in Great Britain* (London, 1892), p. 189.

54 *The Times*, 25 April 1904.

55 Gartner, *op. cit.*, p. 183.

56 Wilkins, *op. cit.*, pp. 93–4, 104.

57 Evans Gordon, *op. cit.*, p. 263 claimed that alien prostitutes were responsible for producing and perpetuating sexual activities which otherwise would be known in Britain only vicariously through the work of Homer and Catullus! In similar vein G. S. Reaney in 'The Moral Aspect' in White (ed.), *op. cit.*, p. 75 accused the alien Jew of importing 'vices common to the deeper depths of continental cities'. The imagination was left to wander on this and no explanation was forthcoming as to what these were.

58 See *RC* II, pp. 44, 280, 446, and W. A. Coote, *A Romance of Philanthropy* (London, 1916), respectively.

59 HO 45 10062/B2386/8, Pauper Immigration. Deputation to Mr Matthews and Mr Ritchie, 15 December 1887. This detail was picked up in the *Briton* no. 1, 30 April 1887 and remarked upon in *ibid.*, no. 6, 4 June 1887. Throughout its ephemeral life the *Briton* – which had, as its slogan, 'For all who love the Mother Country' – took a keen interest in immigration matters.

60 Banister, *England under the Jews*, p. 5.
61 *ibid.*, p. 6.
62 *ibid.*, pp. 79–80. Banister continued to inveigh against Jews in the white slave traffic when he was writing for the Britons. See his pamphlet, *Jews and the White Slave Traffic or Lords of the Hells of Gomorrah* (London, 192?). For perspective on these later charges see S. Salomon (ed.), *The Jews of Britain* (London, 1938), pp. 104–7.
63 *Jewish Chronicle*, 4 June 1886.
64 *ibid.*, 12 October 1888.
65 Gartner, *op. cit.*, p. 185.
66 *ibid.* contains a reference to the conference. Report, London Committee of Deputies of the British Jews (London, 1907), p. 39 refers to the Board's establishment of a special vigilance committee.
67 All these are referred to in Gartner, *op. cit.*, p. 184.
68 *Report to the Board of Trade on the Sweating System at the East End of London by the Labour Correspondent of the Board (John Burnett)*, BPP LXXXIX (1887), p. 8.
69 The *Briton*, 7 May 1887; a similar comment was made in the same year by the deputation which visited the Home Office on the matter of pauper immigration. See HO 45 10062/B2386/8. It was also a continuing concern of W. H. Wilkins. See Wilkins, *op. cit.*, p. 93 and his pamphlet, *The Bitter Cry of the Voteless Toilers. With special reference to the seamstresses of East London* (London, 1893), p. 9.
70 N. Deakin, 'The Vitality of a Tradition', in Holmes (ed.), *op. cit.*, p. 163.
71 C. C. Hernton, *Sex and Racism* (New York, 1965), is a well known work which illustrates this approach.
72 In G. J. Kneeland, *Commercialized Prostitution in New York City* (New York, 1913), pp. 200–201 some of the statistics are made to reveal which offenders were Jewish. But there does not seem to be anything equivalent for Britain.
73 As noted in Gartner, *op. cit.*, p. 184.
74 According to *ibid.*, p. 183 there is a powerful account of the Russian end of the traffic in M. M. Seforim's novel, *Ba Yamin ha Hem* (*In Those Days*), and its Yiddish version *Dos Vinshfingeril* (*The Wishing Ring*). The novel, written in 1880s, was in fact describing the traffic of the 1840s and 1850s but the details seemed contemporaneous with the time of writing. In Britain white slave trafficking was made illegal by the 1885 Criminal Law Amendment Act.
75 Pearson, *National Life*, *op. cit.*, p. 105.
76 Rentoul, *Race Culture*; *or*, *Race Suicide*, *op. cit.*, p. 1.
77 S. Webb, *The Decline of the Birth Rate*, Fabian Tract, no. 131 (1907), printed in *Fabian Tracts, nos. 1–153* (London, n.d.).
78 *Spectator*, 16 August 1902 quoted in G. R. Searle, *The Quest for National Efficiency. A Study in British Politics and Political Thought, 1899–1914* (Oxford, 1971), p. 1. In an earlier work, *Imperialism and Social Reform* (London, 1960), Bernard Semmel had also focused his attention on such matters.
79 See below chapter 7 for a more extensive discussion of macro- and micro-contex's.
80 See Fishman, *op. cit.*, pp. 21–2 for a report on conditions in Russia and W. E. Evans-Gordon's account of conditions which had to be endured in Vilna in *RC* II, p. 456. See also F. H. E. Palmer, *Russian Life in Town and Country* (London, 1901), p. 125.
81 *RC* I, pp. 10–11.
82 Interestingly enough, Richard Burton, whose opinions will be considered in

chapter 4, believed that Jews enjoyed a superiority in resisting disease. See *The Jew, The Gypsy and El Islam* (London, 1898), p. 8.

83 See above p. 45.

Chapter 4

1 W. H. Wilkins in Sir Richard F. Burton, *The Jew, the Gypsy and El Islam*, edited with a preface and brief notes by W. H. Wilkins (London, 1898), p. xvi.
2 Jacket on F. M. Brodie, *The Devil Drives* (Harmondsworth, 1971).
3 In the issue of 24 October 1890.
4 *ibid.*, 4 May 1906.
5 Brodie, *op. cit.*, pp. 311–31 deals with this period of his life.
6 For further details about his removal from Damascus see below pp. 59–61.
7 Burton, *op. cit.*, p. vii.
8 Quoted in Brodie, *op. cit.*, p. 464.
9 See the consecration to I. Burton, *The Life of Captain Sir Richard F. Burton* (London, 2 vols, 1893).
10 Brodie, *op. cit.*, p. 464.
11 R. Burton, *op. cit.*, pp. 115–29.
12 *ibid.*, p. 128. On the Padre Tomaso affair see the brief summary and references contained in *Encyclopaedia Judaica* v (Jerusalem, 1971), pp. 1249–52 and the fuller, earlier account by A. M. Hyamson, 'The Damascus Affair – 1840', *TJHSE* XVI (1945–51), pp. 47–71.
13 The *Athenaeum*, 7 May 1898, pp. 591–2.
14 The *Critic* XXXIV (March 1899), pp. 280–81.
15 The *Bookman*, June 1898, p. 74.
16 *Spectator*, 14 May 1898, p. 696.
17 R. Burton, *op. cit.*, p. x.
18 *ibid.*, pp. x–xi.
19 *ibid.*, p. xi.
20 Brodie, *op. cit.*, p. 464.
21 Board of Deputies, minute book, 13 March 1889 – October 1898, meeting of 14 March 1897.
22 See Law and Parliamentary Committee, minute book 1895 – 1901, meeting 18 March 1897 and 31 March 1897 and *ibid.*, meeting 8 April 1897.
23 *ibid.*, meeting 8 April 1897.
24 *ibid.*, meeting 13 May 1897.
25 *ibid.*, meeting 4 July 1897.
26 *ibid.*, meeting 27 October 1897.
27 Board of Deputies, minute book 13, meeting 17 April 1898. The Board preferred the 'i' to the 'y' in gypsy.
28 *ibid.*
29 Law and Parliamentary Committee, minute book, 1895–1901, meeting 1·2 May 1898.
30 Board of Deputies, minute book 13, meeting 15 May 1898.
31 *ibid.*, meeting 25 October 1908.
32 *ibid.*, meeting 21 February 1909. See also Law and Parliamentary Committee, minute book, 1904–11, meeting 4 February 1909.
33 Board of Deputies, minute book 16, March 1909 to July 1915, meeting 25 March 1909.
34 Brodie, *op. cit.*, p. 464; for Alexander's role in the affair see Board Minute Book 13, meeting 14 March 1897, 17 April 1898, 15 May 1898, 25 October 1908. Alexander was president of the Board of Deputies between 1903 and

1917. Contrary to Brodie's suggestion, Alexander was not Isabel Burton's literary trustee – a claim made in Brodie *op. cit.*, p. 464.

35 *The Times*, 28 March 1911. Alexander had such rights since as president of the Board he was the assignee of the Burton manuscript.

36 See above p. 53.

37 See *DNB*, second supplement III (London, 1912), pp. 666–7.

38 *The Times*, 28 March 1911.

39 C. Roth, *A History of the Jews in England* (Oxford, 1964), pp. 9, 56–7. See above p. 7 for earlier references.

40 *Universal Jewish Encyclopaedia* II (New York, 1948), p. 407, and *Encyclopaedia Judaica* IV (Jerusalem, 1971), pp. 1120–22.

41 M. Samuel, *Blood Accusation. The Strange History of the Beiliss Case* (London, 1967), provides details on the Beiliss affair. The best work is still A. B. Tager, *The Decay of Czarism – The Beiliss Trial* (Philadelphia, 1935).

42 See above p. 50.

43 Board of Deputies, minute book 12, April 1878 – February 1889, meeting 25 May 1881.

44 See below pp. 164–5 for Arnold Leese's charge of ritual murder against the Jewish community in 1936.

45 He wrote: 'So a man will often say 'Judêo-nos', he has jewed us. Jew is still used here in a sense which is utterly obsolete amongst the educated classes in Europe. Had I a choice of race, there is none to which I would belong more willingly than the Jewish – of course to the white family.' Captain Richard F. Burton, *Explorations of the Highlands of Brazil* (London, 2 vols, 1869) I, p. 403. Two brief comments might be made on this. First of all, Brodie, *op. cit.*, p. 334 omits the crucial, qualifying end phrase of Burton's note. Secondly, the perjorative use of the verb 'to jew' was wider than Burton was prepared to admit. It was, and still is, not uncommon in private conversation.

46 Brodie, *op. cit.*, p. 163.

47 *Lord Beaconsfield. A Sketch* by Captain Richard F. Burton (London, n.d. 1882?), p. 4.

48 *ibid.*, pp. 11 and 3.

49 *ibid.*, p. 12.

50 See my references to the hostility of Goldwin Smith and others towards Disraeli in 'Goldwin Smith. A Liberal Anti-Semite', *Patterns of Prejudice* VI (September–October 1972), pp. 25–30.

51 G. Watson, *The English Ideology* (London, 1973), pp. 206–7 coined the phrase 'bright racialism'.

52 Burton, *Beaconsfield*, p. 5.

53 A similar technique was employed by Arnold White in *The Modern Jew* (London, 1899), p. xv.

54 Burton, *Beaconsfield*, p. 5.

55 *ibid.*, p. 6.

56 *ibid.*, pp. 6, 10–11.

57 *ibid.*, pp. 5–6 and Burton, *The Jew*, pp. 4–5.

58 Burton, *Beaconsfield*, p. 5; Burton, *The Jew*, pp. 63–4.

59 Burton, *Beaconsfield*, pp. 4–5; Burton, *The Jew*, pp. 20, 27–8.

60 For further details see *DNB*, second supplement III, pp. 666–7.

61 J. A. Garrard, *The English and Immigration, 1880–1910* (London, 1971), p. 30.

62 *ibid.* On Dunraven see his autobiography *Past Times and Pastimes* (London, 1922).

63 Full details of these publications are as follows: W. H. Wilkins, 'The Immigra-

tion of Destitute Foreigners', *National Review* XVI (1890–91), pp. 114–24; W. H. Wilkins, 'Immigration Troubles of the United States', *Nineteenth Century* XXX (1891), pp. 583–95; W. H. Wilkins, 'The Italian Aspect', in Arnold White (ed.), *The Destitute Alien in Great Britain* (London, 1892), pp. 146–67; W. H. Wilkins, *The Alien Invasion* (London, 1892); W. H. Wilkins, *The Bitter Cry of the Voteless Toilers. With special reference to the seamstresses of East London* (London, 1893).

64 Brodie, *op. cit.*, and Garrard *op. cit.*, both miss the significance of the Wilkins connection, as does B. Gainer, *The Alien Invasion* (London, 1972).

65 Brodie, *op. cit.*, p. 336.

66 See Samuel, *op. cit.*, for the necessary details on this. The event seems to have provided material for Bernard Malamud's novel, *The Fixer*. An inaccurate summary of Burton's book was circulated in Kiev at the time of the trial.

67 For an analysis of British public opinion and the Beiliss affair see S. G. Bayme, 'Jewish Leadership and Anti-Semitism in Britain 1898–1918', unpublished PhD thesis, Columbia University, 1977, pp. 156–61: among the major 'quality' periodicals an important article on the earlier ritual murder incidents is C. H. H. Wright, 'The Jews and the Malicious Charge of Human Sacrifice', *Nineteenth Century* XIV (1883), pp. 753–78.

68 See *The Times*, 21 May 1912; 28 May 1912; 27 May 1912.

69 Wright, *op. cit.*, p. 778.

70 See *Leading British Christian Theologians, Men of Letters, Scientists, Politicians and others Protest. Protest signed to (remove?) the hideous charge of Ritual Murder – known as the 'Blood Accusation' against Judaism and the Jewish People* (London, 1912). Jewish opinion was reflected in a *Jewish Chronicle* publication, *The Ritual Murder Accusation and the Beilis Case* (London, 1913).

71 In fact, contrary to Floyer's claim, the book did nothing of the kind – as other opinion had clearly emphasized. The letter appeared in *The Times* 30 May 1912. Prior to this Floyer had enjoyed some correspondence with Moses Gaster, one of the leading figures of Anglo-Jewry, but after reading the letter Gaster ended the correspondence. Floyer was told: 'Dr Gaster greatly regrets to find a scholar in the twentieth century subscribing and evidently believing in one of the most atrocious and malicious falsehoods which a cruel and perverted imagination could produce. Dr Gaster regards your letter as a deep insult to himself, his faith and his people and he must therefore cease to hold any further communication with you.' Letter of 20 May 1912 by Gaster's secretary to Floyer in the Gaster Papers, Mocatta Library.

72 See above chapter 2 for earlier references to this journal. O'Donnell (1848–1916) was formerly an Irish Nationalist MP. He was also an evident anti-semite. See below pp. 75–6.

73 See the critical letter by H. Cutner in the *New Witness*, 30 October 1913, pp.823–4.

74 *ibid.*, 30 October 1913, pp. 813–15.

75 *ibid.* Burton's stay in Damascus and these incidents are referred to below. For the importance of Burton's life and thoughts to later anti-semitism see below pp. 74–6, 141, 292.

76 Perhaps it should be said here that the nature of Burton's thought is totally lost on M. F. Modder, *The Jew in the Literature of England* (Philadelphia, 1944), pp. 248–50, where, in addition, *The Jew, the Gypsy and El Islam* is inaccurately given a publication date of 1869–71. However, Burton's anti-semitism was not missed by that lynx-eyed, anti-semitic observer of the British scene, P. Aldag, in *Das Judentum in England* (Berlin, 1943), pp. 363–4.

77 S. Dearden, *The Arabian Knight. A Study of Sir Richard Burton* (London, 1936), pp. 276–7.

78 Case of Captain Burton, Late HBM's Consul at Damascus. FO 78/2260, p. 1.
79 See above p. 55.
80 T. Wright, *The Life of Sir Richard Burton* (2 vols, London, 1906) 1, p. 205.
81 FO 78/2260, p. 22.
82 The letters are reprinted in *ibid.*, pp. 24–7. O'Donnell in the *New Witness*, 30 October 1913, p. 813 goes too far in claiming that Burton was recalled in 1871 'at the instigation of two Sephardim Jews', Montefiore and Goldsmid.
83 The details are in Brodie, *op. cit.*, pp. 325–6.
84 A number of sources deal with Burton in Damascus. These include, I. Burton, *op. cit.*, chapters 20 and 21; Dearden, *op. cit.*, pp. 276–302; Brodie *op. cit.*, pp. 311–31; FO 72/2260 contains the fullest account of developments.
85 The traumatic effect of his recall from Damascus is generally commented upon.
86 Brodie, *op. cit.*, p. 334.
87 *ibid.*, pp. 334–6 delves into Burton's psyche in this connection.
88 Wilkins p. viii in his introduction to *The Jew* remarks on Burton collecting material on the Tomaso incident. FO 72/2260, pp. 26–7 contains details of a conversation in which Burton was alleged to have accepted that Jews were responsible for the murder of Tomaso.
89 FO 72/2260, pp. 28–9 contains a letter of protest by S. A. Weiskopf concerning Burton's activities in Syria. See above p. 56 for Burton's views on the Alliance Israélite Universelle. This international organization concerned with the protection of Jewish interests was founded in 1860. See A. Chouraqui, *L'Alliance Israélite Universelle et la renaissance juive contemporaine, 1860–1960* (Paris, 1965), and the shorter account in *Encyclopaedia Judaica* II (Jerusalem, 1971), pp. 648–54. N. Cohn, *Warrant for Genocide* (Harmondsworth, 1970), pp. 61–2 refers to anti-semitic opposition to the organization.
90 See *RC*, pp. 146 and 177 and Garrard, *op. cit.*, p. 63, both of which refer to evidence on this.

Among the works which concerned themselves with religious aspects of Jewish life were: S. A. Bradshaw, *The Trumpet Voice, Modus Operandi of Political, Social and Moral Forecast concerning the East. Based on Authoritative Bible Testimony* (London, 1884), in which the restoration of Jews to Palestine was described as politically urgent and socially necessary. Conversionist sentiment, which had a long tradition to draw upon, was present in W. Gidney, *The Jews and their Evangelization* (London, 1889), in the many works of D. Baron, such as *The Jewish Problem* (London, 1892), and *The Ancient Scriptures and the Modern Jew* (London, 1900), where the theme was, 'In Christ alone will Israel live again and be a blessing to the world', W. O. E. Osterley, *Walks in Jewry* (London, 1901), and P. Dearmer, *Sermons on Social Subjects* (London, 1911). Chaim Lewis in *A Soho Address* (London, 1965), p. 10 could recall some of this activity, such as 'a "Christian Mission to the Jews", which by dispensing free medicine and gospels traded on Jewish ills to work a spiritual regeneration'. His impression was that 'the Jewish sick thirstily imbibed the medicine but remained irredeemably allergic to the Christian doctrine.' Interestingly enough, Arnold White, although hostile towards Jews on a number of counts, had little time for conversionist societies. See *The Modern Jew* (London, 1899), pp. 239–60. A sympathetic history of conversionist activity is W. T. Gidney, *The History of the London Society for Promoting Christianity among the Jews from 1809 to 1908* (London, 1908).

Elsewhere, the suffering rather than the proposed redemption of Jews was concentrated upon and an explanation of anti-semitism as a chastisement upon the House of Israel for its national sin was emphasized in S. H. Wilkinson and A. Wingate, *Antisemitism, its Causes and its Cure* (London, 1907). Wilkinson was a prolific writer on Jewish matters viewed from a religious perspective. Apart from such tracts, a religious concern was also reflected in literature and one of the most popular novels of Edwardian England, Guy Thorne's *When it was Dark* (London, 1903), showed traces of hostility towards Jews expressed within a religious context. Thorne's Jewish villain, Schuabe, was portrayed as trying to bring about the confusion and collapse of society by enlisting the help of corrupted Gentile aides to 'prove' that Christ never rose from the dead. For a full discussion of Thorne's ideas see G. M. Mitchell and C. Holmes, '"*In His Image*": a study of Jews in the literature of Guy Thorne', *Patterns of Prejudice* IX (January–February 1975), pp. 18–24. This concern about the secular consequences which could arise from religious discord was apparent in different form elsewhere. Although he denied its religious implications, Goldwin Smith's hostility towards 'strict Jews' was at heart an attack upon religious Jews and needs to be recognized as such (see above pp. 11–12). And a similar dimension was apparent in the hostility towards Jewish separateness as it was discussed in the *New Witness* (see above p. 29).

Elsewhere, the social implications of Jewish religious practices came under attack. This was evident in J. Banister, *England under the Jews* (3rd edn, London, 1903), pp. 125–8, where an objection to Sunday newspapers was linked to an intention by Jewish newspaper interests to desecrate the Sabbath and a similar concern was present in W. E. Evans Gordon, *The Alien Immigrant* (London, 1903), p. 14, as well as in evidence given to the 1903 Royal Commission on Alien Immigration on the question of Sunday trading – although in this case such comments were laced with obvious economic self-interest. See *RC* II, pp. 260–61. Finally, a slightly different type of fear was expressed by G. S. Reaney, 'The Moral Aspect', in A. White (ed.), *The Destitute Alien in Great Britain* (London, 1892), p. 93, who believed that the presence of Jews encouraged a declining interest in 'Sabbath keeping' among their Christian neighbours. An interesting discussion which combines religious sentiment with a socio-economic hostility towards Jews is 'The Modern Jew', *Quarterly Review* CLXXXIII (1896), particularly pp. 51–7.

91 See above p. 56 for Burton's comment.

92 These qualities are referred to in *The Jew* p. 117 and *Lord Beaconsfield*, p. 8.

Chapter 5

1 N. Cohn, *Warrant for Genocide* (Harmondsworth, 1970), p. 12.

2 *ibid.*, p. 13.

3 See below chapter 9 on *The Protocols*.

4 F. Deml, 'Antisemitismus in German Encyclopaedias', *Wiener Library Bulletin* XXI (autumn 1967), p. 31.

5 *RC* II, pp. 70–71 and *Eastern Post and City Chronicle*, 11 May 1901. Similar comment appears in the *East London Advertiser*, 16 September 1893 and 13 April 1895. The letter which was put before the Royal Commission was used by James Blyth in his vehemently anti-Jewish novel, *Ichabod* (London, 1910), pp. 7–8.

6 On Shaw and the British Brothers' League see below pp. 89–95. His remark appears in the *East London Observer*, 27 June 1913 and is referred to on p. 95 below.

7 *Eastern Post and City Chronicle*, 20 September 1902. E. C. Carter, *The Jewish Question in Whitechapel* (London, 1901), p. 8 referred to a Christian feeling in the East End that a plan of 'literal extermination which would result in Jewish dominance was being ruthlessly pursued against them'.

8 *East London Leader*, 2 June 1883.

9 A. White, *The Modern Jew* (London, 1899), pp. xi–xii. Ten years later in Englishman, *Britons Awake*! (London, 1909), Jewish dominance was described as a fact of life.

10 *ibid.*, p. xv. These sentiments appeared almost word for word in a review by White of Israel Zangwill's *Dreamers of the Ghetto* in the *Academy*, 26 March 1898, p. 342.

11 Arnold White, 'The Jew and Europe: a plea for a European Congress', *Pall Mall Gazette*, 13 October 1897.

12 *ibid.*, 16 November 1897. C. C. Aronsfeld, 'Jewish Bankers and the Tsar', *Jewish Social Studies* XXXV (April 1973), pp. 87–104 is a useful recent discussion of this issue. See also S. M. Fuller, 'The British Press and European Anti-Semitism, 1880–1917', unpublished PhD thesis, University of New Mexico, 1974, pp. 202 ff.

13 A. White, *The Modern Jew*, pp. 157–8.

14 A. White, *For Efficiency* (London, 1902), p. 175.

15 In his own words, elsewhere: 'Cosmopolitan finance is only another name for Jewish finance.' A. White, *The Modern Jew*, p. 199.

16 *Pall Mall Gazette*, 3 November 1897.

17 A. White, *The Modern Jew*, p. xvii.

18 *ibid.*, p. 193.

19 *ibid.*, p. xvii.

20 *ibid.*, p. 200.

21 *ibid.*, p. 12. Such matters continued to exercise White's mind long after 1899. See his article 'The Cosmopolitan Financier', the *Throne*, 19 June 1912, p. 450 for a clear expression of his later concern about those financiers 'whose god is Mammon and country none'.

22 See above p. 42.

23 J. Banister, *England under the Jews* (3rd edn, London, 1907), pp. 1, 2, 86. Banister lamented the short of run of the paper, the *Sunrise*, which was also obsessed with an alleged Jewish domination of Britain. See particularly the issues of 23 November 1901, pp. 15–16 and 14 June 1902, p. 4.

24 J. A. Hobson, *The War in South Africa* (2nd edn, London, 1900), pp. 189, 197, 195. A recent fascinating study of the liquor trade in South Africa in which there is an absorbing discussion of Jewish involvement is, C. van Onselen, 'Randlords and Rotgut, 1886–1903: an Essay on the Role of Alcohol in the Development of European Imperialism and Southern African Capitalism', *History Workshop* II (1976), pp. 33–89. See above pp. 12–13 for additional sources on the role of Jews in southern Africa.

25 J. A. Hobson, 'Capitalism and Imperialism in South Africa', *Contemporary Review* LXXVII (1900), pp. 4–5. See also Hobson *The War*, pp. 193–4.

26 Letter from J. A. Hobson to C. P. Scott, 2 September 1899. I am grateful to Harold Hobson for allowing me to refer to this.

27 Hobson, *The War*, p. 226.

28 Hobson, *Contemporary Review*, p. 16.

29 H. Mitchell, 'Hobson Revisited', *Journal of the History of Ideas* XXVI (1965), p. 399.

30 *ibid.*, p. 397.

31 R. Koebner and H. D. Schmidt, *Imperialism: the Story and Significance of a Political Word* (Cambridge, 1964), pp. 250–56, concentrate on Hobson in their discussion of anti-Jewish hostility during the Boer War, as does P. Aldag, *Das Judentum in England* (Berlin, 1943), pp. 371–4, an important anti-semitic source. See also comments in *Clarion*, 17 March 1900; *Justice*, 3 March 1900

and 24 March 1900.

32 J. S. Galbraith, 'The Pamphlet Campaign on the Boer War', *Journal of Modern History* XXIV (1952), p. 119.

33 *Westminster Gazette*, 17 September 1900, quoted in *ibid.*, p. 120.

34 Galbraith, *op. cit.*, p. 120.

35 *Labour Leader*, 23 December 1899.

36 *ibid.*, 3 March 1900. See also *ibid.*, 24 February 1900 for additional references to the influence of Jewish finance.

37 Quoted in *Clarion*, 24 February 1900. Massingham was squeezed out of the editorship of the *Daily Chronicle* during the course of the war when the proprietor decided to pursue a pro-war policy.

38 *ibid.*, 29 September 1900. Just prior to this the paper had claimed that 'if gold were found in Palestine, in six months legions of Jews would flock there and demand the franchise from the Turks.' *ibid.*, 18 August 1900.

39 *Justice*, 28 January 1893.

40 *ibid.*

41 *ibid.*, 5 July 1890.

42 *ibid.*

43 *ibid.*, 21 January 1893.

44 *ibid.*, 2 May 1896.

45 *ibid.*, 25 April 1896.

46 *ibid.*, 7 October 1899. Beit, Eckstein and Barnato were Jews with financial-industrial interests in South Africa. Oppenheim, Steinkopf and Levi were Jews with press interests. See below pp. 85–6.

47 *ibid.*, 28 October 1899.

48 *ibid.*, 4 and 11 November 1899.

49 There is a detailed discussion of this in C. Holmes, 'J. A. Hobson and the Jews' in C. Holmes, (ed.), *Immigrants and Minorities in British Society* (London, 1978), pp. 190–91.

50 An analysis of the reviews of Hobson's work, *The War in South Africa*, shows that there was little opposition to such a claim.

51 H. Rollin, *L'apocalypse de notre temps* (Paris, 1939), p. 527. Aldag, *op. cit.* is a good example of National Socialist analysis.

52 F. Donaldson, *The Marconi Scandal* (London, 1962), is the standard history. On Cecil Chesterton see *Who Was Who, 1916–28* (London, 1919), p. 193 and B. Sewell, *Cecil Chesterton* (Faversham, 1975).

53 The full range of anti-semitic opinion which developed over the affair is treated in K. Lunn, 'The Marconi Scandal and Related Aspects of British Anti-Semitism, 1911–14', University of Sheffield PhD thesis, 1978. He also extends our general understanding of the scandal. At this point my discussion is restricted to the years before 1914 but the Marconi scandal lived on in anti-semitic circles after this. See below pp. 138, 141, 145, 305.

54 *National Review*, January 1912, p. 679. Details of Maxse's life are provided in the *DNB, 1931–40* (London, 1949), pp. 606–7. Mr H. Snyder is currently working on a full length study.

55 *National Review*, January 1912, p. 688.

56 *ibid.*, March 1912, p. 15.

57 *ibid.*, April 1912, p. 189.

58 *ibid.*

59 *ibid.*, January 1913, pp. 723–4.

60 *ibid.*, December 1912, p. 553.

61 See above pp. 1–2 for the definition of anti-semitism which is being used.

62 *National Review*, April 1913, p. 302.

63 *ibid.*, pp. 215–16.
64 For further details see above p. 28.
65 The *Eye Witness*, 8 August 1912, pp. 230–31. This issue of the journal is crucial for an understanding of its response to the scandal.
66 Samuel to Isaacs, 8 August 1912, Samuel Papers A/38/3. J. Bowle, *Viscount Samuel* (London, 1957), p. 83 refers to Wells's characterization.
67 Asquith's letter is in The Marquess of Reading, *Rufus Isaacs, First Marquess of Reading* I (London, 1942), p. 242.
68 The history of this is given in the Samuel Papers A/38/7, A/38/8, A/38/9, A/38/10.
69 The *Eye Witness*, 8 August 1912, p. 230.
70 *ibid.*, 26 September 1912, p. 455. Perhaps it could be said at this point that the Socialist press did not turn the Marconi affair into an anti-semitic crusade. See *Clarion*, 4 April 1913, 11 April 1913, 2 May 1913 and 27 June 1913 as well as *Justice*, 15 February 1913.
71 The *New Witness*, 26 December 1912, p. 226.
72 *ibid.*
73 *ibid.*, 2 January 1913, p. 258.
74 K. Lunn, MS. on Marconi scandal.
75 The *New Witness*, 26 December 1912, p. 226.
76 Lunn MS. on Marconi scandal. A contrast to the foregoing comments from the *Witness* is provided by the analysis from a Liberal standpoint in 'Ministers and the Stock Exchange', *Round Table* III (June–September 1913), pp. 425–55.
77 The *New Witness*, 27 March 1913, p. 650. Similar claims about *Le Matin* were made elsewhere. The *Outlook*, 29 March 1913, p. 429 referred to it as a 'cosmopolitan organ' and the *Throne*, 26 March 1913, p. 487 said it was a journal which had, if anything, 'a strong pro-semitic tendency'.
78 As mentioned above, O'Donnell (1848–1916) was a former Irish Nationalist MP. See the obituary in *The Times*, 6 November 1916.
79 The *Eye Witness*, 14 March 1912, p. 407.
80 *ibid.*, 28 March 1912, p. 472. See similar comments in B. Lazare, *Anti-Semitism. Its History and Causes* (London, 1967, 1st edn, 1894), pp. 167–8.
81 Some of which, as we have observed, was given over to a discussion of the Beiliss affair and *The Jew, the Gypsy and El Islam.* See above p. 59.
82 The *New Witness*, 16 January 1913, p. 340. Hilaire Belloc thought that Cecil Chesterton, who was editor of the *Witness* when O'Donnell became a regular contributor, allowed the Irishman to go too far in his attacks upon Jews. See Sewell, *op. cit.*, p. 106.
83 The *New Witness*, 6 February 1913, p. 425.
84 *ibid.*, 2 July 1914, p. 267, thereby almost certainly displaying an awareness of the work of Alphonse de Toussenel, whose work *Les Juifs, Rois de l'Epoque* had appeared in Paris in 1845, when, according to H. Arendt, *The Origins of Totalitarianism* (2nd edn, London, 1958), p. 47, its attack upon the Rothschilds had been enthusiastically received by 'the entire left-wing press, which at that time was the organ of the revolutionary lower middle classes'.
85 The *New Witness*, 3 July 1913, p. 270.
86 *ibid.*, 9 October 1913, p. 718.
87 H. Belloc, *Mr Clutterbuck's Election* (London, 1908), pp. 178–80. The foregoing analysis is heavily dependent upon D. Lodge, *Novelist at the Crossroads* (London, 1971), pp. 151–2. In addition to his prose, Belloc's hostility towards Jewish power was also evident in his poetry as in 'Verses to a Lord who, in the House of Lords, said that those who opposed the South African Adventure confused Soldiers with Money-Grubbers'.

88 Letter 23 July 1913. Astor Papers, Reading University Library. I am grateful to Kenneth Lunn for drawing my attention to these papers. It should be said that Belloc wanted to have the best of all worlds. In his novels he could allow characters to speak without restraint about the accumulation of Jewish power but in the *Eye Witness*, 28 September 1911, p. 458 where he was attempting to present a reasoned case against the Jews, he could deny that Jews exercised a dominant influence in finance and the press. And, as we have noticed, he was careful in his handling of O'Donnell.

89 By H. D'Avigdor Goldsmid, 'The Little Marconi Case', *History Today* XIV (1964), pp. 283–6.

90 *Jewish Chronicle*, 15 November 1912 urged the resignation of his seat.

91 Quoted by Bowle, *op. cit.*, pp. 101–2. See also *National Review*, December 1912, p. 552.

92 The *New Witness*, 27 March 1913, pp. 643–4, 1 May 1913, pp. 801–2, 30 October 1913, p. 801, 13 November 1913, p. 46.

The Collected Writings of John Maynard Keynes I, *Indian Currency and Finance* (London, 1971), pp. 101–3. The essay first appeared in 1913. R. Gwynne, 'The Indian Silver Question', *Our Flag*, February 1913, p. 26.

93 See above p. 61.

94 Clearly shown in relation to South African affairs in F. W. Hirst (ed.), *Liberalism and the Empire* (London, 1900).

95 A. J. F. Lee, 'J. A. Hobson, A Study of the Social and Economic Thought of J. A. Hobson', unpublished PhD thesis, University of London, 1970, p. 109. Around the same time a remark by Hobson about 'financial Jews' was defended on the grounds that it was the growing power of finance which was really at issue. See *Ethical World*, 3 June 1899, p. 350. E. Silberner, 'British Socialism and the Jews', *Historia Judaica* XIV (1952), pp. 42–3 provides numerous illustrations from *Justice* to show that the Jew could be treated as the personification of finance capital. See *Justice*, 5 February 1887, 16 March 1901 and 26 March 1904 for comments on the exploitation of Egypt. See below pp. 82–4 for an extended discussion of the role of Jews in finance.

96 See the discussion of the 'Telephone Ramp' in the *New Witness*, 7 November 1912, p. 2. See below p. 270 for a reference to J. Lyons and government contracts.

97 The *Eye Witness*, September 1911, p. 365. See above for an extended discussion of the problem.

98 Samuel Montagu, Lord Swaythling, died on 12 January 1911 and in his will, published in the following March, his bequests to his children and those taking through his children were on condition that, at the time of his death, they should be professing the Jewish religion and should not be married to a person not professing the Jewish religion. He also expressed the hope that no child of his should at any time abandon the Jewish religion or intermarry with persons not of the Jewish religion. He also gave his trustees the right to act against his daughters if they helped to sponser Liberal Judaism – as they had done in the past. *The Times*, 6 March 1911. The Liberal journal, the *Nation* 11 March 1911, p. 951, was particularly sharp in its criticism of the 'attempts of one generation to limit the spiritual freedom of another' and this brought a cryptic, double-edged reply from G. K. Chesterton, who said that Englishmen were prepared to let Jews be anything except Jews. *ibid.*, 18 March 1911, p. 1004.

In the following year Sir Edward Sassoon's will, which ventured a criticism of the death duty on charitable legacies, was also picked up in *ibid.*, 3 August 1912, p. 662. In this instance the letter writer was particularly incensed that

Sassoon had not left any money to British charity because of such penal taxes. In fact, however, Sassoon made it clear that he had given generously to charities during his lifetime – although this did not receive any stress in the *Nation*. See Sassoon's will in *The Times*, 23 July 1912. For comment in the *Witness* on such matters see O'Donnell's reference to Swaythling detesting the touch of an English hand in the *New Witness*, 16 January 1913, p. 340. For a recent reverberation of such a will see the Raphael Tuck case reported in *The Times*, 2 November 1977 and commented upon earlier in G. Bindman, 'Discrimination in Wills', *Patterns of Prejudice* IX (November–December 1975), pp. 23–4.

99 J. Parkes, *The Jewish Problem in the Modern World* (London, 1939), p. 44. To a much earlier observer 'The Jew' was a 'trained man among mere tyros and neophytes' in the competitive conditions of the nineteenth century. P. J. Hughesdon, 'Anti-Semitism: the Other Side of the Question', *New Liberal Review* VI (1904), p. 727.

100 The best discussion of this is in Lodge, *op. cit.*, pp. 149–50.

101 According to one source Maxse was offered the editorship of 'a great colonial newspaper' but it was an offer he refused, saying, 'I must stay in England to warn people of the German danger.' *DNB, 1931–40* (London, 1949), p. 607.

102 E. E. Williams, *Made in Germany* (various editions) captures the paranoid contemporary mood and the issue of German commercial strength is discussed in R. J. S. Hoffman, *Great Britain and the German Trade Rivalry, 1875–1914* (Philadelphia, 1933). Scare stories about a German invasion of Britain started with George Chesney's novel, *Battle of Dorking* (1871).

103 As emphasized a little later in the *National Review*, October 1914, p. 239.

104 *ibid.*, p. 250.

105 See L. J. Maxse, *Germany on the Brain* (London, 1915).

106 It might be of interest to say once again that *The War in South Africa* by J. A. Hobson, which provided the basis for many other discussions of the war, and which emphasized that the war was being fought mainly for Jewish interests, did not receive a hostile critical reception on this account. An analysis of the reviews appears in Lee, 'J. A. Hobson', op. cit., p. 110.

107 W. R. Lawson, 'Kaffir Finance', *National Review*, May 1896, p. 415 refers to the Jewish role in creating an interest in the South African goldfields and the subsequent trading in shares. Lawson, a financial journalist, was closely involved in exposing the Marconi scandal and did not come out of it too well. Maxse had to admit to the select committee of enquiry that he was temperamentally unsuited to be a witness. See Donaldson, *op. cit.*, p. 90. His article in the *National Review* is not slanted towards an attack upon Jewish finance and it provides a useful impression of the ambience surrounding the 'Kaffir boom'. The boom was also discussed in the *Economist*, 3 August 1895, pp. 1010–11, and 2 November 1895, pp. 1429–30. Arendt, *op. cit.*, p. 198 notes the importance of Jewish capital in developing the goldfields, in the course of which she refers to most of the individual Jews referred to here and on p. 203 points to the Rhodes-Rothschild connection.

108 Arendt, *op. cit.*, pp. 202–3. This was accepted later by Mitchell, *op. cit.*, pp. 401–2.

109 *National Review*, September 1914, p. 48 has critical references to 'Sir Edgar –, Sir Ernest –, Sir Alfred – and Mr Alfred –'. The last reference was to Alfred Mond who was in fact born in Britain but, in terms of allegiance, was classified by Maxse as a German Jew. E. Halévy, *The Rule of Democracy (1905–1914)*, (London, 1961), pp. 409–10 refers to 'a disquietingly large proportion of German or German Jewish names in pacifist movements' and mentions Lucien Wolf, Sir John Brunner, Sir Alfred Mond, Sir Edgar Speyer and Sir Ernest

Cassel in this connection.

110 P. H. Emden, *Jews of Britain* (London, n.d.); V. D. Lipman, *Social and Economic History of Jews in England 1850–1950* (London, 1954); C. Bermant, *The Cousinhood* (London, 1971); S. Aris, *Jews in Business* (Harmondsworth, 1973), all provide evidence on this for Britain. Arendt, *op. cit.* and P. G. J. Pulzer, *The Rise of Political Anti-Semitism in Germany and Austria* (New York, 1964), offer evidence for elsewhere.

111 Quoted in Aris, *op. cit.*, p. 53.

112 S. G. Checkland, *The Rise of Industrial Society in England 1815–1885* (London, 1969), p. 207 provides evidence of international initiatives by English banking concerns.

113 Arendt, *op. cit.*, p. 202. See also an earlier comment in H. Withers, *International Finance* (London, 1916), p. 114.

114 For an early comment in the present context see Richard Burton's remarks in *Lord Beaconsfield. A Sketch* (London, n.d. 1882?), p. 5.

115 E. C. Corti, *The Rise of the House of Rothschild* (London, 1928), is a classic study in Rothschild history.

116 Parkes, *op. cit.*, p. 55 and Arendt, *op. cit.*, p. 25.

117 *Justice*, 17 May 1890.

118 *ibid.*, 2 September 1893. The reference to the foreign secretary is to Rosebery who was married to a Rothschild. See above pp. 34–5.

119 *Ethical World*, 27 May 1899, p. 323.

120 As in *Justice*, 25 April 1896; *ibid.*, 16 March 1901; *ibid.*, 6 July 1901. Banister, *England under the Jews*, p. 136 noted the influence of 'Money-bags Rothschild' in the debate over immigration into Britain. Englishman in *Britons Awake! op. cit.*, p. 2, referred to the Rothschilds as 'the paramount influence in the country'.

121 *Labor Leader*, 21 November 1891. 'These Rothschilds can make peace or war at pleasure. Even the aristocratic rulers of Europe are puppets in the hands of this blood-sucking tribe. Gore has always been the means by which the Rothschilds have made their pile. The first, big lift the family got, dates from the battle of Waterloo. The fortunes of the family took root in the bloody quagmire of the battlefield.

And this tradition has been kept up. War today gains more and more in financial matters. Neither kings nor peoples make war, it is the blood-sucking tribe of financiers that start the game and reap their harvest of gold out of human misery. We cannot wonder at the hatred with which these Jewish financiers are regarded in Russia and Germany'. Barbara Hill drew my attention to this reference. J. A. Hobson, *Imperialism. A Study* (London, 1938; first published 1902), pp. 56–7 doubted whether a modern war could be started without the Rothschild influence. The Rothschild connection with modern war and, in particular, the initial enrichment of the Rothschilds through the Napoleonic Wars was not lost upon F. Hugh O'Donnell who referred in the *New Witness*, 23 October 1913, p. 780, to 'Rothschild de Waterloo'.

122 *Labor Leader*, 19 December 1891. Also brought to my attention by Barbara Hill.

123 H. B. Marriott Watson 'The Jew and his Destiny', *National Review*, November 1905, p. 524. See also p. 523.

124 *Society in the New Reign*, by A. Foreign Resident (London, 1904), p. 193. It is of interest that it was not until 1 July 1960 that a non-Rothschild was admitted to a partnership in the firm. See J. Wechsberg, *The Merchant Bankers* (London, 1967), p. 348.

125 T. H. S. Escott, *King Edward and his Court* (London, 1903), pp. 201, 211

discussed the influence with quiet equanimity.

126 See C. C. Aronsfeld, 'Jewish Bankers and the Tsar', *Jewish Social Studies* XXXV (1973), provides clear evidence on this.

127 Emden, *op. cit.*, p. 357.

128 As evidenced in S. Wolf, *The Influence of the Jews on the Progress of the World* (Washington D. C., 1888), p. 39. Emden, *op. cit.*, pp. 355–7, 539–42.

129 See the *Derbyshire Advertiser*, 21 October 1892; the *National Review*, June 1896, p. 579; A. White, *The Modern Jew*, p. XIII and finally Banister, *op. cit.*, chapters 17–24.

130 L. Maxse, in *National Review*, December 1911, p. 499 and *ibid.*, March 1912, p. 15; F. H. O'Donnell, 'The Masters of the New Slave States', the *New Witness*, 2 July 1914, p. 265; J. F. Fraser, *The Conquering Jew* (London, 1915), p. 33.

131 *Justice*, 5 July 1890.

132 See *ibid.*, 21 January 1893; Oppenheim was also mentioned in *ibid.*, 29 June 1901 and Steinkopf in *ibid.*, 5 July 1890; Steinkopf and Löwanfeld are discussed in J. W. Robertson Scott, *The Life and Death of a Newspaper* (London, 1952), p. 272 where reference is made to the sale of the *Pall Mall Gazette*. The reputed purchaser was T. Dove Keighley but there were rumours that 'one Löwenfeld' who was the owner of a non-intoxicating beverage called Kop's Ale and who was described as 'Polish by birth, Jewish by race and Roman Catholic by religion', was the real investor. But this was also denied and 'there was talk of one Steinkopf, a man who had bought a house in the West End and, when he did not like it, pulled it down and built another in its place', being the real purchaser. J. A. Hobson in the *Derbyshire Advertiser*, 21 October 1892, commented upon Jewish finance and the *Pall Mall Gazette*.

133 *Justice*, 21 January 1893, and *ibid.*, 28 January 1893 for a critical comment by W. Jacob on the views expressed in *Justice*.

134 A. J. Lee, *The Origins of the Popular Press in England, 1855–1914* (London, 1976), p. 17 has written: 'There is indeed a great need for a serious history of the British press, even if at this stage it would have to be rather tentative.... The available works on the subject are largely anecdotal, fragmentary, scissors-and-paste studies, usually written by journalists.' He goes on to write that the fundamental work on the structure and development of the press has yet to be done. S. Koss, *A. G. Gardiner, Fleet Street Radical* (London, 1973), p. 6 refers to the press as an untapped source for recent British political history.

135 As in Fraser, *op. cit.*, p. 33: 'Few things are more remarkable than the way Jews control the Press in London, New York, Paris, Berlin, Vienna and elsewhere.' What does this mean?

136 C. Roth, *The Sassoon Dynasty* (London, 1941), pp. 197 ff. refers to Rachel Beer. Harry Oppenheim's involvement was commented upon in J. D. Symon, *The Press and its Story* (London, 1914), p. 194 and Baron von Eckardstein, *Ten Years at the Court of St James' 1895–1905* (London, 1921), p. 52. It has also been noticed recently in Lee, *Press*, p. 163. Harry Marks, like Oppenheim, has not been the subject of a full length study but his role in financial journalism is referred to in the *Financial Times*, 12 November 1969. Emden, *op. cit.*, pp. 539–40 also mentions him and on pp. 357–63 comments on Levy Lawson and the *Daily Telegraph*. H. Bolitho, *Alfred Mond* (London, 1933), pp. 156, 171 refers without much precision to Alfred Mond's press interests. Reuter's is discussed in Emden, *op. cit.*, pp. 355–7 as well as G. Storey, *Reuter's Century* (London, 1951), and a list of shareholders appears in L. J. Maxse, 'Concerning Reuter', *National Review*, December 1914, pp. 595–605.

137 However, Lee, *Press*, in his wide-ranging study of the newspaper world does

not pursue this line of enquiry.

138 It is interesting that the *Eye Witness* and the *New Witness*, which were particularly concerned about the Jewish press, concentrated almost entirely upon a few examples. The *Eye Witness*, 13 July 1911, p. 9 (Mond); 28 March 1912, p. 456 (the Soda Trust i.e. Mond); 4 July 1912, p. 69 (Levi and Mond); the *New Witness*, 10 July 1913, p. 298 (Reuter); 24 July 1913, p. 356 (veiled reference probably to Reuter's); 15 January 1914, p. 329 (Mond); 17 September 1914, p. 534 (Reuter's). Rather later, Ada Chesterton in *The Chestertons* (London, 1941), pp. 45–6 commented that among anti-semites it was claimed that journalists on the *Telegraph* kept away from Gentile companionship to avoid being selected by their colleagues for ritual murder which, it was suggested, was perpetrated annually in the darker recesses of the premises! Some of the most vicious anti-semitism directed against the Levy-Lawson family who controlled the *Telegraph* is to be found in the comments of the Duke of Marlborough, consequent upon a review in the *Telegraph* of Winston Churchill's life of his father. See *Winston S. Churchill, Companion* II, part 1, 1901–1907 (London, 1969), pp. 487–90. The reading of European influences into the British situation is suggested by A. White, *The Modern Jew*, and in F. Hugh O'Donnell's column in the *New Witness*. Both White and O'Donnell were clearly influenced by their impressions of Europe and attempted to argue that Britain was moving in a similar direction. For their part European anti-semites were prepared to accept that Jews exercised a press influence in London. See, for example, J. de Ligneau, *Juifs et Anti sémites en Europe* (10th edn, Paris, 1891), p. 255. For Maxse's confidence about overcoming the Jewish menace see *National Review*, April 1913, p. 189. In sharp contrast to the claims about Jewish press power we have been discussing, Escott, *op. cit.*, pp. 201–2 was abruptly dismissive of any reference to 'Isrealitish dictatorship over Fleet Street'. In his opinion this 'superstructure of fiction' rested upon Baron Lionel Rothschild's contact with J. T. Delane of *The Times* at Gunnersbury where, 'especially on Sundays, men of any position in public affairs or great enterprises of any sort were in the habit of meeting each other.' This simplifies and omits too much.

139 It seriously exercised F. Hugh O'Donnell. See the *New Witness*, 9 October 1913, p. 718. From a different standpoint it was favourably referred to in 'Ministers and the Stock Exchange', *op. cit.*, p. 426

140 The reference to the nature of the entourage is from B. Connell, *Manifest Destiny* (London, 1953), p. 54. See below chapter 7 for further discussion of the emancipation process.

141 C. Roth, 'The Court Jews of Edwardian England', *Jewish Social Studies* IV (1943), p. 356. For opposing views on the court Jews see C. W. Smith, A Manifesto *on International Financial and Commercial Gambling* (London, 1910), p. 18 and *Society in the New Reign*, chapter 11.

142 *Justice*, 17 May 1901.

143 Banister, *op. cit.*, pp. 171–2.

144 A. White, *For Efficiency* (London, 1902), p. 176.

145 W. Paget, *In My Tower* (2 vols, London, 1924) II, p. 474; W. S. Blunt *My Diaries* (London, 1932), p. 716.

146 See above p. 47.

147 *National Review*, December 1911, p. 499.

148 See *Morning Post*, 12 and 14 June 1913 in discussing Marconi and H. Belloc and C. Chesterton, *The Party System* (London, 1911).

149 E. J. Hobsbawm, *Industry and Empire* (London, 1968), p. 162.

Chapter 6

1 See below pp. 110–11.
2 *East London Observer*, 12 April 1902.
3 See the discussion above in chapter 2.
4 *Eastern Post and City Chronicle*, 9 November 1901. M. J. Landa, *The Alien Problem and its Remedy* (London, 1911), p. 77 refers to Evans-Gordon's 'genius for organization' which he applied to the BBL.
5 *East London Observer*, 11 May 1901. Although the BBL has been discussed almost exclusively in a London context, it did have branches in Bradford, Kettering and elsewhere. See M. D. Bleach, 'Nation, Empire and the Birmingham Working Class', unpublished PhD thesis, University of Birmingham, 1975, p. 170.
6 *East London Observer*, 11 May 1901.
7 *ibid.*
8 *ibid.*, 25 May 1901.
9 *ibid.*, 8 June 1901.
10 *ibid.*, 24 August 1901. See also *Jewish Chronicle*, 2 August 1901.
11 *East London Observer*, 23 November 1901. The progress of the BBL is captured most graphically in the *Eastern Post and City Chronicle*.
12 *Jewish Chronicle*, 1 November 1901 and *East London Observer*, 14 September 1901.
13 *East London Advertiser*, 14 January 1902.
14 *East London Observer*, 4 January 1902.
15 *ibid.*, 18 January 1902. There is a further reference to the development of anti-semitism within the BBL and support for this trend in *ibid.*, 1 March 1902.
16 *ibid.*, 18 January 1902. Apologizing for his absence from an earlier meeting in Bethnal Green, he had written, 'You have my best wishes in your crusade', *ibid.*, 19 October 1901. Will Crooks, the mayor of Poplar and a future Labour MP, also found it expedient to accommodate the League in its early days. See *ibid.*, 4 January 1902.
17 *ibid.*, 18 January 1902.
18 *Jewish Chronicle*, 31 October 1902.
19 *Eastern Post and City Chronicle*, 3 August 1901.
20 *Jewish Chronicle*, 1 November 1901.
21 *ibid.*, 25 January 1902.
22 *East London Observer*, 29 August 1903.
23 *ibid.*
24 *RC* II, pp. 283, 292.
25 *Jewish Chronicle*, 31 October 1902.
26 *East London Advertiser*, 6 June 1903.
27 J. A. Garrard, *The English and Immigration 1880–1910* (London, 1971), pp. 41, 59–60.
28 *East London Observer*, 19 September 1903.
29 *ibid.*
30 *ibid.*
31 Garrard, *op. cit.*, p. 60. The *East London Observer* was suitably impressed by the meeting. It had passed without 'the slightest attempt to raise racial feeling or prejudice'. *East London Observer*, 14 November 1903.
32 *East End Argus*, 13 June 1903. See above p. 16 for additional comments. I am grateful to J. J. Bennett for providing me with this reference. His Sheffield MA thesis will be the fullest account we have of East End press reaction to

Jewish immigration.

33 *East London Observer*, 7 March 1903.
34 *ibid.*, 17 October 1903.
35 *Eastern Post and City Chronicle*, 16 January 1904.
36 *ibid.*, 7 January 1905.
37 For further discussion of the 1905 Act see below p. 101.
38 Garrard, *op. cit.*, p. 41. Compare with above p. 93. HO 45/10241/B37811 and *Jewish Chronicle* supplement 27 June 1902 indicate the sympathy of the secretary to the Commission with the League's aims.
39 See above p. 90.
40 Garrard, *op. cit.*, pp. 63–4.
41 *East London Advertiser*, 5 July 1902. A. T. Williams was sympathetic to BBL demands, Eddis was secretary to the Royal Commission on Alien Immigration and Major Gordon was the Tory MP for Stepney.
42 *East London Observer*, 5 April 1902, although the *Eastern Post and City Chronicle*, 5 April 1902 claimed that Shaw continued to be a member of the BBL. *East London Advertiser*, 21 September 1901 refers to Shaw's earlier resignation.
43 *East London Observer*, 16 August 1902.
44 *ibid.*, 5 July 1902 and 27 September 1902 and *ibid.*, 4 October 1902 for criticism of Shaw's behaviour.
45 *Jewish Chronicle*, 31 October 1902. See also *East London Observer*, 27 September 1902, where he describes the League as falling to 'outside politicians – or would be politicians'.
46 *Eastern Post and City Chronicle*, 1 and 15 March 1902.
47 The *East London Observer* badgered the League to produce a balance sheet. The document appeared six months after the assumed date of publication in February 1902. See *Eastern Post and City Chronicle*, 16 August 1902. See also *East London Observer*, 28 March 1902.
48 *East London Observer*, 27 June 1903.
49 Remarks by Shaw which appear in *ibid.*, 22 February 1902 and 24 December 1910 – the latter in connection with the Hounsditch murders – suggest that he was not averse to making specific attacks upon Jewish interests. Finally, there is no record that he objected to his article on alien criminality which appeared in the *Daily Mail* on 16 April 1928 being reprinted in the well known anti-semitic publication, A. H. Lane's *The Alien Menace. A Statement of the Case.* (3rd edn, London 1932), pp. 200–201. File B4/SH1 of 1930 in the Board of Deputies contains correspondence on the possible prosecution of Shaw for anti-semitic libel. In his 1928 article Shaw was still using the title 'Captain' derived from his BBL involvement – to which also he openly referred.
50 See above p. 90.
51 *Jewish Chronicle*, 14 February 1902.
52 *Eastern Post and City Chronicle*, 8 February 1902; see also *ibid.*, 22 February 1902.
53 *East London Observer*, 18 January 1902, reacting to the meeting at the People's Palace. See also *ibid.*, 1 March 1902.
54 *Eastern Post and City Chronicle*, 4 and 11 October 1902.
55 *East London Observer*, 18 January 1902.
56 *ibid.*, 25 January 1902.
57 *ibid.*, 11 May 1901.
58 *ibid.*, 26 April 1902.
59 *Eastern Post and City Chronicle*, 30 May 1903 reprints the manifesto.
60 *East London Observer*, 18 July 1903.
61 *The Times*, 1 April 1904. Letter from Julian Grande.

62 *ibid.*, 5 April 1904.
63 L. Hyman, *The Jews of Ireland* (London/Jerusalem, 1972), pp. 210–11 refers to developing hostility.
64 *The Times* 4 and 12 April 1904.
65 *ibid.*, 12 April 1904; see above p. 7 for the blood accusation.
66 *ibid.*
67 R. Hofstadter, *The Paranoid Style in American Politics* (London, 1966), p. 4.
68 *The Times* 1 and 15 April 1904.
69 *ibid.* A. D. Grimshaw, 'Relationships among Prejudice, Discrimination, Social Tension and Social Violence' reprinted in A. D. Grimshaw (ed.), *Racial Violence in the United States* (Chicago, 1969), pp. 446–53 discusses the importance of external control forces in containing social violence.
70 Minute Book, Board of Deputies, 1904 (London, 1905), pp. 30–32 gives the letter.
71 C. H. L. Emanuel, *A Century and a Half of Jewish History* (London, 1910), pp. 160–63. See also *Jewish Year Book* (London, 1904), p. 465.
72 Minute Book, Board of Deputies, 1905 (London, 1906), p. 30.
73 Hyman, *op. cit.*, pp. 217, 347 refers to several contemporary accounts of the Limerick situation. G. F. Abbott, *Israel in Europe* (London, 1972, reprint of 1907 edition), pp. 471–2 provides some of the bare details. The episode is also mentioned briefly in C. W. Rosenfeld, *Progress or Retrogress, The Reactionary 20th Century, or, Back to the Middle Ages* (London, 1904), p. 38 and S. Rosenbaum, 'The Jewish Question in England', *Jewish Review* II (1911–12), p. 107 as it also is in M. Hunterberg, *The Jew and the Anti-Semite* (London, 1913), pp. 100–101. See also S. G. Bayme, 'Jewish Leadership and Anti-Semitism in Britain 1898–1918', unpublished PhD thesis, Columbia University, 1977, pp. 240–47, who treats the issue as of significance in the internal responses of Anglo-Jewry to the post-emancipation world.
74 *Alien Immigration. Should restrictions be imposed?* Pro. Frederick Bradshaw MA, Con. Charles Emanuel MA (London, 1904), p. 131. The incidents were also picked up by Joseph Banister. See *England under the Jews* (3rd edn, London, 1907), pp. 177–8.
75 *Jewish Chronicle*, 25 September and 2 October 1903. See also *Jewish Year Book* (London, 1904), pp. 465–6 where an attack upon Jewish miners at Dowlais was recorded.
76 See G. Alderman, 'The Anti-Jewish Riots of August 1911 in South Wales', *Welsh History Review* VI (December 1972), pp. 190–91 for details.
77 The disturbances against the Chinese in Cardiff are discussed in J. P. May, 'The British Working Class and the Chinese, 1870–1911, with particular reference to the Seamen's Strike of 1911', unpublished MA dissertation, University of Warwick, 1973. As yet no one has succeeded in conclusively demonstrating that the anti-Chinese riots helped to trigger the later disturbances against Jews.
78 Alderman, *op. cit.*, pp. 192–3. See also O. K. Rabinowicz, *Winston Churchill on Jewish Problems* (Westport, Conn., 1974), pp. 167–72.
79 *Justice*, 2 September 1911. Alderman, *op. cit.*, pp. 193–4 refers to the national press. For scepticism on this kind of analysis see M. Simon, 'Anti-Semitism in England', *Jewish Review* II (1911–12), p. 302. For comment in a source hostile to Jews which explained the riots as a reaction to Jewish oppression, see the *Eye Witness*, 31 August 1911, p. 324.
80 Alderman, *op. cit.*, pp. 195–6.
81 *ibid.*, p. 199.
82 *ibid.* In a reference to anti-semitism in Europe, although with a wider signi-

ficance, P. J. Hughesdon commented that 'popular animosity' against Jews was 'primarily attributable to the treatment which the weaker social classes have experienced at the hands of Jewish usurers'. *New Liberal Review* VI (1904), p. 727.

83 See above p. 100. G. Alderman, 'Into the Vortex: South Wales Jewry before 1914', in *Provincial Jewry in Victorian Britain* (London, 1975), pp. 8–9 deals with 'religious bigotry'.

84 Alderman, 'The Anti-Jewish Riots', *op. cit.*, pp. 197–8.

85 As emphasized in Rabinowicz, *op. cit.*, pp. 169–72.

86 Garrard, *op. cit.*, pp. 36–47 gives the background and provides details. The main classes of undesirable aliens were those unable to show that they could procure the means of subsistence in decent sanitary conditions, lunatics or idiots, the diseased and criminals (excluding political criminals).

87 See above chapters 2 and 5.

88 The *New Witness*, 4 December 1913, p. 132. The work on which Cecil Chesterton collaborated with Hilaire Belloc, called *The Party System* (London, 1911), was also concerned with such matters.

89 The *New Witness*, 18 December 1913, p. 217.

90 D. Low, *Autobiography* (London, 1956), p. 133.

91 The *New Witness*, 3 July 1913, p. 272.

92 *ibid.*, pp. 272–5.

93 *ibid.*, 30 October 1913, p. 811.

94 William Morton Eden (1859–1917), who does not seem to have had any other political involvement.

95 See above pp. 24–6, 64–6.

96 See J. P. Corrin, 'Chesterbelloc and the Distributist Circle', unpublished PhD thesis, University of Boston, 1976, for details. I am also grateful for information from Kenneth Lunn.

97 See below pp. 210–13.

Chapter 7

1 There are also severe limitations on what survey analysis can reveal about anti-semitism which ought to be realized. It has been commented that while it is useful for 'periodic pulse taking' it can hardly capture the intricate complexities which anti-semitism involves. L. S. Dawidowicz, 'Can Anti-Semitism be Measured?', *Commentary* L (July 1970), p. 42.

2 Garrard had to admit that he was unable to discover the extent of anti-alienism at the time of the late nineteenth century Jewish immigration into Britain and in an earlier study which was specifically concerned with anti-semitism Robb had to accept that major problems existed in accumulating evidence on this question. J. A. Garrard, *The English and Immigration, 1880–1910* (London, 1971), p. 71 and J. H. Robb, *Working Class Anti-Semite* (London, 1954), pp. 200–201.

3 *RC* II, pp. 16, 17, a remark which also hints at Jewish influence in the world of communications.

4 P. G. J. Pulzer, *The Rise of Political Anti-Semitism in Germany and Austria* (New York, 1964), p. 32, has a convenient catalogue of liberal values. Garrard, *op. cit.*, p. 145, notes the disreputability of anti-semitism in Britain. Some further discussion of the influences which contained anti-semitism in Britain takes place below in chapters 12 and 14. My paper on the 'German Gypsy Question in Britain, 1904–6', given at the Society for the Study of Labour History meeting in Sheffield in May 1978 is useful for revealing the limits of

toleration in Britain. The comparative study of American and British labour responses to the great Jewish immigration presented by A. T. Lane at the same conference casts doubt upon any natural tendency in Britain towards toleration.

5 The *Briton*, no. 1, 30 April 1887.

6 *East London Observer*, 11 May 1901.

7 See *Parliamentary Debates*, House of Commons LXXXIX (1901), col. 119 and *ibid.* CI (1902), col. 1279.

8 Garrard, *op. cit.*, p. 57.

9 *ibid.*, pp. 59–60. See also above p. 92.

10 *RC* II, p. 105. See above pp. 27–8 for earlier references to his role in the immigration debate.

11 *RC* II, p. 105. But see above p. 94.

12 *ibid.*, p. 17.

13 See Samuel Montagu's evidence before the House of Commons *Select Committee on Emigration and Immigration* I, British Parliamentary Papers XI (1888), p. 766 and *RC* II, p. 619.

14 E. C. Carter, *The Jewish Question in Whitechapel* (London, 1901), pp. 6–7 and *Parliamentary Debates*, House of Commons CI (1902), col. 1281 both refer to the possibility of outbreaks of violence against Jews.

15 L. Gartner, *The Jewish Immigrant in England, 1870–1914* (Detroit, 1960), p. 49. S. G. Bayme, 'Jewish Leadership and Anti-Semitism in Britain 1898–1918', unpublished PhD thesis, Columbia University 1977, is generally useful on the responses of Anglo-Jewry to social problems.

16 Garrard, *op. cit.*, p. 23.

17 S. Kaplan, 'The Anglicisation of the East European Jewish Immigrant as seen by the London Jewish Chronicle, 1870–1897', *Yivo Annual of Jewish Social Science* X (1955), pp. 267–78, offers a useful insight into establishment views.

18 Gartner, *op. cit.*, p. 51 on which the foregoing account is based.

19 A claim frequently made by others hostile to immigration.

20 Gartner, *op. cit.*, p. 54.

21 Garrard, *op. cit.*, p. 15.

22 See above pp. 17, 29.

23 Sir Bernard Cohen, Tory MP for Islington voted for the Aliens Act. P. Foot, *Immigration and Race in British Politics* (Harmondsworth, 1965), p. 99. Garrard, *op. cit.*, p. 15 comments that several others were 'staunch anti-aliens'.

24 See my essay on 'J. A. Hobson and the Jews', in C. Holmes (ed.), *Immigrants and Minorities in British Society* (London, 1978), pp. 127–31.

25 See above p. 16.

26 Gartner, *op. cit.*, p. 273.

27 C. Bermant, *The Cousinhood* (London, 1971), pp. 99–100 provides details on this.

28 R. H. Jenkins, *Asquith* (London, 1964), appendix A, pp. 539–42.

29 W. D. Rubinstein, 'Jews among Top British Wealth Holders, 1857–1969: Decline of the Golden Age', *Jewish Social Studies* XXXIV (January 1972), p. 73. P. H. Emden, *Jews of Britain* (London, 1943), provides information snapshots of these and many other prominent Jews. Although he was attacked as a Jew, it is not clear that Goschen was in fact Jewish. Sources vary on this.

30 See above p. 87.

31 Rubinstein, *op. cit.*, pp. 76–7. Jewish persons were taken to be those of known Jewish faith or descent, those of partly Jewish descent were excluded together with ambiguous cases. *ibid.*, p. 74.

32 Gartner, *op. cit.*, p. 280.

33 H. N. Adler, *The Jews during the Victorian Era. A Sermon preached at the North London Synagogue. Sabbath June 26th 5657, 1897* (London, 1898).
34 Rubinstein, *op. cit.*, p. 73.
35 Quoted in Garrard, *op. cit.*, p. 135.
36 *ibid.*
37 Robb, *op. cit.*, pp. 204–5.
38 E. E. Burgess, 'The Soul of the Leeds Ghetto', *Yorkshire Evening News*, 19 January 1925. Much of this material is impressionistic rather than precise. Oscar T. Schweriner, a German journalist, who wrote a series of articles for the *Daily Mail* called 'A German in England' presented on 28 June 1909 his impressions of Leeds, in the course of which he commented about the Jewish population: 'All the people I have spoken to tell me that they are a law-abiding set, who never give any trouble, and that they have certainly done a good deal towards the general prosperity of the town. And yet I could not help noticing on all sides a slumbering anti-semitic feeling – and not in Leeds alone. I have observed the same thing all over the north. The feeling is not outspoken, sometimes indefinite, sometimes denied, but in spite of all there it is. It does not at all agree with what I believe I have learnt of the English character, and I cannot understand it. Of course, I am speaking of the people only; probably only of a certain kind of people; certainly not of the authorities.' In his autobiographical social history of Salford, Richard Roberts refers to the hostility which was expressed, sometimes in the form of physical violence, towards Jews in another area of settlement in the north of England. See *The Classic Slum* (Harmondsworth, 1974), p. 171.
39 Letter to his parents quoted in J. Namier, *Lewis Namier: A Biography* (London, 1971), p. 101.
40 *Jewish Chronicle*, 25 July 1913.
41 L. Davidoff, *The Best Circles: Society, Etiquette and the Season* (London, 1973), pp. 75–6.
42 Gleik's case referred to in Garrard, *op. cit.*, p. 76 raises race and class issues which are difficult to disentangle.
43 See p. 256.
44 See above chapters 2, 3, 4, 5.
45 See chapters 2, 5 and pp. 228–9.
46 See above p. 12.
47 See above pp. 11–12.
48 See above chapter 2.
49 See above pp. 29–30.
50 See above pp. 39–42.
51 See above chapter 5.
52 T. Farrow, *In the Moneylender's Clutches* (London, 1895), p. 53.
53 *Parliamentary Debates*, House of Commons LXXXIV (1900), cols. 681–733.
54 *ibid.*, House of Lords XIV (1913), cols. 689–91. Newton's bill passed through the Lords but no time was found for it in the Commons. The kind of measures wanted by Newton had the support of *Truth*, which was concerned about money-lending activities and the trading by Jews under assumed names, and referred to the matter constantly throughout 1913. The journal had a reputation for crusading in such an area under the guidance of Henry Labouchere. Newton's campaign in 1913 was sympathetically treated in *Punch*, 9 July 1913, p. 53 which also provided a cartoon representation of Moses and Aaron trading as Crewe and Lansdowne. In the *Truth*, Christmas number, 25 December 1913, p. 15 the moneylender appeared as the MONKEY and was drawn with huge hooked nose, pendulous eye pouches, thick lips and crinkly hair, offering 'loans

on easy terms'. For the general account of Shylock in literature see E. Rosenberg, *From Shylock to Svengali. Jewish Stereotypes in English Fiction.* (London, 1961).

55 See above pp. 19–21, 24.

56 Among Jewish commentators, the value to Britain of such characteristics, was clearly expressed in J. A. Dyche 'The Jewish Workman', *Contemporary Review* LXXIII (1898), pp. 35–50 and 'The Jewish Immigrant', in *ibid.* LXXV (1899), pp. 379–99. For an aggressive counter attack upon Dyche's views see John Smith's article, 'The Jewish Immigrant', in *ibid.* LXXVI (1899), pp. 425–36. See above p. 19 for Liberal rejoicing at Jewish Smileseanism in Great Britain. Although Jewish immigration into Britain produced nothing comparable in literature to Abraham Cahan's *The Rise of David Levinsky* which appeared in New York in 1917 it did lead to something similar in Elizabeth Wheeler's novel *From Petticoat Lane to Rotten Row; or, The Child of the Ghetto; a Jewish Story* (Manchester, 1901), which was also concerned with 'getting on'. And one view, confirming that Jews had 'got on' to an extent that British society could not function properly without them was contained in Violet Guttenberg's 'novel of the impossible', *Neither Greek nor Jew* (London, 1902), in which she described the expulsion of the Jews from England by a hostile home secretary and their subsequent necessary return.

57 See chapter 5, *passim.*

58 And would therefore be regarded as anti-semitic in the light of the definition against which evidence is being measured.

59 See chapter 14.

60 Bernard Levin referred to this campaign and its consequences in *The Times*, 30 November 1976.

61 J. H. Murray (ed.), *A New English Dictionary* (Oxford, 1901), p. 576.

62 *ibid.*, p. 577. The word had a wide currency in this sense. See above p. 249. And, in our own day, it is still not uncommon to hear it said 'I was jewed', implying that a hard, unfair bargain had been enforced or some sharp practice entered into. See the comment on p. 249.

63 M. F. Modder, *The Jew in the Literature of England* (Philadelphia, 1944), p. 351.

64 Rosenberg, *op. cit.*, pp. 14–15.

65 L. G. Zatlin, 'Some of their best Friends were Victorians: The Nineteenth-century Anglo Jewish Novel', unpublished PhD thesis, Emory University, 1974, pp. 189 ff.

66 *ibid.*, p. 212.

67 L. P. Curtis Jr, *Apes and Angels. The Irishman in Victorian Caricature* (Newton Abbot, 1971), p. ix.

68 *Punch*, 9 August 1899, p. 63 and *ibid.*, 9 March 1910, p. 195.

69 *ibid.*, 4 August 1877, p. 37.

70 As shown in *ibid.*, 7 May 1913, p. 369.

71 *ibid.*, 14 October 1914, p. 325.

72 The *Jewish Chronicle*, 10 January 1913 referred to the caricature of Jews in the music halls, much of which came from self styled 'Hebrew character comedians' and the daughter of Rufus Isaacs commented on the prevalence of anti-Jewish 'gags' at the time of the Marconi scandal. See E. Reading, *For the Record: The Memoirs of Eva, Marchioness of Reading* (London, 1973), p. 28. I owe both these references to the kindness of Kenneth Lunn. Some evidence on the image of the Jewish immigrant in the cinema is provided in Cecil Hepworth's 'The Aliens' Invasion'. See R. Low and R. Manvell, *History of the British Film 1896–1906* (London, 1973), pp. 58–9.

73 M. Hunterberg, *The Jew and the Anti-Semite* (London, 1913), p. 7. A converted Jew, like Jacob Prelooker, took a different stand and could write: 'My chief point is that the causes of the antagonism existing between Jew and Christian lie with them both'. *Under the Czar and Queen Victoria* (London, 1896), p. 39.
74 C. K. Salaman, *Jews as they are* (London, 1882), pp. 47 and 65.
75 *The Jewish Question and the Mission of the Jews* (London, 1894), pp. 2–3, 5. The work also appeared in 1899 under Charles Waldstein's name. Waldstein's analysis was essentially a hymn to Liberal optimism.
76 *Aspects of the Jewish Question* by a Quarterly Reviewer (London, 1902), pp. 29–30. Authorship is attributed to Laurie Magnus and the work is not only an attak upon anti-semitism but also upon Zionism. It is argued that, 'the Jews of each country must work out for themselves (with such help as they may receive from better civilised Powers), their emancipation and their religious liberty.' *ibid.*, p. 69.
77 M. Simon, 'Antisemitism in England', *Jewish Review* II (1911–12), p. 301.
78 B. Glassman, *Anti-Semitic Stereotypes without Jews: Images of the Jews in England, 1290–1700* (Detroit, 1975), is useful on this. The durability of stereotypes is also discussed in Rosenberg, *op. cit.*, pp. 14–15.
79 See above pp. 8–9.
80 See above chapters 2 and 5.
81 See above pp. 76 and 110.
82 Disillusionment with Liberalism and the Liberal Party was quite widely present among those who manifested hostility towards Jews. Among the sources showing this might be mentioned A. White *The Modern Jew* (London, 1899), p. xv, where Liberalism was described as 'often but a synonym for the decay of faith'; J. Banister, *England under the Jews* (3rd edn, London, 1907), pp. 192, 193, 201, 203–5. See also the *New Witness*, 30 October 1913, p. 806, and 13 November 1913, p. 43. The National League for Clean Government, with which the *Witness* was linked, was concerned about political corruption, including its manifestation within the Liberal ranks. See also comments in the *National Review*, May 1910, pp. 402–16, December 1911, p. 499 and April 1913, p. 189 upon the Radicals who were described as engaging in anti-British behaviour.
83 See above p. 18 for ideas about a mythical golden age in the East End before the immigrants came. See above p. 88 for Maxse's references to a past glory which could be contrasted with a debilitated present. See the *Morning Post* 12 June 1913 and 14 June 1913 for remarks stimulated by the Marconi scandal, urging a return in public life to the high standards of the past. This was also echoed in the *Outlook*, 5 April 1913, p. 461 and the *Spectator*, 19 April 1913, p. 652. See also H. Belloc and C. Chesterton, *The Party System* (London, 1911), p. 150. See above p. 88 for evidence of the economic and political uncertainty of the late nineteenth, early twentieth centuries.
84 See above chapters 3, 4, 5 for Burton and Banister.
85 C. McWilliams, *Brothers under the Skin* (Boston, rev. edn, 1964), p. 317.
86 J. Higham, 'Anti-Semitism in the Gilded Age', *Mississippi Valley Historical Review* XLIII (1956–7), p. 566. See above pp. 30–35, 47–8, 81, 84, 86 for instances of simplification and distortion.
87 See above chapters 2, 5 and 6.
88 See above chapters 2 and 5.
89 See above pp. 107–8 for responses of the Jewish community.
90 See above chapter 6.
91 Sir R. Burton, *The Jew, the Gypsy and El Islam* (London, 1898), pp. 65–71.
92 See above p. 26.

93 A summary of the details is in R. Patai, *Encyclopaedia of Zionism and Israel* (New York, 1971). Its place in the history of Zionism is discussed, among others, by W. Laqueur, *A History of Zionism* (London, 1972).
94 *East London Advertiser*, 13 January 1906.
95 Banister, *op. cit.*, chapter 7 *passim.*
96 W. Evans-Gordon, 'The Attack on the Aliens Act', *National Review* XLVIII (1907), p. 471.
97 S. Graham, 'Russia and the Jews', *English Review* XIX (1914–15), p. 332. Bayme, 'Jewish Leadership', pp. 297–305 discusses Gentile Zionism between 1898 and 1917.
98 See above p. 30.
99 C. Chesterton, *The Prussian hath said in his Heart* (London, 1914), p. 227.
100 *ibid.*, p. 228.
101 See below pp. 251–2.
102 Hunterberg, *op. cit.*, pp. 107–13. See also below pp. 251–2 for additional references to conversionist activity. In addition, E. E. Burgess 'The Soul of the Leeds Ghetto', *Yorkshire Evening News*, 14 February 1925, refers to the 'harvest of failure' reaped by conversionists in Leeds.
103 The *Outlook*, 31 October 1914, pp. 564–5.
104 B. Gainer, *The Alien Invasion* (London, 1972), pp. 124–5 refers to this aspect of White's thought.
105 H. B. Marriott Watson, 'The Jew and his Destiny', *National Review* CXLVI (1905), p. 525.

Chapter 8

1 *The Times* 10 and 12 May 1915 reported the sinking of the *Lusitania* and the wrecking of German shops which ensued. *ibid.*, 11 May 1915 refers to the suspension of naturalized members of the Stock Exchange of German and Austrian birth. A. Marwick, *The Deluge* (London, 1973), p. 131 has an account of the East End outbreaks of hostility against aliens and S. Koss, *Lord Haldane. Scapegoat for Liberalism* (New York, 1969) deals with the dismissal of Haldane. The 1914 Aliens Act empowered the home secretary absolutely to prohibit immigrants from landing and to deport them. It also required all aliens to register with the police. See below p. 274 for the 1918 British Nationality and Status of Aliens Act. There is as yet no adequate account of the Belgian refugees in Britain. The feline analogy is from Marwick, *op. cit.*, p. 44. L. Poliakov, *Histoire de l'Antisèmitisme: L'Europe Suicidaire* (Paris, 1977), pp. 211–12 has some brief comment on the atmosphere of the time.
2 See above p. 87.
3 *DNB 1931–40* (London, 1949), pp. 828–9. See also the obituary notice in *The Times*, 18 February 1932.
4 Mond's life is discussed in *The Times*, 29 December 1930; H. Bolitho, *Alfred Mond* (London, 1933), and *DNB 1922–1930* (London, 1937), pp. 602–5. Mond was in fact born in Lancashire but the family's German origins were not forgotten. An academic study of Mond is G. M. Bayliss, 'The Outsider: Aspects of the Political Career of Alfred Mond, First Lord Melchett', unpublished PhD thesis, University of Wales, 1969.
5 Thus when we come upon the comment that 'the wild fury aroused by the sinking of the 'Lusitania' in May 1915 intended to hit everything German: it so *happened* that the victims were almost entirely Jews', I would argue that we are not concerned with a situation involving anti-semitism. The quotation is from C. C. Aronsfeld, 'Anti-Jewish Outbreaks in Modern Britain', *The*

Gates of Zion, July 1952, p. 17. Similarly, the internment policy of the British government was not directly specifically against Jews as such, even though Jews were caught up in its consequences. See, for instance, MEPOL 2 1633. Bayliss, 'The Outsider', p. 155 makes a similar stress in discussing the opposition which was directed towards Alfred Mond.

6 Bolitho, *op. cit.*, pp. 210–11.

7 *The Times*, 11 May 1915.

8 *ibid.*, 12 May 1915.

9 *ibid.*, 11 May 1915. A number of the individuals concerned are referred to in a different context in C. C. Aronsfeld, 'German Jews in Victorian England', *Leo Baeck Yearbook* VII (1962), pp. 312–29.

10 H. C. Semon and T. A. McIntyre, *The Autobiography of Sir Felix Semon* (London, n.d.), pp. 294–323, refer to Semon's 'trials' during the war.

11 Much earlier, Arnold White had queried why Cassel should have been made a privy councillor. See *For Efficiency* (London, 1902), pp. 101–2.

12 Makgill was involved in the British Empire Union, a right wing pressure group. See HO 45 10818/318095/2. The case was heard before Rufus Isaacs, then Lord Reading and lord chief justice.

13 *The Times*, 11 May, 13 May, 14 May, 15 May, 17 May, 18 May, 19 May, 20 May, 21 May 1915 contain details of the 'loyalty letters'; *ibid.*, 24 June 1915, 17, 18, 19 November 1915 and 18 December 1915 refer to the action against Speyer and Cassel, which, not surprisingly also attracted the interest of the *New Witness*, 23 December 1915, pp. 210–11; further information regarding Speyer's situation is in *DNB 1931–40*, *op. cit.*, pp. 828–9 and *The Times*, 7 and 9 January 1922 and 19 February 1932. See also Sir A. Fitzroy, *Memoirs* (2 vols, London, n.d.) II, pp. 613–14, 680, 770. The best secondary account of the rich, naturalized Jews and the loyalty issue is C. C. Aronsfeld, 'Jewish Enemy Aliens in England during the First World War', *Jewish Social Studies* XVIII, no. 4 (October 1956), pp. 275–83.

14 *The Times*, 17 November 1915. By contrast his obituary notice in 1921 was quite open about his Jewish origins. *ibid.*, 23 September 1921.

15 *Parliamentary Debates*, House of Lords XXXI (1918), cols. 426, 432.

16 Fitzroy, *op. cit.* I, pp. 97, 102, 387; *ibid.* II, pp. 499, 516 for references to Cassel's and Speyer's origins. *ibid.*, p. 598 which refers to the 1915 situation does not contain any such references.

17 *Parliamentary Debates*, House of Commons, CVIII (1918), cols. 2158–60. 'Once a German always a German', Macneill was led to comment.

18 The *New Witness*, 3 September 1914, p. 502 and 10 September 1914, p. 513.

19 *ibid.*, 10 September 1914, p. 513.

20 See chapters 2 and 5 for a discussion of the earlier activities of the *Witness*.

21 The *New Witness*, 10 September 1914, p. 513.

22 *ibid.*, 29 October 1914, p. 626. See above for a discussion of the Indian silver scandal.

23 *ibid.*

24 On 28 January 1915, p. 150 under the title 'The Roast Beef of Old England', a campaign was started against J. Lyons who were alleged to have delivered to troops at White City meat which was unfit for human consumption. Readers were reminded that in the previous year they had been advised that J. Lyons was a name to watch. The journal cast a critical eye over most government contracts. The chance to expose alleged Jewish corruption was even more welcome.

25 Newman's speech is in *Parliamentary Debates*, House of Commons CVIII (1918), col. 2173.

26 *ibid.*, col. 2196.
27 *ibid.*
28 See above chapter 5.
29 *National Review*, October 1914, p. 229. See also *ibid.*, December 1914, p. 517.
30 *ibid.*, October 1914 p. 232.
31 Those mentioned in *ibid.*, pp. 229–30, for instance.
32 *ibid.*, October 1914, p. 163 and pp. 240–41; December 1914, p. 595; March 1915, pp. 681–93 and 905–16; June 1915, p. 512; implicitly in July 1915, p. 685; September 1915, p. 85.
33 *ibid.*, October 1914, p. 16.
34 *ibid.*, November 1916, p. 293 and October 1917, p. 134.
35 *Jewish Chronicle*, 9 October 1914.
36 E. Levy, 'English Jewry in the Great War' unpublished Master of Hebrew Literature thesis, Jewish Theological Seminary, 1966, p. 42.
37 J. Liddiard, *Isaac Rosenberg, the Half Used Life* (London, 1976), pp. 186–7 refers to Rosenberg encountering anti-semitism within the ranks, but does not provide details. See J. Cohen, *Journey to the Trenches. The Life of Isaac Rosenberg 1890–1918* (London, 1975), p. 127 for a similar brief reference. Siegfried Sassoon, fox hunting man and infantry officer, does not seem to have encountered similar problems. M. Adler, *The Jews of the Empire and the Great War* (London, 1919) was an early study of the Jewish war effort. B. A. Kosmin and N. Grizzard, 'The Jewish Dead in the Great War as an Indicator for Anglo-Jewish Demography and Class Stratification in 1914', confidential paper, Research Unit, Board of Deputies (1974), point out that Jews were over-represented in the armed forces. This was probably due to the younger age structure of the community and the fact that few Jews were in reserved occupations. Altogether 41,500 Jews served in the armed forces. Prior to the introduction of conscription in January 1916, 10,000 Jews volunteered for active service. These were probably from the anglicized section of Jewry. See pp. 2–3. Kosmin and Grizzard shed no light on the Russian-Jewish immigrants' contribution to the war effort, which, as we shall discover, became a contentious issue.
38 *Parliamentary Debates*, House of Commons LXXXV (1916), col. 1839.
39 L. Stein, *The Balfour Declaration* (London, 1961), pp. 488 ff. discusses briefly the responses of Russian Jews in Britain towards the war. L. Greenberg, *The Jews of Russia* (2 vols in 1, New Haven, 1965) II, pp. 94–6, refers to the enlistment of Jews outside Russia in the Tsar's forces but also to a growing disillusionment on account of the continuation of anti-semitic policies by the authorities – in the services and elsewhere. Home Office papers suggest that hostility in Britain was directed generally towards the Russian-Jewish population.
40 V. Jabotinsky, *The Story of the Jewish Legion* (New York, 1945), p. 62.
41 *ibid.*
42 See below pp. 128–9, 132–3. There is some brief discussion of such matters scattered through W. Kendall, *The Revolutionary Movement in Britain 1900–1921* (London, 1965) and in R. Challinor, *The Origins of British Bolshevism* (London, 1977), chapters 6, 7 and 8.
43 *Jewish Chronicle*, 2 October 1914.
44 *ibid.*, 9 October 1914.
45 *ibid.*, 2 July 1915.
46 *ibid.*, 24 December 1915.
47 *Parliamentary Debates*, House of Commons LXXXIV (1916), cols. 178–79.
48 *Jewish Chronicle*, 21 July 1916.
49 See Jabotinsky, *op. cit.*, for details of Jabotinsky and his ideas.

50 *Parliamentary Debates*, House of Commons LXXXIV (1916), cols. 178–9; *ibid.*, cols. 1420–22; *ibid.* LXXXV (1916), cols. 173–77.
51 Aliens classified as hostile were interned.
52 *ibid.* LXXXV (1916), col. 176. In other words the government did not intend to return political refugees to Russia.
53 *ibid.* LXXXIV (1916), col. 1421.
54 *ibid.*, col. 1420; *ibid.* LXXXV (1916), col. 174.
55 HO 45 10821/318095/367 and HO 45 10823/318095/624, /632, /633 are useful on these developments and their repercussions.
56 HO 45 10818/318095/32.
57 See for example, HO 45 10819/318095/110. Bezalel was deported in 1917. See *Parliamentary Debates*, House of Commons XCVIII (1917), col. 1456.
58 HO 45 10821/318095/367.
59 HO 45 10820/318095/309. See below pp. 132–3.
60 HO 45 10820/318095/219.
61 *Parliamentary Debates*, House of Commons LXXXV (1916), col. 178. The government maintained throughout, for instance, that it would never engage in forcible deportation or abrogate the sacred right of political asylum.
62 HO 45 10823/318095/633.
63 HO 45 10823/318095/632 reveals Bolshevik hostility to the 1917 agreement. Some sharp comment was also made in the commons. See *Parliamentary Debates*, House of Commons CIII (1918), cols. 595–6. In a telegram to Lockhart at the British embassy in Moscow, the Foreign Office on 27 June 1918 provided full details of the agreement so that the matter could be comprehensively discussed with the Russian authorities.
64 Kosmin and Grizzard, *op. cit.*, refer to the general Jewish contribution to the armed forces and assess its cost. Jabotinsky, *op. cit.*, is concerned with the fight for a Jewish Legion. See also J. H. Patterson, *With the Judeans in the Palestine Campaign* (London, 1922), pp. 23–5 who notes the difficulty in securing recruits for the Jewish Legion, which was gazetted on 23 April 1917. As for the Russian Jews in Britain, the government maintained a calculated vagueness about the numbers engaged on active service. See *Parliamentary Debates*, House of Commons XCVIII (1917), cols. 9 and 1292–3 and *ibid.* CI (1918), col. 15. For a pessimistic assessment see Stein, *op. cit.*, p. 493.
65 There is no mention of them in E. Krausz, *Leeds Jewry: its History and Social Structure* (Cambridge, 1964); C. C. Aronsfeld, *The Gates of Zion*, July 1952, pp. 15–18, 21 does not quite come to grips with the problem. S.G. Bayme, 'Jewish Leadership and Anti-Semitism in Britain 1898–1918', unpublished PhD thesis, Columbia University, 1977, pp. 23–6 comments on Jews in the war and refers briefly to the situation in Leeds.
66 *Parliamentary Debates*, House of Commons LXXXIV (1916), col. 1420 indicates the government's awareness of a potential conflict situation unless it acted. See also *ibid.* LXXXV (1916), col. 174.
67 HO 45 10810/311932/40.
68 *Yorkshire Post*, 4 June 1917.
69 *Leeds Mercury*, 4 June 1917.
70 *Yorkshire Evening Post*, 4 June 1917.
71 See also *Yorkshire Evening News*, 4 June 1917.
72 *Yorkshire Evening Post*, 4 June 1917 and *Yorkshire Evening News*, 4 June 1917.
73 Based upon *Yorkshire Evening Post* and *Yorkshire Evening News*, 5 June 1917 editions.
74 HO 45 10810/311932/40 for his letter.
75 HO 45 10810/311932/43 letter of 18 June 1917. The *Yorkshire Post*, 4 June

1917, dismissed the disturbances on 3 June as a 'hooligan outrage' but this view was not shared by other sections of the press. The *Leeds Mercury*, 4 June 1917, adopted an agnostic position on the causes of the violence but the *Yorkshire Evening Post*, 4 June 1917, emphasized that the disturbances were related to the military service issue which was mixed with an element of hooliganism.

76 *Yorkshire Evening News*, 5 June 1917, refers to her reaction.

77 HO 45 10810/311932/37.

78 HO 45 10810/311932/46.

79 *Yorkshire Evening Post*, 5 June 1917 comments favourably on police activity.

80 HO 45 10810/311932/46, letter 24 June 1917.

81 HO 45 10810/311932/37.

82 HO 45 10820/318095/309.

83 *Yorkshire Evening Post*, 5 June 1917.

84 In HO 45 10821/318095/336.

85 HO 45 10810/311932/56. See below for a discussion of the later disturbances in London.

86 HO 45 10820/318095/309.

87 HO 45 10821/318095/336.

88 *East London Observer*, 5 August 1916.

89 HO 45 10820/318095/202.

90 HO 45 10820/318095/252 contains the *East London Observer*, 13 March 1917.

91 HO 45 10820/318095/243.

92 HO 45 10822/318095/473.

93 *Daily News and Leader*, 24 September 1917; *The Times*, 24 September 1917.

94 The main details of this account are from a Hackney police station report of 24 September 1917 in HO 45 10822/318095/478.

95 *ibid.*

96 HO 45 10822/318095/478, Report from Hackney Police Station, 25 September 1917.

97 HO 45 10810/311932/56.

98 S. White, 'Soviets in Britain: the Leeds Convention in 1917', *International Review of Social History* XIX (1974), pp. 166–93, is a recent consideration of the conference.

99 *ibid.*, p. 167.

100 S. R. Graubard, *British Labour and the Russian Revolution 1917–1924* (Cambridge, Mass., 1956), is useful on the reactions of British labour to the changing events in Russia.

101 Aronsfeld, *The Gates of Zion*, pp. 18–19 argues along these lines. Alf Mattison in his Diary, Notebook C (1917), pp. 15–16 says that the disturbances had nothing to do with the conference. What is less open to conjecture is that the government kept a close watch on proceedings. HO 45 10810/311932/35/41.

102 J. Fraenkel (ed.), *The Jews of Austria* (London, 1970), pp. 289–92 refers to Galician Jews and the magnet of Vienna.

103 Most of this is based upon, A. G. Duker, 'Jews in the World War. A Brief Historical Sketch', *Contemporary Jewish Record* II, part 5 (September–October 1939), pp. 6–29.

104 *East London Observer*, 13 March 1917.

105 See above p. 87 for antipathy towards the court Jews. In addition to these examples it might be mentioned that Arnold White, in an article called 'The Cosmopolitan Financier', which appeared in the *Throne*, 19 June 1912, p. 450 expressed his hostility towards the activities of a number of financiers – clearly Jewish – who found themselves the subject of vicious comment in the war years. See above pp. 122–5 for the antipathy of 1914–15. The later hostility of

1918 is apparent in the series 'Our Gold Lords', which started in the *New Witness*, 2 August 1918, pp. 267–8 and which ran into the autumn of that year. The use of material from some of these led to the Beamish v. Mond trial, referred to below p. 144. The articles in the *Witness* began to appear in the atmosphere which resulted in the 1918 British Nationality and Status of Aliens Act, the main purpose of which was to introduce widespread powers of revoking certificates of naturalization and to provide machinery for that purpose. This amended the Aliens Act of 1914.

106 As the 'loyalty letters' indicate.

107 The *New Witness*, 13 December 1918, p. 132. See below pp. 145, 166, 216, 305 for further comment concerning the Versailles Settlement.

108 See below pp. 141, 145, 305 for references to the revival of the scandal after the First World War.

109 J. H. Clarke, *The Call of the Sword* (London, 1917), pp. 21–2. This was a theme which was repeated in H. S. Spencer, *Democracy or Shylocracy?* (London, 1918). This book was later reissued by the Britons when it carried an introduction by Clarke. See below pp. 141, 145, 277 for references to this and to Spencer himself.

110 Clarke, *Call of the Sword*, p. 22.

111 *ibid.*, p. 26.

112 N. Cohn, *Warrant for Genocide* (Harmondsworth, 1970), p. 164 refers to the anonymity of the author of *England Under the Heel of the Jew* without revealing that it was Clarke who wrote it. The work was first published by C. F. Roworth in 1918 and then in 1921 by the Britons Publishing Company. Clarke's role in the Britons is referred to in C. C. Aronsfeld, 'The Britons Publishing Society', *Wiener Library Bulletin* XX, no. 3 (summer 1966), p. 32 and H. Blume, 'A History of Anti-Semitic Groups in Britain 1918–1940', unpublished MPhil thesis, University of Sussex, 1971, chapter 3 *passim*. The only obituary of Clarke which I have been able to trace is in the *Homoeopathic Recorder* XLVII (1932), pp. 157–60.

113 *DNB The Concise Dictionary, 1901–1950* (Oxford, 1961), p. 94 provides details of his life and career.

114 I. D. Colvin, *The Unseen Hand in English History* (London, 1917), pp. ix, x. In the same year Arnold White in *The Hidden Hand* (London, 1917), p. 13 was to comment that The Hidden Hand would remain the chief instrument of Pan-Germanism until Germany was obliterated from the map.

115 Colvin, *op. cit.*, p. 238.

116 *ibid.*, p. 227.

117 I. D. Colvin, 'The Germans in England', *National Review*, December 1915, pp. 529–41; *ibid.*, March 1916, pp. 55–64.

118 *ibid.*, December 1915, p. 533.

119 See below for a discussion of this.

120 The attitude of the *Morning Post* towards the Russian Revolution, as well as other reactions which were to become important after the war, are deferred for discussion until later when they can be appropriately and clearly linked with related post-war attitudes. The Balfour Declaration and the growth of Zionism are covered in innumerable publications from which selection is invidious but Stein, *op. cit.* and W. Laqueur, *A History of Zionism* (London, 1972), are both useful.

Chapter 9

1 *Plain English*, 9 April 1921, pp. 291–3, 23 April, pp. 324–5, 30 April, p. 344.

2 J. H. Clarke, *England Under the Heel of the Jew* (2nd edn, London, 1921),

p. 90. See also H. H. Beamish, *The Jews' Who's Who. Israelite Finance. Its Sinister Influence* (London, 1920), pp. 29–40.

3 Clarke, *op. cit.*, p. 60. See also *Jewry Ueber Alles*, June 1920, p. 3 and *Blackwood's Magazine* CCIX (February 1921), pp. 262–3 and V. E. Marsden, *Jews in Russia, with half Jews and 'damped' Jews* (London, n.d. 1921?), p. 5. See also *Plain English*, 18 December 1920, pp. 561–3; 15 January 1921, p. 54, 11 June, pp. 473–6, 18 June, pp. 492–3 and 25 June, pp. 511–2.

4 See the *DNB, 1941–1950* (Oxford, 1959), p. 336 and *The Times*, 27 June 1950 for Gwynne. W. Hindle, *The Morning Post, 1772–1937* (London, 1937), is a history of his newspaper.

5 *Morning Post*, 16 March 1917. Both Marsden and Colvin, it will become apparent, were prominent in contributing to the hostility which developed in Britain towards Jews in the 1920s. On Marsden see the obituaries in *The Times* and the *Morning Post* on 30 October 1920. Colvin appears in the *DNB, The Concise Dictionary 1901–1950* (Oxford, 1961), p. 94.

6 The Morning Post, 6 October 1917.

7 *ibid.*, 9 November 1917.

8 *ibid.*, 6 December 1917.

9 See V. E. Marsden, *Rasputin and Russia* (London, 1920), p. 55 and his *Jews in Russia, op. cit.*

10 Wilton was born at Cringleford near Norwich in 1868 and died in Paris in 1925. He was appointed by *The Times* to St Petersburg in 1903. His father had been a mining engineer in Russia and Wilton had lived there from an early age. There is an obituary in *The Times*, 20 January 1925. See also *The Times House Journal* XV (February 1925), p. 122.

11 In a letter to Wickham Steed on 9 October 1914 he was offering material on German atrocities with the comment: 'It seems to me that it will be a good thing to bring it before the British Public to counteract the pro-German campaign already been waged by the Jews and other Germanophiles.' Copy in the archives of *The Times*.

12 See the letter from Abraham Bezalel to the editor of *The Times*, 4 April 1917. See also the letter from John Buchan, then at the Foreign Office, to Geoffrey Robinson at *The Times*, dated 1 May 1917 and now in the archives of *The Times*, which enclosed a short memorandum prepared by the Intelligence Bureau on Wilton's activities in Russia. Buchan's comment to Robinson was: 'The situation in Russia is very delicate, and I cannot think that Wilton's cables and articles have been always very discreet. Would it be possible for you to keep an eye on him and perhaps give him a hint?' There is some critical comment on Wilton and Marsden of the *Morning Post* portraying the situation in the interests of the old régime in a communication from the conjoint foreign committee of the Board of Deputies and the Anglo-Jewish Association, in HO 45 10818/318095/371. Wilton's writings remained in vogue in anti-Bolshevik and anti-Jewish circles. See the *Patriot*, 20 February 1930, p. 168, 10 April 1930, pp. 364–6, 17 April 1930, pp. 390–92. See also The *Free Press*, October 1938.

13 See the memorandum prepared by the Intelligence Bureau of the Foreign Office and dated 30 April 1917 in the archives of *The Times*. Objections were also raised against Stephen Graham of *The Times*, who was described by Geoffrey Robinson in a letter to John Walter on 8 December 1913 as 'a very remarkable writer about Russia', but whom the moderate socialist paper, *Dyelo Naroda* described as anti-semitic. See Stephen Graham's article 'Russia and the Jews', *English Review* XIX (1914–15), for his views, particularly pp. 324–6. See also the comments in his *Russia and the World* (London, 1915) especially, pp. 134–6.

14 A letter to Wickham Steed from Wilton, written on 9 October 1920, referred to 'a feeling' against him in the office and his comment was: 'My impression was that the Jews were at the bottom of it all.' After leaving *The Times* he joined the staff of the *New York Herald* in Paris and later moved to the *Paris Times. The Times House Journal*, *op. cit.* Wilton's books on Russia were *Russia's Agony* (London, 1915); *The Last Days of the Romanovs* (London, 1920) and a translation of *Kamchatka* (London, 1921?). He has recently figured in A. Summers and T. Mangold, *The File on the Tsar* (London, 1976), pp. 60, 102–4, 148, 159, 161–2, 176 and 277–8. Wilton's view was that 'it was the Jews in charge of the Red Okhrana, the red secret police . . . and not Lenin and Trotsky who decided that the Imperial family should die.' *The Times*, 20 January 1925. See also his reference to the 'Red Jew Murderers' in *The Last Day of the Romanovs*, p. 144.

15 *The Times*, 28 July 1919, 14 November 1919, 22 November 1919, 25 November 1919, 27 November 1919 and 1 December 1919.

16 *A collection of reports on Bolshevism in Russia. Russia No. 1* Cmnd. 8 (1919), particularly pp. 6, 28, 32 and 56.

17 *Jewish Chronicle* 4 April 1919. See also *ibid.*, 28 March 1919. See, however, the letter in the *Morning Post*, 23 April 1919 from a number of prominent Jews dissociating British Jews from the Bolshevik cause. For a detailed general study of Jews and revolution, see R. Wistrich, *Revolutionary Jews From Marx to Trotsky* (London, 1976).

18 W. S. Churchill, 'Zionism versus Bolshevism. A Struggle for the Soul of the Jewish People'. *Illustrated Sunday Herald*, 8 February 1920. Churchill's attitutes towards Jews and Zionism at this time have been discussed recently in M. Gilbert, *Winston S. Churchill* IV, 1917–22 (London, 1975).

19 L. Schapiro, 'Jews in the Revolutionary Movement', *Slavonic and East European Review* XL (1961), pp. 148–67 is valuable on these matters as is C. Abramsky, *War Revolution and the Jewish Dilemma* (London, 1975).

20 Beamish, *op. cit.*, pp. 68–9, where they appear as 'LANDMARKS IN HISTORY'.

21 *The Times*, 2 December 1919. The charges against Mond first appeared in a series called 'Our Gold Lords' by Percival F. Smith in the *New Witness* on 13 September 1918, pp. 387–8 and echoed on at regular intervals to the end of the year. See below p. 274 for additional comment.

22 *The Times*, 2 December 1919.

23 *ibid.*, 13 January 1920 reports the state of Beamish's health; *ibid.* 5 December 1919 refers to Beamish organizing the Britons. The whole case is covered in *ibid.* 2–6 December 1919, 13 January 1920 and 9 March 1920. Beamish's career is discussed in L. W. Bondy, *Racketeers of Hatred* (London, 1946), particularly pp. 130–41 and B. A. Kosmin, 'Colonial Careers for Marginal Fascists – a Portrait of Hamilton Beamish', *Wiener Library Bulletin* XXVII (1973–4), pp. 16–23. There is a file on Beamish in the Wiener Library which includes an obituary in the *Broom*, 27 April 1948. A sympathetic view is contained in the *Free Press*, December 1936, a publication of the Militant Christian Patriots.

24 W. Freeman, *The Life of Lord Alfred Douglas: Spoilt Child of Genius* (London, 1948) and R. Croft-Cooke, *Bosie* (London, 1963), provide biographical information on Douglas. It was in his cell in Wormwood Scrubs in 1924 after the Churchill case that Douglas wrote what he considered to be his greatest poem on 'the leprous spawn of scattered Israel' – see *The Complete Poems of Lord Alfred Douglas* (London, 1928), pp. 131–2. In *The Autobiography of Lord Alfred Douglas* (London, 1931 edn), pp. 302–4, Douglas comments in retro-

spect about his association with anti-semitism.

25 *The Times*, 11–14 December 1923 gives full details of the trial.

26 The case was reported in *The Times*, 18 July 1923. On the Kitchener incident see below p. 145.

27 Spencer was the author of *Democracy or Shylocracy*? which was first published by C. F. Roworth in 1918 and which was later reissued by the Britons, when it was supplemented with a preface by Dr J. H. Clarke. Spencer bought *Plain English* out of receivership on 3 December 1921 and ran it for the rest of its brief life. It was through such channels that Spencer disseminated his own brand of anti-semitism in the early 1920s. In his capacity as a troublemaker, Spencer was one of the witnesses in the Pemberton – Billing libel case in 1918. See the review of Michael Kettle's book, *Salome's Last Veil* in the *Times Literary Supplement*, 2 December 1977.

28 *The Times*, 14 December 1923. The Churchill-Douglas libel action was revived and referred to in Nazi propaganda in the Second World War. See F. Rose, *Das ist Churchill* (Munich/Berlin, 1940), pp. 57–8.

29 Banister's articles appeared in *Plain English*, 5 March 1921, pp. 193–5, 17 December, p. 1600, 24 December, pp. 1023–4, 31 December, pp. 1041–3; 7 January 1922, pp. 1061–2. The Kitchener incident is referred to in *ibid.*, 10 December 1922, p. 976 and 17 December, p. 997. The *Fascist Bulletin*, 5 June 1926, p. 1 and the *British Lion*, late June 1926, pp. 8–9 which took up the theme at a later date. For an even later reference see W. Joyce, *Twilight over England* (2nd edn, The Hague, 1942, first published 1940), p. 171.

30 See the open letter sent by G. K. Chesterton to Lord Reading (Rufus Isaacs) in the *New Witness*, 13 December 1918, p. 132. See also *Blackwood's Magazine* CCVIII (1920), p. 691 for a remark on 'the Jews supreme at the Conference of Paris'. *Jewry Ueber Alles or The Hidden Hand Exposed*, August 1920, p. 1 refers to the 'Kosher Peace Conference', H. A. Gwynne (ed.), *The Cause of World Unrest* (New York, 1920), pp. xxvii-xxx and chapter 12 *passim* was also critical of the influence of Jews. For later echoes, see *inter alia*, A. H. Lane, *The Alien Menace* (3rd edn, London, 1932), chapter 12 *passim*. More objective comment recognizing the influence of Jews at Versailles is contained in E. J. Dillon, *The Inside Story of the Peace Conference* (London, 1919), pp. 10–11, 201, 423–32 and J. Parkes, *Anti-Semitism* (London, 1963), p. 49. See also I. Sieff, *Memoirs* (London, 1970), pp. 114–21.

31 See 'The Kosher League', in *Jewry Ueber Alles*, May 1920, p. 2 and 'The League of Nations starts', by Uriah the Hittite, *Plain English*, 5 February 1921, pp. 112–13 for two hostile comments from the fringe. More mainstream criticism came from High Tory quarters such as L. J. Maxse, 'The Second Treaty of Versailles', *National Review*, August 1919, pp. 819 and 844; Gwynne, *op. cit.*, pp. XXIX–XXX and the *Morning Post*, 7 September 1921.

32 For comment that the principle of self determination espoused by the League created disaffection within the British Empire see Gwynne, *op. cit.*, p. 170. See also N. Webster, *The Surrender of an Empire* (London, 1931), chapter 2.

33 'In the history of every great nation, there comes a time when it is expedient to take stock of itself.' G. P. Mudge, *The Menace to the English Race and its Traditions of Present-Day Immigration and Emigration* (n.p. n.d. 1919–20?), p. 2. Mudge wrote for the Britons. See *Jewry Ueber Alles*, May 1920, p. 7, June 1920, pp. 5–6; *Jewry Ueber Alles or The Hidden Hand Exposed*, July 1920, pp. 6–7. See also *The Hidden Hand or The Jewish Peril*, February 1924, pp. 21–2, March 1924, pp. 37–8 and April 1924, pp. 55–6. See also the *British Guardian*, May 1924, pp. 70–71 and June 1924, pp. 86–7 and finally *ibid.*, November–December 1924, pp. 159 and 161–2.

34 *Jewry Ueber Alles*, June 1920, p. 3. *Blackwood's Magazine* CCVIII (1920), p. 692 was also hostile to Samuel's appointment for his being a Jew. Viscount Samuel, *Memoirs* (London, 1945), pp. 150–52 gives Herbert Samuel's own recollections of the appointment. See above pp. 70–73 for Samuel and the Marconi affair. J. S. Schneider, 'Anti-Semitism in Britain in the early Nineteen–Twenties', MS. pp. 89–90 carries additional comment on Samuel's appointment.

35 *Plain English*, 8 January 1921, pp. 23–4.

36 *Blackwood's Magazine* CCIX (1921), p. 262.

37 *ibid.*, p. 263.

38 *ibid.*, p. 265.

39 *ibid.*, p. 264. Wordsworth could hardly have imagined that part of his sonnet 'On Venice' would be quoted in such circumstances. Opposition to Montagu was particularly pronounced after the General Dyer incident in April 1919. At Amritsar in that month Dyer opened fire on an unarmed crowd and killed 379 of them. Montagu condemned the action: others defended Dyer as a bulwark of the Raj. See S. D. Waley, *Edwin Montagu* (Bombay, 1964), particularly pp. 205–7.

40 *Blackwood's Magazine* CCVIII (1920), p. 692. See above pp. 86, 122 for earlier opposition to Mond.

41 Beamish worked this appeal into the Mond libel case. See *The Times*, 6 December 1919.

42 See R. Skidelsky, *Oswald Mosley* (London, 1975), pp. 318–9.

43 See R. May and R. Cohen 'The interaction between Race and Colonialism: a case study of the Liverpool Race Riots of 1919', *Race* XVI (1974), pp. 111–26 and G. W. Dimmock, 'Racial Hostility in Britain, with particular reference to the disturbances in Cardiff and Liverpool', unpublished MA dissertation, University of Sheffield, 1975. P. Foot, *Immigration and Race in British Politics* (Harmondsworth, 1965), pp. 103–7 discusses the 1919 Aliens Act in morally indignant tones.

44 P. Abrams, 'The Failure of Social Reform 1918–1920', *Past and Present*, no. 24 (April 1963), pp. 43–64.

45 C. L. Mowat, *Britain between the Wars 1918–1940* (London, 1976 edn), chapters 1 and 2; A. J. P. Taylor, *English History 1914–1945* (Oxford, 1965), chapter 4 *passim* are generally useful on the 'atmosphere' of these years.

46 Belloc's work is discussed below p. 211.

47 The publication is discussed by, among others, H. Rollin, *L'apocalypse de notre temps* (Paris, 1939), – a work which was sought out and destroyed by the Germans after their invasion of France in 1939. Later comment is contained in J. S. Curtiss, *An Appraisal of the Protocols of Zion* (New York, 1942); N. Cohn, *Warrant for Genocide* (London, 1967), and H. Bernstein, *The Truth about 'The Protocols of Zion'* (New York, 1971, with an introduction by Norman Cohn; first published 1935). Two more recent works of relevance are, J. Webb, *The Occult Establishment* (La Salle, Illinois, 1977), and J. R. von Bilberstein, *Die These von der Verschwörung 1776–1945* (Bern/Frankfurt, 1977). Both are reviewed by N. Cohn in the *Times Literary Supplement*, 17 June 1977.

48 Cohn, *Warrant For Genocide* (Harmondsworth, 1970 edn), pp. 164–72, does this but as will become apparent my comment takes account of new information. All future references are to the Pelican edition.

49 *ibid.* casts no light on this.

50 *The Universal Jewish Encyclopaedia* IV (New York, 1948), p. 58. This report was based upon an account given in the anti-semitic *Highland Post*, 17 May 1936, which was published at Highland, New York. The account was later

reprinted in the *American Gentile*, June 1936.

51 Robert Cust to H. A. Gwynne, 11 February 1920 (Bodleian Library). Cust's letter indicated that Shanks had translated the British Museum copy. This would be *Velikoe v Malom i Antikhrist* (Tsarskoe Selo, 1905), by S. A. Nilus.

52 Cohn, *op. cit.*, chapter 6 deals with the hawking of *The Protocols* by Russian emigrés in Germany. See also W. Laqueur, *Russia and Germany* (London, 1965), chapter 6. See also the references to Major General Cherep Spiridovitch, below p. 150. Correspondence in the archives of the Britons between F. D. Fowler, Shanks, J. H. Clarke and Eyre and Spottiswoode (Printers), conducted in the summer and autumn of 1920, conclusively confirms Shanks as the translator of *The Jewish Peril* and the original owner of the copyright. I am grateful to the Britons for granting me access to this material. See also below note 72.

53 *Morning Post*, 11 February 1920.

54 *Jewry Ueber Alles*, February 1920, p. 4.

55 See *The Nation*, 27 March 1920, pp. 890–91 and the *Jewish Guardian*, 5 March 1920. At the end of March a critical question was asked in the House of Commons about *The Jewish Peril*, drawing attention to its anti-semitic origins. See *Parliamentary Debates*, House of Commons CXXVII (1920), col 919. It might be noticed that the occult world, traditionally a source of much conspiratorial thought, was not unanimously sympathetic to *The Jewish Peril*. See A. E. Waite, 'Occult Freemasonry and the Jewish Peril', *Occult Review* XXXIII (September 1920), pp. 142–53. See Webb, *op. cit.* for a lively discussion of anti-semitism and the occult.

56 'The Jewish Peril', *The Times*, 8 May 1920. The article was anonymous but Gordon Phillips, the archivist of *The Times*, informs me that it was written by Steed.

57 See *ibid.*, 10, 11 and 12 May 1920. Maude's letter appeared in the last issue. The issue of 10 May carried comment from J. H. Clarke whose role in British anti-semitism is discussed elsewhere. See above p. 139 and below p. 157. The fact that *The Times* did not condemn the publication outright was seized upon and exploited by the Britons. See *Jewry Ueber Alles*, May 1920, p. 8.

58 The *Spectator*, 15 May 1920, p. 640.

59 *ibid.*, p. 641. *ibid.*, 5 June 1920, pp. 750–51 and 12 June, pp. 782–3 included a discussion of 'Disraeli on the secret societies of the Jews' in the light of *The Jewish Peril*.

60 H. A. Gwynne in the introduction to Gwynne (ed.), *op. cit.*, p. viii. The work appeared in London in 1920.

61 *ibid.*, chapters 1–5 and 8 particularly.

62 *ibid.*, p. xii.

63 Preface to American edition by H. A. Gwynne.

64 H. Blume, 'A History of Anti-Semitic Groups in Britain 1918–1940', unpublished MPhil thesis, University of Sussex, 1971, p. 49 refers to Colvin as the likely author. Schneider MS. p. 62 attributes authorship to H. A. Gwynne and V. E. Marsden.

65 See my article 'New Light on "The Protocols of Zion"', *Patterns of Prejudice* VI (November–December 1977), pp. 13–21.

66 Letter H. A. Gwynne to Grant Richards (Publishers), 23 July 1920. Gwynne Collection, Bodleian Library. I am grateful to Vice-Admiral I. L. T. Hogg, for allowing me to quote Gwynne's correspondence.

67 *Morning Post*, 24 July 1920.

68 L. Wolf, *The Jewish Bogey and the Forged Protocols of the Learned Elders of Zion* (London, 1920).

69 As in *Jewry Ueber Alles or The Hidden Hand Exposed*, August 1920, pp. 5–6 and *The Hidden Hand or Jewry Ueber Alles*, October 1921, p. 1.

70 *Plain English*, 17 July 1920, p. 28 referred in complimentary terms to the articles in the *Morning Post*. Details of Spirodovitch's life are provided in *ibid.*, 25 September 1920, p. 265. His articles started in *ibid.*, 21 August 1920, p. 149. In 'New Light on "The Protocois of Zion"', I identified the wrong Spiridovitch. In fact, he lived between 1858 and 1926 and was the author of *The Secret World Government* (New York, 1926). He was present at the second meeting of the Britons held on 31 January 1920. See the Minute Book of the Britons.

71 Laqueur, *op. cit.*, p. 120 engages in some scathing comment.

72 Hitherto, the history of the various issues of *The Protocols* in Britain has been obscure. The archives of the Britons makes it clear, however, that Shanks was the translator of *The Jewish Peril* and that the Britons pushed their interest in the publication when Shanks was reluctant to finance another edition by Eyre and Spottiswoode. With the purchase of the plates of the book by the Britons the copyright was transferred through Shanks to the Britons. Under the new arrangement Shanks was to receive 3*d.* per copy in royalties on copies of the book sold after 11 August 1920. Correspondence also established that Shanks wanted to separate himself from his work, although discussion about royalty payments as late as 1930 indicate a continuing financial interest on his part. It was the difficulty in dealing with Shanks which encouraged the Britons to bring out the Marsden translation of *The Protocols*. Letters of 18 September 1920, 23 June 1930, 17 July 1930, 11 December 1957 and the legal agreement between Shanks and the Britons provide details in such matters. G. Volz-Lebzelter, 'Political Anti-Semitism in England 1918–1939', unpublished DPhil thesis, University of Oxford, 1977, is the only other research which has unearthed this information. Dr Lebzelter is to publish her thesis and has therefore requested that I do not discuss her work before it appears in print. Suffice it to say that I have read her thesis, I have examined the major new sources of information which are available on inter-war anti-semitism and I do not wish to change any of the detail or nuances of my argument. The *Universal Jewish Encyclopaedia* IV (New York, 1948), p. 58 suggests that T. and T. Clark, printers of Edinburgh, refused to print a version of *The Protocols* to the commission of the duke of Northumberland. In a letter to the author on 26 August 1977 the firm declared that they did not have any records which would shed light on the claim. Those interested in the wider context of *The Protocols* would be advised to direct some attention to the Gwynne papers in the Bodleian.

73 The *Spectator*, 16 October 1920, p. 503 which contained a review of *The Cause of World Unrest*.

74 *Blackwood's Magazine* CCVIII (1920), pp. 689–92.

75 *Jewry Ueber Alles*, March 1920, p. 3. See also *ibid.*, April 1920, p. 3 and *Blackwood's Magazine* CCVIII (1920), p. 692.

76 It is interesting to note that H. A. Gwynne of the *Morning Post* was not convinced about the authenticity of *The Protocols*. However, he was prepared to recommend V. E. Marsden's translation of them to Grant Richards. This suggests that while he was inclined to present a 'reasoned' case against Jewish interests in *The Cause of World Unrest*, he was not averse to more extreme conspiratorial forms of hostility being encouraged into publication – provided he were not associated with them. Letter H. A. Gwynne to Grant Richards (Publishers), 23 July 1920 in H. A. Gwynne Collection, Bodleian Library.

77 On Philip P. Graves (1876–1953) see *Who Was Who, 1951–1960* (London, 1961), p. 447. On the exposé see, *inter alia*, the early publication by P. Graves, *The Truth about The Protocols* (London, 1921); J. Gwyer, *Portraits of Mean*

Men. A Short History of the Protocols of the Elders of Zion (London, 1938), chapter 3 *passim*; Curtiss, *op. cit.*, refers to evidence on the facts of the forgery; J. Parkes, *An Enemy of the People: Anti-semitism* (Harmondsworth, 1945), p. 42; Cohn, *op. cit.*, pp. 78–80. See my article 'New Light on "The Protocols of Zion"', *op. cit.* for a documentary account of the exposé.

78 Letter, Raslovleff to Graves, 12 July 1921, in the archives of *The Times*.

79 Letter Raslovleff to Graves, 13 July 1921.

80 Graves to Steed, 13 July 1921. For some discussion in Wickham Steed's attitudes towards Jews see S. G. Bayme, 'Jewish Leadership and Anti-Semitism in Britain 1898–1918', unpublished PhD thesis, Columbia University, 1977, pp. 132–5.

81 Raslovleff to Graves, 13 July 1921.

82 Graves to Steed, 13 July 1921. The book by Wolf was *The Jewish Bogey*. See above p. 150.

83 In a letter to the foreign editor of *The Times* – Basil Kellet-Long – he wrote, on 25 July 1921: 'I am trying to find a British subject who is leaving for England shortly who will take the book and under certain circumstances will offer him a fee of £10 as messenger. The trouble is that people travelling just now whom I know are slapdash sort of fellows who might conceivably stop two or three times 'pour faire la noce' on the way home at Venice or Paris and increase the risk of loss.' In a PS his sense of anxiety was underlined by a remark that: 'As it may be some days before a messenger leaves here need I say that the matter should be as little mentioned as possible at P. H. Square: the Jews manage to hear a great deal everywhere.'

84 A copy of the agreement is in the archives of *The Times*.

85 The exposé appeared in *The Times*, 16, 17, 18 August 1921.

86 Letter, V. Barker, Agence Continentale, *The Times*, Paris, to the manager, *The Times*, 24 January 1924.

87 *The Times* to Barker, 25 January 1924.

88 *The Times* to Barker, 27 January 1927.

89 Letter, Raslovleff to Agence Continentale, *The Times*, Paris, 4 February 1927.

90 Memorandum, Graves to editor, 28 February 1935.

91 Letter, Neville Laski to *The Times*, 26 April 1935.

92 Letter to *The Times*, 2 May 1935 from Berne. *The Times* spoke to Neville Laski over the 'phone about the matter.

93 Memorandum, Graves to the manager of *The Times*, 28 April 1937.

94 Neville Laski to the manager, *The Times*, 6 May 1937.

95 On 10 March 1939, Geoffrey Dawson, the editor, reminded Graves that the material relating to the exposé remained the property of *The Times*. In a letter of 18 February 1939 to Dawson, Graves had requested the use of the material for an intended book on *The Protocols*.

96 In his letter to Steed on 13 July 1921 Graves wrote that in Raslovleff's opinion 'the Jewish peril lies in the materialism of the Jews rather than in his (sic) revolutionary idealism'.

97 See above note 83 for his reference to Jews having their listening posts in many places: his opposition to political Zionism appears in his book *Palestine: the Land of Three Faiths* (London, 1923), pp. 3–4, while it is reinforced in letters of 20 October 1931 to Dr Nimr, as well as those of 24 November 1931 and 10 November 1932 to C. D. R. Lumby. *The Times*, 14 April 1911 and 28 September 1912 contain earlier reports by Graves on the Young Turk Revolution and Palestine, respectively, which display suspicions about German-Jewish involvement, which themselves lean towards the conspiratorial.

98 See, for instance, letter from Geoffrey Dawson to Graves, 10 March 1939.

99 Cohn, *op. cit.*, pp. 171–2.

100 Baron Sydenham of Combe, 'The Jewish World Problem', *Nineteenth Century* XC (1921), p. 889. This article was later reprinted by the Britons with the title *The Jewish World Problem* (London, 1922). See the favourable review in *Plain Speech*, 7 January 1922, pp. 187–8. On Sydenham see the *DNB 1931–1940* (London, 1949), pp. 181–2. His private correspondence with J. St. Loe Strachey, now kept in the House of Lords Record Office, is a revealing source for his anti-semitism and his belief in *The Protocols*. See the letters of 26 January and 23 November 1920, 10 and 15 June 1921 and 5 January 1922.

101 Cohn, *op. cit.*, pp. 201–2 refers to a conversation about *The Protocols* between Hermann Rauschning and Hitler which revealed that Hitler was of a similar frame of mind. 'He did not care two straws, he said, whether the story was historically true. If it was not, its intrinsic truth was all the more convincing to him.'

102 N. Webster, *Secret Societies and Subversive Movements* (London, 1964, first edition 1924), pp. 408–9. There are further references to Mrs Webster on pp. 156–60 below. There is an obituary in *The Times*, 18 May 1960.

103 *ibid.*, p. 414

104 As recorded in Admiral Sir Barry Domvile's autobiography, *From Admiral to Cabin Boy* (London, 1947), pp. 82–3.

105 See below chapter 10.

106 *Blackwood's Magazine* CCX (1921), p. 559. This was written in October 1921.

107 *Plain English*, 20 August 1921, p. 663. The series 'John Brown on The Protocols of Zion' had begun on 4 June 1921, pp. 451–2. The articles continued to appear after Graves's exposé had been published in *The Times*. In a review of H. S. Spencer's *Democracy or Shylocracy*?, Dr J. H. Clarke commented: 'The "Protocols of the Learned Elders of Zion" are no forgery – they are facts. The *origin* of the document may be a subject of dispute, just as any other scriptures may – including the Jews' own Scriptures – but the document itself is corroborated by all sorts of other documents and by all that is now happening all over the world.' *Plain English*, 21 January 1922, p. 1102. The additional documentary evidence to which Clarke referred was *The World Significance of the Russian Revolution* by George Pitt-Rivers – a favoured and favourite work in anti-semitic circles.

108 The *Fascist Bulletin*, 15 August 1925, p. 2.

109 The *Free Press*, April 1937 noted that Jews in Manchester had presented a copy of *The Protocols* to the public library. They were congratulated on such a move! *ibid.* carried another piece on *The Protocols* taken from Henry Ford's *Dearborn Independent*. See the *Free Press*, September 1937, October 1937, November 1937, January 1938, February 1938, March 1938, April 1938, May 1938, June/July 1938, September 1938 for further details.

110 The aims of the *Patriot* were given in the issue of 9 February 1922, p. 1. References to *The Protocols* include those in issues of 9 January 1930, pp. 38–9, 16 January, pp. 64–5, 23 January, pp. 85–6, 30 January, pp. 105–7; 28 November 1935, p. 427. A fuller discussion of the ideas in the *Patriot* occurs below pp. 207–8. See below p. 201 for the *National Citizen's* flirtation.

111 Cohn, *op. cit.*, p. 172.

112 *Universal Jewish Encyclopaedia*, *op. cit.*, p. 59 notes the street corner distribution.

113 *Action*, 2 December 1937. I am indebted to Richard C. Thurlow for this reference. An infiltrator at a BUF meeting noticed that *The Protocols* was on sale. See 'Mosley's Luncheon at the Criterion'. A copy is in the Wiener Library. The date of this document is in doubt.

114 The only published study of the Britons is C. C. Aronsfeld, 'The Britons Publishing Society', *Wiener Library Bulletin* XX (summer 1966), pp. 31–5. This study is misleading, however, in some of its detail relating to the journals of the Britons and misses other nuances by not having had access to primary material. The Minute Book of the Britons for 17 February 1932 reveals the separation of the Britons from the Britons Publishing Company. On Beamish, see above note 23. Beamish was president until his death in 1948. During his absences J. H. Clarke, who was chairman and vice-president from the inception of the organization until 1931, assumed control. See the obituary in the *Homoeopathic Recorder* XLVII (1932), pp. 157–60. Walter Crick, a Northampton boot manufacturer was a vice-president between 1925 and 1946. See the *British Guardian*, 3 April 1925, pp. 97–8. For Crick's financial views see the *Northampton Independent*, 25 August and 22 September 1939. See his obituary in *ibid.*, 17 January 1958 which indicated that he had not visited England since 1939. See also file B4/CR2 in the Board of Deputies for an interest in his monetary writings.

115 Various journals are the best source for the ideas of the Britons. The publications in question are: *Jewry Ueber Alles* which appeared in February 1920; in July and August 1920 this appeared as *Jewry Ueber Alles or The Hidden Hand Exposed*; between September 1920 and September 1923 the name changed to *The Hidden Hand or Jewry Ueber Alles*; from October 1923 to April 1924 this appeared as *The Hidden Hand or The Jewish Peril*; in May 1924 this became the *British Guardian*, which ran until June 1925. The Wiener Library has a copy of the *Investigator*, for January 1937, published and edited by G. E. Thomas, which contained the slogan: 'ARYANS OF ALL LANDS UNITE: YOU HAVE NOTHING TO LOSE BUT THE JEW.' It would seem that there were other issues of this journal but none appears to have survived.

116 *The Hidden Hand or Jewry Ueber Alles*, May 1921, p. 1 and June 1923, p. 1.

117 Beamish, *The Jews' Who's Who*, p. 15: 'THE JEWS ARE A RACE NOT A RELIGION'; *Jewry Ueber Alles*, March 1920, p. 3 stated: 'With Jewry the tribe is the unit. With white people every adult is a responsible individual: a Jew is not an individual – he is only a bit of his tribe.' See also *ibid.*, April 1920, p. 3 for 'The Blood Test: The Jew is not the White Man's Brother'. See also *The Hidden Hand or Jewry Ueber Alles*, May 1921, p. 1 where it was stated that Jewry was 'the most deadly enemy of every other nation; it is the cancer of humanity. The only remedy is to give it the isolation it claims, to cut it out from the body politic, body economic, body social of every other nation, and then the White nations will have a chance of achieving each for itself its own destiny.' See also Clarke, *England under the Heel of the Jew*, pp. x, 61.

118 *Jewry Ueber Alles*, February 1920, p. 1: 'We are convinced Zionists, and whilst we are out to secure Britain for Britons, we are no less out to secure Zion for the Jews.' See also *Jewry Ueber Alles or The Hidden Hand Exposed*, July 1920, p. 1 and *The Hidden Hand or Jewry Ueber Alles*, June 1923 p. 1 where it was commented: 'Zionism is political, and has nothing to do with mystic Zion. Therefore Madagascar will do for their national home infinitely better than Palestine, and will afford ample room for the development of a national culture and art.' On the history of ideas about a Jewish settlement in Madagascar see J. Tenenbaum, *Race and Reich* (New York, 1956); Madagascar was suggested as an alternative location by the Britons because of difficulties which settlement in Palestine inevitably created. A similar awareness was behind the suggestion that a National Home might be established in Australia. See the pamphlet *The Jewish Peril* (London, n.d.), p. 3.

119 *Jewry Ueber Alles or The Hidden Hand Exposed*, July 1920, p. 1.
120 *The Hidden Hand or The Jewish Peril*, January 1924, p. 13.
121 *Jewry Ueber Alles or The Hidden Hand Exposed*, August 1920, p. 1; *The Hidden Hand or Jewry Ueber Alles*, May 1921, pp. 4–5; *ibid.*, November 1921, p. 4.
122 Beamish, *The Jews' Who's Who*, p. 7 refers to his intention to make plain the 'garotte-like grip of Finance when dominated by the International Jew'. *Ibid.*, pp. 42–53 is devoted to 'Our Jew Dominated Press'. See Clarke, *England under the Heel of the Jew*, *op. cit.*, p. 61 for an attack upon pernicious Jewish finance. The *British Guardian*, May 1924, p. 68 comments on Jewish press control. The influence of Jews on finance and the press was widely raised in anti-semitic groups in the inter-war years (see below pp. 166–87) and the matter ought to be commented upon at this point. Hostility of this kind was not new. We have already discussed its manifestations before the First World War at which time it was heard not only in Britain but in many other countries. After the war the charges had probably less validity in Britain than they did before 1914. The great days of Jewish banking fortunes were over [W. D. Rubinstein, 'Jews among the Top British Wealth Holders, 1857–1969: Decline of the Golden Age', *Jewish Social Studies* XXIV (January 1972), pp. 73, 76–9] and many of the merchant banking houses which had been founded by Jews had come under more diffused control. But the origins of such houses were not forgotten and the undoubted prominence of concerns associated with Jews in fixing the price of gold was also a magnet to those interested in the power of Jewish finance [P. Arnold, *The Bankers of London* (London, 1938), discusses such mysteries of the City]. As for the press, it was still possible to find Jews who achieved prominence in Fleet Street but, as in the world of finance the influence of Jews was less than it was before the war [S. Salomon, *The Jews of Britain* (London, 1938), pp. 49–52 is critical of suggestions of Jewish press influence. For other comments see Lord Camrose, *London Newspapers. Their Owners and Controllers* (London, 1939), which provides a detailed analysis of press ownership and gives no support to the claims of Jewish press control]. The claim that Jews dominated the placing of newspaper advertisements is almost impossible to assess since as yet we do not have sufficient worthwhile evidence on which to base a reasonable assessment. Finally, the responses of the British press to the Hitlerite persecution of Jews would hardly indicate a strong Jewish influence over newspaper opinion. See A. Sharf, *The British Press and Jews under Nazi Rule* (London, 1964), pp. 165–6 and 173–4.

The associated claims about Jewish influence in the cinema had more to support them. Some indication of the interests of Jews in the British film industry is in F. D. Klingender and S. Legg, *Money Behind the Screen* (London, 1937). Of course, the influence of Jews outside Britain in the world of finance was also stressed and the undoubted importance of individual banking houses such as Kuhn Loeb and Warburgs which had strong Jewish influences magnetized attention [see the *British Guardian*, 13 February 1925, pp. 44–5, 6 March 1925, pp. 69–70 and 20 March 1925, pp. 83–4. On Warburgs see E. Rosenbaum and A. J. Sherman, *M. M. Warburg and Co., 1798–1938. A Hamburg Private Bank* (London, 1978)], and the influence of individual Jews as Hollywood directors almost certainly added to impressions of Jewish power within the international cinema world. [P. French, *Movie Moguls* (Harmondsworth, 1971), discusses these colourful characters] Even if it is possible to locate the presence of certain influential Jews in Britain and elsewhere in finance, the press and the cinema, this does not prove, of course, that they acted in concert in some kind of Jewish interest. But, it might be suggested that the presence of individual Jews added to the historical tradition of suspicion and fear concerning the activity of Jews in finance and communications and helped to create an impression of Jew power, particularly among those who viewed the world through the medium of *The Protocols*.

123 The sexual undermining of society is the theme of J. Banister, *Jews and the White Slave Traffic, or Lords of the Hells of Gomorrah* (London, 192?), copy in the Wiener Library. *The Alienization of the British Services. A danger which besets our national life* (London, 1924), is a pamphlet issued by the Loyalty League and printed by the Britons which not only refers to underground influences at work in the armed forces but outlines the major fear that Britain was coming under the control of Jewish influence.

124 *The Hidden Hand or Jewry Ueber Alles*, November 1920, p. 2.

125 The threat of Jewish Bolshevism is referred to in *Jewry Ueber Alles*, February 1920, p. 6, April 1920, pp. 7–8, May 1920, p. 7, June 1920, pp. 5–6 and *Jewry Ueber Alles or The Hidden Hand Exposed*, July 1920, pp. 6–7. See also Sydenham of Combe, *The Jewish World Problem*. See also *Halt Gentile! And Salute the Jew* (London, 1931), pp. 15–17; *Why are the Jews Hated* ? (London, 1937), p. 8; A. Howard, *The Beast Marks Russia* (London, 1938). In common with others hostile towards Jews, concern was expressed about the activities of revolutionary Jews outside Russia. See the comments on Bela Kun in *Jewry Ueber Alles*, March 1920, p. 3. See also Gwynne, *op. cit.*, pp. 150–54. See above p. 145 for reference to the League of Nations.

126 The British Guardian, May 1924, pp. 69, 74–6. See also *The Hidden Hand or Jewry Ueber Alles*, March 1921, p. 1 and *The Hidden Hand or The Jewish Peril*, February 1924, p. 27.

127 *Jewry Ueber Alles or The Hidden Hand Exposed*, July 1920, p. 5 and August 1920, p. 3; *The Hidden Hand or Jewry Ueber Alles*, April 1921, p. 4 and January 1923, p. 2; the *British Guardian*, May 1924, pp. 74–6; See also Sydenham of Combe's *The Jewish World Problem* where Disraeli's work was liberally quoted and *The Alienization of the British Services*, pp. 2–4.

128 *Why are the Jews hated*?, p. 13. On Röhling see P. G. J. Pulzer, *The Rise of Political Anti-Semitism in Germany and Austria* (New York, 1964), pp. 163–4 and *Encyclopaedia Judaica* XIV (Jerusalem, 1971), p. 223.

129 Sombart was very widely used. See the heavy indebtedness of J. H. Clarke, *England Under the Heel of the Jew*, etc., as well as H. S. Spencer, *Democracy or Shylocracy*? (London, 1923, 3rd edn). Both of these works were first published in December 1918. See also J. H. Clarke, *White Labour or the Jew and International Politics* (London, 1920), pp. 4–5 where *The Jews and Modern Capitalism* is referred to as 'that very notable book'. See also the journal references in *Jewry Ueber Alles*, February 1920, p. 4; *The Hidden Hand or Jewry Ueber Alles*, March 1921, p. 1; *The Hidden Hand or The Jewish Peril*, February 1924, p. 27; the *British Guardian*, May 1924, p. 67.

130 The Britons, *A Short History of the Jewish Race* (London, 1921), is indebted to Chamberlain. On the reaction of British public opinion to Chamberlain's work see my article, 'Houston Stewart Chamberlain in Great Britain', *Wiener Library Bulletin* XXIV (1970), pp. 31–6.

131 This was another work quoted with great frequency. A particular attraction of it was the preface which was written by Oscar Levy. See *The Hidden Hand or Jewry Ueber Alles*, May 1921, p. 4 which quoted Levy to the effect that the Jews were 'the world's seducers, its destroyers, its incendaries, its executioners'. See also Banister, *Jews and the White Slave Traffic*, *op. cit.*, which quotes the same sentence on its introductory pages; H. H. Beamish, *Jew World Plot: A Catechism for Britons* (London, n.d. n.p.); Clarke, *White Labour*, p. 7. See also Clarke's introduction to H. S. Spencer, *Democracy or Shylocracy*, p. viii;

Halt Gentile!, p. 15; *The Jewish Peril*, p. 4; *Why are the Jews hated*?, p. 3.

132 *The Hidden Hand or Jewry Ueber Alles*, July 1921, p. 1 discusses *World Revolution* and the *British Guardian*, September 1924, pp. 126–8 reviewed *Secret Societies and Subversive Movements.*

133 See above note 72.

134 Hence the continuing advertisements for the publication in the journal, the catechistic appendix to *Halt Gentile*!, pp. 22–4 and the continued offering of *The Protocols* which now appear as *World Conquest Through World Government.* This is Marsden's translation. The exposé in *The Times* was specifically attacked by the Britons in *The 'Times' on The 'Protocols'* (London, n.d.).

135 N. Cohn in his introduction to Bernstein, *op. cit.*, p. ix, provides details on such developments.

136 See chapter 5 for these earlier expressions of concern about Jewish power. For similar comment see Bayme, 'Jewish Leadership', pp. ii, 101, 167.

137 The anti-semitic emphasis upon Jews in finance and the press at this time is assessed on pp. 284–5 below. Apart from the political influence of Jews which has been referred to in the text, Walter Rathenau in Germany received considerable scrutiny as an agent of Jewish interests. See *The Hidden Hand or Jewry Ueber Alles*, September 1921, pp. 5–6, *ibid.*, June 1922, p. 3 and *The Alienization of the British Services*, pp. 4–5.

138 See above pp. 141–7.

139 See below chapter 10.

140 See above pp. 149–51.

141 See above note 76. The *Jewish Guardian* noted that restrained anti-semitism could lead to more irresponsible expressions. See the discussion in the *Morning Post*, 26 April 1922.

142 See above p. 155.

143 See above pp. 104–5.

144 See below chapter 12 for a discussion of such matters.

145 Cohn, *op. cit.*

146 *ibid.*, p. 12.

147 In an article in a Japanese newspaper of 17 September 1936, which forms part of a file in the Wiener Library, Beamish reaffirmed his belief that 'the Jewish machinations are responsible for all wars, civil wars and uprisings in various countries of the world.' He prefaced his remarks with: 'You might think I am crazy . . .'. See also the remarks about Beamish's obsessions made by the South African judge in the Grahamstown trial in 1934, which are quoted in Bondy, *op. cit.*, p. 133. Leese's anti-semitism is discussed below, pp. 161–74. A copy of *An admonition on the moral insufficiency of the British Government in the matter of the fearful tolerance of the great Communist Conspiracy cum Economic Piracy directed against the United Kingdom and prosecuted by the Jews* (Liverpool, 1935), a wierd concoction which strains the bounds of credulity which was printed, published and distributed by the Conservators of the Privileges of the Realm, is in the Wiener Library.

148 Nesta Webster's psychology is certainly intriguing, to say the least. Her obituary notice in *The Times*, 18 May 1960 noticed that 'a strange literary obsession came over her that she had lived in eighteenth-century France'. Her autobiography, *Spacious Days* (London, 1950), reveals very little. A much more fascinating if speculative probe into her psyche is taken by Richard Thurlow in his unpublished paper, 'The Creation of the English Volk'.

149 C. McWilliams, *Brothers under the Skin* (rev. edn, Boston, 1964), p. 317; J. Higham, *Strangers in the Land. Patterns of American Nativism, 1860–1925* (New York, 1965), p. 402; W. Laqueur, *Commentary* XLIV (July 1967),

pp. 80–84, in a review of *Warrant for Genocide* makes a number of interesting and relevant comments on such matters. J. M. Roberts, *The Mythology of Secret Societies* (London, 1972), pp. 351–2 has some sharp comment on psychological and psychoanalytical explanations of why individuals have believed in the activities of secret societies. However, he has little to offer by way of a social explanation of such beliefs.

Chapter 10

1 See below chapter 11.
2 H. Blume, 'A History of Anti-Semitic Groups in Britain, 1918–40', unpublished MPhil thesis, University of Sussex, 1971, and R. J. Benewick, *The Fascist Movement in Britain* (London, 1972), are useful for detail.
3 For more details see A. S. Leese, *Out of Step* (Guildford, 1947).
4 *Stamford News*, 5 March 1924 refers to local developments.
5 The political flavour of the British Fascists is apparent from 'British Fascist Principles', *British Lion*, 28 August 1926, pp. 10–11 and the 'British Fascist Manifesto', *ibid.*, October–November 1927, p. 3. See Benewick, *op. cit.*, pp. 27–36 for more details.
6 See above pp. 156–8 for a discussion of the Britons. On Kitson see the obituary in *The Times*, 4 October 1937 and L. Wise, *Arthur Kitson* (London, 1946). For further evidence of Kitson's influence see H. S. Spencer, *Democracy or Shylocracy?* (London, 1918), pp. 41–8 and the *Fascist Bulletin*, 15 August 1925, p. 2.
7 Leese, *Out of Step*, p. 50; *Gothic Ripples*, no. 375, May 1948, p. 2. See above chapter 9 for references to Beamish.
8 Leese, *Out of Step*, p. 50.
9 J. Morell, 'The Life and Opinions of A. S. Leese. A Study in Extreme Anti-Semitism', unpublished MA thesis, University of Sheffield, 1975, p. 25.
10 A. S. Leese, *The Jewish War of Survival* (Guildford, 1945).
11 Morell, 'A. S. Leese', p. 47.
12 *ibid.*, p. 49. A sample of his work is currently being offered in the anti-semitic monthly, *Christian Vanguard*, the official publication of the New Christian Crusade Church based in Hollywood.
13 Leese, *Out of Step*, p. 1. R. Skidelsky, *Oswald Mosley* (London, 1975), p. 390 writes about the nature of Mosley's attitudes towards Jews.
14 The *Fascist*, no. 46, March 1933. But see *ibid.*, no. 8, October 1929, and no. 86, July 1936, for deviations from this.
15 See, for instance, A. S. Leese, *The Jewish War of Survival* (Guildford, 1945), p. 75.
16 The *Fascist*, no. 45, February 1933, no. 47, April 1933; IFL, *Race and Politics* (London, n.d.), p. 6. See L. L. Snyder, *The Idea of Racialism. Its Meaning and History* (Princeton, N. J., 1962), pp. 39–53 and M. D. Biddiss, *Father of Racist Ideology. The Social and Political Thought of Count Gobineau* (London, 1970), for a discussion of Aryanism.
17 IFL, *The Jew. Past and Present* (London, n.d.), p. 1.
18 The *Fascist*, no. 75, August 1935. See also, A. S. Leese, *My Irrelevant Defence* (London, 1938), p. 2: 'The Jews are a nation without a home, not a race; they are a mixture of races, and the racial constituent which is most frequently to be found among them is the Armenoid, or, as it is sometimes called, Hither Asiatic.'
19 The *Fascist*, no. 3, May 1929, no. 21, February 1931.
20 A. S. Leese, *Bolshevism is Jewish* (London, n.d.), p. 2.

21 IFL, *The Wailing Wall of Archer Street* (London, n.d.), p. 1; the *Fascist*, no. 36, May 1932, and no. 106, March 1938.
22 The *Fascist*, no. 86 July, 1936; Leese, *My Irrelevant Defence*. An account of the conversion is given in D. M. Dunlop, *The History of the Jewish Khazars* (Princeton, 1954), pp. 115, 170. Details on the Khazars can be found in the *Encyclopaedia Judaica* x (Jerusalem, 1971), pp. 944–53 and A. Koestler, *The Thirteenth Tribe* (London, 1976).
23 Leese, *My Irrelevant Defence*, *op. cit.*, pp. 1–3; IFL, *Race and Politics*, p. 8; *Gothic Ripples*, no. 78, 28 July 1951, p. 2.
24 See Morell, 'A. S. Leese', pp. 96–101.
25 See above chapters 1 and 4.
26 The *Fascist*, no. 40, September 1932, and, most prominently in *ibid.*, no. 85, June 1936.
27 A reprint of the court notes is available in the Wiener Library, London and at the Board of Deputies of British Jews. An abridged report appeared in *The Times*, 19 and 22 September 1936. On the legal significance of the case see A. T. Denning, *Freedom under the Law* (London, 1949), pp. 42–4. See below p. 198 for further reference to the case.
28 Leese, *My Irrelevant Defence*, p. 7. Leese also mentioned: 'Another festival at which it is thought that Ritual Murder has sometimes been indulged is Chanucah.' Albert Speer in *Spandau. The Secret Diaries* (London, 1977, edn), p. 24 claims that the last words of Julius Streicher before his execution at Nuremburg were '"Heil Hitler! This is the Purim festival of 1946!"' If true, these must constitute some of the most bizarre final words ever spoken. For details on the Purim festival, instituted by Mordecai to celebrate the deliverance of the Jews from Haman's plot to kill them, see *Encyclopaedia Judaica* XII (Jerusalem, 1971), pp. 1390–95.
29 The *Fascist*, no. 86, July 1936.
30 Leese, *My Irrelevant Defence*, p. 6; the *Fascist*, no. 69, February 1935. Modern Chassidism originated in the eighteenth century. It was distinguished by an emphasis upon ecstasy, mass enthusiasm, group cohesion and charismatic leadership. See *Encyclopaedia Judaica* VII (Jerusalem, 1971), pp. 1390–432.
31 Leese, *My Irrelevant Defence*, pp. 4–5.
32 IFL, *The Jew Past and Present*, p. 1.
33 Leese, *The Jewish War of Survival*, pp. 64, 75.
34 The *Fascist*, no. 33, February 1932; *Gothic Ripples*, no. 27, 24 November 1946, p. 3.
35 A. S. Leese, *Bolshevism is Jewish*, p. 6; the *Fascist*, no. 11, February–March 1930, no. 59, April 1934, no. 97, June 1937.
36 Leese, *Bolshevism is Jewish*, p. 2.
37 The *Fascist*, no. 94, March 1937.
38 *ibid.*, no. 29, October 1931.
39 *Gothic Ripples*, no. 7, 30 November 1945, p. 2. See also Leese, *Devilry in the Holy Land*, p. 16; IFL, *The Era of World Ruin* (London, n.d.), p. 7; the *Fascist*, no. 108, May 1938, p. 1 and A. S. Leese, *Gentile Folly: the Rothschilds* (London, 1940), p. 21.
40 Leese, *The Jewish War of Survival*, p. 10.
41 The *Fascist*, no. 82, March 1936, no. 98, July 1937.
42 *ibid.*, no. 49, June 1933, no. 86, July 1936.
43 Leese, *Devilry in the Holy Land*, p. 16.
44 The *Fascist*, no. 79, December 1935. See above for other expressions of this sentiment.
45 Leese, *The Mass Madness of September 1938* (London, n.d.), p. 9; the *Fascist*,

no. 26, July 1931, no. 86, July 1936, no. 8, October 1939.

46 Leese, *Devilry in the Holy Land*, p. 6; the *Fascist*, no. 9, November 1929, no. 66, November 1934.

47 Leese, *The Jewish War of Survival*, p. 94; *Gothic Ripples*, no. 103, 25 July 1953, p. 1.

48 Leese, *The Jewish War of Survival* is devoted entirely to this. As early as 1934 he was threatening: 'We will not fight for the House of Rothschild', The *Fascist*, no. 62, July 1934, and no. 63, August 1934.

49 The *Fascist*, no. 6, August 1929; IFL, *Money, No Mystery* (London, n.d.), p. 5.

50 IFL, *Money, No Mystery*, p.11; The *Fascist*, no. 28, September 1931, no. 71, April 1935, no. 96, May 1937, no. 115, December 1938.

51 Leese, *Jewish War of Survival*, p. 36; IFL, *Mightier Yet*! (London, 1935), p. 17; The *Fascist*, no. 23, April 1931, no. 46, March 1933, no. 59, April 1934, no. 105, February 1938.

52 Leese, *Gentile Folly*, pp. 56–62; Leese, *The Mass Madness of September 1938*, p. 7; IFL, *Agriculture Comes First* (London, n.d.), p. 5; IFL, *Money, No Mystery*, p. 8; IFL, *Political and Economic Planning* (London, 1934), p. 9.

53 The *Fascist*, no. 10, December-January 1930, no. 73, June 1935, p. 1.

54 IFL, *To a Gentile Jester (of the Variety Profession)* (London, n.d.), p. 2; IFL, *The Wailing Wall of Archer Street*, p. 1; IFL, *Mightier Yet*! p. 17; The *Fascist*, no. 35, April 1932, and later, *Gothic Ripples*, no. 36, 20 March 1948, p. 2.

55 IFL, *Money, No Mystery*, p. 9; The *Fascist*, no. 40, September 1932. See below p. 284 for general comment on such matters. See below pp. 186–7 for BUF hostility towards Jews in finance.

56 Leese, *The Mass Madness*, p. 11; *Out of Step*, p. 61. See below p. 284 for a discussion of these matters and below pp. 179, 216 for further concern about Jewish influence of this kind.

57 IFL, *Jewish Press Control* (London, 1937), p. 2; The *Fascist*, no. 24, May 1931, no. 63, August 1934, no. 83, April 1936.

58 IFL, *To a Gentile Jester*, p. 1; IFL, *The Wailing Wall*, p. 2; The *Fascist*, no. 53, October 1933; *Gothic Ripples*, no. 3, 27 July 1945, p. 2.

59 IFL, *The Plan of the Jew* (London, n.d.), p. 1; The *Fascist*, no. 26, July 1931, no. 67, December 1934.

60 Leese, *Jewish War of Survival*, p. 29.

61 IFL, *The Growing Menace of Freemasonry* (London, n.d.).

62 Leese, *Jewish War of Survival*, p. 30; IFL, *Growing Menace*, p. 9; IFL, *Mightier Yet*! p. 26; IFL, *Race and Politics*, p. 3; The *Fascist*, no. 38, July 1932, no. 55, December 1933, no. 86, July 1936; *Gothic Ripples*, no. 20, 25 August 1946, p. 1, no. 91, 28 August 1952, p. 1.

63 IFL, *Our Jewish Aristocracy* (London, 1936), pp. 4–5; the *Fascist*, no. 116, January 1939; *Gothic Ripples*, no. 42, 23 September 1948, p. 3.

64 IFL, *Our Jewish Aristocracy*, *passim*; the *Fascist*, no. 70, March 1935, no. 73, June 1935, no. 76, September 1935, no. 100, September 1937; *Gothic Ripples*, no. 16, 15 June 1946, p. 4, no. 31, 15 July 1947, pp. 1–4.

65 IFL, *Our Jewish Aristocracy*, p. 15; the *Fascist*, no. 60, May 1934, no. 84, May 1936.

66 IFL, *Mightier Yet*! p. 20; *Gothic Ripples*, no. 12, 17 March 1946, p. 3.

67 *The Jewish Yearbook* (London, 1939), p. 345.

68 The *Fascist*, no. 22, March 1931.

69 *ibid.*, no. 7, September 1929.

70 *ibid.*, no. 86, July 1936 and *Gothic Ripples*, no. 126, 19 April 1955, p. 2.

71 *Gothic Ripples*, no. 126, 19 April 1955, p. 2.

72 H. H. Beamish, *The Jews' Who's Who. Israelite Finance. Its Sinister Influence* (London, 1920), pp. 43–45.
73 *The Hidden Hand or Jewry Ueber Alles*, June 1923, p. 1. See above for a discussion of such matters and for the reference to the possibility of settlement in Australia.
74 J. Tenenbaum, *Race and Reich* (New York, 1956), chapter 19, pp. 238–49 refers to Polish and German opinion on the Madagascar scheme but does not direct attention to discussion in Britain.
75 Leese, *Devilry in the Holy Land*, pp. 15–16.
76 IFL, *Mightier Yet*! pp. 20–21; the *Fascist*, no. 40, September 1932, no. 69, February 1935; *Gothic Ripples*, no. 48, 21 February 1949, p. 3 all deal with the Madagascar plan.
77 See above p. 157. L. Lowenthal and N. Guterman, *Prophets of Deceit* (New York, 1949), p. 60 quote a letter from Beamish, Leese's mentor in anti-semitism, which suggests that Beamish excluded extermination as a solution to the Jewish question.
78 The *Fascist*, no. 22, March 1931.
79 *ibid.*, no. 69, February 1935.
80 The *Fascist*, no. 22, November 1931, no. 40, September 1932, no. 69, February 1935, no. 86, May 1936.
81 *Gothic Ripples*, no. 26, 2 October 1946, p. 4, no. 96, 14 January 1953, p. 4.
82 See Benewick, *op. cit.*, p. 27 for the fullest discussion of the transient history of the British Fascist movement. See the *British Lion*, 28 August 1926, pp. 10–11 for 'British Fascists' Principles'. *ibid.*, October/November 1927, p. 3 has 'The British Fascist Manifesto' and *British Fascism*, April 1931 (insertion), contains 'Summary of Policy and Practice', both of which also provide an insight into the British Fascists' programme. An early attempt to discuss Fascist principles was made by the movement's President, Brigadier General R. B. D. Blakeney in 'British Fascism', *Nineteenth Century* XCVII (1925), pp. 132–41. In 1930 the British Fascists became associated with Lt. Col. Oscar Boulton's Unity Band. The demise of the British Fascists was reported in *The Times*, 20 July 1935.
83 Communism and aliens were in fact linked together and presented as a deadly combination intent upon sapping 'our national virility'. The *Fascist Bulletin*, 20 June 1925, p. 1.
84 Blume, 'A History of Anti-Semitic Groups', p. 104 and Benewick, *op. cit.*, p. 30 note the hardening of policy as the movement was whittled down to a hard core. 'A great but stifled problem Germans and Jews', *British Fascism*, January 1932, p. 8, 'Germany and the Jewish Question', *ibid.*, Special Propaganda Number, pp. 6–7, 10–11 and the letter from Kenneth Green in *ibid.*, March 1934, pp. 7–8, as well as the interest taken in the work of Capel Pownall, who was a source for the distribution of German anti-semitica in Britain, reveal the interest in European developments at this time.
85 The *Fascist Bulletin*, 11 July 1925, p. 1. See also *ibid.*, 26 September 1925, p. 7 and 'The War Danger', in *British Fascism*, Extra Autumn Issue, 1933, p. 1.
86 See 'The Death Camps of the Soviets', in *British Fascism*, Extra Autumn Issue, 1933, pp. 6–7.
87 The *Fascist Bulletin*, 15 August 1925, p. 2, *ibid.*, 5 September 1925, pp. 1, 3, 4, and *British Fascism*, October 1932, p. 2, where it was claimed that Englishmen were 'mere hewers of wood and drawers of water, mere serfs of the City Financiers' who were 'mostly Jews and their big rings'.
88 *British Fascism*, May 1934, p. 2.
89 'Why we are anti-semitic', *ibid.*, Extra Autumn Issue, 1933, pp. 6–7.

90 *ibid.*
91 The *Free Press*, October 1935. Benewick, *op. cit.*, p. 276 gives 1939 as the date of origin but this is clearly incorrect. Further details about the group's origins are in dispute. See Blume, 'A History of Anti-Semitic Groups', p. 227 and Bondy, *op. cit.*, p. 149 for a difference of opinion.
92 *ibid.* For an outline of its philosophy by a hostile source see the file on the MCP, Document Box 610 in the Wiener Library.
93 L. Fry, *An Analysis of Zionism* (London, 19?), p. 3; MCP, *Zionism* (London, 193?); MCP, *Zionism and the Christian Church* (London, 193?).
94 The MCP supported the country in the war. When Hitler handed over 16 million Poles to the Russians after the Hitler-Stalin Pact, he was portrayed as betraying the struggle against Communism. German involvement in the origins of Bolshevism was now emphasized and Britons were urged to fight against the 'sinister power' of Bolshevism. The *Free Press*, October 1939. The same issue carried an announcement that the MCP were 'making every effort to support HM the King and the Government in the War against our open enemies'.
95 The co-ordinating activities of the MCP are remarked upon in Blume, ' A History of Anti-Semitic Groups', p. 234 and are evident on a reading of the *Free Press*. Such attempts at co-ordination were unwelcome to Leese. See Morell, 'A. S. Leese', p. 27. See below for a discussion of the Boswell Company.
96 The *Free Press*, January 1936.
97 Fry, *op. cit.*, p. 8.
98 The *Free Press*, October 1935.
99 Fry, *op. cit.*, p. 3.
100 MCP, *Zionism*, pp. 3, 6, 19–20; L. Fry, *The Jews and the British Empire* (London, 193?), pp. 4–7.
101 Fry, *An Analysis of Zionism*, p. 8; the *Free Press*, October 1938 and *ibid.*, October 1939; the *Britisher*, 15 January 1938, p. 2. With its belief in internationally organized threats to Britain's interests there is little surprise that the MCP was quite happy to give publicity to *The Protocols*. See the *Free Press*, January 1936, December 1936, April 1937, September 1937, October 1937, November 1937, January 1938, February 1938, March 1938, April 1938, May 1938, June/July 1938, September 1938.
102 The *Free Press*, October 1935.
103 C. L. Mowat, *Britain Between the Wars 1918 to 1940* (London, 1976 edn), p. 462 which refers to the general interest in economic planning at this time. The hostility to PEP was present in the headlines of the first issue of the *Free Press*, October 1935 under the heading 'Amazing Plan Threatens Freedom. Sinister Monopoly' and the case against it was argued in the same issue under the heading 'Capitalism Has Not Failed'.
104 The *Free Press*, October 1935. See also *ibid.*, September 1938 for another attack. For hostility elsewhere see IFL, *PEP (Political and Economic Planning)* (London, 1934), and 'Letting in the Socialists' by Captain Bernard Ackworth in the *English Review* LX (1935), pp. 411–15. Ackworth ran the Liberty Restoration League which was prominent in attacking PEP and any preference which was shown towards the oil industry in Britain's energy policy. See also the *Patriot*, 11 June 1936, p. 505.
105 The *Free Press*, June/July 1938, October 1938, July 1939, October 1939. See also the article, 'They call it Psychology' in *ibid.*, December 1936.
106 The *Britisher*, 15 October 1937, p. 3. See also, on immigration, the pamphlet *Pro Patria Refugees before Britons! A Menace to the Health of the Nation* which was initially issued by the MCP and later reissued, in 1939, by the Britons.

107 The page in the *Free Press*, January 1936, entitled 'In this year of Grace 1936' captures the mood of anxiety.

108 *ibid.*, April 1936.

109 *ibid.*, October 1936. On Biro-Bidjan see C. Abramsky, 'The Biro-Bidzhan Project 1927–1959', in L. Kochan (ed.), *The Jews in Soviet Russia since 1917* (Oxford, 1970), pp. 62–75.

110 See above p. 157.

111 See above p. 160.

112 Morell, 'A. S. Leese', pp. 110–14.

113 *Gothic Ripples*, no. 90, 8 July 1952, p. 2.

114 R. Hofstadter, *The Paranoid Style in American Politics and other Essays* (London, 1966), discusses conspiratorial fears and the paranoid modes of expression through which they are transmitted. However, he distinguishes between a paranoid style and clinical paranoia (p. 4).

115 N. Cameron, *The Psychology of Behaviour Disorders* (Boston, 1947), p. 441; W. S. Taylor, *Dynamic and Abnormal Psychology* (New York, 1954), p. 597.

116 G. W. Allport, *The Nature of Prejudice* (Cambridge, Mass., 1954), p. 423.

117 Leese's own work suggests that social pressures influenced his plunge into political life. He could not understand 'how it was that although we had won the war we seemed to be losing every yard of the peace which followed. Something I felt must be acting like a spanner in the works.' Leese, *Out of Step*, p. 48. See also the comment in R. M. Gorman, 'Swastika over England: the Life and Thought of Arnold Spencer Leese', unpublished MA thesis, Midgeville, Georgia, 1975, p. 25. An outline of Gorman's assessment of Leese appeared in, 'Racial Antisemitism in England: The Legacy of Arnold Leese', *Wiener Library Bulletin*, XXX (1977), nos. 43–4, pp. 65–74.

118 See above pp. 141–7 for a discussion of these matters.

119 See above pp. 141–7 for reference to the uncertainty following the war and below chapters 11 and 12 for reference to the crisis and depression of 1929–31.

120 We have already noticed that the publication was central to Arnold Leese's anti-semitism and a continuing belief in its message was apparent within the MCP. Among the British Fascists the stress was also present, explicitly or implicitly. See the *Fascist Bulletin*, 15 August 1925, p. 2; *British Fascism*, Special Summer Propaganda Issue, 1933, p. 6. See above pp. 141–7 for evidence of the gathering force of anti-semitic opposition to Jewish Bolshevism, Zionism and the League of Nations.

121 So that, for instance, Disraeli's attitudes and career could be used for anti-semitic ends, see Leese, *Disraeli the Destroyer* (London, n.d.), and *My Irrelevant Defence*, p. 6; the *Free Press* September 1937 and May 1938; L. Fry, *Jews and the British Empire* (London, 193?), p. 5. By way of another example, Richard Burton's career could be recalled in the *Free Press*, December 1936 and his work on ritual murder could be referred to in Leese, *My Irrelevant Defence*, p. 6.

122 Opposition to Jewish finance can be found in the *Fascist Bulletin*, 15 August 1925, p. 2, and 5 September 1925, pp. 1, 3, 4; Morell, 'A. S. Leese', pp. 133–4 discusses Leese's attitudes towards Jewish finance; the *Free Press*, October 1935 indicates MCP hostility towards finance and *ibid.*, January 1939 and February 1939 contain critical comment on Jewish finance. See also Virgil, *The Wars that need not have been fought. The Millions who need not have died* (n.d., n.p.) an MCP leaflet on Jewish finance working through disruption for Jewish ends. The *Free Press*, June/July 1938 and October 1938 are concerned with Jewish finance as an aid to Bolshevism. When the activity of Jews in finance was refracted through *The Protocols* a potent brew resulted. See *World Conquest*

through World Government (85th impression, Chulmleigh, 1972), pp. 75–85 for Protocols 20–22 and a conspiratorial analysis of Jewish conquest through the mysterious processes of finance.

123 Apart from Leese's comments on Jews in the press and in the film world, references can also be found in *British Fascism*, June 1934, pp. 5–6 and in the *Britisher*, published by the MCP between September 1937 and October 1938 (when it appeared as the *Britischer*). *World Conquest* etc., Protocol 12, pp. 50–55 refers to control of the press as a means of acquiring social domination.

124 Morell, 'A. S. Leese', pp. 139–40 refers to Leese's hostility towards monopoly. The *Free Press*, October 1935 and November 1937 reveal a clear opposition to 'Fabian-Zionist' planning. *World longuest* etc., Protocol 5, p. 33 refers to planning as a way of achieving Jewish control. Leese's belief in the importance of agriculture is referred to *Agriculture Comes First* and *Mightier Yet*!

125 Blume, 'A History of Anti-Semitic Groups', pp. 245–99 provides brief comments on most of these, including Lt. Col. Graham Seton Hutchinson's National Workers' Party of Great Britain, the Right Club, E. Lashmar and even Mr Higgs who, we are told, ran an anti-semitic propaganda campaign from his furrier's shop at 471 Romford Road, Forest Gate.

Chapter 11

1 For details on Mosley's career see R. Skidelsky, *Oswald Mosley* (London, 1975), Mosley's own account appears in *My Life* (London, 1968).

2 For a review of the reviews of Skidelsky's work on Mosley see R. C. Thurlow, 'The Black Knight. Reactions to a Mosley Biography', *Patterns of Prejudice* IX (May–June 1975), pp. 15–19, from which these ascriptions are taken.

3 F. Mullally, *Fascism inside England* (London, 1946), pp. 69–71.

4 C. Cross, *The Fascists in Britain* (London, 1961), pp. 118–19, 122, 125–8, 151.

5 R. J. Benewick, *Political Violence and Public Order* (London, 1969), pp. 151–8 which appeared later as *The Fascist Movement in Britain* (London, 1972).

6 W. F. Mandle, *Anti-Semitism and the British Union of Fascists* (London, 1968).

7 Mosley, *op. cit.*, pp. 336–43.

8 *The Times*, 21 October, 24 October, 25 October, 26 October, 28 October, 29 October, 30 October, 31 October, 1 November, 4 November, 5 November, 7 November 1968. The reviewer was N. St. John Stevas.

9 Skidelsky, *op. cit.*, p. 391.

10 *ibid.*, p. 390.

11 Thurlow, *op. cit.*, refers to most of the reviews which have appeared at the time of publication. For some recent comment see W. C. Bader, Jr, 'The Return of Mosley', *Wiener Library Bulletin*, XXX, nos. 41–2 (1977), pp. 62–7 and Skidelsky's reply in *ibid.* XXX, nos. 43–4 (1977), pp. 79–80.

12 C. C. Aronsfeld, 'Old Fascism Writ Large. Mosley's Memoirs', *Patterns of Prejudice* II (November–December 1968), p. 19, refers to a speech in November 1933 when Mosley accused the Jews of not only opposing Fascism but also of 'organizing as a minority race within a nation'; he especially attacked the tiny number of German Jewish refugees for 'taking jobs from Englishmen'. In the spring of the same year *Blackshirt* had been cool towards the adoption of an anti-semitic programme. The change came in the autumn.

13 Skidelsky, *op. cit.*, p. 383.

14 *Daily Mail*, 19 July 1934.

15 *The Times*, 1 October 1934; *Blackshirt*, 5 October 1934. At a slightly earlier meeting in Hyde Park reported in *Blackshirt*, 14 September 1934 he had

accused 'the alien Jewish financier' of supplying left wing hecklers with 'palm oil' to make them yell – an accusation he was repeating in Manchester. For other comments on 'the Sheeny Press' and international finance see *Fascism and the Press* (n.d., n.p.) by A. K. Chesterton.

16 Mandle, *op. cit.*, p. 10.

17 *The Times*, 29 October 1934; *Blackshirt*, 2 November 1934.

18 Quoted Mandle, *op. cit.*, p. 12.

19 *The Times*, 25 March 1935; *Blackshirt*, 29 March 1935. *The Times*, 15 April 1935 gives details of a similar speech at Leicester. See chapters 9 and 10 for a discussion of alleged Jewish influence in finance, the press and the cinema.

20 *The Times*, 24 March 1936.

21 *Daily Mail*, 19 July 1934. Mandle, *op. cit.*, p. 8 claims that Mosley suggested the Jews constituted 6 per cent of the population, but this misreads the evidence.

22 *Blackshirt*, 3 October 1936.

23 *ibid*; *Facism: 100 Questions asked and answered* (London, 1936), Q. 97 and *Tomorrow We Live* (London, 1938), pp. 59–60 discuss such matters. See also Skidelsky, *op. cit.*, p. 390. An unsigned list of the 'opponents' of Zionism in Parliament prepared in the London office of the Zionist organization in November 1922 included Mosley's name. This will be referred to by Dr B. M. J. Wasserstein – to whom I owe the reference – in volume XI of *The Letters and Papers of Chaim Weizmann* in note 2 to the letter of 28 February 1922.

24 Quoted V. Bogdanor 'A deeply flawed hero', *Encounter* XLIV (1975), p. 71.

25 There are those who would classify this as racism, but I have used that term only with reference to a genetic-based hostility. See J. Rex, *Race Relations in Sociological Theory* (London, 1970), pp. 157–9, for a wider use.

26 *Blackshirt*, 6 September 1935. The interests of certain prominent Jews such as Lord Bearsted in the oil industry caused some agitation in Fascist and other circles. See W. Joyce, *Twilight over England* (The Hague, 1942, first published 1940), p. 111. The Liberty Restoration League run by Captain Bernard Ackworth was particularly concerned about such influences.

27 L. Lowenthal and N. Guterman, *Prophets of Deceit: A Study in the Techniques of the American Agitator* (New York, 1949), pp. 52–8 offers a valuable discussion of anti-semitic imagery, useful not only in relation to Mosley but also to Joyce and Chesterton, who are discussed below. See below pp. 228–9 for additional comment, relevant to the present categorization of Mosley's views.

28 See above pp. 176–8.

29 For an early statement of his views see *Blackshirt*, 4 November 1933; for further reference to this issue see below pp. 190 and 297.

30 See above note 12.

31 See above pp. 177–8.

32 See above p. 178.

33 See above p. 178.

34 In *My Life*, p. 443 he now describes the charge of a Jewish conspiracy as nonsense.

35 Mandle, *op. cit.*, p. 9.

36 Bogdanor, *op. cit.*, p. 76. See also R. Skidelsky, 'The Problem of Mosley', *Encounter* XXXIII (1969), p. 86 for the remark that Mosley was incapable of holding the balance between 'the politics of self-discipline' and 'the politics of self-expression'.

37 Mandle, *op. cit.*, p. 6.

38 J. A. Cole, *Lord Haw Haw – and William Joyce* (London, 1964).

39 On Beckett see my entry in J. Saville and J. Bellamy (eds), *Dictionary of Labour Biography* (forthcoming).

40 William Joyce, *Fascism and Jewry* (London, n.d. 1936?), p. 3.
41 See Mosley, *My Life*, p. 338 where, with reference to his Albert Hall speech in October 1934, he makes the same points.
42 Joyce, *Fascism and Jewry*, p. 3.
43 Mosley, *My Life*, pp. 336–43.
44 Joyce, *Fascism and Jewry*, pp. 4, 5, 6; Mosley, *op. cit.*, p. 339.
45 Joyce, *Fascism and Jewry*, p. 7. For Mosley's references on the same theme see his Albert Hall speech of 24 March 1935, referred to on p. 178 above.
46 Cole, *op. cit.*, p. 75.
47 Mandle, *op. cit.*, p. 9.
48 Joyce, *Fascism and Jewry*, pp. 4, 8.
49 *New Statesman and Nation*, 31 October 1936, p. 666. Letter from Theodore Besterman, corroborated by other sources.
50 Joyce, *Fascism and Jewry*, pp. 4, 6, 8.
51 Joyce, *Twilight over England*, pp. 58, 70, 94, 98, 116, 144 embraces such sentiments.
52 Skidelsky, *Mosley*., pp. 343–4. For additional details see *Arthur Kenneth Chesterton, M. C.* (n.p., 1973).
53 R. C. Thurlow, 'Ideology of Obsession', *Patterns of Prejudice* VIII (November–December 1974), pp. 23–9 is a detailed discussion of Chesterton's ideas.
54 A. K. Chesterton, 'The Apotheosis of the Jew', *British Union Quarterly* V, no. 2 (April–June 1937), p. 51.
55 *Blackshirt*, 25 July 1936.
56 *ibid.*, 24 October 1936.
57 *ibid.*, 31 October 1936.
58 *ibid.*, 8 January 1938.
59 *ibid.*, 15 February 1935.
60 See his comment in the *British Union Quarterly*, pp. 46, 50–51 and his article, 'The Cancer of Jewish Culture', in *Action*, 24 July 1937.
61 A. K. Chesterton, *Oswald Mosley. Portrait of a Leader* (London, 1937), p. 126.
62 *Blackshirt*, 27 December 1935.
63 Chesterton, *British Union Quarterly*, p. 54.
64 *Blackshirt*, 5 September 1936.
65 In *My Life*, p. 336, anti-semitism is defined as an attack upon Jews on account of race or religion.
66 Sir Philip Game, the police commissioner.
67 Skidelsky, *Mosley*, pp. 400–401.
68 *ibid.*, p. 400.
69 Mandle, *op. cit.*, has a good selection of such comments.
70 *Blackshirt*, 3 October 1937. The series began on 26 June 1937 with an anti-semitic piece on the Commune Warbler.
71 Mullally, *op. cit.*, p. 165, quoting BUF *Speaker's Notes*, no. 21.
72 As in *Blackshirt*, 2 January 1935.
73 *Action*, 25 August 1938.
74 *ibid.*, 2 September 1939.
75 *Blackshirt*, 28 February 1936.
76 *Fascist Quarterly* I (April 1935), p. 119.
77 *ibid.*, 30 September 1933.
78 *Action*, 7 January 1939.
79 *ibid.*, 13 January 1939.
80 *ibid.*, 21 January 1939.
81 BUF, *Britain and Jewry* (n.d., n.p.), p. 8.
82 Benewick, *op. cit.*, pp. 18, 152.

83 Mandle, *op. cit.*, p. 23. M. D. Biddiss, 'Fascism and the Race Question: a Review of Recent Historiography', *Race* x (1968–9), p. 261 refers to this as 'Mr Mandle's admirable summary of the reasons for the British Union of Fascists' eventual adoption of anti-semitism'.
84 Mosley, *My Life*, p. 336.
85 Skidelsky, *Mosley*, pp. 365–421. See note 11 above for reference to the continuing debate on such matters.
86 D. Marquand in the *Guardian*, 3 April 1975; R. E. Dowse in the *Times Higher Education Supplement*, 18 April 1975.
87 Mandle, *op. cit.*, pp. 20–23.
88 Cole, *op. cit.*, pp. 30, 34.
89 R. Merton, L. Brook and L. Cottrell, *Sociology Today* (New York, 1959), p. 379.
90 M. Banton, *White and Coloured* (London, 1959), p. 25 has some comment on these matters. See also his *Race Relations* (London, 1967), p. 299. For a similar point of view at the other end of the ideological spectrum, see J. Rex and R. Moore, *Race, Community and Conflict* (London, 1974 edn), p. 2.
91 As suggested by J. Vincent, the *Times Literary Supplement*, 4 April 1975.
92 Chapter 13 below discusses anti-semitism outside Fascism. Chapter 12 discusses those forces opposed to anti-semitism and attempts an explanation of why the BUF's anti-semitic campaign ended in failure.
93 As at Stratford Town Hall in the East End. See *Blackshirt*, 2 August 1935.
94 O. Mosley, *The Greater Britain* (London, 1934 edn), p. 19.
95 *Britain and Jewry*, p. 8; Hill, *op. cit.*, p. 7. It was also given full expression in William Joyce's *National Socialism Now* (London, 1937), pp. 70–71, written for the National Socialist League. The well worked attack upon chain stores could be approached in a similar way. See, for instance, P. Heyward, *Menace of the Chain Stores* (n.d., n.p.), p. 3.
96 Mandle, *op. cit.*, p. 15. 'We must not ... deny the importance of the Jewish factor in creating anti-semitism. Jews are undeniably different and to an extent have chosen to remain so.' See also E. Bonacich, 'A Theory of Middleman Minorities', *American Sociological Review* xxxviii (1973), pp. 591–3.
97 As Bogdanor, *op. cit.*, p. 72 points out.
98 See *ibid.* for critical comment on the Fascist reaction to Jews over this matter. Skidelsky, *Mosley*, p. 384 discusses the BUF and the Jewish boycott.
99 See the discussion of IFL ideas in chapter 10.
100 Mosley, *The Greater Britain*, pp. 158–9. See also *Fascism Explained. 10 Points of Fascist Policy* (nd., n.p.), p. 7. *Tomorrow We Live* is full of such opinions. Skidelsky, *Mosley*, pp. 140–41 notes his early hostility to the forces of finance.
101 In *Break the Chains that bind us, Our Financial Masters* (n.d., n.p.).
102 *Fascism and Jewry*, pp. 5–6.
103 *Britain and Jewry* (n.d., n.p.), pp. 2, 3.
104 See above pp. 173–4 and below p. 208.
105 See chapters 9 and 10.
106 Mandle, *op. cit.*, pp. 29–30. See also above pp. 166–7. The most recent general study of the BUF's economic and political ideas is N. Nugent and R. King (eds), *The British Right* (Farnborough, 1977), pp. 133–64.
107 Mandle, *op. cit.*, pp. 18–19, 23; Skidelsky, *Mosley*, p. 433; J. D. Brewer, 'The BUF., Sir Oswald Mosley and Birmingham, M. Soc. Sci. thesis, Birmingham University, 1975, pp. 159–62.
108 See *The Times*, 13 October 1936; Mullally, *op. cit.*, p. 69 and Mandle *op. cit.*, p. 18.
109 Skidelsky, *Mosley*, p. 393.
110 *New Survey of London Life and Labour* vi (London, 1934), p. 287. Mosley in

My Life, pp. 336–7 refers to the 'execrable' conditions which prevailed in the area.

111 Skidelsky, *Mosley*, p. 396.

112 As recognized by Mullally, *op. cit.*, pp. 69–71.

113 Skidelsky, *Mosley*, p. 393.

114 H. Roberts, 'Jew and Blackshirt in the East End', *New Statesman and Nation*, 7 November 1936, p. 698. For critical comment on some of this article see A. Sharf, *The British Press and Jews under Nazi Rule* (London, 1964), p. 195. For a more romantic view of the situation in the East End at this time, see G. Lansbury, 'Anti-Semitism in the East End', pp. 133–4, *Spectator*, 24 July 1936. This was reprinted by the Board of Deputies.

115 V. D. Lipman, *Social History of the Jews in England 1850–1950* (London, 1954), pp. 168–9 notes the declining Jewish population of the East End. Simon Blumenfeld's novel, *Jew Boy* (London, 1935), captures some of the tension in the area. See also W. Goldman, *East End My Cradle* (London, 1940).

116 *ibid.*, p. 394. See Herbert Morrison and Harry Pollitt's attempts to convey this to Neville Laski in my 'East End Anti-Semitism, 1936' in the *Bulletin of the Society for the Study of Labour History* XXXII (spring 1976), pp. 26–33.

117 Skidelsky, *Mosley*, p. 395.

118 *Jewish Chronicle*, 22 and 29 January 1936 and 5, 12, 19 and 26 February 1937 discuss the sweated trades in an attempt to place Jewish involvement in perspective. *Evening Standard*, 3 November 1936 refers to sweating by Jewish employers in the clothing industry and the existence of a 'simmering' anti-semitism before Mosley came on the scene. *Daily Herald*, 14 and 23 December 1938 and *The New Survey of London Life and Labour* II (London, 1931), pp. 218–19 discuss sweating and Jewish involvement in it in the furniture trade; M. Freedman, *A Minority in Britain* (London, 1955), pp. 214–16 comments on allegations of price-cutting by Jews in the grocery trade and also the use which the BUF made of this. See also below pp. 205–6. For general comment see Skidelsky, *Mosley*, pp. 394–5.

119 W. E. D. Allen, 'The Fascist Idea in Britain', *Quarterly Review* (October 1933), pp. 223–38 attempts to argue that Fascism was not alien to British traditions.

120 J. Higham, *Strangers in the Land. Patterns of American Nativism, 1860–1925* (New York, 1963), p. 402 has some perceptive words about interaction of this kind.

121 See above pp. 42, 160, 172–3, 180–83.

122 The phrase is taken from N. Cohn, *Warrant for Genocide* (Harmondsworth, 1970), p. 14 in a discussion of *The Protocols*. See above pp. 180–83 for the ideas of Joyce and Chesterton.

123 See below p. 194.

124 See Bogdanor, *op. cit.*, p. 73 on this. Some additional comment is also called for. In *My Life* (p. 346) Mosley has remarked that whereas Jews wanted a war to prevent the persecution of Jews in Germany, his concern was to protect the lives of young Englishmen. Each side, he has said, 'held its opinion and principle with passionate conviction'. This is now written about as a reasonable conflict of interests. But, as Skidelsky has emphasized, this was *not* the argument Mosley was using in the 1930s. At that time his claim was that a war was being engineered by Jewish finance against world Fascism because the latter 'had challenged the dictatorship of that finance', (p. 389). What was being expressed was still a conflict of interests but of a rather different kind from that which is now being suggested.

125 Well illustrated in his speech at Stratford Town Hall in 1935, which is an important source for the nature of Mosley's anti-semitism. In it Jews are

presented as manipulating British society for their own ends. See *Blackshirt*, 2 August 1935. Major-General J. F. C. Fuller's article, 'The Cancer of Europe', *Fascist Quarterly* 1 (January 1935), pp. 66–81, is a good example of Jews being treated as the vitiating agents of modern life. For a discussion of Fuller's attitudes towards Jews, see A. J. Trythall, *'Boney' Fuller. The Intellectual General 1878–1966* (London, 1977), pp. 184, 194, 201.

126 *Action*, 7 November 1936. See above pp. 178–9 for Mosley's solution.

127 *ibid.*, 26 June 1937. See also *Blackshirt*, 31 July 1937, for a discussion of the 'means of eradicating this pest from England once and for all'. All this was a far cry from the attempt to distinguish between the 'low type of foreign Jew' and 'the better type of Jew' who had 'become thoroughly British in outlook'. However, this was Joyce being expedient. See *The Letters of Lucifer and Leading Articles from 'The Blackshirt'* (London, 1933), pp. 100–102.

Chapter 12

1 W. F. Mandle, *Anti-Semitism and the British Union of Fascists* (London, 1968), p. 41, notes the involvement of the BUF in violent anti-semitism in the East End.

2 *ibid.*, pp. 50–51.

3 See above pp. 187–9.

4 See chapters 2 and 8. *The Times*, 20 October 1936 commented: 'The big Jewish immigration of the nineties is still remembered.' The speech made by E. G. 'Mick' Clarke on 23 June 1937 in Bethnal Green is similar in its argument, nuance and even choice of phrases to those which were made at BBL meetings. MEPOL 2 3115 contains Clarke's speech. The end section is particularly significant regarding this verbal tradition.

5 R. Skidelsky, *Oswald Mosley* (London, 1975), p. 393.

6 C. Russell and H. S. Lewis, *The Jew in London* (1900), pp. 16 and 17 is one of many contemporary sources to refer to the impact of Jews on the nineteenth-century housing market. See also B. Gainer, *The Alien Invasion* (London, 1972), p. 44. H. L. Smith (ed.), *The New Survey of London Life and Labour* (London, 1930–35) III, pp. 140, 353 refers to improvements in the area. J. H. Robb, *Working Class Anti-Semite* (London, 1954), p. 57, M. Young and P. Willmott, *Family and Kinship in East London* (Harmondsworth, 1969), p. 110 refer to the East End concept of rootedness as does D. Englander, 'The National Workmen's Housing Council', unpublished MA dissertation, University of Warwick, 1973, pp. 11–12.

7 Skidelsky, *op. cit.*, p. 395.

8 The predominant theme of Robb, *op. cit.*

9 N. Deakin, 'The Vitality of a Tradition' in C. Holmes (ed.), *Immigrants and Minorities in British Society* (London, 1978), p. 166.

10 See *ibid.* for evidence of this.

11 C. Cross, *The Fascists in Britain* (London, 1961), p. 70.

12 A. Oberschall, *Social Conflict and Social Movements* (New Jersey, 1973), p. 333.

13 See William Catmur's comments in the *East London Observer*, 6 January 1906.

14 Skidelsky, *op. cit.*, p. 395.

15 Cross, *op. cit.*, p. 151. See the letter in *The Times*, 14 June 1978, from the Rev. Kenneth Leech, on the sense of political betrayal felt by certain young people in parts of the East End, the movement of the National Front into this vacuum and the consequences this has had for the Bengali community, for evidence of a continuing problem of this sort.

16 R. J. Benewick, *Political Violence and Public Order* (London, 1969), p. 217

and Mandle, *op. cit.*, p. 53.
17 For details see Skidelsky, *op. cit.*, p. 397.
18 *ibid.*
19 *ibid.*, pp. 402–3.
20 See below pp. 225–6 for additional discussion on violence.
21 Cross *op. cit.*, pp. 159–61 provides one of the many accounts of Cable Street. F. Brockway, *Inside the Left* (London, 1947), pp. 271–2 gives an eye-witness account. Skidelsky, *op. cit.*, p. 406 quotes a Fascist reaction.
22 For details see Mandle, *op. cit.*, pp. 57–8.
23 MEPOL 2 3043/37B. A vivid personal memory of the campaign is provided in Mrs Lena Jeger's letter in *The Times*, 15 December 1977.
24 Mandle, *op. cit.*, p. 56.
25 Full details of the Fascist performance in the 1937 municipal elections are given in the report of the co-ordinating committee of the Board of Deputies, 7 October 1937.
26 Mandle, *op. cit.*, p. 66.
27 All from *ibid.*, p. 67.
28 *ibid.*, pp. 64–5.
29 See below pp. 221–6 for similar comment relating to the years between 1876 and 1939.
30 J. Stevenson and C. Cook, *The Slump* (London, 1978), pp. 266–7. See below for further discussion.
31 See Mandle, *op. cit.*, p. 65 and Stevenson and Cook, *op. cit.*, pp. 215–16 and 265–82. See below pp. 221–6 for comment on comparative matters.
32 Mandle, *op. cit.*, p. 65.
33 As indicated in Gordon Allport's, *The Nature of Prejudice*, Gunnar Myrdal's *An American Dilemma* and in J. A. Garrard's *The English and Immigration.*
34 'The working class may well be uncontaminated by the political inhibitions of the bourgeois mind, large sections of it are singularly free likewise from bourgeois standards of public morality and respect for the rights of others that go with them.' R. Skidelsky, 'The Problem of Mosley', *Encounter* XXXIII (1969), p. 80. On Clarke see above p. 183. See above chapter 7 for additional related comment.
35 See above pp. 176–8.
36 For comment on the 'rules of the game' and 'a civilized framework of public life', see Skidelsky, *Encounter*, pp. 80–81. See below p. 306 for comment by prominent public figures indicating that they stared in the non-theoretical hostility towards Jews which was present in Britain.
37 G. E. Simpson and J. M. Yinger, *Racial and Cultural Minorities* (4th edn, New York, 1972), chapter 5 *passim* discusses the nature and influence of cultural traditions. See above pp. 104–5 for similar comment.
38 A. D. Grimshaw, 'Factors Contributing to Colour Violence in the United States and Britain' *Race* III (1962), p. 18; see also his article 'Relationships among Prejudice, Discrimination, Social Tension and Social Violence', *Journal of Intergroup Relations* (autumn 1961), p. 303. See below chapter 14 for a more extensive discussion of such matters.
39 MEPOL 2 3043/1A contains an *aide memoire* of 16 July 1936 by Sir John Simon, the home secretary, on such matters and MEPOL 2 3047/57A includes a memorandum from the commissioner of police of 29 June 1937 indicating the seriousness with which he viewed the task of surveillance and reporting.
40 Benewick, *op. cit.*, pp. 254–6.
41 *ibid.*, pp. 239–40 and Skidelsky, *Mosley* p. 416 are convenient sources for details. *ibid.*, pp. 415–21 has a comprehensive discussion of law and order

issues and the major question of free speech. See also his article in *The Times*, 17 October 1977, at the height of recent controversy over such matters.

42 Benewick, *op. cit.*, pp. 235–59 and Skidelsky, *Mosley*, pp. 416–21 discuss these issues. See also Stevenson and Cook, *op. cit.*, pp. 240–43.

43 MEPOL 2 3069/98, /23A, /23B, all of which deal with the selling of *Blackshirt*. See also MEPOL 2 3074/5A, /35E; MEPOL 2 3077/22A, /32A; MEPOL 2 3104. See also the comment in Stevenson and Cook, *op. cit.*, p. 237.

44 MEPOL 2 3043/10A. Leese's trial is referred to on p. 164 above.

45 MEPOL 2 3043/10A.

46 See above pp. 180–83.

47 MEPOL 2 3127/43A, /39A, /45A. The Minutes of the Jewish Defence Committee for 6 December 1939 give a list of slogan daubing.

48 This fundamental issue was raised in the Beckett libel case in 1936. See Skidelsky, *Mosley*, p. 536 and my entry on Beckett in J. Saville and J. M. Bellamy (eds), *Dictionary of Labour Biography* (forthcoming).

49 See P. Piratin, *Our Flag Stays Red* (London, 1948), for reminiscences.

50 See above p. 188.

51 For further details see Deakin in Holmes, *op. cit.*, pp. 168–70.

52 See above for reference to the activities of the Stepney Tenants' Defence League against Jewish landlords. Skidelsky, *Mosley*, pp. 365–6 refers to the activity of the CP. G Sacks, *The Intelligent Man's Guide to Jew Baiting* (London, 1935), is a trenchant polemic expressing the general Marxist position. From 1934 the National Council for Civil Liberties – which was alleged to be a Communist front organization although evidence on this is open to dispute – also took an active interest in combating anti-semitism from a less theoretical standpoint than the CP. See Benewick, *op. cit.*, pp. 254–6, for an account of some of its activities. A more jaundiced view is present in Skidelsky, *Mosley*, pp. 357, 398–9.

53 Co-ordinating Committee Minutes 12 and 25 November 1936. A memorandum of 21 July 1938 also indicates the intentions of the Board of Deputies towards the Jewish People's Council.

54 Six copies of this undated memorandum were made. One of these is in the Anglo-Jewish Archives in the Mocatta Library and reference throughout is to that source. Salomon was the editor of *The Jews of Britain* (London, 1938), a sane and well balanced defence of Jewish interests, which was published on behalf of the Board of Deputies.

55 N. Laski, *Jewish Rights and Jewish Wrongs* (London, 1938), p. 131. 'In the fight against anti-semitism we have been careful, in the first place, not to put purely Jewish interests before those of the State of which we are citizens.' See *ibid.*, p. 132 for his comments in this connection on the boycott of German goods.

56 This was reflected in *ibid.*, p. 113: 'One might say that the English nation is predisposed by the very nature of its culture and civilization to look favourably on the Jews.'

57 Publications Sub-Committee of the Board of Deputies, 26 October 1936.

58 Co-ordinating Committee Minutes, 12 November 1936 and 15 July 1937 indicate something of the influence with the BBC.

59 Salomon, Jewish Defence Committee, p. 24.

60 See F. A. Renton, *Jewish Defence Campaign Speakers' Handbook* (London, 1937), for an instructional guide and *Anti-Semitic Lies Exposed* (London, 1937), for a collection of pamphlets recommended for use by speakers.

61 Co-ordinating Committee Minutes, 14 June 1937 and 15 July 1937 discuss these developments.

62 Salomon, Jewish Defence Committee, p. 6 wrote: 'For a considerable number of years past it has been easily the most venemous anti-semitic paper in this country, all the more dangerous as its anti-semitism has been of an insidious and subtle nature. Efforts have been made both in public and private to combat this policy. There are forces behind [it] which are obviously of a powerful nature, but they keep carefully in the background. We have not yet, however, abandoned hope of forcing them out into the open.' For additional comment see A. Sharf, *The British Press and Jews under Nazi Rule* (London, 1964), pp. 202, 217.

63 Benewick, *op. cit.*, pp. 40–42 discusses the National Citizens' Union. See the *National Citizen*, January 1937, p. 11, February 1937, p. 19 and April 1937, p. 56 for the developments referred to here.

64 *National Citizen*, May 1937, p. 807.

65 *ibid.*, June 1973, p. 837. Meriel Buchanan was the daughter of Sir George Buchanan, British ambassador in St Petersburg between 1910 and 1918. See *Ambassador's Daughter* (London, 1958).

66 Salomon, Jewish Defence Committee, pp. 6–7. On Beamish see below p. 276.

67 Salomon, Jewish Defence Committee, pp. 14–16. On Ramsay see Benewick, *op. cit.*, pp. 40, 266, 287, 289, 290. See also the obituary in *The Times*, 12 March 1955.

68 Salomon, Jewish Defence Committee, pp. 13–14. An interesting report by an infiltrator is 'Mosley's Luncheon at the Criterion' which is in the Wiener Library. This is dated 'probably late 1936' but Salomon, Jewish Defence Committee, refers to March 1940. On the Nordic League, see H. Blume, 'A History of Semitic Groups in Britain, 1918–40', unpublished MPhil thesis, University of Sussex, 1971, pp. 248–50.

69 Laski, *op. cit.*, p. 130 commented that, 'the work of the Board has been conducted quietly, without advertisement or publicity'.

70 *ibid.* The furniture trade was given a good deal of attention. Conditions here were such that Mosley found the trade a profitable recruiting ground. The Jewish Defence Committee, Retrospect and Prospect (December 1938), p. 5 refers to the approach to the furniture trade and a document, Resumé of Cases Reported and Investigated (March 1939) reports on Jewish landlords. Both these are in the Board of Deputies.

71 See the advice of Herbert Morrison and Harry Pollitt, given to Neville Laski in a private conversation reproduced in my edited document, 'East End Anti-Semitism, 1936', *Bulletin of the Society for the Study of Labour History* XXXII (spring 1976), pp. 26–33.

72 Defence Committee Minutes, December 1938, p. 3 of the secretary's report.

Chapter 13

1 H. S. Ashton, *The Jew at Bay* (London, 1933), p. 9.

2 L. Browne, *How Odd of God* (London, 1935), pp. 216 and 226.

3 P. Harlow, *The Shortest Way with the Jews* (London, 1939), pp. 227–8.

4 W. Lewis, *The Jews. Are they Human?* (London, 1939), pp. 111 and 109.

5 G. Sacks, *The Jewish Question* (London, 1937), p. 11 and throughout. See also his other publication, *The Intelligent Man's Guide to Jew Baiting* (London, 1935).

6 See chapter 9 for the discussion of hostility towards Jews in such sources.

7 *Jewish Chronicle*, 9 January 1931.

8 *ibid.*, 18 December 1931. For a complaint about an incident in Margate, see *ibid.*, 7 April 1933.

9 *ibid.*, 29 December 1933. See also *The Times*, 19 December 1933; *North Eastern Daily Gazette*, 19 December, 21 December, 22 December, 27 December, 28 December, 1923 and 2 January, 4 January, 6 January, 8 January and 9 January 1924. The Middlesborough incident was a clear instance of discrimination against Jews as Jews; for a less certain case involving a country club in south Wales, see *Jewish Chronicle*, 31 August 1934.

10 *Jewish Chronicle*, 21 September 1934. H. Blume, 'A History of Anti-Semitic Groups in Britain 1918–1940', unpublished MPhil thesis, University of Sussex, 1971, p. 306 refers to a number of additional instances of alleged anti-semitic discrimination.

11 See Board of Deputies file C13/3–9 for details on all this.

12 Letter 28 September 1937 in the Board of Deputies.

13 See File C13/3–10 in the Board of Deputies on employment matters.

14 The *Grocer*, 8 February 1936, p. 47.

15 *ibid.*, 23 July 1938, p. 38. 'Although assuming good old English and Scottish names, they are, of course, under the skin Jews; and, of course, the private trader is being gradually ousted by them and keenly feels the position.'

16 *ibid.* See also *ibid.*, 6 August 1938, p. 32.

17 *ibid.*, 30 July 1938, p. 31. But see *ibid.*, 6 August 1938, p. 32.

18 *ibid.*, 13 August 1938, p. 32. But see *ibid.*, 20 August 1938, p. 36.

19 *ibid.*, 6 August 1938, p. 32 and 20 August 1938, p. 37 gives comment by 'Ipso Facta' and *ibid.*, 23 July 1938 and 6 August 1938, p. 32 carry the views of 'Always Merry and Bright'.

20 *ibid.*, 9 December 1933, p. 63 and 7 November 1936, p. 88. S. Aris, *The Jews in Business* (Harmondsworth, 1973), has gossipy vignettes on figures such as Montague Burton, Jack Cohen and Isaac Wolfson, as well as on the Marks family, all of whom were involved in retail and trading developments. See also R. Redmayne, *Ideals in Industry – the Story of Montague Burton 1900–1950* (Leeds, 1951); I. Sieff, *Memoirs* (London, 1970), particularly pp. 144–61; and M. Corina, *Pile it High, Sell it Cheap* (London, 1970), for details on Jack Cohen. For BUF attempts to exploit developments in the retail sector see the *Grocer*, 7 November 1936, pp. 88–9, P. Heyward, *The Menace of the Chain Stores* (n.d., n.p.) and F. D. Hill '*Gainst Trust and Monopoly* (n.d., n.p.). S. Salomon, *The Jews of Britain* (London, 1938), pp. 52–5 tries to place such accusations in an economic perspective. J. B. Jefferys, *Retail Trading in Britain 1850–1950* (London, 1954), discusses general developments in the retail trade.

21 A. J. Sherman. *Island Refuge. Britain and Refugees from the Third Reich, 1933–1939* (London, 1973).

22 A. Sharf, *The British Press and the Jews Under Nazi Rule* (London, 1964), pp. 159–60. A similar response was apparent towards the persecution and subsequent immigration of Russian Jews in the late nineteenth century. See S. M. Fuller, 'The British Press and European Anti-Semitism, 1880–1917', unpublished PhD thesis, University of New Mexico, 1974, pp. 1–2.

23 'We have ever been the refuge of the oppressed and exiled, but surely, as the profession is already overcrowded, charity begins among ourselves.' Letter, *British Medical Journal*, supplement, 16 December 1933, p. 311. The letter had a populist strain in it, in the sense that it was expressed as a defence of the small man against 'the nonchalance and excessive gallantry' of those with 'established reputations and incomes' whom the immigration would not adversely affect. A calmer view at this time was reflected in the *Medical World*, 1 December 1933, p. 333.

24 *British Medical Journal*, 30 December 1933, p. 323.

25 *ibid.*, 13 January 1934, p. 15, as well as elsewhere. See, for instance, Yaffle's comments in *Reynolds News*, 11 September 1938 and the remarks in *Everybody's Weekly*, 17 September 1938, p. 6.
26 Sherman, *op. cit.*, pp. 123–4. Viscount Templewood, *Nine Troubled Years* (London, 1954), p. 240 contains ministerial reflections on such matters.
27 *Sunday Express*, 19 June 1938; more examples are provided in Sharf, *op. cit.*, p. 168. The other side of the coin, evidenced in a warm welcome is conveyed in a letter by Freud, written in July 1938. See E. L. Freud (ed.), *Letters of Sigmund Freud* (London, 1961), p. 443.
28 Sharf, *op. cit.*, p. 161.
29 See D. Reed, *Disgrace Abounding* (London, 1939), pp. 242 and 245. Reed had joined *The Times* in 1921 and worked for the paper between 1928 and 1938 in central Europe. He resigned in October 1938. See the interesting, informed and allusive obituary in *The Times*, 23 September 1976. The Board of Deputies was soon considering what to do about *Disgrace Abounding*. See Publications Committee Minutes 27 March 1939.
30 Blume, 'A History of Anti-Semitic Groups', chapter 4 *passim* provides an outline history of the Boswell Printing and Publishing Company. On Northumberland (1880–1930) see *DNB 1922–1930* (London, 1932), pp. 662–3 and *The Times*, 15 August 1930. In the 1930s the *Patriot* received financial support from Lady Houston, who ran the *Saturday Review* from 1932 until her death in 1936. See J. Wentworth Day, *Lady Houston. The Woman who won the War* (London, 1958), pp. 55 and 82. When the Boswell company was dissolved in 1950 the Britons Publishing Society assumed the copyright over its works.
31 See above pp. 41–51 for the *Morning Post's* role in post-war anti-semitism in Britain. W. D. Rubinstein, 'Henry Page Croft and the National Party 1917–22', *Journal of Contemporary History* IX (January 1974), pp. 144–5 discusses the interest this group took in Jews.
32 Blume, 'A History of Anti-Semitic Groups', p. 90.
33 The *Patriot*, 27 October 1927, p. 387 referred to the opening of an enquiry centre under Nesta Webster. Prominent among the books published by the Boswell Company were Webster's *World Revolution* (London, 1921), *Secret Societies and Subversive Movements* (London, 1924), and *The Socialist Network* (London, 1926).
34 The *Patriot*, 9 February 1922, p. 1.
35 *ibid.*, 16 March 1922, pp. 1–2.
36 I. D. Colvin, *A Wreath of Immortelles* (London, 1924), pp. 41, 54. For earlier references to the activity of Colvin see above pp. 139–41, 149.
37 The *Patriot*, 5 September 1929, pp. 217–19 in an article called 'Anticipating The "Protocols"'.
38 *ibid.*, 23 October 1924, p. 186, 30 January 1930, p. 107, 20 February 1930, pp. 167–8, 20 September 1934, pp. 220–21. N. Webster, *World Revolution*, chapter 10, refers to German-Jewish Bolshevism. See also Northumberland's speech in the Lords in *Parliamentary Debates*, House of Lords LIII (1923), col. 808. A. H. Lane, *The Alien Menace* (3rd edn, London, 1932), chapter 11 is concerned with the threat of Bolshevism supported by international finance. See also A. Homer, *Judaism and Bolshevism* (London, 1934), pp. 2–3.
39 The *Patriot*, 5 September 1929, pp. 217–19.
40 The cartoon in *ibid*, 15 July 1926, p. 57 conveys this in dramatic fashion.
41 *ibid.*, 21 July 1927. pp. 49–51 in a piece called 'Anti-Semitism'. See also the trenchant analysis of Cobbett, *Jews and the Jews in England* (London, 1938), p. 89.
42 See above chapters 2, 7, 9, 10 and 11.

43 The *Patriot*, 6 February 1930, pp. 129–30 comments on alien influences in the City and *ibid.*, 18 July 1929, pp. 49–52, 20 February 1930, pp. 167–9 and 8 March 1934, pp. 181–2 refer to alleged press influences. See below p. 284 for general comment on such allegations.
44 *ibid.*, 9 November 1922, p. 223, 18 October 1923, p. 167 and 2 October, 1924, p. 142 provide a sample of the fears of Jewish political manipulation. *ibid.*, 4 January 1934, pp. 9–10 contains a comment from A. H. Lane on immigration. Lane's book, *The Alien Menace* – essentially the Jewish menace – was published by Boswell and went through a number of editions.
45 The *Patriot*, 5 July 1923, pp. 349–50, 23 October 1924, p. 186, 21 July 1927, p. 50, 29 November 1934, p. 416. See above pp. 141–51 for the attitudes of the *Morning Post*.
46 The *Patriot*, 5 July 1923, p. 349.
47 *ibid.*, 21 July 1927, p. 50.
48 *ibid.*, displays the tendency to attack a section of Jews; Cobbett, *op. cit.*, pp. 14, 17 and 114–15 displays a racist hostility.
49 The *Patriot*, 5 July 1923, p. 349.
50 *ibid.*, 4 May 1922, p. 4, 15 June 1922, p. 4 and 8 March 1934, p. 183. Cobbett, *op. cit.*, pp. 115 ff wrote about the need to aviod inter-marriage as a solution to the Jewish question and stressed instead the need to exclude Jews from positions which could affect national life and the necessity to pose an alternative philosophy to the Jewish way of life. In February and March 1939 the *Patriot* ran a series of articles attacking Zionism as a solution to the Jewish question. Zionism, it was argued, encouraged the mobilization of Jews and that could be dangerous.
51 See J. L. Finlay, *Social Credit. The English Origins* (Montreal and London, 1972). This book contains a discussion of Douglas's life and ideas. Brief details on his life are in *Who Was Who, 1951–1960* (3rd edn, London, 1964), p. 314.
52 Finlay, *op. cit.*, p. 103.
53 *ibid.*, pp. 104–5.
54 C. H. Douglas, 'The Jews', *Social Credit*, 26 August 1938, p. 8.
55 *New Age*, 28 February 1924, p. 215.
56 *ibid.*, 30 October 1924, p. 12. The cartoon was based upon a woodcut by Haydn Mackey.
57 *ibid.*, 6 May 1926 until 29 July 1926.
58 *ibid.*, 22 April 1926, pp. 289–90, and 18 June 1936, pp. 47–8, for instance.
59 *ibid.*, 30 March 1922, p. 282.
60 *ibid.*, 9 January 1930, p. 113.
61 *ibid.*, 8 May 1930, p. 18. See above pp. 39–42, 66 for Banister's anti-semitism.
62 *ibid.*, 15 May 1930, p. 29 and 22 May 1930, pp. 37–42.
63 *ibid.*, 21 July 1932, pp. 141–2, 28 July 1932, pp. 152–3, 4 August 1932, pp.162–3. See *ibid.*, 11 August 1932, p. 179 for a reply.
64 The extensive discussion of 1926 was instigated by S. P. Abrams.
65 See above
66 A. E. Day 'The Story of G. K.'s Weekly', *Library Review* XXIV, no. 5 (spring 1974), pp. 209–12 provides an outline of the journal's history.
67 G. K. Chesterton, *The New Jerusalem* (London, n.d. 1921?), pp. 264 and 269. In his *Autobiography* (London, n.d. 1936?), p. 77 he said they were 'foreigners; only foreigners that were not called foreigners'.
68 Chesterton, *The New Jerusalem*, p. 265.
69 *ibid.*, p. 271.
70 *ibid.*, p. 272.
71 *ibid.*, p. 280–81.

72 *ibid.*, pp. 267–8. See also C. Hollis, *The Mind of Chesterton* (London, 1970), pp. 133–4.
73 C. Sykes, *Nancy: the Life of Lady Astor* (London, 1973), p. 135.
74 See the articles which appeared in the *Eye Witness* between 7 September and 26 October 1911 and Belloc's *The Jews* (London, 1922). The references to Bolshevism and the Jews which appeared in the latter were not present, of course, in the articles. C. L. Klein, 'English Anti-Semitism in the 1920s', *Patterns of Prejudice* VI (March–April 1972), pp. 23–8 discusses Belloc and Galsworthy. For a defence of *The Jews* see R. Speaight, *The Life of Hilaire Belloc* (London, 1957), pp. 452–4. Needless to say the Marconi scandal remained a strong memory for Belloc, thereby indicating another link with pre-war years. See *The Jews*, pp. 51, 245.
75 D. Lodge, *Novelist at the Crossroads* (London, 1971), p. 157.
76 See above pp. 29–30.
77 Chesterton's distributist articles were collected together in *The Outline of Sanity* (1926). See J. M. Thorn, 'An Unexplored Chapter in Recent English History: Distributism and the Distributist League', unpublished PhD thesis, Wisconsin University, 1976, for details of policy. Belloc's early distributist ideas can be found in *The Servile State* (London, 1912).
78 *G. K.'s Weekly*, 6 June 1925, p. 246.
79 *ibid.*, 14 July 1938, p. 341.
80 *ibid.*, 18 July 1925, pp. 399. In making this suggestion Chesterton wrote, 'The Editor of this paper, in his personal capacity, has not the smallest intention of denying that he wishes for the wholesale conversion of the Jews and everybody else to Roman Catholicism. He does not, however, think this probability one that presses so closely upon us as to be a substitute for any other policy about Jews.'
81 G. K. Chesterton, in *The New Jerusalem* had, in 1921, displayed sympathy towards Zionism. For critical comment by Chesterton, see, *inter alia*, *G. K.'s Weekly*, 6 June 1925, p. 246, 18 July 1925, p. 399. Belloc commented in *ibid.*, 25 June 1936, pp. 233–4, 15 October 1936, pp. 96–7; the *Weekly Review*, 14 July 1938, pp. 341–2 and 22 September 1938, pp. 38–9.
82 *The Weekly Review*, 14 July 1938, p. 342. In other words we were back with Belloc's solution proposed in *The Jews* and even earlier in the *Eye Witness*.
83 See the letters to the editor of the *Catholic Herald* on 8 January 1924 and 5 March 1924 in file B4/CAR 11 at the Board of Deputies. For the activity of the Board in combating Fascist anti-semitism see above pp. 200–202.
84 File B4/CAR 11 contains accounts of protests made in 1928, 1929, 1933 and 1935.
85 File B4/CAR 13 and B4/CAR 16 in the Board of Deputies contain information on such matters. The *Catholic Gazette* carried an article on 'The Jewish Peril and the Catholic Church' which contained a Protocols-like analysis of the danger which Jews posed to the Catholic Church. The item was reprinted in the *Patriot*, 20 February 1936, pp. 157–9.
86 File B4/CAR 14 in the Board of Deputies contains the details. See above pp. 50–51 for reference to the Tomaso incident. *Encyclopaedia Judaica* II (London, Jerusalem, 1971), p. 1122 comments on the Holy Child of La Guardia. See above pp. 200–202 for other activities of the Board in fighting anti-semitism.
87 See above p. 144 for comment on this.
88 J. A. Morris, 'T. S. Eliot and Anti-Semitism', *Journal of European Studies* II (1972), pp. 172–82, is a recent analysis which refers to earlier studies.
89 See the remarks of David Daiches in the *Observer*, 11 June 1967.
90 Morris, *op. cit.*, pp. 175 and 180. See Eliot's own comment in *After Strange*

Gods (London, 1934), pp. 19–20.

91 Eliot, *After Strange Gods*, p. 48. A. Hamilton, *The Appeal of Fascism* (London, 1971), p. 276 refers to the 'greater serenity' of his later work.

92 Morris, *op. cit.*, p. 182. See also J. Harrison, *The Reactionaries* (London, 1966), p. 183.

93 See Harrison, *op. cit.*, p. 183. D. H. Lawrence, *Kangaroo*, chapter 12 is particularly revealing.

94 D. H. Lawrence, *The Virgin and the Gipsy* (Harmondsworth, 1974), p. 55.

95 G. M. Mitchell, 'John Buchan's Fiction: a Hierarchy of Race', *Patterns of Prejudice* VII (November–December 1973), p. 29.

96 G. Himmelfarb, 'John Buchan – an Untimely Appreciation', *Encounter* XV (September 1960), pp. 46–53 is a critical account of Buchan's work drawing attention to his references to racial types. See the defence by Buchan's son in *ibid.* (November 1960), p. 83. Mitchell, *op. cit.*, follows Himmelfarb and adds to the detail of the discussion. See particularly her use of Buchan's pamphlet *The Novel and the Fairytale* for Buchan's views on what novel writing was intended to achieve. D. Daniell, *The Interpreter's House: a Critical Assessment of the Works of John Buchan* (London, 1975), attempts to answer the charges of racism, anti-semitism, snobbery with violence and careerist values emphasized by Buchan's detractors. In an earlier study, *John Buchan* (London, 1965), p. 117, Janet Adam Smith drew a distinction between Buchan's attitudes at various stages of his career, suggesting that Buchan might have been genuinely anti-semitic in his early days but that he mellowed later.

97 Comment on Sapper's work is provided by G. M. Mitchell, 'Caricature of the Bulldog Spirit', *Patterns of Prejudice* VIII (September–October 1974), pp. 25–30, particularly, pp. 29–30. The fiction of Dornford Yates is discussed by J. Morris in 'Best-selling Prejudice', *ibid.* XI (July–August 1977), pp. 23–30, particularly pp. 28–9.

98 J. Hitchman, *Such a Strange Lady* (London, 1975), p. 123.

99 *ibid.*, pp. 124–5.

100 See above for Fascist interest in the retail trades.

101 See above pp. 141–7 for an account of this atmosphere.

102 The opinions of the *New Age* on the Marconi scandal are referred to in Kenneth Lunn's PhD thesis. See the bibliography for details.

103 'Chips' Channon's suggestive comment on Leslie Hore-Belisha, to the effect that 'he is an oily man, half a Jew, an opportunist, with a Semitic flare for publicity', quoted in R. R. James, (ed.), *The Diaries of Sir Henry Channon* (London, 1967), pp. 23–4, was not unusual. Evelyn Waugh, for instance, could refer to the pianist, Solomon as 'an appalling little Jew and great musician'. See M. Davie (ed.), *The Diaries of Evelyn Waugh* (London, 1976), p. 66. The pianist, Leslie Hutchinson (Hutch) was a 'nigger'. *ibid.*, p. 281. Gratuitous references to Jewish origins, in a variety of circumstances, appeared in *ibid.*, pp. 266, 293, 423, 433. For similar remarks see H. Nicolson, *Diaries and Letters 1930–1939* (London, 1966), p. 327, where he refers to a retort by Lady Astor and M. Gilbert, *Sir Horace Rumbold* (London, 1967), p. 49 for comment by Rumbold. At a different level similar hostility was encountered by Bernard Kops, when his fellow school children shouted, 'Dirty Git! You killed our Lord.' See his autobiographical account of East End life just before the war and afterwards in *The World is a Wedding* (London, 1963), p. 35. See also p. 33. This tradition of non-theoretical anti-semitism was also reflected in literature. See G. Sacks, *The Intelligent Man's Guide*, pp. 12–13 and S. Orwell and I. Angus (eds), *The Collected Essays, Journalism and Letters of George Orwell* (3 vols, London, 1968) III, p. 338.

104 T. W. H. Crosland, *The Fine Old Hebrew Gentleman* (London, n.d. 1922?), chapter 14. Various Jewish organizations complained to the publishers about this book and the content of such correspondence encouraged Crosland to think in terms of starting legal proceedings. See File B4/CR5 in the Board of Deputies.
105 Crosland, *op. cit.*, pp. 78–9.
106 M. G. Murchin, *Britain's Jewish Problem* (London, 1939), pp. 142–4.
107 Speaight, *op. cit.*, p. 456.
108 But see above note 48 for references to racist hostility in 'Cobbett' and below p. 228 for Belloc. See above pp. 157, 169, 190 for Fascist genocidal references. See below p. 288 for the definition of racism which is intended here.
109 Crosland, *op. cit.*, chapter 10 *passim* refers to Jews in the First World War. C. H. Douglas, in *New Age*, 3 June 1926, p. 51 comments upon the influence of Jews at Versailles, as does Belloc, *The Jews*, p. 19. Crosland, *op. cit.*, p. 141, Douglas, *loc cit.*, p. 51 and Murchin, *op. cit.*, pp. 142–4 discuss an alleged involvement by Jews in Bolshevism, planning and collectivism respectively. Belloc, *The Jews*, p. 281 argued that the direction and the staff of Communism depended upon Jews but to go further than this was to lapse into anti-semitism. Hostility towards Jews on account of their alleged activities during the war and at Versailles and their role in Bolshevism were heavily emphasized by the right wing anti-semites we discussed in chapter 9.
110 Murchin, *op. cit.*, pp. 12–13 and 38–56 made a good deal of the refugee problem, as did, for instance, the *Sunday Express*. See above note 27. Undercutting was the major feature of the debate in the *Grocer*, see above pp. 205–6, and was touched upon by Murchin, *op. cit.*, p. 96. Jewish filtration and threat of dominance was present in Crosland, *op. cit.*, pp. 14, 20, K. Williams, *Money Sense* (London, 1937), pp. 224 and Murchin, *op. cit.*, pp. 24–37.
111 C. H. Douglas in *Social Credit*, 26 August 1938, p. 8 referred to the Bank of England being under Jewish control. See also Williams, *op. cit.*, pp. 218–20.
112 Crosland, *op. cit.*, pp. 155–8.
113 Reed, *op. cit.*, pp. 233, 242.
114 Crosland, *op. cit.*, p. 50. The whole of the Chesterbelloc runs along these lines. See above pp. 210–12. See also 'Ipso Facta' in the *Grocer*, 6 August 1938, p. 32 and Reed, *op. cit.*, pp. 222–3, 237 and 246–7.
115 See above p. 36 for information on Pearson and his work.
116 K. Pearson and M. Moul, 'The Problem of Alien Immigration into Great Britain illustrated by an Examination of Russian and Polish Children', *Annals of Eugenics* I (1925–6), p. 7. We still await a good study of Pearson, on whom see the entry in the *DNB*, *1931–1940* (Oxford, 1949), pp. 681–4.
117 Pearson and Moul, 'Alien Immigration', *op. cit.*, p. 127.
118 *ibid.*
119 *ibid.*
120 *The Hidden Hand or Jewry Ueber Alles*, June 1922, p. 1. See also A. H. Lane, *The Alien Menace* (3rd edn, London, 1932), pp. 49–52. In an attempt to counteract the Pearson survey the Board of Deputies sponsored a reply in the form of 'An Investigation into the Comparative Intelligence and Attainments of Jewish and Non-Jewish School Children', by Mary Davies and A. G. Hughes. This appeared in *The British Journal of Psychology* XVIII (July 1927), pp. 134–46. The major conclusion of this research, which received help and guidance from Professor Cyril Burt, and which was based upon IQ tests, was that: 'On an average, both in General Intelligence and in attainments in English and Arithmetic, Jewish children are definitely superior to the non-Jewish children attending the same school, the superiority being more marked with the boys

than with the girls' (p. 145). For the involvement of the Board, see Board of Deputies, *Annual Report 1927* (London, 1928), p. 40.

121 On the political use of IQ tests see L. Kamin, *The Science and Politics of IQ* (Harmondsworth, 1977).

122 See, for instance, the letter in the *Grocer*, 6 August 1938, p. 32 with its references to the 'sorrowing creditors of those "who fold their tents and disappear into the night"', the comments on 'Fire kings and share pushers', and the guest setting out to take the house from his host, which rightly encouraged the host of kick him out, all of which was rounded off with an open admiration of Hitler, 'for giving Germany back to the German'.

123 Crosland, *op. cit.*, pp. 9, 11, 22, 23, 68. Crosland was an associate of Lord Alfred Douglas and had involved himself in the activities of *Plain English*. See above pp. 144–5 for references to this journal. On Crosland see W. Sorley Browne, *The Life and Genius of T. W. H.* Crosland (London, 1928). Williams, *op. cit.* contains a section on 'Jewish Gentlemen in Business' and the cartoon on p. 217 sums up the viciousness. Murchin, *op. cit.* was described on the dust cover as 'a critical but strictly impartial analysis'.

124 Reed, *op. cit.*, pp. 232–3, 242–3, 245.

125 Orwell commented upon such pressures. See *The Collected Essays, Journalism and Letters of George Orwell* III, pp. 336–7. Murchin, *op. cit.*, has frequent references to the atmosphere which surrounded the discussion of anti-semitism. But mild anti-semitism by some could encourage others to go further. See the comments of the *Jewish Guardian* suggesting that the anti-semitic policy of the *Morning Post* 'encouraged editors of minor importance to pursue a similar policy with even less reticence and restraint'. Quoted in the *Morning Post*, 26 April 1922.

126 See my article 'New Light on "The Protocols of Zion"', *Patterns of Prejudice* VI (November–December 1977), pp. 13–21, for documentary proof of Colvin's reluctance. *Jews and the Jews in England* was published by the Boswell Publishing Company in 1938. The quotation is from the preface.

127 The reference to Murchin is taken from the dust cover; as is the reference to the author of H. S. Ashton, *The Jew at Bay* (London, 1933).

128 See above pp. 164 and note 64, p. 290.

129 In a discussion of his anti-semitism it has been written: 'He lived to see where such attempted witch-hunting led in Germany and in his last years he regretted that he had ever soiled his hands with it, loathing Nazism with a hearty and verbose hatred that comes out in his letters.' R. Croft-Cooke, *Bosie* (London, 1963), p. 293. The poet Roy Campbell had no such difficulty in accommodating Hitler's treatment of a 'dissolving, softening, undermining and vulgarizing' race. See his *Broken Record* (London, 1934), pp. 45–6. For a general impressionistic comment upon the impact of Hitlerite anti-semitism on unsystematic anti-semitism in Britain, see Himmelfarb, *op. cit.*, p. 50.

130 See 'The Horse and the Hedge' by G. K. C. in *G. K.'s Weekly*, 30 March 1933, pp. 55–6. See also comment by him in *ibid.*, 27 September 1930, pp. 34–5, 4 May 1933, p. 135 and 22 March 1934, pp. 39–40.

131 *ibid.*, 18 May 1933, p. 166 and the *Weekly Review*, 14 July 1938, p. 342.

132 *The Weekly Review*, 1 December 1938, pp. 274–5. See the comment on Belloc's position by Bernard Bergonzi in 'Chesterton and/or Belloc', *Critical Quarterly* I (1959), p. 65. See the 1937 edition of *The Jews*, pp. XL–XLI, for a condemnation of Nazi atrocities.

133 See his article, 'The Jews' in the *Sunday Express*, 12 February 1922.

134 M. Muggeridge, *The Thirties*, 1930–1940 (London, 1940), p. 243.

135 See the review by John Vincent of Skidelsky's biography in the *Times Literary*

Supplement, 4 April 1975.

136 See above p. 104 for comment.

137 *Daily Dispatch*, 17 October 1932, quoted in Sharf, *op. cit.*, p. 194. *ibid.*, chapter 7 discusses in an impressionistic way how widespread anti-semitism was and concludes that it was less pervasive than was often believed and of less significance than Nazi observers wished it to be. See above pp. 1–2 and below p. 227 for comment on the forms of anti-semitism to which reference is being made.

138 By the 1919 Act any alien could be refused entry into the United Kingdom at the discretion of the authorities. In general aliens were not allowed into the country for more than three months unless they held a Ministry of Labour permit for work or had visible means of support. Any alien could be deported by the home secretary if he deemed it were for the public good. A general exception to this was that anyone likely to be persecuted on his return to his own country should be granted political asylum. For anti-semitic tones in the parliamentary discussion see, for example, *Parliamentary Debates*, House of Commons CXX (1919), cols. 58 and 86.

139 Sherman, *op. cit.*, p. 222, stresses that the avoidance of any financial commitment for the emigration and settlement of refugees and a fear that the influx of immigrants might generate anti-semitism were the major principles determining British policy.

140 See above chapter 12 and below chapter 14.

141 See below pp. 221–6.

Chapter 14

1 B. Dobson, *The Jews of Medieval York and the Massacre of March 1190*, Borthwick Papers, no. 45 (York, 1974), discusses this incident.

2 See above pp. 18, 30, 118–19, 168, 171–2, 178–9.

3 See above p. 101.

4 See above chapter 1.

5 See above chapter 5 *passim.*

6 See above p. 113 and below pp. 228–9.

7 As those who held such attitudes were keen to emphasize. On Sampson Levi, a caricature of a certain type of Jew, see Arnold Bennett's novel, *The Grand Babylon Hotel.*

8 R. Skidelsky, *Oswald Mosley* (London, 1975), covers both sets of hostility. The wider implications of attacks upon blacks by the nationalist right are not lost on the Jewish community. See the letter in *The Times*, 27 August 1977 from the chairman of the defence and group relations committee of the Board of Deputies.

9 R. E. Harwood, *Did Six Million Really Die? The Truth At Last* (Richmond, 1974?), and A. R. Butz, *The Hoax of the Twentieth Century* (Richmond, 1976), are two recent publications in English which set out to question the Holocaust experience. On the National Front see M. Walker, *The National Front* (London, 1977). An academic committee of the Yad Vashem has recently been established in Britain to examine 'the problems of the Holocaust' and to counteract such hostile interpretations of recent history.

10 J. Higham, 'Anti-Semitism in the Gilded Age', *Mississippi Valley Historical Review* XLIII (1956–7), p. 571. In the following footnotes which relate to anti-semitism outside Britain, I have restricted my choice of sources to those which students are likely to find readily available.

11 L. Greenberg, *The Jews of Russia* (New Haven, 1965), and S. W. Baron, *The Russian Jew under the Tsars and Soviets* (New York, 1964; new edition

1977), both provide general histories of Jews in Russia.

12 L. Wolf (ed.), *The Legal Sufferings of the Jews in Russia* (London, 1912), is a good contemporary account of such problems.

13 P. Aldag, *Das Judentum in England* (Berlin, 1934), p. 363.

14 Brief extracts from significant sections of the Nuremberg Laws are conveniently available in L. L. Snyder, *The Idea of Racialism. Its Meaning and History* (Princeton, 1962), pp. 163–5. In addition to Germany, official anti-semitism was strong in Poland. See C. S. Heller, *On the Edge of Destruction* (New York, 1977).

15 Such matters are discussed in R. Byrnes, *Antisemitism in Modern France* (New Brunswick, 1950), D. Johnson, *France and the Dreyfus Affair* (London, 1966), and M. R. Marrus, *The Politics of Assimilation: a Study of the French Jewish Community at the time of the Dreyfus Affair* (Oxford, 1971); L. Dinnerstein, *The Leo Frank Case* (New York, 1968); A. B. Tager, *The Decay of Czarism: the Beiliss Trial* (Philadelphia, 1935), and M. Samuel, *Blood Accusation: the Strange History of the Beiliss Case* (London, 1967).

16 S. Joseph, *Jewish Immigration to the United States from 1881 to 1910* (New York, 1914), pp. 43–8 and Baron, *op. cit.*, pp. 82–3, 97, 106 ff., are useful on the Russian situation. On Germany see H. Valentin, *Anti-Semitism, Historically and Critically Examined* (London, 1936) chapter II; W. E. Mosse (ed.), *Entscheidungsjahr 1932. Zur Judenfrage in der endphase der Weimarer Republik* (Tübingen, 1965), pp. 87–131 provides evidence on the socio-economic structure of Jewry as Hitler came to power; W. Laqueur, *Weimar, A Cultural History* (London, 1974), pp. 72–7, offers general comment. N. Cohn, *Warrant for Genocide* (Harmondsworth, 1970), p. 192 and his introduction to H. Bernstein, *The Truth about 'The Protocols of Zion'* (New York, 1971 edn), p. xxi show how Jewish influence could be exaggerated on the basis of specific examples. On Britain see W. D. Rubinstein, 'Jews among Top British Wealth Holders 1857–1969: Decline of the Golden Age', *Jewish Social Studies* XXIV (1972), pp. 73–84 for an attempt to discuss Jewish power. J. Gould and S. Esh (eds), *Jewish Life in Modern Britain* (London, 1964), p. 27 refers to the difficulty in obtaining statistics on Anglo-Jewry. S. Aris, *The Jews in Business* (Harmondsworth, 1970), pp. 3, 7 comments on the same and the possible under-playing of Jewish influence. See below p. 284 for some comment on Jewish influence – or lack of it – in certain areas of British life. A good starting point for a discussion of such economic and political influence for the inter-war years would be a rigorous, critical analysis of the later chapters of Aldag, *op. cit.*

17 Greenberg, *op. cit.*; Baron, *op. cit.* and Cohn, *op. cit.* are all useful on such issues. See also Joseph, *op. cit.*, who gives the background to Jewish immigration to America; S. M. Dubnow, *History of the Jews in Russia and Poland*, trans. I. Friedlander (3 vols, Philadelphia, 1916–20), and J. Frumkin, *et al. Russian Jewry, 1860–1917* (New York, 1966). C. E. Black (ed.), *The Transformation of Russian Society* (Harvard, 1960), is valuable on wider, related developments in Russia.

18 P. W. Massing, *Rehearsal for Destruction* (New York, 1949); E. Reichmann, *Hostages of Civilization* (London, 1950); P. G. J. Pulzer, *The Rise of Political Anti-Semitism in Germany and Austria* (New York, 1964); G. Mosse, *The Crisis of German Ideology* (New York, 1964); F. Stern, *The Politics of Cultural Despair* (New York, 1965); R. S. Levy, *The Downfall of the Anti-Semitic Political Parties in Imperial Germany* (New Haven, 1975), and F. Stern, *Gold and Iron, Bismarck, Bleichröder and the Building of the German Empire* (London, 1977), are crucial sources on anti-semitism in Germany before the War.

In the case of Hitler we need to remind ourselves that he had grown up in Austria, where there was a powerful anti-semitic tradition. See Pulzer *op. cit.*

19 Cohn, *op. cit.*, p. 195 and in Bernstein, *op. cit.*, p. xxii notes such influences.

20 See below p. 226 Pulzer, *op. cit.*, pp. 293–333; L. Dawidowicz, *The War against the Jews 1933–45* (Harmondsworth, 1975), chapters 1–6 are two sources, drawn from many, which discuss German anti-semitism before the Second World War. W. Laqueur, *Russia and Germany* (London, 1965), p. 94 notes the influence of Russian emigrés upon anti-semitism in Germany. John Vincent, in a review of Skidelsky's *Mosley* in the *Times Literary Supplement*, 4 April 1975, succinctly draws a contrast between Britain and Germany in terms of factors which helped to create anti-semitism.

21 L. Schapiro, 'The Russian Background of the Anglo-American Jewish Immigration', *TJHSE* xx (1959–61), pp. 215–31 is an excellent compact account of anti-semitism in Russia before the Revolution and vividly illustrates the power of the autocracy and the failure of liberal forces to make an impression upon policy.

22 T. Kemp, *Industrialization in Nineteenth-Century Europe* (London, 1969), p. 142.

23 L. Poliakov, *Harvest of Hate* (London, 1954); H. Arendt, *The Origins of Totalitarianism* (2nd edn, London, 1958); R. Hilberg, *The Destruction of the European Jews* (Chicago, 1967); Cohn, *op. cit.*; Dawidowicz, *op. cit.*, collectively provide the main features of Nazi anti-semitism.

24 See Higham, *op. cit.*, p. 571.

25 See above pp. 221–5.

26 See Cohn, *op. cit.*

27 See above chapters 7 and 12.

28 S. Orwell and I. Angus (eds), *The Collected Essays, Journalism and Letters of George Orwell* (3 vols, London, 1968) III, p. 105. See also B. Zawadzki, 'Limitations of the Scapegoat Theory of Prejudice', *Journal of Abnormal and Social Psychology* XLIII (1948), p. 136.

29 See. W. Laqueur, in *Commentary* XLIV (July 1967), p. 84.

30 Levy, *op. cit.*, p. 1.

31 See the comments by Michael Banton in his *Race Relations* (London, 1967), pp. 20, 298–9 and in S. Zubaida (ed.), *Race and Racialism* (London, 1970), pp. 22–4. C. Bolt, *Victorian Attitudes to Race* (London, 1971), J. M. Winter, 'The Webbs and the Non-White World: a Case of Socialist Racialism, *Journal of Contemporary History* IX (January 1974), pp. 181–92 and a good deal of the wild debate in *Encounter* beginning in March 1976 over Beatrice Webb's attitudes towards Jews, all offend these principles. See below pp. 230–31 for further reference to the problem of prejudice.

32 E. P. Thompson, *The Making of the English Working Class* (New York, 1963), pp. 12–13.

33 Cohn *op. cit.*, moves in this direction. R. C. Thurlow, 'The Creation of the English Volk', unpublished MS. does even more so.

34 I have referred elsewhere to the various ways in which anti-semitic thought was expressed before 1914 and this present discussion, concerned with the essence of anti-semitic expressions, builds upon that earlier analysis. See C. Holmes 'J. A. Hobson and the Jews', in my edited *Immigrants and Minorities in British Society* (London, 1978), pp. 148–52.

35 See above pp. 221–6.

36 See above pp. 110–11.

37 G. Anderson, *Victorian Clerks* (Manchester, 1976), pp. 60–65 discusses the German 'Clerical Invasion'; J. P. May, 'The Chinese in Britain', in Holmes,

op. cit., p. 116 refers to the Chinese.

38 See above pp. 203–5.

39 J. T. Sinclair, *A Defence of Russia and the Christians of Turkey* (London, n.d.), pp. 124 and 129: 'The lion can no more change his skin or the leopard his spots than the Jews can lose their distinguishing characteristics both of appearance and disposition; and even to this day the hook nose, the shambling gait and the peculiar accent of the race are unmistakable.' We mixed with them, he wrote, like oil and vinegar. Aldag interpreted this as a reference to miscegenation but this reads too much into it. See Aldag, *op. cit.*, p. 363. Following after Sinclair, Joseph. Banister could write: 'It is the Jew's nature and race which render him objectionable, not his religion.' See J. Banister, *England under the Jews* (London, 1901), p. 98. O'Donnell commented on Rufus Isaacs: 'The mean treachery of the Isaacs person is, of course, manifest. But that is of less moment. Isaacs had it in his blood and tribe. . . . Israel like the leopard changes his habitat but not his spots.' The *New Witness*, 9 October 1913, p. 718.

40 See above pp. 182–3.

41 See above pp. 183–4.

42 A. M. Ludovici, *A Defence of Conservatism* (London, 1927), pp. 19, 61–2, 116, 149; 'Cobbett', *Jews and the Jews in England* (London, 1938), pp. 14, 17 and 114–5.

43 H. Belloc, *The Jews* (London, 1922), chapter 4 *passim* and pp. 297–8. See also his earlier comment in the *Eye Witness*, 7 September–26 October 1911. It should be emphasized, however, that Belloc's work is not always easy to classify on this score.

44 And differences could open up on this account. See the critical remarks in the *British Guardian*, September 1924, pp. 126–8, concerning Nesta Webster.

45 See above pp. 11–12.

46 See below pp. 251–2 for evidence of religious attacks upon Jews. For further evidence that anti-semitism equalled anti-Judaism, see the evidence of Arnold White in *Report from the Select Committee on Immigration and Emigration* (Foreigners), British Parliamentary Papers XI (1888), p. 87.

47 See above chapters 2, 5 and 9.

48 Banton, *Race Relations*, p. 8.

49 Particularly by those who have studied European anti-semitism.

50 M. Harris, *The Rise of Anthropological Theory* (London, 1968), p. 130.

51 G. W. Stocking Jnr, 'Lamarckianism in American Social Science 1890–1915', *Journal of the History of Ideas* XXIII (1962), pp. 239–56 and his *Race, Culture and Evolution*: *Essays in the History of Evolution* (New York, 1968), pp. 243–69 provide food for thought on these matters and will hopefully encourage a similar study for Britain.

52 A. White, *The Modern Jew* (London, 1899), pp. 57–64.

53 S. and B. Webb, *Problems of Modern Industry* (London, 1902), chapter 2 *passim*.

54 So that Ralph Neville K. C. giving evidence before the *Inter Departmental Committee on Physical Deterioration* Cd 2175 (1904), p. 192 could refer to 'the true Lancashire race'. Churchill could also use the word in a cultural sense. Hence his last work could appear as *This Island Race* (London, 1964). See George Watson's article, 'Race and the Socialists. On the Progressive Principle of Revolutionary Extermination', *Encounter* XLVII (1976), pp. 15–18 for an emphasis upon these early concepts of race. For a differing emphasis see M. D. Biddiss, 'Myths of the Blood', *Patterns of Prejudice* IX (September–October 1975), pp. 11–19. M. Banton, *The Idea of Race* (London, 1977),

chapter 3 carries comment on the various historical meanings attached to the concept of race.

55 J. Rex, *Race Relations in Sociological Theory* (London, 1970), pp. 158–9 argues that cultural theories of difference can also be deterministic and should be subsumed under racism, together with genetic based hostility. More reflection needs to be given to this. See Banton, *The Idea of Race*, pp, 159–62 for some comment on the suggestion.

56 See above chapter 5.

57 Rubinstein, *op. cit.*, pp. 73 and 76 is very useful on Jewish wealth and influence.

58 It is surprising that Cohn, *op. cit.*, does not recognize this. The point is taken, however, in S. G. Bayme, 'Jewish Leadership and Anti-Semitism in Britain 1898–1918', unpublished PhD thesis, Columbia University, 1977, pp. ii, 101, 167. The temptation to start in 1919 is a great one but it does seriously distort the history of anti-semitism in Britain if it is assumed that there were no earlier fears of Jewish power on which to draw. Sometimes *recherché* examples could be drawn from the past, as when the *Patriot* in 1927 reprinted *The Hebrew Talisman*, which had been published by the Theosophical Society in 1888. See J. Webb, *The Occult Establishment* (La Salle, Illinois, 1976). p. 233 for some discussion of this. Conspiracy theories are not, of course, confined to Jews. D. B. Davis, 'Some Themes of Counter-Subversion: an Analysis of Anti-Masonic, Anti-Catholic and Anti-Mormon Literature' *Mississippi Valley Historical Review* XLVII (September 1960), pp. 205–24, discusses conspiratorial theories which have been attached to such groups. For an interesting charge of conspiracy in Britain before 1914 see 'Vigilant', *Revolution and War or Britain's Peril and her Secret Foes* (new and revised edn, London, 1913). This was written by Mary Frances Cusack with the intention of revealing 'the gigantic efforts which the Jesuits and the Church of Rome are secretly making to effect the overthrow and ruin of the British nation'.

59 See above for the London Society for Promoting Christianity and *G. K's Weekly*, 18 July 1925, p. 399 for Chesterton's comment.

60 White, *op. cit.*, pp. 274–5 refers to Turkish Armenia as a possible settlement. B. Gainer, *The Alien Invasion* (London, 1972), pp. 121–7 is the best attempt so far to come to grips with White's work.

61 Banister, *op. cit.*, p. 26.

62 See chapters 9 and 10. There were therefore those opposed to Jews who could support Zionism. See also above p. 18.

63 See above pp. 28–30, 211.

64 See above pp. 157, 167–8, 190.

65 See above pp. 167–8 for the qualifications by Leese.

66 Of the kind referred to by H. J. Eysenck, 'Politics and Personality', in his *Sense and Nonsense in Psychology* (Harmondsworth, 1960), pp. 265–307.

67 An early attempt to survey the literature on the psychodynamics of prejudice can be found in J. H. Robb, *Working Class Anti-Semite* (London, 1954), chapter 2, *passim*. A later source which provides references to key material and attempts to discuss these psychodynamic dimensions is W. F. Mandle, *Anti-Semitism and the British Union of Fascists* (London, 1968), pp. 14 and 19 ff. Similar ideas, although expressed much more generally and with considerably less sophistication, have been used in the discussion of early radical activity. See F. K. Donnelly, 'Ideology and Early English Working Class-History: Edward Thompson and his Critics', *Social History* II (May 1976), pp. 229–30.

68 See above pp. 39–42.

69 See below p. 286, note 147.

70 See above pp. 162–3 and the letter from Joyce, then in Brixton, to Leese, dated 12 July 1945. This is in the archives of the Britons.
71 See above p. 61 for a discussion of Burton.
72 C. McWilliams, *Brothers under the Skin* (rev. edn, Boston, 1951), p. 317 and J. Higham, *Strangers in the Land. Patterns of American Nativism, 1860–1925* (New York, 1965), p. 402 both make key statements on this issue and D. B. Davis, *The Fear of Conspiracy: Images of Un-American Subversion from the Revolution to the Present* (Ithaca, 1972), p. xiv notes that even conspiracy theories can have a basis in reality. Stern, in *The Politics of Cultural Despair*, pp. XVI–XXVII, emphasizes how personal and social factors did combine in Imperial Germany to produce anti-semitism.
73 Higham, 'Anti-Semitism', p. 571 has some relevant comment.
74 On the general significance of the 'folkways' affecting attitudes towards minorities, see G. E. Simpson and J. M. Yinger, *Racial and Cultural Minorities* (4th edn, New York, 1972), chapter 5 *passim.* See L. Stone, *The Causes of the English Revolution 1529–1642* (London, 1975 edn), for a similar analysis but in a different context.
75 Zawadzki, *op. cit.*, Robb, *op. cit.*, p. 191, Higham, 'Anti-Semitism', p. 566 and Pulzer, *op. cit.*, pp. 14–15 move in this direction. More recently two key articles supporting on interactionist approach to ethnic conflict are E. Bonacich, 'A Theory of Ethnic Antagonism: the Split Labor Market', *American Sociological Review* XXXVII (1972), pp. 547–59 and her article, 'A Theory of Middleman Minorities, *ibid.* XXXVIII (1973), pp. 583–94. See also Bayme, 'Jewish Leadership', pp. 25, 167.
76 Levy, *op. cit.*, p. 6, records an opposing view.
77 For instance, a fear of the influence exerted by Jews in society had more objective evidence to support it before 1914 than afterwards. See Rubinstein, *op. cit.*, pp. 76–80.
78 G. W. Allport, *The Nature of Prejudice* (Cambridge, Mass., 1954), p. 217 and Higham, 'Anti-Semitism', p. 569 both emphasize this.
79 As, say, in the Marconi scandal, in the issue of Jewish Bolshevism and in allegations regarding Jewish finance. N. Laski, *Jewish Rights and Wrongs* (London, 1939), p. 33; L. Namier, *Conflicts, Studies in Contemporary History* (London 1942), p. 131 and Stern, *Gold and Iron*, p. 497 all emphasize the lust for generalization.
80 See the comment by Tawney in his inaugural at the LSE in 1932 which is all too little kept in mind: 'When I reached the years of discretion – which I take to mean the age at which a young man shows signs of getting over his education – I found the world surprising. I find it so still. I turned to history to interpret it and have not been disappointed by my guide, though often by myself.' See N. B. Harte, *The Study of Economic History* (London, 1971), p. 89, where the lecture is reprinted.
81 See above chapters 9, 10, 11.
82 See below pp. 306, 316.
83 Anderson, *op. cit.*, pp. 60–65.
84 Kenneth Lunn's paper, 'Reactions to Polish Miners in Lanarkshire 1880–1914', given at the Society for the Study of Labour History conference in May 1978 is useful on this issue.
85 J. P. May, 'The British Working Class and the Chinese 1870–1911', unpublished MA dissertation, University of Warwick, 1973, pp. 28–38.
86 K. Little, *Negroes in Britain. A Study of Racial Relations in English Society* (London, 1948), pp. 60–62. J. Walvin, *Black and White: the Negro and British Society, 1555–1945* (London, 1973), is a more recent general survey of Blacks

in Britain.

87 HO 45 11843/139147 and HO 45 10649/210615 are full of information on this.

88 J. E. Handley, *The Irish in Scotland* (London, 1943), p. 288 shows the persistence of this.

89 Little, *op. cit.*, pp. 215–20.

90 I touch upon this briefly in 'Germans in Britain 1870–1914', in J. Schneider (ed.), *Festschrift für Hermann Kellenbenz Zum 65 Geburtstag* (Erlangen/Nuremberg, forthcoming).

91 May, 'The British Working Class and the Chinese', is concerned with these issues.

92 R. May and R. Cohen, 'The Interaction between Race and Colonialism: a case study of the Liverpool Race Riots of 1919', *Race and Class* XVI (October 1974), pp. 111–26 and G. W. Dimmock, 'Racial Hostility in Britain, with particular reference to Disturbances in Cardiff and Liverpool', unpublished MA dissertation, University of Sheffield, 1975, provide the basic details on these incidents and lay the ground for further analysis.

93 See Higham, 'Anti-semitism', p. 569 on the value of comparative work.

94 In the sense that gypsies have been accepted as entertainers, Chinese as restaurateurs.

95 Of the kind satirized by 'Robert Tressell': 'We're overrun with em! Nearly all the waiters and the cook at the Grand Hotel where we was working last month is foreigners ... and then thers all them Hitalian horgan grinders an' the blokes wot sells 'ot chestnuts'. *The Ragged Trousered Philanthropists* (London, 1977 edn), p. 22. See also the comments by Percy Cohen in 'Race Relations as a Sociological Issue', in G. Bowker and J. Carrier (eds), *Race and Ethnic Relations. Sociological Readings* (London, 1976), pp. 23–4.

96 See the remark by Louis Namier in *Facing East* (London, 1947), p. 146. It is an insular comment and overstates the case but it contains an important kernel of relevance.

97 See above pp. 221–6.

98 As suggested by E. H. Flannery, *The Anguish of the Jews: 23 Centuries of Anti-Semitism* (New York, 1965), pp. 193–4 and M. D. Biddiss, 'Racial Ideas and the Politics of Prejudice', *Historical Journal* XV (1972), p. 572.

99 The Burton blood libel, the South African War, hostility arising during the great immigration, the Marconi and Indian silver scandals and the Jutland myth were all possessed of great durability.

100 Joseph Banister, William Stanley Shaw, Hilaire Belloc, G. K. Chesterton, H. H. Beamish, Arnold Leese and A. K. Chesterton have all been shown as displaying hostility towards Jews over a considerable period of time and it was also noted that the Chesterbelloc vehicle, the National League for Clean Government, provided an organizational bridge between pre-war and post-war hostility.

101 *Pall Mall Gazette*, 3 November 1897 and in evidence in *RC* II, p. 15.

102 See the *New Witness*, 6 February 1913, p. 424 and 2 July 1914, p. 267.

103 D. Lodge, *Novelist at the Crossroads* (London, 1971), p. 152.

104 See above pp. 148, 150.

105 See above pp. 164, 187.

106 In the sense that actions could involve polite exclusion or organized violence. The exposure of anti-semitic attitudes could also vary considerably. For example, *Clarion*, 27 June 1911 carried an article called, 'Among the Foreign Aliens. A Russian Ghetto' by Victor Grayson which hedged its bets by using two 'spokesmen' and juxtaposing pro-Jewish and anti-Jewish sentiments. Barbara Hill drew my attention to the use of this technique. Furthermore,

the private correspondence between the duke of Marlborough and Winston Churchill indicated that some hostility could be expressed more viciously in private than in public. Marlborough complained to the *Telegraph* about an 'un-English' review of Churchill's book on his father but in private he went further and clearly relished what he imagined to be his trouncing of Harry Levy-Lawson, of the *Telegraph*, referring to him as, 'that dirty little Hebrew' and commenting, 'I don't allow Jews to say members of my family are dishonourable without giving them back more than they expected.' See R. Churchill, *Winston S. Churchill, Companion* II, part I, 1901–7 (London, 1969), pp. 487–90. None of this discretion was apparent in the *Britischer*, October 1938, p. 2 which as a final fling against Jews, and almost certainly under Joseph Banister's influence, could carry items such as, 'Nervous? Your BO will never be noticed at the Lion's Den any night of the week. Kosher cuisine guaranteed.'

107 See Orwell's comment in Orwell and Angus, *op. cit.* III, p. 341 on the need to locate hostility within ourselves. See also the dangers of delusion referred to in Zawadzki, *op. cit.*, pp. 133–5.

Select bibliography

Since the book is heavily documented, those who wish to follow any particular lines of argument should experience no difficulty in doing so. In view of the abundant documentation there would seem to be no point in repeating specific sources at great length in a bibliography and consequently I have concentrated upon a limited number of easily available items which I believe are central for an understanding of anti-semitism in Britain between 1876 and 1939. Those which discuss developments outside Britain are included because of the generally important insights they contain. I should stress that the inclusion of an item in the bibliography does not necessarily mean that I agree with or accept the arguments it puts forward. Finally, it will be apparent from the footnotes that anyone interested in anti-semitism before 1914 would be well advised to dip generally into the *Eye Witness* (later the *New Witness*), as well as the *National Review*, just as those concerned with anti-semitism in the inter-war years would benefit from a reading of the *Fascist*, *Blackshirt* and *Action*. All these publications offer readers more than insight into the Jewish question but they are useful for an understanding of the forms in which hostility towards Jews was manifested at different times between 1876 and 1939.

P. ALDAG: *Das Judentum in England*. Berlin, 1943.

G. ALDERMAN: 'The Anti-Jewish Riots of August 1911 in South Wales'. *Welsh History Review* VI (1972).

C. C. ARONSFELD: 'Jewish Enemy Aliens in England during the First World War', *Jewish Social Studies* XVIII (1956).

J. BANISTER: *England under the Jews*. 3rd edn, London, 1907.

S. G. BAYME: 'Jewish Leadership and Anti-Semitism in Britain 1898–1918'. Unpublished PhD thesis, Columbia University, 1977.

H. H. BEAMISH: *The Jews' Who's Who. Israelite Finance. Its Sinister Influence*. London, 1920.

H. BELLOC: 'The Jewish Question'. *Eye Witness*, 7 September 26–October 1911.

H. BELLOC: *The Jews*. London, 1922.

M. D. BIDDISS: 'Myths of the Blood'. *Patterns of Prejudice* IX (1975).

E. BONACICH: 'A Theory of Ethnic Antagonism: the Split Labor Market'. *American Sociological Review* XXXVII (1972).

E. BONACICH: 'A Theory of Middleman Minorities'. *American Sociological Review* XXXVIII (1973).

THE BRITONS: *Jewry über Alles; Jewry ueber Alles or The Hidden Hand Exposed; The Hidden Hand or Jewry ueber Alles; The Hidden Hand or The Jewish Peril; The British Guardian*. These run collectively between 1920 and 1925.

J. BUCKMAN: 'The Economic and Social History of Alien Immigration to Leeds 1880–1914'. Unpublished PhD thesis, University of Strathclyde, 1968.
R. BURTON: *The Jew, The Gypsy and El Islam*. London, 1898.
A. K. CHESTERTON: 'The Apotheosis of the Jew'. *British Union Quarterly* V (April–June 1937).
COBBETT: *Jews and the Jews in England*. London, 1938.
N. COHN: *Warrant for Genocide*. London, 1967; Harmondsworth, 1970.
ENGLISHMAN: *Britons Awake*! London, 1909.
H. FREDERIC: *The New Exodus*. London, 1892; new issue New York, 1970.
M. FREEDMAN (ed.): *A Minority in Britain*. London, 1955.
B. GAINER: *The Alien Invasion*. London, 1972.
L. GARTNER: *The Jewish Immigrant in England 1870–1914*. London, 1960; new issue 1973.
A. D. GRIMSHAW: 'Relationships among Prejudice, Discrimination, Social Tension and Social Violence'. In A. D. GRIMSHAW (ed.), *Racial Violence in the United States*. (Chicago, 1969).
H. A. GWYNNE (ed.): *The Cause of World Unrest*. London, 1920.
J. HIGHAM: 'Anti-Semitism in the Gilded Age'. *Mississippi Valley Historical Review* XLIII (1956–7).
C. HOLMES: 'J. A. Hobson and the Jews'. In C. HOLMES (ed.), *Immigrants and Minorities in British Society* (London, 1978).
C. HOLMES: 'New Light on "The Protocols of Zion"'. *Patterns of Prejudice* VI (1977).
W. JOYCE: *Twilight over England*. 2nd edn, The Hague, 1942.
A. H. LANE: *The Alien Menace*. 3rd edn, London, 1932.
A. S. LEESE: *My Irrelevant Defence*. London, 1938.
K. J. LUNN: 'The Marconi Scandal and Related Aspects of British Anti-Semitism 1911–14', Unpublished PhD thesis, University of Sheffield, 1978.
W. F. MANDLE: *Anti Semitism and the British Union of Fascists*. London, 1965.
V. E. MARSDEN: *World Conquest through World Government*. 85th impression, Chulmleigh, 1972.
J. E. MORELL: 'The Life and Opinions of A. S. Leese. A Study in Extreme Anti-Semitism'. Unpublished MA thesis, University of Sheffield, 1975.
O. MOSLEY: *My Life*. London, 1968.
M. G. MURCHIN: *Britain's Jewish Problem*. London, 1939.
F. H. O'DONNELL: 'Twenty Years After'. *New Witness*, 6 February 1913.
B. POTTER: 'The Jewish Community'. In C. BOOTH (ed.), *Labour and Life of the People* (London, 1889).
P. G. J. PULZER: *The Rise of Political Anti-Semitism in Germany and Austria*. New York, 1964.
J. H. ROBB: *Working-Class Anti-Semite*. London, 1954.
H. ROLLIN: *L'apocalypse de notre temps*. Paris, 1939.
E. ROSENBERG: *From Shylock to Svengali. Jewish Stereotypes in English Fiction*. London, 1961.
ROYAL COMMISSION ON ALIEN IMMIGRATION, British Parliamentary Papers, IX (1903).
W. D. RUBINSTEIN, 'Jews among Top British Wealth Holders, 1857–1969: Decline of the Golden Age'. *Jewish Social Studies* XXXIV (1972).
L. SCHAPIRO: 'Jews in the Revolutionary Movement'. *Slavonic and East European Review* XL (1961).
A. J. SHERMAN: *Island Refuge. Britain and the Refugees from the Third Reich*, 1933–1939. London, 1973.
R. SKIDELSKY: *Oswald Mosley*. London, 1975.
G. SMITH: 'Can Jews be Patriots?', *Nineteenth Century* III (1878).

F. STERN: *Gold and Iron. Bismarck, Bleichröder and the Building of the German Empire.* London, 1977.

G. W. STOCKING jnr: 'Lamarckianism in American Social Science, 1890–1915'. *Journal of the History of Ideas* XXIII (1962).

THE TIMES: *The Truth about 'The Protocols'*. London, 1921.

G. VOLZ-LEBZELTER: 'Political Anti-Semitism in England 1918–1939'. Unpublished DPhil thesis, University of Oxford, 1977.

A. WHITE: *The Modern Jew*. London, 1899.

B. ZAWADZKI: 'Limitations of the Scapegoat Theory of Prejudice'. *Journal of Abnormal and Social Psychology* XLIII (1948).

Index of Persons

Index of Places

Index of Subjects